757

WILL THE REAL
IAN CARMICHAEL ...

WILL THE REAL
IAN CARMICHAEL . . .

An autobiography

BOOK CLUB ASSOCIATES
LONDON

This edition published 1979 by
BOOK CLUB ASSOCIATES
By arrangement with Macmillan London Ltd

Printed in Great Britain by
BUTLER & TANNER LIMITED
Frome and London

In memory of LUCY – and for
SAMANTHA, KATE, CHRISTIAN, RUPERT
and any others who may follow in the same line

Also for PYM – who undoubtedly deserves a medal

CONTENTS

LIST OF ILLUSTRATIONS

8   *List of Illustrations*

Besides the photographers mentioned above, the publishers would like to make acknowledgement to any they have failed to trace or whose photographs they unwittingly reproduced.

There are two things to aim at in life: first, to get what you want; and, after that, to enjoy it. Only the wisest of mankind achieve the second.

Logan Pearsall Smith

PART I

1920–1940

Aged about four and all dolled up for a children's fancy dress ball at the City Hall, Hull – an annual charity event which I hated

CHAPTER ONE

IN THE BEGINNING ...

Slap bang in the middle of 1920 – on 18 June to be exact, the day when 105 years previously the Duke of Wellington and a German bloke called Blücher were bashing the living daylights out of Napoleon at the Battle of Waterloo – I was born in a pleasant terraced house in Kingston upon Hull in Yorkshire. The number of the house was 114 and the street rejoiced, most appropriately, in the name of Sunnybank.

No street could have been more aptly named. It faces due south, is a cul-de-sac and, as its houses are on the north side of the street only, it has an uninterrupted view of Hymers College playing-fields – the school which, along with Hull Grammar School, had been attended by my father several years previously. It was my parents' first home – a rented one. The war was over, my father had returned after four years in the army, and their two-year-old marriage had now been blessed, if that isn't too presumptuous, with the arrival of their first child – a son and heir.

My father was the youngest by eleven years of a family of five. His parents were Scottish and had lived in Greenock. My grandfather, Michael Carmichael, worked as a superintendent for the Scottish Legal Life Assurance Society, and in the early 1880s his employers had sent him south with instructions to open up a new division of the organisation in the north of England. He then moved to Hull and there set up home with his wife, Mary, one son and one daughter in a modest street which has long since been swept away by council bulldozers. Later there were to be three more sons, all of whom were born in Hull and who, together with their eldest brother, were to establish a most successful business enterprise in the city.

My memories of my paternal grandparents are one-sided. My grandmother died when I was only seven months old so I have no recollections of her whatsoever; my grandfather, consequently, I can only remember

My grandparents Carmichael

living a widower's existence sustained by his housekeeper, a Miss Ransome. He was a fit, erect, handsome man with a fine figure and an H. G. Wells moustache, and like most Scots he enjoyed his golf. He was kindly, gentle, soft-spoken and wonderful with his grandchildren, of whom he eventually had nine. The first home of his that I remember was a not unattractive, turn of the century terraced house on the Beverley Road right opposite the baths, and it was there that the whole family gathered at Christmas time; its main attraction to the young was exciting cavernous cellars in which he kept a regular record of the height of all his grandchildren, and through which he used to lead us, follow-my-leader style, by the light of a single candle. We were enthralled – it was all very Robert Louis Stevenson. Upstairs in the dining-room at the front of the house the atmosphere was more Dickensian. It housed a long dining-table around which was a set of what seemed to be at least a dozen chairs. Come pudding-time at family gatherings, all the children would get on the floor and crawl through the tunnel made by the legs of the chairs from the bottom end of the table to the top. There they would emerge to receive a spoonful of blancmange from grandfather who presided at the head.

Not long after his wife's death he moved to Kirk-Ella, a small village about five miles north-west of the city, where he bought a charming detached house called Vesper Lodge next to the church and almost opposite the golf-course. Here he held big family parties every Christmas Day. Unlike the remainder of the family who would assemble about noon, my parents always preferred to have Christmas lunch at home, and arrive in the region of three; a blow for independence for which I was always extremely grateful. Nothing is worse than, stocking and presents opened, to have them whipped away without a chance to set one's train out, start transferring one's stamps from old album to new or commence the experiment which will blow the house to smithereens with one's new chemistry set. An additional perk was that we always had goose for lunch while the rest of the family had turkey, a preference I acquired at a very early age and which has remained with me ever since.

My most vivid recollections of Vesper Lodge are Miss Ransome's home-made toffee, an orchard full of the most delicious plums, and the adjacent church bells pealing for Evensong on otherwise peaceful Sunday afternoons.

I have nothing but happy memories of my paternal grandfather. I can never remember him owning a car or going out to work, but this was because all his work was done from home; and by the time I was fifteen he had retired. He died when I was eighteen in a way that all golfers would wish to go: he sustained a heart attack on the eighteenth green from which he never recovered. He was eighty-three.

My maternal grandparents were also kind but cast in an entirely different mould. They didn't have the flamboyance of Grandfather Carmichael. I think perhaps flamboyance is not the right word – I haven't met many flamboyant Scotsmen, come to think of it – but he had a splendid *bon-homie*. His house was always so full of sunshine and fresh air.

Henry Meads Gillett, my mother's father, was by trade a 'Lead, glass, zinc, tinplate, oil, paint, colour, varnish and general merchant', according to his office notepaper (Telegrams: Glass, Hull), and he headed a firm called T. B. Morley & Co. Ltd. which had offices in Jameson Street. The firm, under its new name of Morco Products Ltd, is now run by two cousins of mine in premises on the Beverley Road. As a small boy I remember vividly my grandfather's office smelling strongly of cigar-smoke and containing a mantelpiece on which was aligned a row of small pharmaceutical bottles, each containing a different coloured chemical powder – presumably something to do with the 'oil, paint, colour and varnish' side of the business. But the main commodities I remember the firm trading in, as indeed it still does, were bathroom and lavatory furniture, domestic boilers and electric-light fitments.

Grandfather Gillett married twice. His first wife provided him with a daughter followed by a son, and his second a son followed by a daughter – my mother, Kate. It's interesting to try to fathom the reasons behind the moralities of successive generations; although grandfather's first wife died a natural death, I was in my early teens before my mother told me that he had married twice and that she had only one full brother.

Grandfather Gillett was stockier than his opposite number in the Carmichael family. He too sported an H. G. Wells moustache (*de rigueur*, it would seem, at that time), grey, slightly tinged with nicotine, and a pair of gold-rimmed pince-nez; and in addition to dealing in 'lead, glass, zinc, tinplate, oil, paint, colour and varnish', he was a devout churchgoer and lay preacher. When I was born he was living in Hessle, then a small village some three or four miles west of the city on the banks of the Humber. Certainly once and sometimes twice every Sunday he would walk to his favourite church in the centre of Hull to attend divine service and then walk home again afterwards.

He too ran a happy and contented household but he was a more reserved personality than Grandfather Carmichael. His homes, or certainly the two that I remember, were heavier and darker in furniture and décor and exuded a distinct Victorian atmosphere.

Some three years after my birth he developed – not without reasonable cause, as it transpired – a phobia about being burgled at Hessle, so he sold 'Ardlui', his house on the end of Davenport Avenue, which was quiet and had a sunny aspect, and moved to the darkest, dingiest and most miserable terraced house it has ever been my misfortune to visit. It was situated in Victoria Avenue, a modest but respectable residential street in Hull itself. Apart from peace of mind, the only possible advantages of the move were that my parents were then living two streets away, that it was a 1½d tram-ride from the end of the street to his office, and only a fifteen-minute walk to the Methodist church in Princes Avenue where he worshipped. Whether it was the name Victoria that attracted him to this new dismal location, I know not, but it was certainly appropriate. The tiny front room containing a large, peacock-blue velvet three-piece suite with its obligatory antimacassars, ornate, black wood-backed occasional chairs and tables and a glass-fronted cabinet packed to capacity with various items of china that I can never remember being used. It is interesting to reflect that I have one of those peacock-blue velvet armchairs in my study as I write and it is still as comfortable and sturdy as it was all those years ago; maybe because it was used so little in the 1920s.

After a few years the funereal atmosphere of his new home must have dampened even my grandfather's spirits, as he upped and moved to another house, larger and sunnier, just around the corner in Princes Avenue and even nearer to his church. In this, his last home, every morning after breakfast and before he left for the office the table was cleared, the Bible taken down and family prayers were shared by the entire household, which under normal circumstances would have been just my grandfather, grandmother and their two maids, but if the milkman was delivering at the time he too was invited in.

My mother used to tell me that her father had been sorely tempted to become an actor, and throughout his life he frequently reminded his children how lucky they were that he had not succumbed to the temptation. I have plenty of evidence that he was not without creative talent. When my mother was a little girl and away boarding at Harrogate Ladies' College, he used to write to her copious, long and loving letters, much of them in verse, which he would then sign paradoxically: 'Your loving dear old Dad, H. M. Gillett.' On 4 April 1909, the day before her sixteenth birthday, his letter was completely in verse, the middle stanzas of which are of an amusingly philosophical nature.

> You have learnt both French and Latin,
> You can play at cricket too,
> But have you learnt to wash and cook
> Or make an Irish Stew?
>
> You have studied Art and Music
> And your knowledge daily grows,
> But can you make a pigeon pie
> Out of a string of crows?
>
> You can talk of by-gone heroes
> And can tell off-hand their names,
> But could you clean a bedroom out
> And wash the window panes?
>
> You can tell of styles and fashions
> At a mile a minute rate,
> But if you tried to trim a hat
> Would you spoil it 'sure as fate'?
>
> Now, whilst going in for dancing
> Elocution and the like,
> Try and learn a house to manage
> Some day maids will go on strike!

Grandfather Gillett died when I was fourteen and, being away at boarding-school from the age of eight, I saw much less of him than I

would have done had I been living at home. For this reason, I don't feel
qualified to pontificate about the finer points of his character and I have
had to fall back on more materialistic and outward impressions. In so
doing, if I have painted him as a stern, Victorian paterfamilias I'm sure
I have done him an injustice. Anyone who can write to his teenage
daughter as follows could not have been devoid of a sense of humour.

You will be sorry to hear that mother gave me her influenza to take care of
for her and that I have been busy nursing it for her ever since the weekend!
I have been so anxious to treat it well that I have not been out since Tuesday
until this morning and even then I got into a jolly row all round because I
left it at home and went to church, but people never are satisfied, are they?

His letters to my mother, written in a neat, firm hand, were all full of
humour and loving kindness. Another charming example was a brief note
on a postcard bearing his office letter-heading:

Tom Appleton	JP
Along with	HMG
Will call to see	KG
On Saturday at	3
To take you out to	T
And Harrogate to	C
So you must ready	B
With Dolly & Marjorie	P[school friends of my mother]

So ask Miss J [the headmistress] she'll not say 'Nay',
Instead she'll say, 'Oui, oui.'

Had he lived longer, I am sure Grandfather Gillett and I would have
been great pals.

My maternal grandmother was never, in my eyes, a dominant personality; in fact I can only remember her as an elderly lady who had very little
to say for herself. She died at the age of seventy-three, when I was twelve.

The impression I am left with is that she was not in good health in
her later years. She always seemed to be sitting down, and on entering
or leaving a room she required the use of a walking-stick. She wore long,
voluminous dresses in funereal colours and her staple diet appeared to
be two raw eggs in a tumbler downed in one gulp. My grandparents'
holidays, as I remember them, were invariably spent at spas like Harrogate and Matlock; whether this had anything to do with my grandmother's health, or whether it was occasioned by the fact that my mother
was at school at the former, presents the age-old enigma of the chicken
and the egg. Letters once again provide clues to her character and those
sent to my mother were always tenderly loving.

My grandparents Gillett

On the deaths of both her parents my mother went into deep mourning for several months which meant purchasing entirely new wardrobes.

Lasting impressions? First, my grandfather's crystal set with head-phones, and later his super-het valved wireless with black horned speaker; devouring by the tablespoon Nestlé's sweetened condensed milk which he used to put in his coffee; and a little verse, no doubt one of his own, that he used to recite to me when appropriate at the beginning of a meal. 'Ian,' he would say:

> *'Apple pie is very nice,*
> *And so is apple pasty,*
> *But if you eat it with dirty hands*
> *I'm sure it's very nasty.*

'Go and wash 'em!'

'This could be the start of something big,' quoth the song-writer; little did the eldest Carmichael brother realise what he was starting when, somewhere around the turn of the century, he left school and, for want of any more ambitious employment, started to help his father with his insurance round.

The Scottish Legal Life Assurance Society sold, amongst other policies no doubt, life insurance to the country's industrial labour force. The premiums were modest and were collected by agents in weekly in-stalments which could amount to pennies only. Robert – number one son – was hence put to work as a house-to-house premium collector.

Thinking this was hardly a full-time occupation for an able-bodied young man, grandfather, with all his Scottish and perhaps newly acquired Yorkshire business canniness, encouraged him to try and deal in some form of trading which, without any additional energy, could also be done on the instalment plan at the same time that he was officiating on behalf of Scottish Life. This struck Robert as an eminently sound and practical scheme and without further ado he started buying and selling wristwatches in the manner prescribed.

A few years later number two son, James, left school. He, who also had no particular vocation beckoning him, obtained employment as an office boy with a firm of Hull timber merchants; a trade far removed from the one in which he was eventually to help make the name Carmichael a synonym for distinction and class amongst the Hull retailers.

In due course, with Robert's personal sideline flourishing, it seemed a natural progression for him to raise a loan and buy a small retail jeweller's shop which was for sale in a not very salubrious part of the city; a business in which he was shortly to be joined by James, who then handed in his cards to his timber company employers.

There seems to have been no end to the commodities in which the Carmichael brothers experimented during those early years. For a time they also dealt in coal and had two railway trucks, each with their names emblazoned on the side to advertise the fact.

The next recruit to join Carmichael enterprises was son number three, Herbert, and several years later, after new premises were found in George Street, a better trading area, he became their expert in gems and jewellery. Several years after that a final move was made to the opposite side of the street, where the shop, which no longer belongs to the Carmichael family but which still bears its name, stands to this day. Such then was the position when my father left school eleven years later. A small jewellery business had been successfully established by his three senior brothers, but was there room in it for him, and, anyway, did he want to join them?

My father, Arthur, but known to most of his friends as Mike, was the baby of the family and was looked upon as such by some throughout his life. He was kind, thoughtful towards others, generous, forgiving and, if nothing else, a perfect gentleman. I never heard anyone speak unkindly of him during his lifetime, or since. Of all the brothers, he alone decided that he would have some specialist knowledge unallied to commerce so that he could be self-reliant. Consequently, he decided to become an optician. He studied at the University of London, qualified in October 1914, and was awarded the Freedom of the City of London on 8 December of the same year at the age of twenty-one. On the certificate awarding him the Freedom he is described, strangely, as a 'Citizen and Spectacle Maker'. After qualifying, he returned to Hull and opened up a practice in the George Street premises of his brothers' firm, now fully designated R. P. Carmichael & Co. Ltd., Jewellers and Silversmiths, his skills thus adding yet another anomalous service to the business.

From chats that I had with him later in life, it was clearly important for my father to attempt to plough his own furrow; he was reluctant just to follow his brothers automatically into an already established business, albeit at that time a small one. Many years later, after he had got over the disappointment of his only son not wishing to enter the family firm, I know full well that he inwardly admired my decision to branch out and do my own thing. I can remember him on more than one occasion saying to me that he envied me the independent life I had made for myself and that he wished he had had the courage to do the same thing himself when he was younger. What it was that he wished he had done I am not sure, because he was the most courageous, patient, painstaking, industrious man and made a success of everything that he set his hand to in the commercial world. Nevertheless, in 1914, like his son twenty-six years later, the immediate task of launching himself on a career was temporarily interrupted by an arrogant and belligerent Hun, and very soon he was to find himself a subaltern in the East Riding Royal Garrison Artillery manning anti-aircraft guns in the Humber estuary.

My mother was a very beautiful woman and the apple of her father's eye. She was also small and slight, weighing under seven stone at the time of her marriage. In fact, she was rarely any heavier during her entire life. She was the same age as my father, both of them being twenty-five when they went to the altar. Her figure was sylph-like and her complexion as per peaches and cream, the latter quality being inherited by all her children and grandchildren. Throughout her life she was passionately fond of little china figurines – particularly of ladies in crinolines and poke-bonnets – and pictures of old English gardens – thatched-roof cottages surrounded by hollyhocks, foxgloves and delphiniums; these were tastes that somehow reflected her own personality, which was petite, uncomplicated, very feminine and slightly old-world. She was also vivacious and totally unsophisticated. Whenever my parents came to visit me at boarding-school, I always glowed with pride; she was, to me, without any question, the most beautiful mother on the campus.

My mother and father

She had a talent for drawing and water-colouring which, after leaving
school, she neglected completely, and she shared with my father a great
love of poetry. During their courting years their invariable presents to
each other were books of verse – many of them the size of a pocket diary
containing but one poem, say, *Sohrab and Rustum* or Tennyson's *Morte
d'Arthur* enchantingly bound in covers of coloured suede.

But though she had the outward appearance of frailty, she was wiry
and never failed to look after herself. I hardly knew a day during my
boyhood when she failed to go upstairs and have an hour and a half's
lie down on her bed after lunch.

It has been suggested to me in later years that she had a touch of selfish-
ness about her (which it has also been suggested I have inherited), but
if this is true it dovetailed perfectly with my father's total selflessness.

When my parents first met I'm not sure, but they became engaged in
1915 when my mother was nursing with the St John's Ambulance Brigade,

and in so doing entered a state of suspended animation in which they had to remain for two and a half years, a result of a persistent battle with my mother's father over the date of the wedding. As my father had been earning his own living only a matter of a month before the outbreak of war, his accumulated capital was negligible. In addition, his present occupation as a serving officer in an armed struggle which was to develop into the bloodiest in world history, made him, in grandfather's eyes, to say the least, a pretty lousy bet as a home-builder for his devoted younger daughter. He had nothing against my father as a man, but he was defending like a stag at bay the risk of the beautiful Kate Gillett becoming a penniless widow when she was barely twenty-two. Marriage after the war had his fondest blessing; marriage during it had his implacable opposition. He was not the only father in either 1914–18 or 1939–45 who failed to understand that a girl in love would, in the event of being widowed, without question have preferred to have lost a husband rather than never to have owned him at all. In the end my parents' persistence, coupled with thinly veiled threats of taking the law into their own hands, broke grandfather's resistance and they were married on 14 May 1918 at the Presbyterian Church in Prospect Street, Hull – the church in which all their children were subsequently christened and from the ashes of which, after recent demolition, the phoenix of a new public library has arisen.

After the ceremony they left for a brief honeymoon at the Royal Marine Hotel in Ventnor on the Isle of Wight, and settled a few days later into digs in Carisbrooke, where my father was stationed. Ten days later he wrote: '... we have never been so happy in our lives as we have during the last ten days, in fact we never knew what real happiness was until we got married'. My mother also wrote about 'ten days of *absolute bliss and happiness*'. There was no doubt at all that they were deeply in love and that at last they were enjoying the total togetherness that had been denied them for so long, a state of euphoria which was to be cruelly shattered the day my father returned to duty. Awaiting him were his posting orders to embark for France in only ten days' time.

But fortunately the armistice was not far away and it was only a matter of months before he could return home to reopen his practice and establish his young bride in their first home in Sunnybank.

CHAPTER TWO

HULL

Earliest Memories

When I was two we moved half a mile away into Westbourne Avenue. Now, first of all I must explain to you about 'the Avenues'. There were four of them running parallel to each other: Marlborough, Westbourne, Park and Victoria, and they were crossed at right-angles by Salisbury Street about a third of the way down, and Richmond Street two-thirds of the way down. At either end ran Princes Avenue at the bottom and Chanterlands Avenue at the top. The whole made a rectangle patterned rather like the streets and avenues of Manhattan and inside it was a highly desirable middle-class residential area about a mile from the city centre. At the time, if you were a professional man, were self-employed, or were an executive white-collar worker in the middle income bracket and had to live in Hull, 'the Avenues' were the place to drop anchor. If I were to place them in order of desirability, I would put Westbourne at the top of the list, followed by Park, Victoria and then Marlborough. Westbourne Avenue was the broadest and consequently the most sunny. Between the footpath and the road there was, on either side, about ten yards of grass verge planted at intervals with beautiful chestnuts, sycamores and plane trees. The Avenue was a mixture of terraced and semi-detached houses, with the occasional detached property, and embraced a variety of architectural styles, mostly emanating from the early part of the century: good, solid, not unattractive family houses of varying sizes and, no doubt, prices. At the intersections of Salisbury Street with Westbourne Avenue, and also with Park Avenue, there was a magnificent lead fountain about fifteen feet high that provided a roundabout; the only sadness was that they didn't 'fount', if you follow me – at least, in my day they didn't. Nor, to my certain knowledge, have they ever done so since. Today some heathen in local government has decreed that they be painted a variety of psychedelic colours. They now look exactly like outsize versions of one of those more revolting and exotic ice-lollies.

'Ian aged one', it says in the family album

Anyway, it was in this highly desirable enclave that my father bought our first house – No. 32 Westbourne Avenue. It was a semi, definitely one of the more modest houses in the street and very plain indeed, but it was, oh bliss, on the sunny side of the street.

A number of milestones in my life established themselves during our stay in Westbourne Avenue. The first and most important: my mother being delivered of Mary, the first of her identical twin daughters, in her own bed at 5.30 a.m. on 4 December 1923 – immediately after which every light in the house fused. My father, in a breathless panic, just managed to restore them in time to illuminate the birth of his second daughter, Margaret, twenty minutes later.

As I have already explained, my mother was a small woman, and the birth of my sisters left her weak and exhausted. A month later, after she had got up (they didn't rush things in those days), the doctor recommended that she should be sent away somewhere for a complete rest. So in January my father despatched her to Torquay for a recuperative holiday where she remained for three months. During her absence considerable anxiety set in at home as neither daughter would put on an ounce of weight. In March signs of improvement were detected, so telegrams were despatched to Devon to inform the distraught mother.

5 March. Twins gained one ounce each since Sunday. Mike.

12 March. Twins gained quarter pound each. Mike.

Such optimism was, however, short-lived. At the age of six months both of them still only scaled their birth weight.

Eventually, a friend of the family who lived in Brough (Ronald Coleman's sister, actually) recommended that my parents should take the pair of them to see a particular children's specialist in Leeds, which they immediately did. He reported that they were perfectly healthy children and that there was nothing wrong with them that the correct diet and plenty of it wouldn't put right. My parents returned home, sacked the old nurse, engaged a new one, laid in the caviare and truffles, started stuffing them like a couple of Strasburg geese – and neither of them looked back.

The second milestone was the removal of my tonsils and adenoids on the nursery table (first floor back) two years later, at the age of five. A Dr – or maybe it was a Mr, I'm not sure – Ritchie Rogers was responsible for executing the dirty deed. Actually I malign him; he was the top local ear, nose and throat man and was supposed to be pretty hot at that sort of thing. Ts and As that he removed were gone for life; no ancillary roots or suckers were left behind to sprout again. Maybe that's impossible anyway, but it was, nevertheless, the gist of the tea-table chat that passed between my mother and any stray visitors who happened to call in at that time. In retrospect, it is, I suppose, some consolation for a pretty hair-raising experience for one so young.

I remember being escorted along to the nursery by my mother on the morning concerned, wearing my pyjamas and a camel-hair dressing-gown. I was totally unaware of what was about to happen to me. There I found two gentlemen in their shirt-sleeves, one of whom looked quite absurd sitting on a tiny nursery chair belonging to one of my two-year-old sisters – the sort they provide for the chimpanzees' tea-party at the

With my sisters who hardly look as if they are suffering from malnutrition

zoo. He was struggling with a dark-brown rubber balloon, which looked for all the world like an inflated sponge-bag. It was, of course, the primitive instrument for administering the anaesthetic with which I was just about to be scared out of my wits. A nurse in white uniform approached, put a brown swimming-cap on my head, my mother left the room and all I remember thereafter is being forcibly held down on the table, screaming for my life until I finally succumbed to insensibility.

My mother, I was later informed, remained outside the nursery door wringing her hands in an anxiety only exceeded in its intensity by my own terror. Seldom have I been so frightened.

An interesting corollary to this experience which illustrates how sensitive, even logical, the minds of the young can be occurred about a year later. My parents were having some friends round to dinner. I can't remember who or how many there were, but the occasion must have been important because my mother had hired a special maid for the evening. She was middle-aged to elderly and arrived during the afternoon resplendent in uniform – a black dress surmounted by a snow-white apron and bib with crossed braces at the back, white starched cuffs and collar and some sort of white cap. The moment I saw her, a total stranger to me, imperious and authoritarian in manner, terror struck again. My mother was at a loss to understand what had come over me. For a time I was too frightened even to ask questions, but eventually I flung my arms round her and with the most agonising *cri de cœur* pleaded: 'I'm not going to have another operation, am I?'

Over the years I have been fortunate to be a fairly fit man. My brushes with doctors have mercifully been few and far between – maybe that's why hospitals always frighten me a bit; but my third milestone in Westbourne Avenue was also of a medical nature.

A year after that last experience I became aware of a heavy thumping pain on the top of my head. In fact, a headache, but of a rather odd nature and in an unusual place. Apart from that I felt perfectly normal – no temperature or anything of that sort. This foxed the medicos for a while, but one morning I was told to remain in bed until the doctor came. When he arrived he conducted a fascinating examination, employing a stethoscope, small, steel, retractable ruler and an indelible pencil. I bared my chest and he started listening and making marks on my left bosom with the pencil. This finished, he pulled out his ruler and started measuring. He then made the astonishing announcement that my heart had swollen half an inch on one side and three-quarters of an inch on the other. I've always been mystified as to how you assess 'sides' of an object which is, to all intents and purposes, spherical. However, that's what he said, and he then prescribed total rest with six weeks in bed, and I mean *in bed*. I wasn't allowed to leave it even to go to the loo. Bedpans were to be the order of the day, or, to be more accurate, the order of the six weeks. For a seven-year-old boy who is feeling perfectly fit (the headaches vanished the moment I got to bed) to be so confined is a deeply frustrating experience.

My bedroom was a single one over the front door, and my bed was moved to a position across the window so that I could watch the *va et vient*. All sorts of interesting people and things passed up and down the Avenue at that time. The Corporation dustcart drawn by a beautiful Shire-horse; the tricycle of the Eldorado ice-cream man – STOP ME AND BUY ONE; a barrel-organ; the occasional motor car; and, in the evening, the lamplighter, with his tall pole aflame at the top to light the gas street-lights. It was spring or early summer. The big chestnut tree opposite the front of the house was in full leaf. The sun shone in and I was able to have the lower sash of the window open for most of the time. So I suppose things could have been worse.

Necessity, they say, is the mother of invention, and I soon invented a piece of apparatus to relieve my boredom. I tied a piece of string to my bedpost and had the other end secured to one of the railings at the bottom of the front garden beside the gate. On to this was threaded the handle of a small shopping basket to which I tied another string so that the basket could be dropped down the first one to the garden railings and pulled back up again by means of the second. Into this device the postman always placed our letters (there used to be two or three deliveries a day at that time) and I would haul them up into my bedroom. Occasionally a kindly housewife returning home from shopping stopped to call out, 'Let down your basket' – or something equally biblical – and a bar of chocolate (Rowntree's Motoring, no doubt) or some sweets would be put into it for me.

When eventually I was allowed up, my exercise was very strictly con-trolled. I wasn't even allowed to walk to the end of the Avenue, so my parents were instructed to obtain a Bath chair for me. This 'floored' them a bit because even then such items were becoming a rarity. In due course, however, after advertising, a second-hand one was acquired and for several weeks I was pushed around the area in one of those basketwork antiquities that have two big wheels at the back and one small central one at the front. The latter I had to steer myself by means of a long con-necting rod and handle, while someone else propelled the contraption from behind. It must have been a strange (and heartrending) sight; an invalid carriage normally associated with geriatrics occupied by one so young.

The last Westbourne Avenue milestone concerns the beginning of my education. At the age of four I was sent to the Froebel House School in Marlborough Avenue, but was removed after one term because, I was told, of the appalling language that I was bringing home. It would be fascinating to know what constituted bad language in 1924. I was then sent to The Lodge School in Pearson's Park, a fifteen-minute walk away, but all I can remember about it is that it was a co-ed kindergarten, I helped to build a model in a sand-tray of a set for *Hiawatha* ('On the shores of Gitche Gumee,/Of the shining Big-Sea-Water'), and I won a mauve bulb-bowl for growing the best hyacinths. I remained there until, at the age of seven, I was taken away and sent to board at Scarborough College.

The Westbourne Avenue era contains my earliest memories and generally speaking they are happy ones. Many of them are quite vivid and they supplied a fairly clear, if somewhat limited, picture of the 1920s upon which I was able to draw later in life. I remember a ukulele with a green baize covered plectrum that my father was trying to teach himself to play. I remember many of his gramophone records by 'Whispering' Jack Smith, Layton and Johnstone, and Ray Noble and his orchestra (a few of which I still possess). One of my earliest party tricks, long before I was able to read, was an astonishing ability to select any record requested and place it on the machine without ever making a mistake. 'Miss Annabelle Lee', 'My Blue Heaven', 'Constantinople' or whatever. How I acquired this uncanny skill remains a mystery to this day. I remember my father's first car, a Bean, in which the windscreen was competely perpendicular and if it rained the wiper (driver's side only) had to be operated by hand. I also remember a much sportier chariot which was driven by a bachelor friend of his who, in his gauntlet-gloves and long woollen scarf wrapped several times round his neck, always took a running athletic leap over the side and into his seat as it contained no doors. I remember the advent of what were known as 'balloon' tyres; a considerable advance on the solid variety which were hitherto the only ones available. I remember the first spoked wheels, very dashing, and a red triangle painted on a rear mudguard which indicated that the car was fitted with 'four-wheel brakes' – a startlingly new mechanical innovation. I remember Oxford bags, plus-fours, cloche hats, two-tone (co-respondent) shoes, and adults asking for gin-and-limes and gin-and-Its. I remember maids – i.e.

domestic servants – of which, in those days, all but the lowliest of households employed certainly one, if not two – a cook and a housemaid. I remember a vast motorcade driving Amy Johnson through streets thronged with people from Paragon Station to her parents' house in adjacent Park Avenue after returning from her solo flight to Australia; I had a ringside seat in the window of a first-floor bedroom in the house right opposite. I remember the windows of the Hull trams being lined on the inside with chicken-wire during the General Strike, and I also remember my first lady-love.

Maureen was a year older than me, an only child who lived three doors away. One summer our respective families rented adjacent houses in Hornsea, an inexpensive seaside resort on the east coast, and during that holiday I 'married' her. For the ceremony, which took place in the front garden of their house, she wore some sort of white veil while I sported an inverted beach-bucket on my head in lieu of a top hat. I was definitely 'sweet' on Maureen and our romance went swimmingly until we left Westbourne Avenue to better ourselves.

One other incident concerning the fair sex also comes to mind. The Lodge School rented some sort of modest playing-field off Richmond Street and there, one evening a week in the summer, we all used to meet to play unisex cricket. During my first-ever game it transpired that our side won the toss and elected to bat. I think I must have been put in about fifteenth wicket down (we were a large class) because when my turn came I had for some time been lying peacefully in the long grass enjoying myself thoroughly in the company of two of the girls. Such an unwarranted intrusion on my privacy was not to be countenanced for a moment. I strode out to the pitch, grabbed the bat which the previous combatant had abandoned at the crease and, so that there could be no shadow of doubt about my dismissal, on receiving my first ball, I quite deliberately hit my own wicket fair and square. I then dropped the bat exactly where I had found it and returned immediately to my two bits of crumpet before any other male could muscle in on my new-found preserve. To acquire two at the same time at such a tender age showed, I think, considerable enterprise.

But the spring of 1928 started a new chapter in my life and from that date onward I was never again to spend more than one-third of any year at home.

CHAPTER THREE

SCARBOROUGH

Unwillingly to School

The main buildings of Scarborough College, at that time, were two in number. The original imposing structure, very scholastic in style with colonnade-type cloisters against its front elevation and a clock-tower over its front door, looked south over its own playing-fields and comprised classrooms, dormitories, dining-hall, library, a few studies for the senior boys, accommodation for the headmaster – and it was illuminated by gas.

The second building, which was referred to as the New Building, had three extra classrooms and an excellent modern gymnasium. This, as its name implied, was a more recent addition and was equipped with new-fangled electricity. The hall and corridors of the main building were festooned with almost as many glass cases containing specimens of stuffed wildlife as the Natural History Museum. The dining-hall displayed a similar number of silver cups, each under its own glass dome, and the library more wildlife, including mounted swordfish snouts and some positively horrific First World War bayonets.

The establishment was, and still is, situated at the top of a high bank on the Filey Road, on the right as one leaves the town heading south.

A quarter of a mile away, down what was then an unmetalled road leading to the sea, there stands another property on the side of which, engraved in stone, are the words 'Fashoda House 1898'; but in my days it was known unaccountably as Holbeck House. This was the prep school. Built, I would imagine, as a private residence for a well-to-do Victorian family, it is detached, double-fronted, and in the 1920s and 1930s had a good quarter of an acre of back garden. The house has now been converted into flats and the garden, which was sold off separately, contains further 'units', as I believe developers heartlessly refer to them, which live cheek by jowl with the original property. In those days it was ostensibly a house in which the younger boys could live, all lessons and games being conducted up the road at the College proper. Again there was no electricity; it was gaslit throughout.

The school was a private one, took boarders and day-boys, played cricket, soccer and hockey, and boasted no uniform except perfectly ghastly white, starched, Eton collars which were worn over the top of the jacket collar. This resulted in a permanent plague of boils on the neck amongst the younger boys. After the age of thirteen – the age of transferring from the junior to the senior school – this ceased to be so prevalent, as the Eton collar was then replaced by the normal adult variety – like those worn in any good, old-fashioned city office.

A piece of useless information about Eton collars, should you ever have occasion to wear one, is that if you are caught in the rain with it on you must immediately place it inside your jacket collar, otherwise the rain reduces it to the consistency of a pocket-handkerchief.

Anyway, this whole establishment was presided over by two brothers, the Armstrongs, both bachelors to the end of their days. They were a classic Laurel and Hardy combination. Percy, the elder, who had a corpulent Oliver Hardy figure, was the Supremo and lived 'up top', while his younger brother Laurence, a tall, stooping bean-pole of a Stanley Laurel, reigned over the prep school. The latter was always known as Plute, or Pluto – King of the Underworld, you understand; and it was on the steps of this underworld that I was deposited by my father and mother, complete with trunk and tuck-box, bewildered and very tearful, a few weeks before my eighth birthday.

I cannot in all honesty claim that I enjoyed Scarborough. Discipline, at least at the prep school, was Dickensian. Laurence Armstrong, I'm sure, was a kind old gentleman at heart, but I cannot ever remember seeing him smile. Corporal punishment was dished out at the drop of a minor misdemeanour, like talking after lights-out, with the heel of one's own very substantial indoor shoe on a pyjama-clad bottom. Another Nemesis was having to sit cross-legged with one's arms folded behind one's back, totally motionless, against and facing the wall of his study for what seemed interminable periods. When, eventually, he decided that you had been suitably corrected, he never imparted the information to you in a civil tone of voice; one received an indecipherable grunt and a kick up the bottom from a very sharply pointed, highly polished brown boot. By this time rigor mortis had set in and it was practically impossible to stand up anyway.

There were other privations. One, which seemed unnecessary if not actually insanitary, was the weekly bath in six inches of water. This was the only hot water one ever saw – a.m. and p.m. ablutions being carried out in the dormitories in cold provided in one's personal, white, Victorian, earthenware water-jug and basin; on winter mornings one frequently had to break the ice on the water first. Then at breakfast, when large 'doorsteps' of dry white bread were placed on the table together with a small dish of butter and a large bowl of either marmalade or golden syrup, one was never allowed to take butter *and* marmalade or syrup, it had to be butter *or* marmalade or syrup; to be caught having both would have meant another half-hour cross-legged in the study that evening.

Percy Armstrong was a much jollier creature altogether. 'Let me have men about me that are fat,' said Caesar, and as far as Scarborough College was concerned I am in complete agreement with him.

Once a term all the boys were weighed and measured and this was carried out personally by Percy (or 'Snot' as he was so endearingly misnamed) in a study blue with tobacco smoke. It was a tiny, dark room full of old pipes and Victorian and academic clutterment, in the centre of which, occupying almost the entire floor area, was his large roll-top desk. His scales with measuring rod and tape stood next to the fireplace in which burned an open fire nine months of the year. Periodically throughout the term the boys would, when called for, leave their classrooms and file along to his study six at a time, the maximum number that could be shoe-horned into the room at one go, still allowing the door with its draught-curtain on a brass rail to close behind them. Once inside, with difficulty, they stripped to the waist and submitted themselves to have their vital statistics recorded. With the younger boys, the eight- to ten-year-olds, he behaved like a lovable old Santa Claus in a department-store at Christmas time. More than once I was bounced on his knee, which was ample enough to accommodate two at a time, and frequently it did.

His ebullient approach to life was also characteristically displayed on the cricket field. Both the Armstrong brothers played frequently with a master-augmented first eleven. Laurence's approach, somewhere about number six, was all Trevor Bailey at his most resolute, but when Percy replaced him, emerging on to the field from their bell-tent – a personal retreat separating, as it were, the 'gentlemen' from the 'players', which was always erected on the boundary opposite the pavilion – a buzz of expectancy filled the air. As already explained, the headmaster, who must have been in his early sixties, was no slave to the dieticians; it was, in fact, a debatable point as to who or which would have caused the most

Early cricketing days at Scarborough College, self on extreme left

damage to a crumbling pitch, he or the heavy roller. But, to be fair, he also had a gammy leg and, between them, these two disabilities necessitated his being met at the wicket by a runner, who was invariably redundant. Percy Armstrong dealt exclusively in boundaries, mostly sixes over long-on.

The boys at Scarborough college were in general pleasant enough, but there is always one tyrant in any community, and the prep school of Scarborough College was no exception. He had red hair and a small posse of henchmen always ready and willing to carry out his instructions to make some poor soul's life a misery. If you were 'in' with this boy, your life was a bed of roses, but if you were 'out' it was purgatory and there was no end to the bestialities that he would order his hoods to execute. One of the most unpleasant was for one hood to engineer some excuse to cause the unsuspecting victim to leave the dormitory for a few minutes at bedtime when, during his absence, hood number two would throw back the bedclothes and pee in his bed. This not only meant that the victim had to sleep all night in a wet bed, but he also received whatever punishment was meted out to bed-wetters the following morning.

On the credit side of the ledger, however, Scarborough was only an hour-and-a-half's drive from home, and my parents came over to take me out every third Sunday, the statutory period allowed, from after

Matins, which we attended at a church in the town, until Evensong, which was celebrated in the dining-hall back at school.

I learned to play cricket and soccer, both of which I played for the prep school first eleven, and both of which I enjoyed enormously. At soccer I played in goal, and during the term I held that responsible position I succeeded in helping them to lose every single match; I let in more goals than most people had had the proverbial hot suppers. After one home game I remember being particularly relieved because I had only let in four; I was obviously coming out of my bad patch.

I also learned to play chess, but swimming eluded me. During the summer term we swam every day in the municipal pool on the south shore. That is to say, everybody else swam, I only bathed. Swimming was a pastime I never took to. For some reason I was always frightened of water; maybe it was because we saw so little of it back at Holbeck House.

I saw the Graf Zeppelin, with its huge Nazi swastika on the tail, floating across the bay in a clear blue sky; and I managed to rid myself of several juvenile complaints like measles, German measles and chicken-pox.

We were given the occasional whole holiday to celebrate some senior boy's scholastic prowess in a university examination, during which we were allowed to wander free-range around the beach, the cliffs or the Mount. Places of entertainment, however, were strictly taboo, even when accompanied by parents, in case one should come into contact with infectious diseases.

We were taken on a school picnic in charabancs one whole day every summer term to Goathland, now the centre of the North Yorkshire Moors National Park, and we had a magnificent firework display every 5 November.

We had innumerable lantern-lectures ('click-click, next slide please') on such arresting subjects as 'The Great Wall of China', 'The Battlefields of Flanders' and 'Across Tanganyika on a Mule'. These were, invariably, deathly dull and were illuminated by black-and-white slides made from photographs of the most monumentally amateur standard taken by the lecturer himself, and thrown on to a tatty white screen in the dining-hall by a lantern powered by something contained in a metal cylinder; there was, you may recall, no electricity in the building. The main attraction of these lectures was that we got off prep. on the nights on which they were held.

Once a term a Mr Kettle, a local photographer, brought along a 35 mm ciné projector, which was powered via an electric cable festooned across from the New Building, and entertained us with an actual movie, albeit a silent one. *Joan of Arc* I remember, starring Fay Compton, and an all-action drama called *The Battle of the Falkland Islands*. In the middle of the latter a senior boy called Knapp was despatched into the kitchen by the headmaster to acquire a large tin tray which, on his return, he struck loudly with a gong-stick every time a man-of-war's guns went off, thus adding verisimilitude to the entertainment.

There were two annual events that the whole school assembled to listen to in the dining-hall on an enormous uncabineted wireless-set which simply bristled with coils, wires, terminals and illuminated valves: the Boat Race, and the Cenotaph service on Armistice Day. The passing of the latter I regret very much. I remember hearing Leonard Cheshire expressing the same sentiment on television several years ago, and he attributed its diminishing interest as a national event to the time it was moved from 11 November to the nearest Sunday. I agree with him, though I do understand the reason why it was moved. I remember the days, even in the late 1930s, when all men removed their hats when they passed the Cenotaph even if they were on the top of a bus. How quickly people forget.

There were amateur theatricals at Scarborough College too – the usual school plays – but I was always too young to take part and, anyway, I can never remember having had any desire to do so. They were all plays of a light nature: *The Private Secretary* and *Ambrose Applejohn's Adventure* are two that come to mind. They were produced by the music master, a Mr Littlewood, who always took the leading role himself. They were classics of everything that is invariably laughed at in amateur theatricals. Nobody learned more of his part than was absolutely necessary. Pages from the script (Samuel French's acting edition) were removed and secreted all over the set – behind an ornament, on the mantelpiece, flat on a desk, even inside a performer's hat – anywhere, in fact, where it could be read instead of committed to memory. I don't know why I should label such a practice as being amateur. In this television age of high-pressure, sausage-machined soap-opera in umpteen episodes which are churned out with the minimum possible rehearsal time, professional actors are doing it daily. Provided one isn't seen to be doing it I suppose it can be excused, but an instance when Mr Littlewood failed to take such precautions remains in my memory. He was playing a scene in which he was bound to a chair – the chair being adjacent to a table on which lay his script. He was reading away, quite merrily undetected, until he had to free one hand from his fetters in order to turn over the page. This he did quite unashamedly, returning it afterwards to where it came from.

I remained at Scarborough College trying to assimilate a little knowledge until I was thirteen. When the time came for me to leave I solemnly swore that if I ever saw Scarborough again it would be too soon. The town, and everything connected with it, stood to remind me of the unhappier side of school life and its separation from home and family. I don't consider that to be abnormal; no boy, I think, ever looks upon his schooldays as the happiest of his life – not, at least, until he has reached man's estate and even then it is invariably self-delusion – but if anyone had told me at that time that within seven years those views would alter so dramatically that eventually the town would hold only the very happiest of memories for me, I would not have believed him; but this is exactly what happened.

CHAPTER FOUR

ELLOUGHTON

The Sunlit Holidays

By the end of the 1920s the family firm in Hull was going from strength to strength. My father had given up his ophthalmic work – another optician had been employed to keep the practice open – and he had started developing a wholesale side to the business which was largely concerned with importing ornamental cut-glass.

Also at the time an adjacent sweet-shop was acquired so that alterations could be made to enlarge the firm's premises. This was a development in which we children, too, became tangible beneficiaries. The shop was bought with all the stock, and my father arrived home from work one evening in a car loaded with huge bottles of sweets. This acquisition, together with the purchase of an off-licence premises a few years later, gave the R. P. Carmichael building a proud frontage of some fifty yards.

The steadily improving fortunes of the firm inspired my father to better his own family's lot, and he started looking around for a new home for us all out in the country. In due course he found the most beautiful stone-built house, the front section of which was five hundred years old, in a little village called Elloughton, ten miles west of Hull. It stood in two and three-quarter acres of overgrown garden which also contained another stone-built, tiled-roof, two-storey structure known to us as the Garden House. This was, in fact, one of the oldest and largest pigeon-cotes in the north of England, and it stood the height of the house itself. When we arrived it had long since ceased to be a home for pigeons and had been converted for human occupation.

It was entered by double, gothic-shaped, lattice-windowed doors which opened into a huge room containing an open fireplace in one corner. It also had a small lattice window in one wall and a large bay-window, also in lattice, in the opposite one. The walls were faced with timber planks which had been stained and varnished. In the corner opposite the fire there was a broad, staircase-like ladder which led up to a

Elloughton Garth

trap-door in the ceiling, through which was an enormous loft. The loft itself had two small gothic casement windows, one in either of the side walls, but the four walls themselves contained, from floor to raftered roof, row upon row of stone nesting-boxes, each only one foot from its neighbour, actually built into the masonry of the building. At the top of both gable-ends there was a triangle of six exit holes through which the birds could come and go. It was a fantastic sight, and if the timber planks had been removed from the walls in the room below they too, I always understood, would have exposed a continuation of the nesting-boxes right down to ground level. This was a paradise for us children and the ground floor was used as a games room until we too, like the white fantail pigeons with which we eventually stocked the loft, finally fled the nest.

My father paid, believe it or not, £1,800 for the entire property, but it had been empty for some time and was in a pretty ropey state of repair. The workmen went in and each day brought more troubles; my father's anxiety plummeted to rock-bottom. The front part of the house, the oldest section, contained beautiful oak beams. It was not only my parents to whom those beams had appealed; they had also proved a fatal attraction to the largest colony of woodworm ever to be assembled under, or perhaps 'in' would be a better word, one roof. The house had three storeys and at one stage of its renovation you could stand in any of the ground-floor rooms and look straight up to the sky. Every single timber had to come out and be renewed. Each night after he had finished work my father drove out to see how the workmen were getting on and what new disaster had been unearthed. Long after we children had gone to bed he would return to Hull and share his growing concern with my mother. Would they ever be able to pay for it all? After several weeks the work had got so far behind that the house was nowhere near ready for occupation when the time came for us to vacate Westbourne Avenue, so a furnished house had to be rented in adjacent Park Avenue until such time as it was. My father became very thin on top quite early in life and it would not have surprised me to learn that his financial worries induced by the renovations at Elloughton had been largely responsible. However, six weeks later the last of the workmen moved out, we moved in and an enchanting family home it became.

The garden, although neglected, was perfect for adults and children alike. Again, a lot had to be done, but the basics were there; it was merely a question of time, hard work and a certain amount of money. There was a gravel drive flanked by a splendid border of evergreen shrubs laid out and planted by my father; a stream divided by waterfalls, into two pools, each of which we stocked with goldfish, and in which the Golden Orfe grew to the size of healthy trout; and two large lawns separated one from the other by a magnificent herbaceous border. The second lawn was known as The Paddock because that was really all it could be called on our arrival. The grass, if I may borrow from Oscar Hammerstein II, was 'as high as an elephant's eye' but it was patiently mowed and tended over the subsequent months until it could be fairly described as a lawn, and on which I was allowed to play football and cricket.

I had two main colleagues who joined me in these pursuits; a boy called Bobby Saunders, step-son of my uncle Bob, the eldest of the Carmichael brothers, who lived three-quarters of a mile down the road at Brough and who was about three years my junior; and a chum called Peter Kidd, an exact contemporary, who had been a near neighbour of ours in Westbourne Avenue and whose main passion in life was the Corporation tram-cars. Not even the local government officer in charge of the city's transport could have been as filled-in as Peter was about those vehicles. He could tell you, at any time, exactly which particular number was travelling which route, which were 'in dock' and in which particular tram-shed they were being repaired. He was also morbidly fascinated by holes in the road and all who worked in them. These two lads were my immediate, and practically my only, permanent and regular male companions during this period; being away at boarding-school, I have noted, has never been conducive to the formation of local friendships. However, when neither of them was available, my sisters were press-ganged into bowling to me or providing the opposition in a sprightly kick-about; the only drawback to playing cricket with one's younger sisters is that one has to use a soft ball, thus depriving one of any ability one may have for using the seam. In my case the deprivation was minimal. After a couple of years the paddock had a grass tennis-court laid out on it and many were the juvenile tennis parties that my mother organised for us during the school holidays; these, I hasten to point out, were never allowed to interfere with my training to become the next generation's replacement for Herbert Sutcliffe, Harold Larwood or Dixie Dean.

The second lawn, although slightly larger, was strictly ornamental, and on no account was I allowed to set foot on it with a ball of any sort. Beyond both lawns was a wild area, wooded with gracious old trees, which was absolutely packed in spring with golden daffodils and pheasant's-eye narcissi.

Down one whole length of the garden, and separated from the lawns by a hedge, was the kitchen garden, and in it we grew absolutely everything. Potatoes, cabbages, broccoli, onions, lettuces, leeks, carrots, celery, peas, beans, cauliflowers, asparagus, marrows, apples, raspberries, strawberries, gooseberries, loganberries, blackcurrants and, in the cold frames and greenhouse, tomatoes, cucumbers and melons. You name it, we grew it; everything in the fruit and veg. line that we ate in the house was homegrown. It fed all the Carmichaels plus two maids, Miss Airey, a non-liveried nanny who looked after my sisters, periodic daily helps and a full-time gardener and his family of five. Later my father also took to keeping bees and we stocked ourselves up with excellent honey too. In fact, if we had had to withstand a siege at any time, we could have pulled up the drawbridge without a qualm. All this, it is interesting to reflect, was in the days before the domestic deep-freeze was marketed; my mother used to spend hours slicing beans and pickling them between layers of salt in tall stone jars.

Nearer the house was 'the garden beautiful' – beds of roses and yet another herbaceous border. We also boasted two magnificent copper beeches and a large and prolific walnut tree.

Le tout ensemble was known as Elloughton Garth, and it stood in the main street of the village which led down to another village called Brough on the north bank of the Humber one mile away. Where one stopped and the other started was difficult to say as they merged one with the other.

Of the Elloughton-cum-Brough complex Elloughton was, in those days, the quieter of the two. Brough was slightly larger and contained several splendid houses which were owned by the more well-to-do Hull businessmen; it also embraced a few streets of ribbon development which housed workers from the nearby Blackburn Aircraft factory, an industry that engendered no mean excitement for a young boy in the early 1930s, as the sky was always full of aeroplanes. The principal product appeared to be a bi-plane called the Blackburn Dart, but on the river they were also launching a trio of magnificent flying-boats. Bobby Saunders was my constant companion down by the airfield where we watched the landings and take-offs on what was, quite literally, a field with one windsock – no tarmac runways in those days. Bobby was always a bit grabbed by the idea of flying, so it was no surprise that he should go on to achieve the rank of Group Captain in the RAF. He is now retired from the service and, the wheel having turned full circle, can be found today once again back on the same site, this time in the capacity of Chief Security Officer for Hawker Siddeley who took the place over many years ago.

My holidays from school were spent almost entirely in the open air. We all had bicycles and we used them endlessly, riding about the surrounding countryside, much of which was very beautiful. When we weren't on our bicycles or playing cricket, football or tennis, we were collecting birds' eggs and butterflies.

Being away at boarding-school delineated the seasons with a crystal-like clarity. One was at home either in the summer, which seemed to contain day after day of uninterrupted sunshine year in, year out, or in winter, which was cold and wet, but which was always alleviated by a huge fire in the sitting-room at home and the glitter of coloured lights in the Hull shops at Christmas time. Spring and autumn were like ships that pass in the night.

It was about this time that I became hooked by the dance music of the period and developed a craving to play the drums. Somewhere along the line I had acquired a toy set and used to amuse myself for hours accompanying my father's gramophone records on them. In fact, such was my keenness and, no doubt, juvenile talent, that eventually he thought it worth advertising in the *Hull Daily Mail* to try and find someone who might be prepared to give his son proper lessons. As a result, a few weeks later I started studying under a local 'gigster' called Laddie Moses.

Mr Moses was about thirty. He was small, dapper and the possessor of sleek Brilliantined black hair which he parted at the side and brushed straight back; the overall effect thus created being that of patent leather. He lived in a grey-brick, terraced house with fire-brigade-red woodwork and appurtenances adjacent to what was, before Dr Beeching was given his head, the Botanic Gardens railway station – a wayside halt on a local line in the vicinity of 'the Avenues'. He was a pleasant young man who knew his job, and on my arrival for the first lesson he ushered me into the small front room in the corner of which stood his drum kit. Not exactly the Rolls-Royce affair that the virtuosi of the 'name' bands of the period were currently to be seen ensconced behind, but it was a *real* one and comprised a bass drum (which Mr Moses pronounced as if it were a bottle of beer), a side drum, two cymbals and a couple of other ancillary items of percussionry. Also in the room was an upright piano.

'Right, lad,' said Mr Moses, 'to start with, let's see what you can do; get behind that lot and get yourself adjusted.' (A similar line was addressed to me by the instructor at my first driving lesson in exactly the same area of Hull a few years later.) This done, he plonked himself on the piano-stool and, subsequent to giving four hefty, rhythmic thumps on the floor with his left foot, he launched himself into a couple of choruses of 'I Can't Give You Anything But Love', bidding me to join him.

I'm rather square, I suppose; I have never actually experienced an L.S.D. trip, but had I done so I cannot believe that it would have turned me on any more than those two choruses did, accompanying a piano and not a gramophone record on a real set of skins and not some cheap toy.

'Not bad, not bad,' he said eventually as I struck and damped one of the cymbals a crotchet after he had come to rest, as was the current vogue. 'Now – let's see how you hold your sticks.' I showed him, and that, even though I had been 'not bad, not bad', I was apparently doing all wrong. The lesson continued.

That hour passed as though it had been five minutes and at six o'clock, after he had finished work at the office, my father called to pick me up. 'Very promising, very promising,' reported Mr Moses. 'He's got a good sense of rhythm; he should make a rattlin' good little drummer.'

He then imparted an unexpected twist to the conversation and, most persuasively, managed to convince my father that for me to continue with the lessons would be a complete waste of his money unless I had some proper instruments on which to practise. Father, not really knowing a cow-bell from a temple-block, nevertheless saw the logic of this, and Mr Moses, with his eye to the main chance, promptly negotiated the sale of his to us and then went out and bought himself a better set with the proceeds.

All this was, perhaps, the burgeoning of my interest in the arts, an interest which obtained additional stimuli by my sitting glued to the corner of the bandstand during the *thé dansant* sessions in the Spa Ballroom at Bridlington during summer holidays, absolutely riveted to the antics of the drummer in Herman Darewski's orchestra, and also by attending the performances of the pierrots on the sands at the same resort. This gallant troupe of entertainers (three Ms and three Fs), clad in black pierrot costumes with orange pom-poms, performed morning and afternoon with an upright piano on what was really nothing more than a few trestle tables. Their remuneration was obtained by taking the hat round the audience during the second half while, more like than not, the poor tenor was giving out with 'The Road to the Isles'.

I was also going through a cowboy period about this time. My idols were Ken Maynard, Buck Jones, Tim McCoy and Hoot Gibson. I saw as many of their films as I could persuade someone to take me to, and I also bought a weekly magazine called *Boys' Cinema* which told of their exploits. As far as I can see, exactly the same plots are still being used by 'horse opera' producers today.

On the sports front I was an ardent supporter of Hull City FC, and Peter Kidd and I attended every home game that we could at their old ground on the Anlaby Road, remaining behind afterwards to acquire the autographs of the current colossi. We also considerably improved our vocabularies of invective and expletives by standing below the frosted glass window of their dressing-room at the back of 'best stand' while they were wallowing in their communal post-match bath.

In the summer I attended many a Scarborough Cricket Festival with my parents to watch the 'greats' of the day. On one occasion one of Yorkshire's more celebrated batsmen, who was not playing in the current match, was standing with a glass of ale outside one of the bars a few rows in front of which we were sitting in a sparsely attended section of the ground. The anecdote he was relating to his companion was liberally peppered with the word 'bloody'. Finally, my father, unable to stand it a moment longer, rose, worked his way along to the end of the row and approached the gentleman concerned. He asked him politely if he would be kind enough to moderate his language in the presence of a lady and a small boy. He would, I'm afraid, have had a bit of a shock if he had come autograph collecting with me at Hull City on Saturday afternoons.

I only heard my father swear once during his entire life. I had made myself a three-feet-long plaited leather whip for rounding up cattle in one of my many cowboy games. It was a fiendish weapon, resembling the sort of thing with which the man in charge meted out punishment to recalcitrant galley-slaves. It had four loose thongs at the end, and we were at Elloughton, in a small reception room known as the Smoke Room, when the accident occurred. I had been cracking it, in many no doubt irritating attempts to make it go off like a revolver shot. For one of them I was standing rather too close to my father and the four thongs went right up his nose, which must have been very painful indeed. His hand flew to his face in agony and he turned puce in an effort to suppress his fury; but this time it was no good – the lid flew off the kettle.

'That *damned* whip!' he exploded.

Not to put too fine a point on it, I was a lucky boy. My father, who had started with little, had worked hard and done well and consequently his family was now benefiting. But apart from material things, we were a happy family. My parents were devoted to each other and their

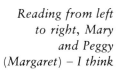

Reading from left to right, Mary and Peggy (Margaret) – I think

devotion and contentment radiated throughout the home. My sisters, being three and a half years younger than me and of the opposite sex, posed a bit of a companionship problem but we were all compatible one with the other and there was no acrimony. They were strictly regimented by Miss Airey whom I found a bit of a tartar, but her authority did not extend over me. It has been suggested in later years by contemporaries of my parents who outlived them that my youth suffered with the arrival of two pretty little identical twin sisters between whom nobody but my parents and I could differentiate. This assertion I strenuously deny. I was never at any time conscious of not receiving parity of treatment in the bestowal of parental favours. In fact, if there *was* any such disparity I would claim that it was I who was the beneficiary, not my sisters.

But by now my thirteenth birthday was looming up on the horizon and that was to herald a new period of my life.

CHAPTER FIVE

THE BROMSGROVE YEARS

The Happiest Days of Your Life ...?

I was entered for Oundle, and had I attended there I would have been the contemporary of two boys, both of whom were destined to become my brothers-in-law, and I would also have preceded my three nephews, all of whom were to follow their fathers to the same seat of learning. As it was, a couple of terms before I was due to leave Scarborough College the brothers Armstrong decided to go into well-deserved retirement and were succeeded by a gentleman called Woolley.

Mr Woolley had been a house tutor at a school called Bromsgrove in Worcestershire, and he promptly persuaded my parents to change their minds and to send me there instead.

My departure from home for my first term at Bromsgrove, in the spring of 1933, meant more to me than just reporting to a new school. I was almost thirteen years of age but hitherto had never set foot outside the East Riding of Yorkshire. Going back to Scarborough at the beginning of a term was a mere hour and a half's car ride, and rather less returning home at the end of it by train; LNER direct Scarborough to Hull – no problem. To reach Bromsgrove, a hundred and sixty miles away, was, for me, a journey across uncharted stretches of our scepter'd isle and required not only changing trains in Sheffield but stations too. In fact, from the LNER to the LMS, with different coloured engines and coaches to boot. The weather became warmer as one progressed south-west. People started talking with a different brogue. More boys, recognisable by the uniform school suit, a sort of blackish bird's-eye, climbed aboard at various stops on the route – Chesterfield, Derby and penultimately at New Street Station, Birmingham, which provided a veritable deluge of juvenile humanity. One more stop, down the Lickey Incline to Bromsgrove and then a mile walk up Station Road to the school.

It must have been about five or six o'clock in the afternoon when I arrived and, as always in my youth, the sun was shining and the air was balmy. Neither fact, unhappily, provided me with much solace. Even now I hate first days of any new gathering, or being a first arrival at a function peopled by strangers; I am shy and uncomfortable. As a young teenager I was downright terrified. My first objective impressions of the school, however, were not unfavourable; the new boy's lot in relation to certain tyrannical groups of older boys was, on the other hand, another matter but that was not to manifest itself for a further twenty-four hours.

The Bromsgrove School complex is situated but a stone's-throw from the busy High Street; it is on high ground rising up from it and is so placed that once you are in the complex itself you are in another world, totally isolated from any outside influences. The whole area, including the playing-fields, covers about fifty acres. The buildings are at the summit of the high ground and are dispersed round two large, well-tended lawns which themselves are partially surrounded by a row of magnificent chestnut trees, between which a plethora of yellow, mauve and white crocuses grow in the spring.

Bromsgrove School –
The new boy

In my day the buildings included the headmaster's House, several class-room blocks of varying ages of antiquity, an assembly-hall, laboratories, tuck-shop, handicraft workshops, armoury, swimming-pool, squash-courts, a splendid chapel designed by Sir Giles Gilbert Scott, and two residential houses – School and Gordon. I was in the latter, which looked out over one of those lawns known as The Green, and as it faced due south it was invariably bathed in sunshine. The school also embraced four other residential houses which were situated in the town itself, out-side the main complex.

The curriculum was not arduous. During the two winter terms we played games – rugger during one and hockey and athletics during the other – every afternoon from lunch until about four, with two complete half-holidays each week. During the summer term we had lessons imme-diately after lunch until about four and then played cricket for the rest of the afternoon, with three half-holidays per week. Rugger I did not take to, and athletics I found held even less appeal; cricket I continued to enjoy. I played for the school junior colts and subsequently the colts, but there my prowess rested its laurels. Maybe I wasn't good enough to be selected for the first or second elevens anyway, but by the time I had moved out of the colt stage I had decided what I wanted to do with my life and all my waking hours were spent, maybe dissipated might be a better word, day-dreaming about my future stardom. Stardom was cer-tainly my dedicated goal, but whether I was to succeed Noël Coward, Fred Astaire or Harry Roy I had not made up my mind.

At cricket my skills lay in the bowling department. I arrived at Broms-grove a budding seamer, but the coach there soon altered all that. He decided that I was a natural wrist spinner and put his heart and soul into turning me into one. Up to a point he succeeded. I did learn to bowl a consistently good length and in so doing I managed to deceive many opponents into thinking that I was a very much better bowler than I actu-ally was. Exercising this gamesmanship ploy in conjunction with moving my field about in a fairly flamboyant manner, I managed to pick up a few wickets. I don't, however, in all honesty, ever remember moving a ball in the air or off the pitch during my entire playing life. Many, many years later, when I had returned to the game for charity purposes, I reverted to my original style of slow-medium, 'straight up and down' pretended seamers, and while playing for the Lord's Taverners against HMS *Mercury* on Broadhalfpenny Down, Ben Barnett, the ex-Australian wicket-keeper who was behind the stumps at the time, assured me that I was moving them in the air quite considerably. A kindly piece of encouragement rather late in my life, but I knew full well that this was due more to a force nine gale which was blowing directly across the pitch from port to starboard than to any skill of mine.

Four out of five of my years at Bromsgrove seem to have been scarred by permanent brushes with authority. The first year and a half, these were with older boys – the self-appointed guardians of the school's traditions, a task which was a euphemism for some pretty medieval bullying – and during the next two and a half they were with the masters, and were caused principally by my natural inclination to be bone idle. My last year was something quite different. My previous altercations had stamped me as being totally unreliable and hence someone on whom it was unwise to thrust responsibility; consequently, I remained until the end of my time a ranker, a pleb, and yet by length of service I was senior to all those other boys who had been placed in a position of authority over me. I was a sort of elder-statesman, a minister without portfolio, and nobody would say me nay. When the time came, I had no desire to leave Bromsgrove at all – I had become omnipotent. But in the beginning the end could not be envisaged.

The pecking order started immediately on arrival. No time was lost in making the new boy's life as miserable and as terror-stricken as possible. The process of making him 'efficient' on the one hand and subservient on the other was enacted in my house by two groups: firstly, the previous two terms' new boys who, having been through it all themselves, were determined that their successors should undergo the same humiliation; and secondly, a self-appointed group called the Round Table. This consisted of the six senior boys in the house who had not yet been appointed as monitors or prefects – call them what you will; we called them 'jouts', actually.

Apart from various initiation ceremonies and unofficial examinations on the history and traditions of the school, all of which were pretty harmless (with one notable exception), the new boy, who was confined in a study with the younger of the two aforementioned groups, was beaten at the drop of a hat for the most trivial misdemeanours several times a day. The instrument of punishment varied according to the ingenuity of the administrators. My term on the receiving end it was an extremely painful piece of knotted rope which was manufactured in front of us with loving hands during our first week. 'And what happened during the two subsequent terms when you were in the position to mete out such punishment?' would be a fair question, so I will anticipate it. By that time the housemaster had got wind of this despotism and we returned from the following holidays to find that the study in question had been transformed into a reading-room and that the former inmates had been separated and split up amongst the other studies in the house, thus totally destroying their strike-power. Wolves always hunt in packs, you may recall.

The initiation ceremony which was an exception to the harmless variety was known as a 'christening' and took place in one of the larger dormitories on a Sunday morning before breakfast. The inmates of the dormitory numbered about fifteen. Towels were put on the floor on which, in a supine position, lay the hapless victim to be christened. His head was held in a vice-like grip between the knees of the largest and strongest boy present, who knelt astride his head, and all the remaining boys, with the exception of one, spreadeagled the recipient of the ceremony and held him down totally immobile. It took a very strong boy indeed to shake himself free. The remaining inquisitor, armed with two half-pint jugs of cold water, then proceeded to pour them one at a time as slowly as possible on to the dimple above the top lip, just below the nose. If the head was held correctly, there was only one way for it to flow – up. The skill was to make the drowning process last as long as possible and to do the changeover from one jug to the next without a break in the stream which might enable the victim to grab a quick breath. This mediaeval torture was also discovered and stopped the term after my initiation as it had been administered to a frail young lad with sinus or chest trouble, I forget which, and although no permanent damage ensued the news had filtered back to his parents and all hell, I am delighted to say, was let loose.

My housemaster at Bromsgrove was a stern man who demanded a healthy respect. His name was 'Freddie' Wallace-Hadrill. He was of medium height, sharp-featured, and the top of his head, which was almost flat, was thinly thatched. He was dark and he brushed his hair straight across his high forehead from east to west. His eyes were also dark and deep-set, and I believe he was blind in one of them – the result of an accident on a tennis-court, we always understood. He was a neat and tidy man who, sartorially, turned himself out, if not with the elegance of the Savile Row trendies, always with dignity and correctness. His suits were invariably of plain grey flannel and all included a waistcoat. The latter he wore throughout every season of the year and in all weathers. In midsummer the boys were frequently told that they could remove their jackets in class; rarely, however, or perhaps it would be fairer to say, with reluctance, in Freddie's classes, and it was at this time that his waist-

Gordon House, Bromsgrove School – overlooking the Green

coat came under discussion.

'Look at me,' he would say. 'I'm wearing a waistcoat. Do you know why I'm wearing a waistcoat, Carmichael?'

'Yes, sir. You're wearing it to keep the heat *out*.'

'Correct' – and as head physics master it was difficult to argue with him.

In the summer he would always wear a small button-hole – a corn-flower or rose picked from his garden – of which he was very proud, and every evening, except Sundays, he changed into a dinner-jacket and boiled shirt even if he was dining alone with his wife.

I think Freddie was a great rarity among schoolmasters – a first-class scholar and also an excellent administrator. He was the school's second master, and was also head of both the mathematics and physics faculties. In both subjects he was a splendidly lucid teacher. He had the ability to make subjects which were, in my eyes, highly complex appear so easy, so logical and so simple. In his house he could be a tartar, but in the classroom the Mr Hyde in him reverted to Dr Jekyll and he became almost human. I think he enjoyed teaching much more than being a housemaster; but it was as the latter that he was to exert the most influence on me. If I was sent for at any time, I suffered immediate, though temporary, heart arrest. 'What have I done?' was the instantaneous, involuntary question that flashed through my brain. He was never – for me, at any rate – a man to be sought out; always one to be avoided. On this subject my attitude was to change towards the end of my schooldays but they were a long time a-coming. In most of his charges I think he inspired awe and fear in varying degrees, and in everyone never less than respect. He had a sense of humour, I'm sure, but I personally supplied him with very little to laugh at. He was also, I'm equally sure, a good husband and father (he had three boys and, if memory serves me right, one daughter) and possessed plenty of compassion, but in my early years it was the sergeant-major in him that predominated; the friendly psychiatrist was not much in evidence.

The reasons for my regular visits to his study were rooted as much in my innate laziness as in actual law-breaking. I don't think I was more of a felon than the next boy although it frequently seemed so, but my aversion to work was reported to him again and again at the periodic (and dreaded) masters' meetings. Whenever I saw the staff assembling in the masters' common room during an afternoon's games period, I knew it was only a matter of time before I was going to be quaking on Freddie Hadrill's carpet. On these occasions I was invariably dished out with a work card. This had to be signed at the end of every lesson by the presiding master and an appropriate code letter had to be recorded. E – Excellent, G – Good, S – Satisfactory, N – Not Satisfactory and B – Bad. At the end of the week the card was returned to one's housemaster for scrutiny and a single 'N' would be sufficient to warrant the issue of yet another card for the following week. A 'B' brought fire and brimstone down on one's head and two 'B's almost certainly stood for 'beating'. I rarely seemed to be without one of the beastly things.

I was also a frequent visitor to Mr Hadrill's study to collect imposition paper for my law-breaking offences. Impositions – 50 lines (rare), 100 lines (general), 200 lines (for heinous offences) – could be meted out by masters and jouts alike. First of all, the 'lines' had to be copied out of Virgil which ensured that one could not rattle on apace as one could do in the 'write out a hundred times "I must not. ..."' variety. Nevertheless, a few daring lads who enjoyed dicing with death would slip in a quick 'Freddae Hadrillum est a congenitalum nincompoopus' for good measure. The really irksome thing about these impositions, however, was not that they had to be written in Latin but that they had to be done on special green paper available only on application to one's house-master. This of course meant that the latter always knew exactly how much hot water one was getting into because to acquire the necessary stationery one had to file up to him and tell him all about it. On issue of the necessary, the details of both crime and punishment were then duly recorded in a register which was retained in his study. There was a statutory number of lines, I forget how many, which were considered permissible. If this number was exceeded, in addition to the imposition which, so to speak, hit the jackpot, one was also summarily beaten. The register was then returned to nought and the count began all over again.

There was an interesting system of barter concerning impositions. A recipient was legally allowed, should he so wish, to trade his imposition for a beating at the rate of one stroke per fifty lines. The beating (all official ones were by cane) was administered by the donor – a factor which would be taken into consideration by the recipient before making his decision: was he a hefty front-row forward or only a light-weight wing-threequarter? As far as jouts were concerned, however, they had to obtain permission from the recipient's housemaster to carry out the chastisement, so one's sins always came home to roost whichever punishment one elected for. I rarely accepted the beating in lieu; beatings I did receive on many occasions but they were always awarded as beatings *per se* and had nothing to do with the exchange-and-mart system. I was beaten by my housemaster as well as by the jouts and once by the headmaster – an extremely rare accolade. I cannot for the life of me remember what my crime was, but in 1977, when I returned to the school as Guest of Honour at their Commemoration celebrations, my old headmaster, now in his eighties, said to my wife, 'He'll tell you I beat him. Don't believe him – it isn't true.' It is.

My brushes with the Round Table, though of an unofficial variety, were nonetheless terrifying. This small body of senior boys, which was peculiar to Gordon House, I can only liken in its reign of terror to the Gestapo or the KGB. Their self-appointed authority seemed to be designed solely to intimidate and crush any individuality, exuberance or even contentment that may have been shown by the junior members of the roll-call. They would meet in one of the studies (all other occupants having been summarily booted out) on a Sunday evening after chapel. They would then decide which of the young and fearful in the house were, in their eyes, getting above themselves and hence in need of deflation. The 'guilty' would then be summoned to appear before their 'kangaroo' court.

The fact that a Round Table meeting had been convened flew round the juniors in the house like a firecracker and fear struck at the very marrow.

The study concerned would have had the table pushed up to one end of the room and the six would be assembled behind it. To the thirteen- or fourteen-year-old arraigned in front of them in the manner of 'When Did You Last See Your Father?' they all appeared tall and menacing.

'Where the hell have you been?'

'What do you mean?'

'Where the hell have you been? Are you deaf? We sent for you three minutes ago.'

'I came as soon as I got the message.'

'Don't argue, you little tick. You're getting above yourself, Carmichael. Aren't you?'

Silence.

'Aren't you?'

Pause.

'Am I?'

'I told you not to argue.'

Silence.

Another inquisitor: 'You're a tick, that's what you are, a bloody little tick.'

Another inquisitor: 'Who was the First XV playing yesterday?'

'Downside.'

'Who won?'

'Downside.'

Another: 'What was the score?'

'19–5.'

'Who scored the try?'

'Roxby.'

'Who was the sixth man down on the list when the team was published on the notice-board?'

Pause.

Another: 'Well, come on, you little tick, who was he? Do you know or don't you?'

'Thompson?'

Derision all round. 'Thompson!'

'Tudor?'

'Which one?'

'A.H.?'

'A.H.! A.H.! You're not only a tick, you're bloody inefficient as well.'

Original inquisitor: 'I saw you round the back of the chapel yesterday in the pouring rain with your mackintosh collar up.'

Pause.

'You know very well, Carmichael, that you're not allowed to have your collar up until you've been here two years.'

Silence.

'Well, do you or don't you, you little tick?'

'Yes.'

'You'd better watch it, you know, or you're going to be in dead trouble.'

Fourth inquisitor: 'And *stand up straight!*'

And a great deal more besides. Finally one was told to, 'Get out and tell Ashton we want to see him – NOW.'

Then, as one was vanishing through the door, a terrifying threat would more often than not be thrown at one: 'And you can look forward to your foot-bath at the end of term!'

I never knew a boy who actually received a 'foot-bath', it was more of a threat than anything, but nonetheless terrifying for that; particularly to me who was frightened of water. There was, in the changing-room, a foot-bath in which feet and legs could be washed after games. It was, I suppose, about two feet deep. The foot-bath treatment was to fill this bath to the very brim, dump the offender inside it and then place the adjacent duck-board on top so that he couldn't get out. This done, several of the administrators would sit on it so that it was impossible for it to be removed from below. The significance of 'at the end of term' was, of course, that, should the authorities find out about what had taken place, on the last day, it was by then too late for the offenders to be punished.

The teenage gregarious male, I have come to the conclusion, can be a very unpleasant person indeed.

But with the first few terms behind me, during which time my only thought was survival, my yearnings to become a performer became more and more magnetic. I say 'performer' as I wasn't really sure in which direction I wanted to travel – in which particular field my talents really lay. I wanted to act, I wanted to sing and dance and, with equal enthusiasm, I wanted to make music. As already mentioned, dance music was my penchant and I had an encyclopaedic knowledge of the British dance-bands of the thirties, their musicians and the hotels and restaurants in which they all played. Harry Roy and Nat Gonella were my idols but I worshipped them all. They were big money in those days and in popularity stakes were the equivalent of the pop idols of today. I never got to London to see any of them but periodically they topped the bill on a provincial tour of the Moss Empire music halls, and when they arrived at the Palace Theatre in Hull nothing would keep me away.

My father, who knew the theatre manager, a magnificent figure of a man who stood before his box-office prior to every performance resplendent in top hat, white tie and tails, always handed my autograph book to him on our arrival. Such an evening was the very pinnacle of excitement for me.

The top of the bill always closed the show and the formula for presentation never varied. The pit orchestra 'played off' the penultimate act which appeared in a front-cloth. A moment of silence and then from behind the number one runners came the sound of the band concerned playing its signature tune. The difference of quality and sound between the pit orchestra and that of Roy Fox, Henry Hall, Ambrose or whoever, was akin to that between the Archangel Gabriel's brass section greeting an arrival at the pearly gates and a Boy Scout bugle band. It never failed to bring hysterical applause and after eight bars the curtains rose to disclose the spectacle. A dozen or so musicians looking pristine in white evening shirts, black ties and tastefully coloured jackets, and a row of glistening gold instruments. In the centre at the back, raised on a rostrum behind a chromium-plated console festooned with tomtoms, cymbals, temple-blocks and invariably a Chinese gong, sat the drummer threshing flamboyantly away at his charges, and in the front of the whole ensemble stood the idol himself, immaculate in white tie and tails. What a sight! What a sound! What a thrill! Well, it was to me, anyway.

Twice a week at Bromsgrove the boys were allowed to go down to the town during the afternoon. I always made straight for Mr Watton's record-shop where I remained for a solid hour and a half sampling the new current releases. Mr Watton, an emaciated, bird-like old gentleman with scant grey hair and gold-rimmed spectacles, kept a small shop at the north end of the High Street. The road swells at that point like the glass bulb at the bottom of a thermometer, and the swelling in those days accommodated several bus stops. It was a bit like the hub of a wheel and public transport left from it in all directions – for Birmingham, Stourbridge, Redditch or Worcester. The building that housed Mr Watton's tiny little shop, which overlooked this scene of activity, was very old and, consequently, rather like Mr Watton himself – a bit decrepit. It is still there and could well be a listed building; Mr Watton, on the other hand, must, I feel sure, have passed on many years ago. He was a dear, kind man who always looked faintly down-at-heel, thus giving the impression that the only trade he ever did was that exacted during those two afternoons a week when the boys of Bromsgrove School invaded his premises; and 'invade' is, I think, the right word. We swarmed over them like wasps round a jam-pot. The current releases held in a wall-rack by the door and the remainder of his stock tucked tightly into shelves behind the counter were all fingered and pawed by small boys who were more curious than affluent. He had a radiogram squeezed into one corner on which we were allowed to sample his wares, and during those bi-weekly sessions everyone seemed to have a record in his hand and to be waiting impatiently for an opportunity to jump the queue and appropriate the turntable.

Gramophone records in those days were ten times more breakable than they are today, considerably more scratchable in view of the steel needles and heavy pickup arms, and on those afternoons the vulnerability of Mr Watton's stock presented a pretty lousy insurance risk. Under the circumstances I consider Mr Watton, who just stood there impassively while all went on around him, to have been a jolly good sport. I seldom had any money but somehow or other I usually managed to scrape together sufficient roubles to acquire each month's Harry Roy and Nat Gonella releases. Both recorded for Parlophone (1s 6d each) and while Harry Roy gave out with the current dance-music pops, 'My Kid's a Crooner', 'Boo-Hoo', 'It's a Sin to Tell a Lie', 'Is It True What They Say About Dixie?' *et al.*, Nat Gonella confined himself more to jazz standards. Also, when I could afford it, I invested in Joe Daniels and his Hot Shots, who recorded for the same label. I still possess the majority of the old seventy-eights that I bought from Mr Watton forty years ago.

During my last year Mr Watton moved to a new and slightly larger shop a hundred yards further down the High Street in which he extended his stock to include penny-whistles, mouth-organs, ukuleles and sheet music. It was situated in a parade of several new shops and was totally characterless.

I had a chum in Gordon House called Partridge who shared my interests and enthusiasms. He was a Nat Gonella and Fats Waller fan and we used to play our purchases on a portable gramophone every half-holiday between games and tea – the only time officially allowed and which amounted to about three hours' needle-time a week. A pretty meagre allocation, you might think. So did we, so we used to play them unofficially on several other occasions too, with a needle held in the hand at the end of a paper funnel or, alternatively, with a sharpened safety-match, similarly harnessed to an empty matchbox in order that nothing could be heard outside the study door. To be fair to the authorities, we were, in addition, allowed to play gramophones (wirelesses were strictly taboo for some unaccountable reason) between Evensong and supper on a Sunday evening but during that session strictly classical music only, which wasn't our scene.

My actual technical knowledge of music was, at that time, absolutely nil, so I decided to learn the piano. Being the possessor of an impatient and dilatory nature, I found the whole process somewhat slow and smacking of hard work, so I decided to join Partridge and have lessons on the alto-saxophone instead. With that I only had to read one note of music at a time instead of whole fistfuls on the pianoforte. After one term, during which my work had left rather more than usual to be desired, my housemaster's comments on my end of term report ran: 'Ian will never make any progress with his scholastic studies until he learns to concentrate on his lessons and abandons his craving for negroid music.'

The only outlet for my musical talents that achieved official approval was when I became the solo drummer and consequently in charge of the drum section of the OTC band. There were eight of us all told, and by dint of the sort of hard work that didn't worry me, we were soon playing and drilling with a precision that would have done credit to the Brigade of Guards. We won several band competitions at OTC camps and for this I received a certain amount of credit.

But in addition to making music I also wanted to act, to sing and dance, and I wanted to make people laugh. So I suppose it was only natural that Noël Coward, Fred Astaire and Jack Buchanan should also have

L/C I. G. Carmichael with his corps of drums. My
first real achievement of which I was justly proud

been my idols. The Astaire–Rogers musicals bracketed my years at Bromsgrove, and of these too I had an encyclopaedic knowledge. Noël Coward and Jack Buchanan I was to meet later in life and, blessed be it, they both lived up to the hero-worship I held for them during my youth.

There was a prop-man at Shepperton Studios who had worshipped a certain Hollywood superstar for years. Eventually she came to make a film in England and he was assigned to work on it. Her behaviour on the floor generally and, on occasions, to him personally left the poor lad with all illusions shattered. He became a broken man. Luckily this didn't happen to me.

There was, however, one serious drawback to my being able to practise for the craft that I had, by then, decided I would follow. No boy at Bromsgrove was allowed to join the Literary and Dramatic Society, membership of which was the only entrée to appearing in an official school play, until he was a member of the fifth form, a position rarely attained until one was reaching the end of one's time at the school. However, a kindly young master, an Oxford rugger blue called Peter Hordern, brother of the actor Michael Hordern, came to my aid and agreed to sponsor the forming of a Junior Literary and Dramatic Society for those too young or, alternatively, too backward or lazy to assail the dizzy heights of the fifth form. We weren't given the right to perform but at least we met about three times a term in Peter Hordern's study to read plays; which was, as we say in Yorkshire, 'better than nowt'. Eventually, during my last year, and after obtaining a solitary pass in geography at my second, if not third, attempt at School Certificate, I graduated to the senior society and was cast in the minute part of a maid in Goldsmith's *She Stoops To Conquer*. As the day of the performance drew near, an epidemic of chicken-pox hit the school with all the ferocity of a biblical plague. The cast was decimated. Four days before curtain-up the boy playing Hastings, the second male lead, became a victim and the master who was producing the play sent for me and asked if I thought I could learn the part in the time remaining. Yes, I responded without hesitation. And so, freed from all scholastic chores until the night of the performance, I girded my loins to accept my big chance. All went swimmingly. I crammed the lines in, a job I have never found easy, and at the end of the dress rehearsal twenty-four hours beforehand, I was reasonably confident, not to say cock-a-hoop, and determined to walk away with the metaphorical notices. On the morning of the actual performance I too woke up with chicken-pox and never left my bed. During my entire schooldays I never appeared in one official school play.

But though Bromsgrove School fully occupied two-thirds of my life during these years, there was always another third of each year during which I would return to the welcoming arms of my family and friends in Elloughton and Hull, and school holidays home from boarding-school brought joy and rapture unconfined.

Between the summer pursuits of collecting birds' eggs and butterflies, I also spent innumerable hours in the many Hull cinemas. These were the golden years of the Hollywood studios and their output was prolific. Movie after movie was turned out and most of them were of a consistently high standard – or at least highly professionally made. Each studio had its large stable of stars, and movies were tailored specifically to showcase those stars because it was them the public wanted to see.

Historical subjects, Westerns, epic spectaculars like *San Francisco* and *Hurricane*; romances and comedies from the boy-and-girl-next-door type epitomised by the Andy Hardy series to the more sophisticated, high-society variety of *The Thin Man*; child prodigy stuff, Shirley Temple, Mickey Rooney, Judy Garland, Deanna Durbin, Freddie Bartholomew; gangsters, glamorous musicals with Dick Powell, Don Ameche, Alice Faye, Eleanor Powell and the aforementioned Astaire and Rogers; biographies from *Emile Zola* to *The Great Ziegfeld*; and novels galore, which culminated in the first film long enough to incorporate an intermission, the legendary *Gone With The Wind*. All these and more besides, because I haven't mentioned the British studios and Alexander Korda's contribution, were showered on a voracious public, which soaked them up like blotting-paper.   .

Going to the pictures was a way of life in the 1930s. Programmes in all but the most underpopulated areas were continuous from 2 until 10.30 p.m. It was to the 'flicks' that one took one's girl and many cinemas had double seats in the back rows to accommodate the young lovers. On Friday and Saturday nights queues used to extend round the block for the final performance of successful movies, and, by Jove, you got value for money. In addition to the main feature, you were given the news, a cartoon, a comedy short featuring, if you were lucky, Laurel and Hardy, Chester Conklin, or some lesser known broad comedians, and a travelogue, invariably a Pete Smith production. In the larger cinemas you got a double feature; two full-length presentations. Then there was fifteen minutes of a gentleman, whose Christian name was invariably Reginald, who ascended through the floor of the orchestra pit playing a mighty organ which was surrounded by what appeared to be illuminated Edinburgh Rock and which changed colour every sixty seconds; and quite frequently a stage show incorporating two or three live acts as well. Not bad value for about three-and-sixpence top, and sixpence bottom.

It was the first matinée performance of the day that I usually attended and, to be quite honest, even at the risk of bursting the balloon that I have just inflated, the audiences at that time of the day, in Hull anyway, were, not to put too fine a point on it, sparse. Nevertheless, I lapped up the whole scene. Hey diddle-di-dee, an actor's life was undoubtedly for me.

There were also innumerable weekly film magazines on sale in the paper-shops during this era. *Picturegoer*, *Picture Show*, *Film Weekly* and many more, all of which I bought to read about the private lives of my idols, to cut out pictures of them in revealing bathing costumes by their swimming-pools or posing with their borzois and Hispano Suizas, and also to bone up on their future plans.

I found the cinema infinitely more glamorous than the live theatre. The rewards, too, seemed to be more attractive, both from a monetary and from an exposure and publicity point of view. This judgement was no doubt influenced by the fact that I saw little of the live theatre, for which Hull was notoriously badly served. During this period it had two variety houses and one small repertory theatre only. No chance ever of seeing any opera, ballet or current West End successes with their original, or even touring, casts. The repertory company, however, was a good one and very popular in the town. It presented a different play each week and many members of its ranks during those years have risen to distinguished positions in today's theatre and TV studios. I saw several of their productions, but 'The Little' never had the same magnetism for me as did the Regal, the Cecil or the Dorchester cinemas.

I am frequently asked which media I prefer working in most. The answer is a complex one and one which I will enlarge upon later, but in general my view hasn't changed a great deal since those days.

But the entertaining bug was biting deep. In my early teens I had erected curtains, lights and a switchboard across the width of my playroom at Elloughton and anyone whom I could press-gang into performing with me in this improvised theatre was not spared. My sisters were the chief victims, but I managed to cajole other friends into having a go too, and for the pleasure of watching such entertainments my long-suffering parents were persuaded to part with a penny or twopence entrance fee.

I also mounted cinematograph entertainments. My projector was a primitive, hand-cranked, toy machine for which you could purchase small reels of 35 mm. film, culled from copies of the real thing – the ones made for the cinema proper. They used to last for about three minutes or maybe less, depending on how fast you cranked the handle. I remember finding one of these in a toy-shop which, upon examination of the first few frames, proved to be a close-up of Maurice Chevalier in his straw boater. This was the first time I had actually identified a fully fledged movie star amongst these clips. I quickly bought it, rushed it home and slapped it on to the projector. That night the whole of Elloughton Garth was going to be treated to a film entertainment starring the one and only Maurice Chevalier. Three minutes later, to my horror, disappointment and anger, roughly in that order, I discovered that it was the same close-up from beginning to end. Furthermore, it was what is known as a reaction shot – in other words, a shot of the subject listening to, or watching whatever is being said or done off-screen behind the camera. It was the best sort of reaction shot too, I was to learn twenty years later – he didn't move a muscle throughout; hardly sufficient to warrant the increased admission fee that I had in mind.

But the year 1937 was almost at hand, and that was the year during which my musical expression reached its zenith. In the following year it suffered its decline and fall, but that was twelve months away. I entered 1937 in a spirit of confidence and optimism quite unbelievable in its naïveté.

On three consecutive days early in 1936 I placed the following advertisement in the personal column of the *Hull Daily Mail*:

WANTED, anyone under seventeen join new juvenile amateur dance band during school holidays – Ian Carmichael, Elloughton Garth, Brough.

This didn't actually produce the deluge of replies for which I had hoped. 1936 was not, apparently, a vintage year for amateur juvenile musicians in Kingston upon Hull. What it did produce, however, was a motley selection of the most unlikely and quite useless instrumentalists for forming the shimmering array of reeds and brass that I had seen myself fronting in a white tuxedo. A pianist who was obligatory, a saxophonist (E flat alto), a violinist (only useful, in my then bigoted opinion, for palm court ensembles), five accordions and a twelve-year-old xylophonist – big deal! It also brought the odd application from budding female crooners who fancied themselves as Hull's answer to Phyllis Robbins or Elsie Carlisle and who could also, they explained, tap dance, should it be necessary.

One of the accordionists was a personal friend of mine and, having a musical mother, he also played the saxophone. In addition, his father was Sheriff of Hull that year, which gave us a certain éclat, if not actual influence. The last time I saw Denis Townsley he was playing the trumpet for Edmundo Ros at The Bagatelle in wartime London, so, you see, in him we had a musician not to be sneezed at. In addition to this versatile array of talent, Bobby Saunders had also by now followed my trail-blazing and become a budding percussionist, which was useful in an emergency but only, let it be said, in an emergency, because that was to be my prerogative. In fact, I wanted to do everything; play the drums, wave the baton, do the vocals and turn out the absolutely stunning arrangements with which we would establish our own totally irresistible style.

Well, we met for our first rehearsal at the Young People's Institute in George Street. After the preliminary introductions I decided that we would have an initial canter with a topical number of the day called 'Goody, Goody'. I handed copies of the ordinary sheet-music piano part, which had a bizarre picture of somebody or something in red on the front, to the pianist and the accordionist (I decided to employ only one of the latter – after all every number couldn't be a tango) and 'top lines' that I had copied from them onto manuscript paper to the two saxophones and the fiddle. 'Intro and three choruses,' I announced, and off we went. Somewhere around the middle of the first chorus it was plain to Ian Carmichael and the entire personnel of his band that something was rotten in the state of Denmark Street. I pulled them all up short, looked over the pianist's shoulder at his music totally perplexed but trying not to show it and said, 'Hmm – yes, well, let's try it again shall we?' And we did – with the same disastrous results. It was then pointed out to me by my first E flat alto saxophone that their parts would have to be transposed if I wished the final result to sound in any way harmonious. ...

'A beat' – as the American playwrights say when trying to indicate how to time a line in their scripts.

This was something quite new to me. Transposed into what, I wondered? What I actually said was, 'Ah, yes, of course, silly of me.' And I was just about to say, 'Take five,' to give me time to think, when my bacon was saved for me because the lads concerned were, glory be, able to do this at sight, which saved me from total humiliation within the first quarter of an hour on the first day of rehearsals.

We then assailed 'Alone' from the Marx Brothers' *A Night at the Opera* and 'Did I Remember' from some film of Jean Harlow.

Further rehearsals were conducted one afternoon a week at the

The first line up of Ian Carmichael and his Band for their initial concert at the Metropole Hall in Hull

Metropole Hall in West Street. At about the third of these my father came in to listen to the last half hour, prior to driving me home. After we'd cleared the outskirts of Hull, having made no comment at all thus far, he said, 'You know, I'll tell you what I think's wrong, Ian. There are far too many instruments playing the melody.' He was, of course, dead right. They all were. The trouble was – and now it must be told if it hasn't been painfully obvious all along – that, though my heart was in the right place and my enthusiasm and confidence knew no bounds, I was a quite appalling, if not non-existent, musician. I think I played the drums well, although I never worried very much about reading, but I wasn't a very good saxophonist and my knowledge of theory and orchestration was, not to put too fine a point on it, nil.

However, I learn quickly when I want to and, though I never assimilated sufficient knowledge to do the job properly, with co-operation from my musicians we managed to put on a couple of concerts in aid of local charities which were patronised by as many relatives and friends as we could all muster. The first of these, I see from my records, benefited the Victoria Hospital for Sick Children by £2 15s 3d. I also see that '... the band rendered a varied selection of popular melodies played in a bright and snappy way', and that 'conjuring tricks by Ian Carmichael, leader and drummer of the band, who also arranged and produced the entire show, provided another high note' (*Hull Daily Mail*)! Whenever, over the intervening years, I have been asked to appear in cabaret I have always said, 'I'm sorry, I have no material to do in cabaret.' Maybe, like an iceberg, I have a submerged four-fifths that I should explore more frequently.

During these early weeks I started doing a bit of a line with one of my employees – a young strawberry-blonde by the name of Hazel Rowe. I had engaged her as a crooner and with her I sang several duets – 'When did you leave heaven?' being one little gem that comes to mind. After rehearsals I used to walk her to her bus at the back of the Regal cinema in Ferensway and frequently, *en route*, we would repair to a convenient telephone-booth in a dark and secluded corner of Paragon Station. Hazel Rowe was, I think, the first girl I ever kissed in hot blood and such was her surprise at my initial assault that she promptly spilt the entire contents of her powder compact down my overcoat when attempting to repair the damage.

However, my confidence and bravado were not, as yet, unduly shaken by the discovery that I had limitations which might possibly cramp my aspirations to excel as a musician. So it was in this phlegmatic mood that I was sitting in a study at Bromsgrove one afternoon during the following term, reading a copy of the *Melody Maker* when I should have had my nose buried in an algebra textbook preparing for my first assault on School Certificate, when the headlines of an article leapt off the printed page and hit me with all the impact of the opening bars of Beethoven's fifth symphony. 'JUVENILE DRUMMER WANTED' it screamed.

The Controllers of the Royal Kiltie Juniors Band are anxious to secure the services of a talented juvenile drummer between the ages of 14 and 17. He must be able to read, and although it is not essential that he plays xylophone, this asset will influence preference. Apply at once direct to Messrs International Theatrical and Musical Corporation, 42 Deansgate, Manchester.

It then went on to explain that the Royal Kiltie Juniors Band (of whom I had never heard) had just concluded a successful variety tour and were about to go to Brighton for the summer with a new revue. It also stated that they had twice 'faced the movie cameras'.

Well now, offers of employment for 'talented juvenile drummers' do not, as they say, grow on trees. This may not only be the first but also the last that might ever come my way. I did not play the xylophone and my reading was fairly non-existent but this in no way deterred me from applying for the job. Down came a sheet of the best die-stamped school notepaper, complete with crest and motto: *Deo, Regi, Vicino* – For God, For King, For Neighbour – and for young Carmichael too, on this occasion; the letter was written and posted in a trice.

Now you must try and get what I did into a bit of perspective. I was imprisoned at boarding-school, a hundred and sixty miles from home, without a bean to my name except the shilling-a-week pocket-money which was handed over to us each Friday. My shilling had always been spent by the Saturday night anyway, so the odds are that if I had any money at all it was in the form of a few postage-stamps. These were, incidentally, accepted as legal tender at the tuck-shop, and writing home for some more stamps always had a better ring about it than asking for more money. I was also about a hundred miles from Manchester, so what I had intended doing about it should I be invited to attend an audition I had never for a moment stopped to consider. The enormity of a decision to walk out of a boarding-school is probably difficult to appreciate in this far more scholastically permissive and lenient age but in 1937 it would, believe me, have been the equivalent of breaking out of gaol.

A few days later a reply arrived on notepaper surmounted by possibly the most ornate letter-heading that I have ever seen before or since; it took up very nearly a third of the paper. 'The International Theatrical and Musical Corporation' was blazoned across the top in enormous letters and in the centre there was a huge insignia of a very beautiful lady with a highly alluring figure clothed, all except for her right breast, in a full-length white Grecian frock. Her right arm was holding, shoulder high, a lyre, and in her left hand, the bottom of which rested on the ground in the manner of Britannia, she held a large, futuristic-looking shield containing what I can only describe as masonic hieroglyphics. Looking at it again in my maturity, I think the latter may be meant to represent a composite of the masks of Comedy and Tragedy, but that is pure conjecture. The lady herself is superimposed on a building which looks as if it is by the Acropolis out of the Royal Exchange, and that, in turn, is superimposed on a rising sun of Hollywood proportions over which hangs the type of cloud that normally only appears in paintings of the Ascension. Below this, in another colour, is the address, on one side of which, in a circle the size of a fivepenny piece, it informs the recipient of the Corporation's telephone number and telegraphic address. Directly opposite, on the other side of the address, for all the world as if the paper had been folded down the middle and blotted while the ink was still wet, there is an identical circle in which the same information is repeated. If viewed through the right glasses, perhaps the information would appear in stereo – I know not. The bottom inch of the paper is taken up by a few ornate lines in two different colours, and a statement in the very smallest of type that any offer in the letter does not constitute a contract.

In the limited amount of space available between all this, there was a message informing me that, if I had all the qualifications specified in the advertisement plus, it now added, the ability to play tympani (of course I could, no problem there; it was merely a question of hitting the darned things), I should 'make my way through' (*sic*) to the Empire Theatre, Newport, Mon., tomorrow, where the manager of the band would give me an audition.

The moment of truth had arrived. What was I to do?

Well, I suppose it is really rather a wet end to an otherwise determined effort to assert my independence. I had, under the circumstances, no alternative but to go to my housemaster and confess all. He took it rather well, considering. I hadn't exactly been his favourite pupil over the years, in fact I think it would be fair to say that I had been a bit of a problem to him on many scores, but this time he seemed to accept the situation with resignation. To help us both out without losing too much face, I suggested that he should ring the Empire Theatre, Newport, Mon., and explain that as I did not play tympani it would be pointless my attending for an audition.

At Christmas 1937 the band was engaged to play at an NSPCC dance at the Hull workhouse, now demolished in favour of a fine new hospital building which has been erected on the site. It was our first professional engagement. Being of both Scottish and Yorkshire stock, and pretty impecunious as well, I was very quick to jettison the amateur status at the first opportunity.

This engagement was notable for an incident that took place at about 10.30 p.m. In the middle of a number – 'One, Two, Button My Shoe', I think it was, an old Bing Crosby favourite – I decided to execute a piece of showmanship to demonstrate my versatility and authority. I removed a cymbal from one of the rocker-arms and, with it in one hand and a drumstick in the other, I abandoned my drum-kit and moved forward to the front of the band, playing it the while. This had the advantage of not only drawing attention to myself as a musician but also indicating that I was in charge. After a moment or two I saw a couple endeavouring to work their way through the other dancers towards the bandstand. As they approached I knelt down towards them to hear the number that they were obviously going to request. On arrival the young man said,

'Are you the leader of the band?' 'Yes,' I replied. 'Then I suggest you go home and pull the plug,' was his rapier-like response. ...

Over the next eighteen months the band changed a good deal and always for the better. This was occasioned almost entirely by my absences at school. The others stuck together throughout, weeded out most of the dead wood like accordions, roped in more accomplished young musicians with more appropriate instruments and played at many more local dances, far more successfully without me.

I was never actually asked to leave but my student days in London were rapidly approaching, and as I spent less and less time in Hull I just sort of faded out of the picture and left them all to it.

Also in 1937, spurred by my continued enthusiasm for the film industry and no doubt wishing to boost a bruised morale caused by an initial brush with the world of music, I decided to make my own feature film. A simple, unpretentious little domestic drama, written by myself, called *What Happened At The Gables*.

What did happen at The Gables was as follows:

An inoffensive suburban housewife, played with no previous acting experience by the daughter of the house next door to my band's pianist, one Geoffrey Hibbert, left home on the morning concerned to go shopping. During her absence two housebreakers, Hibbert himself (First Housebreaker), Denis Townsley (second E flat alto saxophone doubling accordion; Second Housebreaker), having been informed of her departure by myself (Third Housebreaker and 'lookout'), from a nearby GPO call-box, forced an entry and bound and gagged the domestic servant – the latter being played by an attractive bit of local skirt who occasionally appeared in the odd *ingénue* role at the repertory theatre when the company was at full stretch; it was a piece of casting which was considered to be a great coup. Robbery was then committed. Betty Atkinson, for such was the name of the only semi-pro in the cast, wriggled her way along the floor like a demented python and, with her shoulder, skilfully shook an occasional table on which the telephone was situated. With more shaking and even greater skill she then managed to dislodge the handpiece. This attracted the attention of an alert telephone operator played by my sister Peggy (Margaret), and was shot on the small switchboard in my father's emporium on a Sunday. She promptly relayed her suspicions to the police. The only two members of the Force to which we could run (we could only raise two uniforms), friends of Geoffrey Hibbert, then left the station hot foot in Townsley's father's Hillman.

Townsley and Hibbert, by some wheeze that I can't remember, got wind of the imminent confrontation and beat a hasty retreat from The Gables (the real-life residence of Mr Hibbert senior) in my mother's Morris Ten. Then followed a car chase that puts the one in *The Italian Job* well and truly in the shade, and I choose my words carefully. Some of ours appeared to have been shot in brilliant sunshine and the remainder in heavy cloud. As I myself, however, was both the director and the camera-man, this fault, I felt sure, could only have lain with the laboratories. In addition, in ours it was at times difficult to fathom who was actually chasing whom, but this only seemed to add to the excitement. The whole eventually culminated in a smoke-filled room – the gang's HQ (EXT – local tennis club. INT – a back room in Mr Townsley senior's house) – where five more lads of the village, average age seventeen, were playing cards and doing their best to represent the remainder of a gang of hardened criminals. If you looked hard, one of them could be identified as Derek Monsey, a future novelist and film critic of the *Daily Express*. Round-up of miscreants and roller credits superimposed over the upturned card-table and chairs on the floor of the empty room. Fifteen minutes packed with high drama and suspense.

The whole was shot on my father's 16 mm camera, edited the following term at school by myself and a colleague, and fell to pieces every time it was shown.

Nobody can say that I hadn't thoroughly explored every branch of the entertainment industry before deciding which particular one I wished to follow – and that decision I now made. It was a positive and irrevocable one, though it was also one that I was to have grave doubts about in ten years' time.

I can't remember the actual moment when I announced to my parents that I wanted to become an actor. In fact, I'm not even sure there ever was such a moment. After all that had been going on during the past few years, I think it was just taken for granted. Nevertheless, since we had, as a family, no connections whatever with the theatrical profession, some fairly positive decisions had to be made concerning how I should go about it, so I have no doubt that at some time or other I must have made a specific declaration of my intention.

It must have been an enormous disappointment to them, poor dears – particularly to my father. After all, I was his only son and Carmichael's was by this time a flourishing luxury-goods store. Its wares embraced jewellery, gold and silver, with such ancillary spinoffs as watches, clocks, cutlery, fountain-pens and cigarette-lighters; also glass and china, leather goods, antiques and an optical department which sold barometers, binoculars and cameras. On the first floor of the building my father had taken over responsibility for a check trading company (a form of easy-payments business particular to the industrial north) called The North British Supply Co., which was older than Carmichael's and probably had its roots in my uncle Robert's door-to-door watch-trading at the start of his career. Nevertheless, it was now a thriving enterprise with an annual turnover that exceeded that of the retail shop downstairs. The four brothers who had founded, built up and were now running this little empire had only produced three male issue between them. The eldest had left school several years previously and was now ploughing his own furrow elsewhere. The second in line had gone to Cambridge and was giving every appearance of wanting to carve out an independent career for himself in accountancy. The third was myself. My decision to turn my back on all this must have been a bitter blow to my father, but to their eternal credit, once my parents realised my mind was made up, they were superb. The family business was never mentioned again. For myself, I'm ashamed to say, I never for a moment considered any other course of action. The glittering prize of such an inheritance tempted me not one jot or tittle. The impetuosity of youth, plus an unbelievable confidence, were my Sword Excalibur.

The decision made, how to go about it was the next question. I had not the remotest idea where to start so, any port in a storm, my father approached my housemaster to see if he could tender any advice. The news of my eccentricity didn't surprise that gentleman one little bit. He had had to live with and suffer my vagaries for the past four and a half years. He advised that I should try and get into the Royal Academy of Dramatic Art, admission to which did not appear to be over-selective at that time.

Accordingly, I set out to prepare myself for the entrance examination, which consisted of performing two pieces on the stage of its Little Theatre, one to be selected from a half-dozen or so provided by the faculty, the other of one's own choice. Of the former, it was a toss-up between an excerpt from Galsworthy's *The Silver Box* or a speech of Professor Higgins from *Pygmalion*. I think I chose the latter. For the piece of my own choice I again flew to my housemaster for advice. Suddenly my visits to his study were assuming an entirely new aspect: they were now very much of a man-to-man nature which I was actually enjoying.

'Why not try a spot of Shakespeare?' he said.

Elementary, of course – why hadn't I thought of it? Well, I'll tell you why I hadn't thought of it. I was, as I have already recounted, a bone-idle scholar. I had always known that I would adopt one of two callings. I would either enter my father's business or else I would become an actor, and for neither would I require School Certificate. Why then, I reasoned, should I work myself to a frazzle at lessons, all of which I hated? It was a totally reprehensible attitude of which I have been deeply ashamed ever since. I have also been deeply regretful ever since of lost opportunities. However, that was my attitude at the time, and one of the lessons which I found particularly tedious and unrewarding was the study of the Bard of Avon; consequently my knowledge of his plays was scant. Neverthe-less, one of the advantages of being a member of the Junior Literary and Dramatic Society, which Peter Hordern had so kindly taken under his wing, was an outing once a term to see a matinée at the Shakespeare Memorial Theatre at Stratford. This term we had witnessed *Macbeth*, which was still fresh in my memory. James Dale, a distinguished actor who would eventually become known to millions in his radio role of Dr Dale, as immortalised in his wife's journal, had played the main part and his histrionics in the delivery of the dagger speech had struck me as being good, strong, meaty stuff. So – believe it or not – the dagger speech it was to be. I swotted it up and a few weeks later I again repaired to my housemaster's study, our new-found friendship spurring me on, and requested that he should sit down and allow me to perform both pieces for him. It must have been quite alarming for the poor man, but suffer it he did. I can't remember what sort of a reception I received – kindly, I suspect – because he must, while watching me, have felt both thankful and secure in the knowledge that in three weeks' time I would be leaving Bromsgrove and his jurisdiction for ever.

CHAPTER SIX

LONDON

Freedom

There was once, I am told, a certain celebrity who, having gone through a bad bout of alcoholism during six years of his life which he eventually conquered, upon sitting down to write his autobiography, put an advertisement in *The Times* which read: 'If anyone knows what I was doing between 1951 and 1957, would they please get in touch with me, earliest.' I know exactly how he must have felt.

From leaving school at Christmas 1938 until reporting for military service twenty-one months later, my life, though reasonably ordered at the time, appears to me now as one zonking great chronological mess. During those twenty-one months I lived, it now seems, practically a lifetime. It was a period of unconfined joy, occasioned by my finally shaking off the shackles of school discipline and being able to mix daily with young men and women who shared my interests and enthusiasms. This joy was, nevertheless, being tempered daily by the worsening European situation. The fear that now, just as I was standing on the threshold of a future that I had dreamed about for years, the whole thing might be snuffed out like a candle was too unbearable to contemplate.

My memories of that period are truly kaleidoscopic – an endless variety of highly coloured, ever-changing patterns. Some rapturous, some garish and jarring. I suppose the scene did change more during those months than in any similar period of my life.

Having been accepted for RADA, I arrived in London to take up my studies in January 1939, very much the unsophisticate, the innocent abroad. I had been to London only twice in my life, once at the age of sixteen when my parents took my sisters and me on a three-day holiday to see the sights, and once a year later when I was allowed a similar brief holiday with Peter Kidd during which we spent the entire time in cinemas and theatres.

I was very green to the old metrop, as indeed were my parents. We

My mother just
before the war

had no friends or relatives living there, and money, despite a flourishing family business, was tight. The latter point might appear questionable, but I was to find out much later in life that, although we had hitherto lived a comfortable family life, it had been a very hand-to-mouth existence. My parents had sacrificed practically all their cash and many personal ambitions and desires to provide their children's education. So now, as I always knew would happen once I left school, I was to start to feel the pinch.

Under the circumstances, therefore, as far as accommodation was concerned, it had to be the most economical, and this was provided at an address in Adelaide Road, Chalk Farm. It was recommended in the RADA brochure – I think they even called it a hostel – but it was, in effect, a tall, semi-detached, semi-basement Victorian house which was presided over by a genial, middle-aged character-actor called Christopher Steele. He was still a practising performer and obviously ran his establishment to augment his professional income.

Mr Steele himself occupied a large room at the back on the ground floor, and his housekeeper, a Miss Thorburn, a single room on the top floor. Miss Thorburn was a jolly, tolerant spinster of indeterminate years who had a great deal of dark-auburn hair all gathered together in a sort of cock's-comb which earned her the pseudonym of 'Carrot Top'. In addition there were, if memory serves me right, seven other bedrooms. These were furnished with functional furniture rather than with an eye to

aestheticism, and each contained its own metered gas fire. From a communal point of view there was one bathroom with an old-fashioned tubular
gas-geyser, also on a meter; a sitting-room which contained a large,
white, marble mantelpiece, ground floor front and seldom used as intended; and a dining-room and kitchen in the semi-basement where
Carrot Top cooked up breakfast and an evening meal.

The occupants of the house, upon my arrival, included a friendly Scotsman called, if you don't mind, Scottie, with whom I established an instant
rapport, and a very intense student called David of whom I have never
heard from that day to this. David practised his voice production and
elocution lessons either in his bedroom or in the communal sitting-room
at full lung power during every available off-duty moment; if industry
counts for anything, he should be head of the National Theatre by now.
There was also a likeable young Lancastrian who had just about every
attribute necessary to prevent his success as a thespian, and who is now
a prop-man in a TV studio, and a very large, pint-swilling Australian
who had only one suit of clothes but a drawer full of contraceptive pes-
saries. He smoked incessantly and was never to be seen without his nose
in a paperback. I got on famously with Bill, probably because we both
enjoyed our tipple. He used to teach me to box in the communal sitting-
room when it wasn't being used as a sounding-board by David. Bill
entered the National Fire Service on the outbreak of war and later served
in the army. Subsequently he returned to Australia, I'm told, where he
married, had three children and then died of a heart attack.

Another inmate was not a student at the RADA. He had the largest
room on the letting list, his own piano and a small Morris. He also,
I suspect, had rather more money than the rest of us. He was a good-
looking lad and a student baritone with an ambition to follow in the
shoes of Nelson Eddy. There was also in residence a young actor. A fully
paid up member of British Actors' Equity, albeit he appeared to be out
of work most of the time. It was a motley throng but we all seemed to
get along very well together.

The RADA itself at that time did not seem to take its responsibilities
as seriously as it does now. It appeared, in many respects, to be a glorified
finishing-school for girls, who outnumbered the men by about five to one,
and it was obvious from the outset that the percentage of talents that
would ever reach the professional theatre, let alone succeed in it, was
not a generous one. However, mine was not to reason why, neither did
I wish to. 'It's a great life as long as you weaken,' someone once said,
and I was prepared to all along the line. *Les girls* were my main weak-

ness, but you must understand that life in a boys' boarding-school is monastic to say the least, and to be transferred suddenly, a normal, not to say lascivious, male, at the age of eighteen, into a co-ed establishment in which the dice were so disproportionately loaded in the male's favour was heady stuff. But if everything else was in my favour, there was one thing that was not – money. Or to be more explicit, the supply of it. My father paid for my board and lodgings direct to Christopher Steele at the beginning of each term and I, personally, was allowed £1 a week pocket-money, out of which I had to pay for all my fares to and from the Academy in Gower Street, and also my mid-day meals. Even in 1938, I assure you, that left me precious little at the end of the week with which to enjoy myself, let alone lavish hospitality on girl-friends. One of my contemporaries, a boy called Peter Felgate who became a great chum, was a Londoner and knew his way around better than I did, which was invaluable. Very early on, he introduced me to the Brasserie at both the Oxford and Coventry Street Lyons' Corner Houses, each of which served an excellent three-course lunch for 1s 6d – or 7½p, would you believe, in today's money. But after food and fares I was left with only 10s, or 50p, at the outside. Once a week to the pictures at either the Swiss Cottage or Haverstock Hill Odeon, or the Gaumont, Camden Town, cigarettes and the odd pint of beer left me more than anxious for the mail every Monday morning when the next £1 note would be included in a letter from my father.

Yet, despite the straitened circumstances, life was good at the RADA. It was, nevertheless, disappointing to find that, even when I was at last training for a vocation in which I dearly wanted to succeed, my natural inclination to be lazy was still in the ascendant. All the classroom subjects like voice production, elocution, dancing and fencing I considered were, up to a point, necessary evils – some more necessary than others. Voice production – fine. I did learn to project my voice properly and it has stood me in good stead ever since. Elocution, certainly most useful. It was interesting to me, after having arrived at Bromsgrove with what I was told was an appalling Yorkshire accent, to arrive five years later at the RADA with what my elocution master assured me was an equally disastrous Brummagem one. But dancing was largely the rudiments of ballet, and fencing I considered to be of even more doubtful use to a bloke who saw his future in modern drawing-room comedy. I would like to stress at this point that this was the attitude of a rather indolent teenager; my sense of values today is something quite different.

During my first term we performed three plays. Two classics: *The*

Merchant of Venice and *The School for Scandal*, and one modern: Priestley's *Time and the Conways*. In my second we did *The Taming of the Shrew* in which I had a bash at Petruchio, which I thoroughly enjoyed, and *Iphigenia in Tauris*, a spot of Greek tragedy, which I didn't. We also assailed Thornton Wilder's *Our Town*, a modern play containing neither props nor scenery, which was interesting and, no doubt, cheap to mount.

In the Greek opus, which I found monumentally boring, I played King Thoas. It was a very small part, practically non-speaking if I remember rightly. My first entrance was made in the middle of a solemn procession which proceeded from the wings, along a rostrum at the back of the stage parallel to the footlights, turned left centre stage and advanced towards the audience down a flight of steps, and then split up right and left where it mingled with a dozen or so barefoot young ladies in what appeared to be pale-lemon nightdresses who represented the chorus. Our one and only performance was given in the Academy Little Theatre to a 3 p.m. matinée audience. At lunch-time on the appointed day, my pint-swilling Australian chum, Bill Bennett, and another colleague called Bill Squire (now a distinguished Welsh actor) took me round to the nearest local hostelry in Store Street and poured down me at least one too many. Also in very good order themselves by the time we came to leave, they insisted on helping me to make up. This they accomplished with the aid of some sticks of green and mauve greasepaint that they managed to find somewhere – colours, I might add, that an actor may have occasion to use once in a lifetime and this was certainly not the one for me. They then pointed me in the general direction of the stage and went round to watch the result of their handywork from the gallery. I was not too sloshed to know precisely the impression I intended to make on the unsuspecting audience. The procession commenced, all the participant characters – soldiers, prisoners, handmaidens, you name them – being spaced correctly at about a yard apart. I was somewhere about the middle of it all, and when it was my turn to enter I let those preceding me carry out the complete manœvre until they were all in position and static. Momentarily the stage was still, everyone looking up at the rostrum to see what had happened. At this point, I made the most impressive of entrances on my own. I wore a heavy black beard, a hat which resembled a peacock-blue tea-cosy, and a tiger-skin cloak. Hilarity invaded the ladies of the chorus as I shakily negotiated the steps and finally took up a postion on a stone bench for the rest of the act, from which I proceeded to tickle the feet of the chorus with my tiger-skin. Hilarity too, I might add, emanated from the majority of the audience, which was always rather sparse for Greek tragedy, and which was made up almost entirely of fellow students who by then had been appraised of an impending disaster and had been herded into the gallery by my friends, the two Bills. All quite unforgivable, of course, but it was, I suppose, all part of my effervescent irresponsibility and new-found freedom.

The social scene was all sweetness and light during this period. Few of us had 'the ready' to frequent the accredited night spots, but this mattered little; we made our own fun. Regular parties at fellow students' flats or bed-sits were the order of the day – or rather, the night. About a dozen of us would assemble, each taking a couple of quart bottles of beer, which was cheap. The host or hostess provided the sandwiches and we played actors' games like Charades or The Game until the beer took over, the lights went out and the necking started. But it was all largely clean, innocent and hugely enjoyable.

We used to finish afternoon work at the Academy round about tea-time and a gang of us would always go along to the second floor of the Oxford Street Corner House after it was over to drink tea, eat rum babas and dance to quite a large orchestra that played there six days a week.

At the beginning of my second term I was to make my first professional appearance on the stage. There was at that time a company installed at a theatre called the People's Palace in the Mile End Road, Stepney, which performed weekly repertory, and included in its programme for May of that year was a play called *RUR*, which stood for Rossum's Universal Robots. It was written by a Czech couple called Karel and Josef Capek and was a sort of science-fiction offering about man-made robots who finally rebel and take over their masters. Not very original now, but possibly it was then. Eight extras were required for the rebellion scene and for these the director had applied for eight students from the RADA. I was one of those selected and for a whole week I made my way down the Mile End Road each night to dress up in a suit of brown dungarees, a tall tubular hat made of brown linoleum, and for the second and last time in my career I made up my face, this time as instructed, with green and mauve greasepaint. The remuneration we received was ten shillings and sixpence for the entire week which, on returning home after the final performance on the Saturday night, I 'blew' in its entirety on a Knicker-bocker Glory in the Strand Lyons' Corner House. Though this was my first professional appearance on any stage, I cannot report that I look back upon it as any sort of milestone. It was a dull play performed in a cold and uninspiring theatre and my particular contribution required absolutely no acting talent whatsoever. In addition, the director appeared to be both bad-tempered and indecisive, at one point instructing me to stand still and in the next upbraiding me for immobility. 'Get a move on, boy – don't just stand there like Banquo's ghost!' The whole exercise was totally unmemorable.

Not so, however, a most unexpected accolade that I was to receive a few weeks later. When that arrived I was to discover for the first time the quite indescribable elation that an actor experiences upon being awarded the part of a lifetime. It wasn't actually the part of a lifetime but the circumstance in which it was offered to me made it very special indeed.

The full course at the RADA at the beginning of 1939 was two years and, at the end of my first term, selected students who were in their final year appeared, during the following holidays, in a special production of *A Midsummer-Night's Dream*. Directed by a fine interpreter of Shakespeare called Neil Porter, it had been designed with brand-new costumes and was presented twice daily, once in the morning and once in the afternoon, for a period of four weeks in the larger of the Academy's two theatres, for the express benefit of LCC schoolchildren.

When the Academy reassembled for the following term, this production was the main topic of conversation among the students; the whole building seemed to be redolent with praise for its achievements.

Two individual performances were singled out for special mention and the two actors were, in the rarefied atmosphere of student hysteria, in danger of becoming legends in their own lifetime. One, a splendid actor called Ion Rhys Jones who, tragically, was to be killed during the war, played Bottom. The second was a tall, erect, crinkly-haired, sharp-featured young man with the bearing of a guardsman and a rather camp sense of humour called John Hewitt, who played the small part of Flute the bellows-mender. Flute is the 'rustic' who plays Thisbe in the final play scene, and such had been Mr Hewitt's comic impact that anyone not knowing the play and hearing only the plaudits could have been excused for assuming that his had been the leading role.

Well, towards the end of my second term, during which the foregoing legends had established themselves, in the middle of an elocution class when I was half way through a delivery of the Prologue to Act II of *Henry V*, a messenger entered the classroom and informed Mr Wallace Evennett, our tutor, that Sir Kenneth Barnes, the principal of the Academy, wished to see Ian Carmichael in his study.

Suddenly I was back at Bromsgrove. What had I done wrong? Visions

The RADA student

of Freddie Hadrill's wrath, a big stick and green imposition paper floated before my eyes; I don't think I had, at that time, ever spoken to Sir Kenneth personally. He had addressed me from a distance, a mere silhouette in a box at the back of a darkened auditorium during my initial entrance audition and I had, no doubt, along with the remainder of my contemporaries, been the recipient of an opening 'jolly-up' from him at the beginning of our first term; but I had never, as yet, been received in solo audience. What could the man want? Well, there was only one way of finding out. Mr Evennett excused me and I made my way downstairs to Sir Kenneth's office which was on the right of the main entrance door.

I knocked.

'Come in.'

I entered.

'Ah, Ian,' he said. That was a good start. If we were on christian-name terms obviously whatever my misdemeanour had been it was not of too serious a nature.

'What are you doing during the next holidays? During the summer – got any plans?'

What was the fellow building up to?

'I haven't really thought,' I replied. 'I've no plans at the moment.'

'Ah, good,' said Sir Kenneth. 'Well, we're going to repeat Mr Porter's production of *The Dream* for the schoolchildren this coming September. So-and-so who played Lysander last time is leaving and won't be available, so we're giving the part to John Hewitt.'

I didn't have time to anticipate what was coming next because he rushed straight on without drawing breath.

'Mr Porter and I wondered whether you'd like to take over from him and play the part of Flute.'

I ran back to my class two stairs at a time 'with winged heels' like one of those 'English Mercuries' about whom I had, only a few minutes previously, been declaiming. I was speechless with excitement. What had just happened to me was as inconceivable as it was unexpected. That I, a lowly second-term student, should have been given the role, the recent performance of which had been the talk of Gower Street, produced in me an elation of cocaine-sniffing proportions. It was an unbelievable reward so early in my student career and the receipt of it gave me added stature among my classmates. The men's reaction seemed to be a mixture of envy and awe, and the effect on the girls was all that I could have wished. Now I couldn't wait for the summer holidays.

During most student productions a play was performed once only and even then it was invariably only 'scenes from' and not the whole work. On such occasions when the whole play was performed, the parts in it would, more often than not, be split between the over-abundance of students so that throughout a performance of, say, *The Merchant of Venice* there could be as many as five different Shylocks. Now, for the first time, I was about to appear in forty-eight consecutive performances of a whole play, correctly cast.

At the end of term I went home to Elloughton holding my head up high and feeling as proud as a peacock. On arrival, I typed out my part from a large volume of the *Complete Works* and spent the next fortnight wandering round the garden learning it, thinking about the character and wondering what I could do with it to live up to, if not better, Mr Hewitt's past glory.

Two weeks later I returned to Mr Steele's in Adelaide Road and on the first morning of rehearsals I left the house with Bill Bennett, who played Snout the tinker. Now, however, poised on the brink as it were, more than a *soupçon* of apprehension was beginning to make its presence felt. The cast remained largely unchanged from its former production and the actors were all senior to me, established in their roles and well known to each other – I was the new boy, and the nearer the tube drew us to Goodge Street station the more the butterflies in my stomach proliferated. Finally we arrived in the large rehearsal room on the top floor of the Academy's rear building in Malet Street and introductory pleasantries were exchanged. The first thing I noticed was that many people were smoking. This in itself immediately presented a new, relaxed and professional approach to the proceedings – during term-time smoking was never allowed during rehearsals, only in the refectory. Introductions over, an initial read-through began. All went swimmingly until we came to my first line. I delivered it as privately rehearsed in the garden at Elloughton Garth.

'What on *earth* are you doing, dear boy?' rang out the sonorous tones of Neil Porter, himself a distinguished Shakespearian actor. 'The man's not mentally deficient. Why are you speaking in that *extraordinary* manner?'

First blood to Mr Porter. He was right, of course. In an attempt to be funny at all costs I was committing practically every crime in the book – like not thinking about the character, not thinking about what I was saying and grossly overacting, to mention but three. It is difficult to get a laugh on a line like, 'Here, Peter Quince,' but I was determined to, come what may. However, suitably corrected and feeling as if I had been squashed as flat as an intruding cockroach, I threw away all my preconceived ideas and placed myself in the good and capable hands of Mr Porter. This was not the last time that I was to question the wisdom, and frequently the waste of time, of an actor doing a lot of pre-rehearsal study on his role before meeting and discussing it with his director.

Rehearsals for *The Dream* settled in and a most enjoyable and rewarding experience I found them. Neil Porter, a tall man with aquiline features and a huge Roman nose, had the ability of making the most complicated Shakespearian text understandable to a child of five, and his simple, logical and enthusiastic approach made rehearsals stimulating and exciting for his actors.

But heartbreak and disappointment are the stuff an actor's bad dreams are made on and this production was to be the first but by no means the last that I was to experience.

It was a fun production, full of enchantment, and the thought of going to the theatre every day for four weeks, playing an enjoyable part and associating generally with a cast of talented and entertaining people filled me with contentment.

We opened in what is now called the Vanbrugh Theatre on the morning of 1 September, the same day that Hitler's troops invaded Poland. In the middle of our afternoon performance the king signed the order for the general mobilisation of the army, navy and the air force, and after our curtain rang down, because of the imminence of war which would necessitate the evacuation of London schoolchildren, we were informed that our run was to close there and then after only the two performances. We were numbed.

Bill Bennett and I packed up our make-up and returned dejectedly to Adelaide Road. We were accompanied, I think, by Bill Squire too. Having dumped our props at 187, our lodgings, we headed for what is known today in theatrical circles as a greasy spoon 'caff', in Swiss Cottage, where we ordered waffles with maple syrup and cups of coffee. We had bought copies of the evening papers *en route* and there we sat on our drugstore-type bar-stools assimilating the dismal and depressing news that was emblazoned across their front pages. Somewhere up above an aeroplane droned and I know that we each independently reflected, 'Hello, already? Is it one of theirs or one of ours?'

We sat there for some time debating what to do. The RADA had closed, at least until the start of the following term, and none of us had a job; where did we go from here? 'Lord, what fools these mortals be!' I reflected philosophically, had been the most appropriate line spoken in the Vanbrugh Theatre on that day.

I made up my mind fairly quickly. War seemed to be only hours away. What sort of a holocaust would be unleashed on London when the moment came, nobody knew, but judging by what had been going on in Poland over the previous twenty-four hours it could be devastating. I decided to get out of the capital there and then. I bid a fond and sad farewell to my two colleagues, not knowing when, if ever, I would see them again, and returned to Christopher Steele's. There I packed my belongings, said goodbye to my landlord and dear old Carrot Top and caught the next train out of King's Cross for Hull and Elloughton.

CHAPTER SEVEN

LONDON REVISITED

From Exhilaration to Anguish

Two days later, at 11.15 in the morning Prime Minister Neville Chamberlain made his historic radio announcement from 10 Downing Street, informing the nation that, as no undertaking had been received from the German Chancellor to withdraw his troops from Poland by 11 a.m., the country was consequently at war with Germany.

The family listened to the melancholy announcement in stunned silence. For the remainder of the day my father and I filled sandbags and piled them up outside the two windows of the smoke-room. The walls of Elloughton Garth were about eighteen inches thick and built of solid stone, so, short of a direct hit, we considered that we could transform it into a shelter that would at least be blast- and splinter-proof.

By dusk we had only half completed our task but with sandbags up to a height of about four feet we were assured of protection in an emergency, provided we lay on the floor. Shortly after midnight, when we were all in bed, the first sirens of the war sounded in our area. The whole family donned dressing-gowns and went down to the smoke-room. We sat there speechless and apprehensive, then my mother burst into tears and said, 'Oh, dear God, not again. Please, not again.' It was, of course, barely two decades since her young husband had returned to her from the last affray. I looked at her frail, weeping figure and I knew exactly what she was thinking. It was her children who were her prime concern and of the three of us it was the thought of her son, just ripe for cannon-fodder, that caused her the greatest anguish. My father behaved stoically and was full of comfort but he was hard pressed to hide his own anxiety. My sisters, who were only fifteen, were, I think, just bewildered, whereas I was not a little afraid. After about an hour the 'All clear' sounded and we trooped wearily back to bed.

A week or so later I received a letter from the registrar at the Academy informing me that, in view of the uncertainty of the immediate future, the establishment would not now be reassembling for the next term on 29 September as originally announced, and that, until such a time as the governors could separate the wood from the trees, it would remain closed indefinitely.

What was I to do now? I had just entered my twentieth year so obviously I would be required for military service fairly soon. Should I try to beat the gun? If I hung around and waited to be called up, the chances were that I would have little or no control over my destiny. If, on the other hand, I volunteered for military service I might, with luck, have a certain amount of choice in the matter. Good sound thinking, I decided, so with this in mind I hied myself to whichever local government office was responsible for disseminating information concerning the employment of manpower at that time and I returned home with a pile of instructive leaflets on the subject. Wading through them all I came across one headed 'Officer Cadet Reserve'. This, it transpired, was a reserve list of candidates who, provided they had the correct qualifications, were at liberty to volunteer for commissions in the army. I had the qualifications required as a result of my service in the OTC at Bromsgrove; so all in all the Officer Cadet Reserve seemed to be the ideal body to whom I should offer my services. I filled in the necessary form, despatched it and then started looking around for a way to occupy myself during the period of waiting.

The month of August had been brilliantly sunny and I soon discovered that a neighbouring farmer, a kind old soul called Prescott, was looking around for as many willing hands as he could muster to help gather in his harvest. With him I promptly threw in my lot. I worked hard for several weeks from dawn till dusk, the fresh air and manual labour keeping me fit and out of mischief. The only things I found difficult to swallow (literally) were the massive buttered and curranted scones that were delivered to the fields with canisters of tea both mid-morning and mid-afternoon. They were the size of saucers and three times as heavy. Mr Prescott and his regular farm-hands could down about three each during the ten-minute break, whereas I found extreme difficulty in disposing of the half with which I toyed manfully in order not to offend Mrs Prescott, who ran them up personally – on a lathe, I would imagine.

In the middle of September a reply arrived from the Officer Cadet Reserve people and I was instructed to report for an interview in Leeds at 11 a.m. on 2 October. On arrival I produced various credentials that I had been instructed to take with me, answered a long questionnaire which I then signed, and finally I took the oath swearing that I would

'... bear true allegiance to His Majesty King George the Sixth, His Heirs and Successors ... and his Generals and Officers set over me'. I then received the king's shilling and set off for home. As far as I was concerned there had been only one small hiccup throughout the entire interview. When asked in which branch of the army I wished to serve, I had requested the Royal Artillery, and if I was allowed to be more specific I would prefer, I said, the anti-aircraft section of it. I opted for this purely because it had been my father's regiment during the previous punch-up and it had also crossed my mind that manning anti-aircraft guns might give me a good chance of remaining in England. It appeared, however, that I was not qualified for the Gunners. To obtain a commission in the Royal Artillery at that time certain mathematical qualifications were required and these I did not possess. This piece of information mystified every Royal Artillery officer I met throughout the entire war, but it was, nevertheless, what I was told on that morning in Leeds.

'What's your second choice?' said my interviewer. 'Ever thought of the Royal Armoured Corps?'

'You mean tanks?' I enquired.

'More or less,' he replied.

The Great War had been concluded two years before I was born so I had no first-hand knowledge of it, but I had seen many horrific photographs of the slime and mud of the trenches and many newsreel shots of marching Tommies singing 'It's a long way to Tipperary', 'Keep the home fires burning' and similar ditties to spur them on in their miles of foot-slogging. Anything had got to be better than those trenches and the risk of getting a bellyful of cold steel, and having marched mile after mile with the Bromsgrove OTC carrying a Lee-Enfield rifle which was, at that time, practically as heavy as I was, anything had got to be better than marching to war. So, not knowing what I was letting myself in for except that I would be able to, as it were, get a lift into battle, I agreed to put my name down for the RAC.

Finally, before leaving I was informed that my services would not be required until I was twenty and that when my time came I would, first of all, be called up into the ranks, after which my progress towards an OCTU and ultimately a commission would depend entirely on my ability and aptitude. So I was by no means home and dry, but volunteering had achieved what I had hoped it would: a choice of service and a head start in the promotion stakes provided I could show that I was worthy of it.

During September England sat holding its breath waiting for the wrath of Hitler's Luftwaffe to unleash itself upon, if not its green and pleasant land, at least its dark satanic mills. But the expected onslaught never came. Slowly the routine of daily life recommenced; decisions that had been made hurriedly in the light of the emergency were reassessed and, rather like a dog emerging from a swim, the population shook itself, snorted and went unaffectedly on its way. It was then, in the light of this reawakening, that the registrar at the Academy sent out yet another letter to its students. 'After a reappraisal of the situation', it informed us, the Academy would now be reopening in ten days' time. This was good news. On the day before the reopening I returned to Christopher Steele's and on the following morning reported for work in Gower Street.

It was good to see old friends again, but it was in many ways a different Academy to which we had all returned. Every pane of every window in the whole of its tall, red-brick facade had had strips of brown paper affixed to it, diagonally, in the manner of a St Andrew's flag. The second change was in the constitution of the student body itself – many had not returned. Some had already been called up and some, both male and female, had already volunteered for one of the many national services. Several had presumably thought it prudent not to return to the capital city at that time and others, for a variety of reasons, had made a re-appraisal of their personal situation and aspirations. The effect of the smaller number of students was that the faculty had reduced the course from two years to one, and half the classes had been telescoped into the other half. This gave me many new friends and the ones that I acquired then are largely the ones who linger in my memory.

Some song-writer once wrote a lyric which ran: 'I fall in love too easily, I fall in love too fast.' I wonder how he found out about me.

I had another eleven months to go before I was to be called upon to throw my inconsiderable weight behind the Allied war-machine and those eleven months were to be some of the happiest of my life. I adored my work, I adored London – even war-time London; I had a host of true and amusing friends and my path throughout that time was strewn with a string of successful and unsuccessful, fulfilled and unfulfilled, rap-turous and heartbreaking romances.

Back in my band days in Hull I had become close chums with Geoffrey Hibbert. Geoffrey, as I have already mentioned, was the pianist in the ensemble and from the word go he and I established a huge rapport. He was the son of one Arnold Hibbert, an insurance broker who was also a leading light in the local amateur operatic world, a director of the Hull

Geoffrey Hibbert as he appeared in the film of Love on the Dole *in 1939/40*

Repertory Theatre and a distinguished member of the community. Geoffrey was also stage-struck and determined to carve out a career for himself on the boards. He was dark, on the short side, moon-faced with a pale complexion, and off-stage always wore horn-rimmed spectacles. We remained the closest of friends until several years after the war when we became separated by the simple but inexcusable disruption of geography and ultimately his untimely death in 1969 at the age of forty-six. Though younger than me he had preceded me to London and had become a student at the Webber–Douglas School of Dramatic Art in South Kensington; he 'digged' in a small but bright and clean bed-sit in Roland Gardens not far away. His room was part of a large Victorian house of the servants' basement variety with several steps leading up to an imposing front door. It was run by a kindly and tolerant lady called Marjorie Fox and her equally amiable brother Tony. It is difficult when a teenager to assess the age of those several years older than oneself but I would say that the Foxes were at that time in their early to mid-thirties. I used to visit Geoffrey regularly, and always returned to Adelaide Road feeling thunderingly dissatisfied with my own accommodation. I had no quarrel whatever with my affable landlord, but my actual room left quite a lot to be desired. It was the size of a rabbit-hutch, possessed only half a window as the result of a conversion which had turned one room into two with a partition wall which ran straight down the middle of it, and was painted a dismal green throughout. All of which, together with its steel bedstead, uninspired furniture and northern aspect, combined to make it, in comparison with Geoffrey's, dark and unfriendly. Also to be taken into consideration was the fact that 187 (now demolished) contained only one bathroom and a single, coin-operated telephone which was situated very publicly on the wall in the hall.

The rooms in 12 Roland Gardens, on the other hand, were painted white throughout, had large windows, smartly covered divan beds, comfortable and attractive furniture generally, and each room had its own telephone and h. and c. washbasin. In addition, I found South Kensington considerably more agreeable than Chalk Farm and Swiss Cottage. In fact, all in all the disparity between our two life-styles at that time seemed to present an inequality up with which I was no longer prepared to put.

I asked Geoffrey if he would let me know the moment one of Miss Fox's rooms became available.

'There's one available now,' he replied. 'A large double one. How would you feel about sharing?'

'It wouldn't worry me,' I said. 'How about you?'

'Let's take a look at it,' he said.

We did. It was a beautiful light and airy room on the top floor and it appealed to both of us instantly. In addition, we discovered that, by pooling our resources, we would be no worse off than we had been before. We took it there and then and within twenty-four hours I had packed up in Adelaide Road, said goodbye to Christopher Steele and Carrot Top, piled all my belongings into a cab and set off to begin a new life in the more gracious environs of South Kensington.

In ten years' time I was to return to Chalk Farm a contented family man, a householder and a successful actor with a rosy career ahead of me, but that I was unable to foresee in 1939.

Moving in with Geoffrey was a huge success, and as far as 12 Roland Gardens was concerned it was the beginning of a snowball. We shared the same likes and dislikes, the same sense of humour (probably the most essential quality necessary for successful cohabitation) and identical financial resources. Geoffrey was a very funny man and our lives together became hilarious. We used to play a game which either of us would initiate at a moment's notice. We called it 'Make You Laugh In Two Minutes' and it started with the initiator making that simple assertion to the other one. The second party would then immediately assume a stern poker-face while the first party would proceed to try and do just that. Frequently shock tactics had to be employed. On one occasion I was sitting on my bed in my dressing-gown having just had a bath. It was midsummer and both our windows on the fourth floor were wide open.

'Make you laugh in two minutes,' Geoffrey suddenly announced.

'You're on,' I replied.

Whereupon he picked up every item of my clothing which lay on a nearby chair and in a single movement threw the lot out of the window. Not very hilarious out of context, I quite agree, but I can assure you it worked.

Poor old Geoffrey must have had a thing about windows. He was at a party once in another large Victorian house, this time in Hampstead. At some stage around midnight he disappeared upstairs to one of the bedrooms with a particularly attractive ash-blonde. Some time later, when they decided to rejoin the party, he discovered that some wag had locked them in. Geoffrey, ever gallant and a little bit worse for wear after several quarts of pale ale, told his amour not to worry, he'd have her out of it in a trice. He then walked over to the window and, not realising that he was on the second floor, lowered himself over the sill, let go and broke both his legs. I have no doubt he laughed at that too, though I was not there at the time and cannot bear testimony to the fact.

Hilarity is infectious and our respective senses of humour were so in tune that we became a sort of off-stage, real-live double-act and people flattered us by seeking our company.

Before long another of Geoffrey's Webber–Douglas student friends moved into 12 Roland Gardens. He was a super fellow called David Baker, who was later killed in the war. A few weeks after that David introduced his sister, a most attractive blonde to whom he was devoted, to the *ménage*. Then another chum moved in, then another, and within a matter of months practically every room in the Fox house was occupied by student Thespians.

There was one room, however, that was not and that was rented by a totally inoffensive gentleman who, because he was the odd man out, became rather a figure of fun. He had a double-barrelled name, a dark military moustache and was always dressed as formally as we were in-formal – a dark suit, white shirt with white starched collar, a club tie, curly brimmed bowler and rolled umbrella. We never did find out what he did for a living or where he went when he went out. He was a tolerant cove; I'm quite sure that we were as eccentric to him as he was to us.

Marjorie Fox, however, is the one who really deserved a medal for tolerance. The deal at 12 Roland Gardens was really bed and breakfast (served in one's room on a tray) and service as far as cleaning the rooms and making the beds was concerned. If, however, we wanted a bite in the evening and it was within her power, she would always rustle something up for us. These impromptu, extra-curricular meals ran purely to a 'fry-up' – eggs, bacon, chipolata sausage and Heinz baked beans – which the dear lady started to oblige one of us, once, as a favour. Unhappily for her, however, her generosity turned out to be the thin end of the wedge. It was also a monotonous diet but it was cheaper than eating out and consequently extremely popular. Geoffrey and I occupied the largest room and as a result it fast became the green-room. Somewhere around seven o'clock on most evenings, therefore, it was invariably our telephone that was used for ringing down the order for nosh. Generally it would go something like this.

'Miss Fox?'

'Yes.'

'Ah, Ian here – do you think we could have something to eat, dear?'

'How many of you are there?'

'Five, actually.'

Long-drawn-out sigh.

'All right, then, what do you want?'

'Oh, good, you are a dear. Well, Geoffrey would like one fried egg, two sausages, baked beans and a piece of fried bread, and I would like the same but only one sausage and a fried tomato as well. Oh, and a pot of tea for the two of us, please. Got that? Good. Now Vivienne would like two poached eggs on toast, two rashers of bacon, no sausages, no baked beans and a cup of coffee; David wants one egg – sorry, hold on – no, sorry, dear – no eggs for David, baked beans, a tomato and a couple of sausages, and Peter would like no baked beans, two fried eggs, two sausages, a piece of fried bread, toast and a glass of milk. Will that be all right, dear?' And invariably it was. She had no help apart from her brother and she carried it all upstairs from the basement to the top floor of the house, each order on a separate tray. Yes, she was a jolly good sport was Marjorie Fox. After the war one of the boys devotedly nursed her through a fatal illness.

A few months later Geoffrey's father bought him a piano and we moved into the front room on the ground floor which had a big bay-window to accommodate it. This was a splendid new attraction and our lives became filled with music. We started writing songs together, most of which we performed ourselves in a 'Songs at the Piano' act that we put together and with which we used to entertain at parties. One of our efforts called 'Champagne for Breakfast' eventually found its way into a revue at the Windmill in 1942, but we wrote primarily for ourselves.

It was an extraordinary life in Roland Gardens, because although I was studying at the RADA all my social and off-duty hours were spent with my new-found pals from the Webber–Douglas in the heart of whose territory I had now settled. My girl-friends, however, I drew from both sources of supply and from the day I returned to the Academy after the outbreak of war I was never without one. Two years later, when I was in the army, I had as many as eight framed photographs of different beauties proudly displayed on a shelf over my bed. I don't think I was attracted to any particular type – blonde, brunette or redhead – but they had to be pretty, that was essential. I was a great believer in flower-power and any spare cash I had I spent on flowers which I invariably purchased from a very smart florist's which I passed every day on my way to the tube in the Old Brompton Road. My standard present, however, was a small, gold identification bracelet on which I had the recipient's christian name engraved in my own handwriting. These I always obtained at Carmichael's in Hull where I got an excellent discount and my credit was good. There were quite a few of them dangling around fair wrists in our capital city in 1939–40. But though I somehow managed to finance flowers and baubles, the rest of the wooing process was always tinged with austerity. My first date ever at the RADA I worried myself sick about for weeks in advance. There was one fellow in my class who always managed to take his birds to the Coconut Grove, the Bag of Nails and similar racy haunts, but it was no good, I just hadn't got the 'ready' – so poor Betty Atkinson, who had already reached the Academy a couple of terms prior to me, had to put up with a 1s 6d three-course dinner-dance at the Coventry Street Corner House. It wasn't in the Brasserie either, where the décor was acceptable and the lighting, if not subdued, at least reasonably controlled; after 6 p.m. the 1s 6d package-deal was moved up to the second floor, which was furnished in a scarcely more imaginative way than the same company's many tea-shops that were scattered about the metropolis like confetti, and the lighting had, I am convinced, been arranged by whoever was responsible for illuminating the Aldershot Tattoo. The whole thing was agony – not through any fault of Miss Atkinson's, I hasten to add; I was just desperately sorry for her. She was worth much more than all that.

For some reason we never took girls back to Christopher Steele's and I honestly can't remember why. I don't think it was actually banned; perhaps we reasoned that the atmosphere and surroundings, though on the whole acceptable to a handful of bachelor males, could be a bit of a turn-off if pressed into use as a seductive love-nest.

Things improved considerably when I moved to South Kensington.

This didn't actually do anything to help the cash-flow, but many of the girls had their own rooms in less institutionalised houses, which was a great bonus. There was also a better choice of cinema and several modest but pleasant little eating places. Also, right opposite Gloucester Road tube station, there was even a good, old-fashioned, London coffee-stall which the proprietor, who looked as if he had crawled out from under a stone, kept open all night. Taxis, however, were almost entirely taboo. One of my girl-friends who was a student at the Webber–Douglas (and was also the recipient of a gold bracelet) lived at Weybridge. Frequently I took her out after the day's work and then, at the end of a long evening, I would dutifully set out from Roland Gardens in the blackout, escort her on the fifteen-minute walk to South Kensington station, accompany her on the tube all the way to Waterloo, put her safely on her train home and then return the same way. Greater love had no man. ...

But it was worth it. They were lovely – all of them.

During the Christmas holidays in 1939 I obtained a job in a company which was assembled expressly to perform *Charley's Aunt* for two weeks only at the Palace Court Theatre in Bournemouth. I was engaged as Assistant Stage Manager, to appear in the small part of the college scout and to understudy all three of the male leads. The latter duty would have meant learning practically the entire play so I decided that, as all the performers concerned looked fairly hale and hearty, I wouldn't learn a line – a practice I would not advise any young actor to emulate. It was a bitter cold and icy Christmas and I shared digs with an elderly character-actor who played the manservant, Brassett, and who had piles and appalling arthritis. His arthritis was so bad that he was unable to carry a tea-tray as required in Act II so I had to accompany him on the stage and carry it for him. In the digs he never stopped regaling me with long and pointless stories about his days with Frank Benson. At the end of the final performance I got all the company to sign the prompt-copy, which I still possess. My companion signed his: 'Yours tragenically'. The only other item of interest in an otherwise unmemorable production is that the Aunt was played by an actor called Derrick Penley, the grandson of W. S. Penley who created the role in the original production.

1940 was packed with incident for me, as it was for most other people. In January I began my last term at the RADA, during which I appeared in the current Public Show at the Strand Theatre in February. The RADA Public Show always took place in a West End theatre during an afternoon when the advertised attraction did not have a matinée. It was a sort of 'passing-out parade' during a student's final term, and was composed of a series of scenes from various plays. Afterwards three distinguished adjudicators made a number of awards. My party-piece was the wooing scene from *Henry V* and my Katherine (another gold-bracelet holder) was an attractive girl who looked exactly like I always imagined Trilby should look. I found the scene a funny one and so, I'm delighted to say, did the audience. To be fair, the majority of laughs were probably coming from all my Roland Gardens colleagues whom I had herded into the pit for moral support, but nevertheless I have, during all the intervening years, considered that my performance as 'Hank Cinq' was a favourable one. It was disillusioning, therefore, when I looked out my reports the other day, to read that Sir Kenneth Barnes had commented, 'You were unsuited to Henry V but you got your diploma because Mr George Arliss [who was one of my judges] insisted that you had a talent for modern comedy acting – I think he is right.' I am interested in Sir Kenneth's choice of words – '... *insisted* that you had a talent for modern comedy acting' rather implies, I think, that Dame Sybil Thorndike and Miss Irene Hentschel, my other judges, were in violent disagreement with him.

We rounded off the term with another Neil Porter production for the LCC schoolchildren – this time *Twelfth Night* in which I played Fabian – and this time we took the play to them; three weeks of touring and seeking them out in their evacuated premises all around the Home Counties. As the final performance approached I began to develop, not for the last time in my life, a feeling of impending isolation and helplessness. I was about to sever, after nearly twenty years, the umbilical cord of dependence on others. When that final curtain came down, I would be on my own. My student days would be over and I would move out into the big, wide, mercenary world without a single prospect of employment. During the final performance one of the cast told me of some job or other that might possibly be available somewhere; the details have long since faded, but I was given the name of someone to telephone first thing the following morning. I took an eyebrow-pencil and wrote it inside the lid of the small Woolworth's attaché-case in which I kept my make-up. To this day every time I unpack that case the name of Mrs Bowen of WEL 9617 stares me in the face, but what it was all about, heaven knows.

I was lucky, however; I was not out of work for long. Ronald Kerr, one of my producers at the Academy, was about to stage-direct a new Philip King comedy called *Without The Prince*, which was to open shortly

at the Whitehall Theatre, and he offered me the job of Assistant Stage
Manager and understudy. I accepted and found myself sharing a dressing-
room with a young man called David Evans, whom I was to 'cover', and
Michael Hordern, now one of our most distinguished actors and brother
of my benefactor at Bromsgrove. The only problem with my duties in
this production was that David had to make one entrance every night
carrying a real, live hen which, until it was required to give its performance, was kept in a coop on the theatre roof. Luckily David was a fit
young man and I never had to play for him. If I had had to I don't know
what I would have done. I am absolutely terrified of birds. I have never
touched one in my life and nothing whatever could induce me to do so.
One descended our sitting-room chimney a few weeks ago – I was out
of the door before you could say 'Ring-Ouzel'. Even though the room
contains several reasonably valuable pieces of Bristol glass and Stafford-
shire pottery, I was totally helpless. I had to telephone my wife, who was
five miles away with her mother at the time and ask her if she would
kindly return home to cope with the situation.

This production, however, was my first experience of going to work
every night in a West End theatre, and I found it an enjoyable one. The
cast were friendly but I was at a loss to know how to address many of
them. I was only nineteen and was occupying the most lowly position
in the company. 'Darling' is, of course, the usual mode of address between
all and sundry in theatrical circles, but on the rare occasions when terms
of endearment were not used nobody, it seemed to me, was ever addressed
more formally than by his or her christian name. Maybe I was unfortunate but I never heard a soul addressed as Mr So-and-So or Miss So-
and-So and, consequently, to adopt such an approach myself seemed to
be not only unnecessary but, as it were, 'not done'. This I found worrying.
It was unnatural for me to go around addressing my seniors by their christian names and diminutives, but in an effort to behave in a manner that
I thought was expected of me I either became so familiar that it was mistaken for insubordination or, alternatively, I used neither name nor
'handle', which was marginally worse. I put up, I'm sure, many 'blacks'
while trying to wrestle with these social mores. One I certainly put up
a few weeks after we had opened could have been disastrous for me.

On the jungle drums I had heard that Herbert Farjeon was about to
put out a post-London tour of his revues *Nine Sharp* and *The Little
Revue*. Farjeon I doted on. His after-dinner, satirical revues, which had
been enjoying a considerable success at the charming, Adam-designed
Little Theatre in the Adelphi, were absolutely my cup of tea and to be

able to appear in even a tour of them would, for me, be nothing short of manna from heaven. So, regardless of the kindness of Ronnie Kerr, this was an opportunity not to be missed. 'Fools', they say, 'rush in.' 'The end justifies the means,' they also say and I was fully prepared, if necessary, to make a complete jackass of myself to join Mr Farjeon. Not knowing him from a cake of soap, there was only one way of tackling the problem and that was to look him up in the telephone book and give him a ring, which I promptly did.

'Mr Farjeon?'

'Yes.'

'I'm afraid you don't know me from a cake of soap, but my name is Carmichael. I'm a young actor and I hear you're casting a tour of your little Revues. Is that so, and if it is, is there any chance of me joining you?'

He was utterly charming.

'Yes, it's quite true,' he said. 'But the show is being presented by Paul Remlinger and all the casting is being done through an agent called Felix de Wolfe. I'm afraid you'll have to get on to him.'

'Thank you very much indeed,' I replied.

'And good luck,' he added before he put the telephone down.

That night, at the theatre, I gingerly and rather ashamedly tackled Ronnie Kerr on the subject. It seemed a beastly way to behave – asking him to release me almost as soon as we had opened, particularly after he had gone out of his way to give me employment as soon as I left the Academy. However, I explained to him, in my view, the extenuating circumstances. I was, I pointed out, at the Whitehall merely as an Assistant Stage Manager and understudy. Though menial, both were important jobs, I agreed, but in the tour of *Nine Sharp*, as it was to be called, I would, I hoped, actually be performing.

'Well, you'll have to go and see the boss,' said Ronnie.

The boss was a Mr Ide who had an office in the building. I decided to go up and see him straight after the next day's matinée. Mr Ide, too, was kind and understanding but my current social hang-up very nearly ruined it all for me. Had I addressed him as 'Mr Ide' at the time there would have been no problem. In the event, I rapped on his door, stuck my head round the corner and in a bright and breezy manner said, 'Oh, Pat – could I have a word with you a moment?'

Momentarily, Mr Ide seemed to have trouble with a mouthful of tea.

Taking this as an assent, I jollied in, assuming a hail-fellow-well-met bearing (which, incidentally, I certainly didn't feel) and proceeded to place my case before him. Mr Ide remained poker-faced throughout the interview. Eventually, to his eternal credit, he gave me permission to apply for an audition and to hand in two weeks' notice if, by any chance, I was successful. I left his office in ebullient mood. It was later that evening that Ronnie Kerr, to whom my familiarity had by then been reported, hauled me over the coals and gave me a very stern warning indeed about addressing my employers by their christian name at such a tender age. 'Particularly', he added, 'if you are trying to obtain a release from a legally binding contract and are going to give them a lot of recasting problems into the bargain.'

I met Mr Ide again in the Garrick Club last week. I'm delighted to say he seemed to have forgotten the whole incident; I certainly didn't remind him.

The following morning I was on to Mr de Wolfe and luckily it wasn't too late. Auditions were being held in the Little Theatre during the following week. I then swotted up a charming little song out of a revue which was currently running at the Webber–Douglas's Chanticleer Theatre, and a few days later went round the corner to try it out on a more experienced actor, whom Geoffrey had got to know, called John le Mesurier.

'Very nice, but why are you singing it with that dreadful American accent?' said Mr le Mesurier.

'I wasn't aware that I was,' I replied.

'You are,' he said, 'and it's dreadful. It's a Bobby Howes type number and it's English. Sing it in English.'

The advice must have been sound because when I showed up to sing it to Messrs Farjeon and Remlinger it went down a bundle.

After I had given my all, a disembodied voice from the dark, gaping void of the tiny auditorium asked me to go through the pass-door for a chat. I did so and was met by Felix de Wolfe who walked me up to the back of the stalls.

'Mr Farjeon and Mr Remlinger liked your audition very much,' he said. 'The job would mean ASM-ing and also playing the odd small part. How do you feel about that?'

Well, I knew exactly how I felt about it. My last two jobs had grossed me three pounds a week each. 'This time,' I announced firmly to my pals before leaving Roland Gardens with their good wishes ringing in my ears, 'should I be offered a job, I'm sticking out for a fiver and no ASM-ing, and on that I intend to be adamant.'

'What's the money?' I asked Mr de Wolfe casually, as if I had been negotiating contracts all my life.

'Three pounds,' he replied.

I then tried hard to appear impassive, crossed all my fingers and stated my predetermined requirements.

Mr de Wolfe inhaled through his teeth with a pronounced hiss, uttered a 'tch, tch, tch' sound and shook his head. 'I don't think he'll run to that,' he said.

'Well,' I replied, my heart in my mouth and lying into the bargain, 'I honestly don't think I can ask to be released from my present job, for which I am receiving four pounds a week, unless I can say it is for a better one.'

Mr de Wolfe grunted and went back into a huddle with Mr Remlinger, who held the purse-strings. He returned with a marginally improved offer. Further negotiations were entered into and in ten minutes' time I emerged from the stage-door of the Little Theatre into bright spring sunshine not knowing whether it was Monday, Tuesday or washday. Unbelievably, I'd got it! Even though I had had to accept the Assistant Stage Managership, I had managed to extract four pounds ten shillings a week out of them, which was thirty shillings more than I had ever been paid before.

Apart from the tube journey, I ran most of the way home. As I turned the corner from the Old Brompton Road into Roland Gardens I saw most of my chums sitting on the steps of the house basking in the sunshine.

'I've got it!' I screamed from a hundred yards away, throwing my nonexistent hat into the air. 'I've got it! I've got it! I've got it!'

To a man (and woman) they belted down the pavement towards me in wild, abandoned enthusiasm, and I was kissed and embraced in a manner usually only accorded to a striker who has just rammed home a perfectly poised centre from Kevin Keegan. In those early days the unconfined joys experienced by any one of us when getting a job were shared by all. It was a wonderful camaraderie; the exuberance of youth is incomparable.

Mr Ide had been true to his word and with the arrival of spring, which seemed to be symbolic, I said farewell to the Whitehall and started rehearsals for *Nine Sharp*.

Throughout the whole three or four weeks that we rehearsed I was on another planet. I had now, I decided, arrived. This was it. Here was the total fulfilment of all my aspirations and ambitions. Like the man said, I felt that 'Spring had sprung' and that there were 'Songs to be sung, bells to be rung and a wonderful fling to be flung.' I was in paradise. Intimate Revue, I was convinced, was my ideal scene and in 1940 they didn't come any better than Herbert Farjeon's.

The programme itself was made up of the best items from both its parent revues, much of which I already knew and admired. Of the cast, half were from the original company – and that half included its leading lady, Hermione Baddeley – and one of the feature players, George Benson, who also now directed. It was to be the first of many occasions when I was to work with both of them.

Rehearsals were conducted in the Little Theatre itself, which, un-happily, no longer exists, and we had our lunches from high stools in the pleasant and convenient little bar under the adjacent Tivoli Cinema in the Strand, which has also disappeared. But though the company was an agreeable one, in certain areas it reflected the artistic gulf that existed between its two principal protagonists.

The marriage between Herbert Farjeon and Paul Remlinger (whose name I have thought it prudent to alter) was a strange one. Bertie Farjeon had style, taste and class; Mr Remlinger had none of them. Bertie was West End and chic; Paul Remlinger was provincial 'tat'. As individual characters, apart from their professional capabilities, they were also poles apart.

Bertie was a literary figure, donnish in appearance and taller than his pronounced stoop made him appear. He was also slim, grey-haired with a tumbling forelock, bespectacled, an inveterate pipe-smoker, and of a quiet and gentle disposition. If allowed only one word to describe him, 'shaggy' would do admirably. As near as anything else Bertie Farjeon, as I remember him, resembled a lovable, underfed Old English sheepdog.

Paul Remlinger, on the other hand, was a presenter of No. 2 touring revues of a much broader variety than Bertie's *revues intimes*. Mr Rem-linger appeared to be as overfed as Bertie was undernourished. His com-plexion was pallid, his skin greasy, and he sported a dark Clark Gable moustache and a matching toupé which was seldom on straight. It is a long time ago now, but I have a mental picture of Paul Remlinger wearing wide-brimmed felt hats, bookmaker's suits, large, chunky rings and in-variably carrying a flamboyant walking stick. If Bertie Farjeon was an Old English sheepdog, Paul Remlinger was the travelling showman out of *Pinocchio*.

We opened a ten-week tour at the Arts Theatre, Cambridge, in May Week; or if it wasn't May Week it jolly well should have been. The weather decided to bless us and put on a radiant display of the English

Herbert Farjeon

summer at its impeccable best. We all spent the entire six days, from practically dawn until an hour before curtain-up, as near naked as the law would allow in the bottom of punts on the Cam. 'Toté' Baddeley was the most entertaining, vivacious and attractive of leading ladies and as such was ever popular and in much demand by the more dashing undergraduates. On certainly two evenings after curtain-down Toté and several of us were guests at a river party that continued throughout the night by the light of a full summer moon and at which the aforementioned young men provided champagne and the full Ascot picnic.

Throughout the period of rehearsals, in view of the threatened imminent departure of a couple of the senior male members of the cast to HM forces, I was given more to do in the show itself than Mr Remlinger had originally envisaged would be necessary and, as a result, my stage-managerial chores were, through no fault of my own, beginning to suffer. It was, nevertheless, a total surprise to me when one night after the show, towards the end of the first week, a rap on my dressing-room door was followed by a familiar head with a mop of copper-coloured hair being poked round the edge of it. It belonged to an old RADA colleague called John Barron.

'My dear fellow, come in. What on earth are you doing here?' I said.

'I've come to take over from you,' he replied.

I think I turned white.

'You've come to do what?' I said.

'I've come to take over from you,' he repeated. 'As the ASM,' he then added quickly, seeing that he had inadvertently delivered a body-blow from which I was just about to keel over.

'Blood returned to the old noodle,' as Bertie Wooster might have said.

The arrival of John Barron was only the first shock in that initial week. The second one the more experienced members of the cast might possibly have anticipated, but certainly not I, a starry-eyed greenhorn. Come the Friday night, there was no money forthcoming to pay us all. Furthermore, Mr Remlinger could not be found anywhere. To be absolutely honest, I remember very little about the incident itself, but it has been described to me by George Benson several times since. Apparently we all sat down in the green-room, off which all the dressing-rooms but the No. 1 lead at the Arts Theatre in Cambridge, and refused to go home until our due was forthcoming. The lines to London were hot during the next hour and poor unsuspecting, innocent Bertie Farjeon was roped in to try and trace the miscreant. In the end, someone, somehow, from somewhere, produced a cheque which the company manager promptly started to hawk round a few local tradesmen and hostelries in an attempt to find some unwitting soul who might be prepared to cash it. Eventually some-one did and we were paid; but it was a long time before we all left the theatre and returned to our digs on that night.

In Cambridge I had been in digs on my own. In Leeds, the following week, I joined forces with Dilys Rees, a member of the original London company, Joan Sterndale Bennett and John Barron, and we became an inseparable quartet for the remainder of the tour. Dilys Rees, as her name implies, was Welsh. She was a soprano and principally in the show for her singing but, like all in revue, she also appeared in various sketches and bits and pieces throughout the evening. I had been very attracted to her during rehearsals. She was of medium height, as pretty as a picture with a trim little figure and she had a head of dark tumbling locks. She was kind. She was friendly, always an attraction to a newcomer who feels a bit shy and out of things, and she had an engaging sense of humour. Very soon indeed I fell in love with Dilys, hook, line and sinker. This was a love much more complete and overwhelming than anything I had ever experienced before, and it exploded inside me bringing an ecstasy of happiness. A few months later it was to bring a despair and pain that was almost disembowelling. For the heartrending tragedy of my love for Dilys was that it was doomed from the word go. The fact that she was seven years my senior meant nothing; the fact that she was happily married to a young doctor was earth-shattering. However, for ten weeks

Dilys, Joan, John and I lived in each other's pockets and the joy I found in my nightly performances at the theatre, the close friendship that the four of us shared together, and my unquenchable love for Dilys combined to make the 1940 tour of *Nine Sharp* as memorable as any other ten-week period I have ever experienced in my entire life. It also provided a laugh a line and that is just about as seductive as anything I know.

After Leeds we visited Hull where I stayed at home with my parents. The week was also notable because it embraced my twentieth birthday and the fall of France. I remember buying a copy of the *Hull Daily Mail* from a news vendor in Prospect Street in the mid-afternoon and reading the banner headlines. The war news had been getting worse by the week, but this was a blow from which it was almost impossible to imagine the Allies recovering. The Allies? There were no active Allies left. We were on our own; a tiny pink dot on the map separated, at its narrowest point, by a mere twenty-two miles of sea from the now totally Nazi-dominated mainland of western Europe. The future for our vulnerable little island looked depressingly black. However, the tour sped on and the laughs and happiness generated within our little quartet insulated us to some extent from the cataclysmic events that were taking place in the world around us.

Financially, things were working out reasonably well for me too. Four pounds ten shillings a week may sound a pittance now – it was no fortune in 1940 either – but with it I was able to pay for my digs every week, all my meals, my beer and cigarettes (I was about a twenty-a-day man at that time) and still retain sufficient to buy the odd present for Dilys – usually flowers or cigarettes (du Maurier) and, believe it or not, put one pound a week away into the Post Office.

Towards the end of the tour it was rumoured that Paul Remlinger was planning to reopen the show in the West End, this time at the Criterion Theatre. The Cri held an added attraction for all its patrons; THIS THEATRE, its posters proudly advertised, IS RIGHT UNDER-GROUND. It was during our week in Oxford, therefore, that Felix de Wolfe came down on behalf of Mr Remlinger to interview each member of the cast independently and to offer them a new contract for the proposed London run. Now it so happened that Bertie Farjeon was also planning a new revue for London at that time, and he had quietly tipped off a few members of the cast, myself included, that at the conclusion of the tour, if we wished to hold ourselves available, he would, in due course, be in a position to offer us employment in it. So when Mr Remlinger's London contract was presented to me for signature I made the fact known and, while thanking him very much for the offer, I said I would prefer to hold myself available for Mr Farjeon – a new show always being more attractive than a second-hand one. I was then informed that this matter had already been investigated and that my services were not required by Mr Farjeon, so – a bird in the hand and all that – would I now please sign my contract for the Criterion? I managed to stall for twenty-four hours. That night I telephoned Mr Farjeon and discovered that this statement was totally untrue; he did want me in his new show and was very angry to have been misrepresented.

I did not sign Mr Remlinger's contract.

In the event, however, I was shortly to find that I would have been unable to give my services to Mr Farjeon either as they were to be required almost immediately by His Majesty. Furthermore, His Majesty's 'offer', which was to arrive in the middle of our final week at the Theatre Royal, Glasgow, was one that I was going to find impossible to refuse.

I returned to London after the final night in Glasgow resigned to the military service situation, but distraught at being cheated out of what could have been my first West End appearance, and so lovelorn for the unattainable Dilys that my last few days in town were to be spent in an agony of torment the like of which I never wish to go through again.

Nine Sharp duly opened at the Criterion Theatre under the title of *In Town Again* and, after witnessing the final dress-rehearsal, I was to spend my last night (and penny) buying orchids for my love and escorting her to the Café de Paris where we dined and danced to Ken 'Snakehips' Johnson, the West Indian band-leader who was later to die in a direct hit on the building. I clung to her so tightly on the dance floor and sang 'I can't love you any more, Any more than I do,' into her ear. Around one in the morning, at the table, the conversation finally ground to a halt, held tight in the vicelike grip of emotion. I could hardly see her through eyes that were awash with tears.

Dilys I loved with an intensity that was total. She was a super girl; so kind, so gentle, so understanding, and so tolerant and sympathetic. She was also, I wish to make abundantly clear, so virtuous. Eventually, I feel sure, she gave up the theatre and I have seen her only once since the war. It was a long time ago and was such a brief meeting; a chance encounter in the main concourse at the top of the escalators in Leicester Square tube station. Bells still rang, but they were much fainter.

Back in September 1940, however, I left London the morning after our assignation at the Café de Paris emotionally crippled and feeling that my entire world had collapsed about my ears.

PART II
1940-1946

Pym Maclean – as she was when I first met her

CHAPTER EIGHT

CATTERICK AND CAMBERLEY

A Soldier's Apprenticeship

On 12 September 1940 I reported, as instructed by an intractable War Office, to the 51st Training Regiment, RAC, Catterick Camp, North Yorkshire. I was just twenty – an ebullient, irrepressible, lovesick young man, and my life was now about to be turned upside-down.

After a comfortable middle-class home, RADA and the blissfully care-free life of the professional theatre, the army, and particularly the barrack room, made the Slough of Despond look like the Serpentine in mid-summer. In a trice, Ian Carmichael, the promising singing and dancing juvenile light comedian, became plain Trooper Carmichael, I. G., 7900114.

Luckily I have always been a good mixer; the English social strata and class system have never meant anything to me. I have always, I think, had the ability to get on with my fellow man, but oh, how I missed the theatrical environment. I was like a starving, two-month-old babe that had been torn from its mother's breast; a hardened junkie, who had just dropped his syringe down the loo. I had, while I'm mixing metaphors, just tasted the fruit and, snatch! – it had been whipped away from me and there was no more left in the shop. For this, for a very long time, there was no replacement. The other problems posed by a complete change of environment, a circle of friends with whom I had little or nothing in common, caused me no worries. The frustrations, the anger, the utter futility, or what appeared to be the utter futility, of army 'bull', which was always at its worst for new recruits, I could take in my stride and, at times, even laugh at; but the yearning for the theatre, my theatrical friends and above all for Dilys was practically intolerable.

I don't know how many there were in our intake – maybe thirty. Anyway, we were assigned to two barrack room huts in Hooge Lines. There were three other lads amongst us, apart from myself, who were candidates for a commission: a Nordic blond in the next bed to me called

Jackson-Stops, a sandy-haired young man called Dillon, whose uncle was the commanding officer of an adjacent training regiment, and a tall youth with an open-air complexion called Gilbey. Of the other characters in the hut I can remember but three, all older than me, as was the majority of the squad. I remember the face but nothing more of a bloke called Hall; the face but not the name of a kindly, gentle Christian Scientist; and a rough character who slept on the other side of Jackson-Stops, who had been a male nurse in an insane asylum and who woke up every night, without fail, on the stroke of 2 a.m. and 4 a.m. for a cigarette which he smoked in bed. He also kept a large saucepan under it for occasions when he had supped too many pints of ale in the NAAFI. This always fascinated me, as the ablutions that joined the two huts together were probably nearer to him there than the loo had been to his bedroom back in the asylum. Also in the squad, but in the other hut, was the stage-door-keeper of the New Theatre in Hull, at which we had played with *Nine Sharp* only three months previously. He was amiable and chatty, so presumably I had tipped him sufficiently at the end of the week. I remember hearing later that the officer in charge of our squad had been deeply concerned about the content of his new intake because, on studying the nominal roll the week before our arrival, he was horrified to discover that the civilian occupation of sixty per cent of his charge was listed as being a Red Leader. It wasn't until we were all assembled under his wing that he discovered that this was the trade name of a brand of metal worker and in no way reflected a political calling.

Life in the 51st Training Regiment RAC provided the perfect background for a man who, fifteen years later, was to be chosen to play Stanley Windrush, the affable idiot and leading role in *Private's Progress*, but fifteen years hence was light years away and I had no way of knowing that at the time.

For the first month of basic training we were confined to camp. No one was allowed to step outside until he knew how to carry himself with a soldier-like bearing and during that time – indeed, during our entire stay at Catterick – our lives were ruled over, dawn to dusk, by two NCOs: a regular sergeant of the 1st King's Dragoon Guards, and a wartime lance-corporal. I was never aware of an officer having anything to do with us at any time except on pay parade. At my first such parade, however, he taught me something that I have remembered for the rest of my life. I signed, saluted, picked up my money and made for the door.

'Count it!' boomed a voice behind me as I was thrusting it into my pocket. 'How do you know it's right?'

From that day to this I have always opened every pay envelope and counted it before the company manager has left my dressing-room or before I have left the cashier's window when cashing a cheque at the bank.

There must have been other things I learnt which are more useful in after life than square-bashing; but one forgets.

But if Sergeant Slade was our father during that period, Lance-Corporal Bottomley was our mother, and both were ramrod straight in both deportment and discipline.

Slade was on the short side for a drill sergeant but he was stocky and had the flat, 'splatted' face of a prize-fighter. He was rarely seen without his Alsatian dog and not only us, but Lance-Corporal Bottomley too, always sprang to attention whenever he so much as opened his mouth. Lance-Corporal Bottomley was younger, slighter, had fair, straight, greased-down hair, short back and sides, a small toothbrush moustache, and was equally awe-inspiring in his own way.

After our first month's square-bashing and boot toecap boning we were allowed out of camp for the first time – fit, the authorities no doubt assumed, to mix with the outside world without casting slurs on His Majesty's uniform. The first evening of our new-found freedom, Jackson-Stops and I left camp in immaculate boots, best battledress, green blancoed gaiters and belt, brass buckles shining like burnished gold, and each carrying a gas-mask, tin hat, and wearing a white lanyard and a GPO-red forage cap. The latter two items of equipment distinguished the cavalry in particular and the RAC in general from other riff-raff who also inhabited Catterick Camp. We stepped out in true parade-ground fashion, proud as peacocks, four miles to the nearest pub, and rolled home gloriously sloshed three hours later – thus casting certain doubts on the authorities' judgement of our ability to behave in a manner befitting soldiers of the king.

It was bitterly cold in Catterick that autumn and the British soldier's natural ability to improvise and make the best of adverse circumstances soon began to manifest itself. The ablutions, of course, supplied cold water only, so the early-morning routine was to get to the mess hut early – it would still be dark – armed with one's knife, fork, spoon, mess-tin and pint-pot, have breakfast and then return to the barrack room with a second pint of hot tea, which one used for shaving in lieu of hot water. But generally speaking we were kept so busy that there was little time for brooding. Any spare time I did have I spent in the Quiet Room of the YMCA, writing letters to Dilys to which she used to reply in green ink. On Sunday mornings, after church parade, I always used to ring her from a public telephone-box on a crossroads just outside the camp. A few moments of bliss, talking to her and hearing the gossip from West End theatreland, and then back to our hut at a very low ebb indeed.

After a few weeks I thought I would try and get into the regimental concert party. I was advised to seek out a Sergeant Clarkson (3rd Hussars) who was its leading light, producer and NCO in charge. When I eventually found him he proved to be the most unlikely looking character. He was a regular soldier, very large, with a dark moustache and receding hairline and was invariably to be seen wearing a peaked hat and a pre-war cavalry greatcoat. The greatcoat was knee-length, non-waisted and had a centre vent at the back – the better to sit a horse, you understand. Despite his 'regularity' he was a jolly man and although he commanded respect one didn't actually tremble in front of him. The concert party was of a fairly primitive standard, rather like a beach pierrot troupe, and it performed on a stage erected at the end of a large garage the size of a municipal bus station. When directing the ensemble numbers, Sergeant Clarkson had but one instruction to his artistes – 'Come on, lads, bags of movement!' If only it had always been that easy. He eventually gave me a solo spot during which I sang, in white tie and tails forwarded to me by my mother and then retained hidden under my anti-gas cape behind my bed, 'Miss Jones, Are You Coming to Bed?' and 'Only a Glass of Champagne', neither of which I ultimately decided was a suitable choice for the basic tastes of my audience. Or maybe it was me. Perhaps I didn't have enough movement.

After my first performance with the troupe, an officer who had been a pre-war West End producer came round to see me. He suggested that I should swot up some Noël Coward numbers. This I started to do but fortunately I had to leave the 51st Training Regiment in order to advance my military career before I was able to unleash them on an unsuspecting public. I have a feeling that it was just as well – I don't think that *they* were exactly the material for a lot of Red Leaders either.

But nothing lasts for ever, and after ten weeks of being shaken up at Catterick, a period which, seen in retrospect, did me no harm at all, came the news that I had been posted to the Royal Military College, Sandhurst, and that I was to become an officer cadet. Now this was welcome news indeed – the vision of Mecca to a Mohammedan could never have appeared more welcome. Not only would I be leaving my spartan existence at Catterick for an establishment where the cadets slept two to a room and civilian batmen, or servants as they were called, were provided, but the whole was housed in a building of permanence, thus ensuring amenities that after ten weeks in a hutted camp in North Yorkshire seemed to promise Savoy-like luxury. Finally, the RMC Sandhurst is situated in the Surrey town of Camberley, some thirty miles on a good road and excellent train service to my personal Mecca, London's theatreland and Miss Rees.

I was right. Suddenly life took on a rosier glow.

The Royal Military College was administered by the Inns of Court Regiment and I changed my khaki and scarlet dress forage cap for a navy-blue and dark green one which was surrounded by a two-inch white band – the cadets' insignia – new and freshly blancoed each day. We were also allowed to wear proper officers' mackintoshes with collars and belts, and not those dreadful cape/groundsheets that all non-commissioned ranks had to put up with; in torrential downpours the knees and shins got wetter in those, from all the water pouring down off the front, than if one had been wearing nothing at all. They had also been skilfully designed so that the collars could collect the rain as does a gutter, and then, every few minutes, when full, overflow down the wearer's neck.

The drill staff at Sandhurst was provided exclusively by the Brigade of Guards, and there is no getting away from it, if one has to learn army discipline, deportment, drill and what I believe was referred to in the First World War as 'spit and polish', the instructors don't come any better than the Brigade of Guards. The shouting, the abuse, the insults flew just as fast and furious as when we were on parade at our training regiments, the only difference being that now we were Officer Cadets and certain scant respect had to be shown. So the stream of invective was always followed by the word 'Sir'.

'MISTER Carmichael – you 'orrible little man! You aren't in the fuckin' *Desert Song* now. Put yer 'at on straight and try to look like a fuckin' soldier, SIR!'

Drill. Yes, we did a lot of that. It still dominated our lives. We also learned, principally, driving and maintenance, gunnery and wireless. The one thing I can never remember seeing at Sandhurst, however, was a tank. There weren't very many of them about in 1940 and all our tank drill was taught in fifteen-hundredweight trucks. It was a monumental game of make-believe. If it was your turn to be 'tank commander', you stood in the back of the truck yelling things like 'Driver, left,' and 'Driver, right,' as he progressed along one of the king's highways unable to do anything but go straight on. Your gunner looked even more stupid. He stood beside you receiving your orders without a gun to his name.

'Two pounder. Traverse right,' you would bellow, and he, standing upright in the back of the truck with his right arm extended simulating its barrel, would slowly rotate until he was pointing roughly in the direction of the target you had in mind; you then continued: 'Steady. On,' named the target and then, 'Three rounds – FIRE.'

You think *Dad's Army* exaggerates?

Map-reading was a splendid lesson. For that you went out about four cadets to a fifteen-hundredweight, taking it in turns to sit beside the driver and try to get him from A to B without the use of signposts which an inconsiderate government had instructed to be removed as they might assist potential enemy parachutists. The great thing about the map-reading periods was that one saw a lot of the attractive Surrey countryside and the inside of a great many pubs, because every route, more by design than accident, seemed to start and finish at one.

The afternoons were spent largely in the classroom, doing dull stuff like Army Law and King's Regulations, all of which most of us could happily have done without.

Somewhere around Christmas 1940 there was a college ball, a very grand affair held in the gymnasium with the RMC band and a lot of red and white (the RMC colours) awning decked all over the place. Also long frocks, white gloves and all that went with them. I immediately got on the telephone to London and invited Penny Keach, a very dear friend of mine from my RADA days, to come down and be my partner. Penny was a very beautiful girl with a sensational figure. She had hazel eyes and long flowing hair which used to vary its hue, but generally it was round about chestnut. We were contemporaries at the Academy and we had a very close but platonic friendship for the entire period of our course. She was a great girl. We made each other laugh and that, to me, is always like champagne. Pre-war we used to dance together frequently at the Hammersmith Palais and at those Lyons' Corner House tea-dances after afternoon classes. So all in all she was a natural to invite down. She agreed and I got her a room in some local hostelry. We had a great evening and laughed a lot, principally, I'm afraid, at the expense of the many stereotyped cavalry officers and their Joan Hunter Dunns with whom the floor was littered. I was to meet many more of those stereotyped cavalry officers before I was demobilised six years later. Initially, I found them totally unbelievable. Later on, one or two of them I allowed to get under my skin and suffered agonies of fury and frustration as a result. But eventually I learned to live with them and found that, in the main, they weren't such bad types after all.

One such I had to appear before, towards the end of my stay at Sandhurst. He was a pre-war regular officer in a senior cavalry regiment, wore service dress, breeches, highly polished riding boots and spurs. He was, at that time, a sort of casting director for passing-out cadets, and we were all interviewed by him a few months before the end of our course so that, in the event of our being successful, we could state our preference for which particular regiment we would like to join.

Now I, fairly obviously, knew little about the army before 12 September 1940, and what knowledge I had acquired since did not extend further than the weapons and tactics with which I was to be associated. Its history and order of battle were an unopened book to me. The only mob in the Royal Armoured Corps that I really knew anything about was the East Riding Yeomanry, a territorial regiment which a number of my local friends had joined at the outbreak of war. So naturally, when invited by Captain Blank to express a preference, I plumped for them. When he informed me that they were full up and asked what other regiment I would like, it was with total naïveté that I replied, 'What other regiments have you got?' Luckily, this didn't upset his poise overmuch and he started giving me a sales pitch for a new one that had just been formed and for which he was trying to assemble a likely lot of lads – the 22nd Dragoons. Now this sounded really rather grand and for a moment I blanched. The emergency commissioned officer was a bit wary about grand cavalry and guards regiments because, certainly in peacetime, one had to have a private income to hold one's head up in the mess and drink pink-un's and chota pegs with the best of them; not to mention the bills that were liable to be presented by the regimental tailor. The hard, uncompromising fact was, however, that I had absolutely no counter-suggestion of my own. Consequently, for better or for worse, I left the office a candidate for a commission in the 22nd Dragoons.

A few weeks later I received information that I had been accepted, and giving nobody time to change his mind I toddled down to a firm of nationally known outfitters, who had premises right opposite the main gates, to be measured for my uniform. Those particular outfitters, I am here to say, got the contract primarily because nobody in the 22nd Dragoons had informed me who their regimental tailor was and, secondly, because they were the nearest outfitters to the college, an advantage that the enterprising board of directors had no doubt foreseen when they took a lease on the property. Now, apart from the fact that the overcoat worn by the officers of the 22nd Dragoons was a British Warm, which undoubtedly surpassed the normal officer's full-length khaki greatcoat for chic and

pleased me no end, nobody in Camberley had any information at all
about the remainder of the uniform. Quite understandable really, I suppose, as the regiment, I was to discover, had only been formed two
months previously. Nevertheless, an obsequious salesman with his tape-
measure dangling round his neck bade me not to worry. They would
undoubtedly, he assured me, have *all* the details at their London office,
so he would take my measurements and we could arrange a date for the
first fitting.

Now I think I should point out here that in the cavalry practically every
regiment has its own individual design of uniform. They are a very Beau
Brummell lot. Each has its own cloth and cut, and size, shape and layout
of buttons. Shirts and ties are rarely alike, one regiment with the next,
and they come invariably from the smartest of Jermyn Street shirt and
tie-makers. Hats come from Bates' or Herbert Johnson's and they too
are individual in style and material and certainly can't be obtained at
your run-of-the-mill outfitter who supplies the majority of the regiments
in the British army. So it was with a burning curiosity that I turned up
for my first fitting a week or so later. Well, the cloth that had been chosen
seemed to be a fairly commonplace khaki, but the patched, rather than
pleated, pockets showed a certain individuality. The buttons and hat
badge, I was assured, had not yet been designed so I was provided with
a set bearing the General Service badge – the Royal Coat of Arms – which
made me look exactly as if, rather like Fortnum and Mason, I was 'By
Appointment' to the Crown; which in a way I suppose I was.

And so it was, and thus accoutred, that I finally passed out of the Royal
Military College, Sandhurst, in March 1941 – a twenty-year-old (looking
all of sixteen) 2nd Lieutenant I. G. Carmichael, 22nd Dragoons, Royal
Armoured Corps.

I look back with pride at having once passed through the RMC; at
having stood guard outside its main portico, eaten in its dining-hall, slept
in its east wing, and stamped on its parade-ground. I'm proud that I was
once the owner of its red and white permanent pass, and that under its
roof I obtained the king's commission. It was a great experience – and
to think that it took one evil, paranoic, First World War Austrian corporal and peacetime house-painter to get me there!

CHAPTER NINE

WHITBY

From Square-bashing to True Love

Before reporting to my regiment, which was at that time stationed at Whitby, I was given two weeks' leave. My first urge was to spend a few days drinking the heady wine of the metropolis and to show off my newly acquired uniform and solitary pip. So it was to Dilys and Joan Sterndale Bennett that I hastened on my arrival in town. They were both appearing in the second edition of *Diversion*, a new revue written by Herbert Farjeon, which was playing at Wyndham's Theatre. Also in the cast was George Benson, who directed the piece, and it was through these contacts, though not because of them, that I had a few weeks previously been made to feel just about as small as I have ever felt in a theatre before or since. I had nipped up to London for a weekend and both George and Bertie Farjeon had allowed me to sit at the back of the stalls at Wyndham's to watch one of the final rehearsals. I was sitting there happily with a couple of members of the cast whom I knew when Edith Evans, who was the leading lady, suddenly stopped dead in the middle of one of her monologues. She moved to the front of the stage, held up a hand to shield her eyes from the glare of the footlights and, peering out into the auditorium, said to Farjeon who was sitting there with his producer: 'Are we alone, Bertie?'

Farjeon seemed momentarily nonplussed. 'Are we what, Edith?'

'Are we alone, dear?'

Bertie and George looked round the stalls.

'Yes, Edith dear. There's only us here,' said George.

'I mean, there are no *strangers* in the house, are there?' persisted Miss Evans, and she endowed the word 'strangers' with all the disdain that only the imperious Miss Evans could do. I had no doubt whatever to whom she was referring. Feeling smaller than anyone who could have been drawn by H. M. Bateman, I pulled my forage cap from under my shoulder strap and quietly crept out at the back.

Both editions of *Diversion* I enjoyed enormously. They were excellent,

Whitby a hundred years ago, photographed by Frank Meadow Sutcliffe

if perhaps not vintage Farjeon, and sadly they were the last shows that he was ever to write. He died tragically as a result of an accident at his home in St John's Wood only a few months later.

After my brief sojourn in the old metrop. I headed for Elloughton to spend the remainder of my leave at the family home. My father had by now joined the Royal Observer Corps and was doing daily shift-work at the post on Gallons Hill, a piece of high ground overlooking the Humber, about three-quarters of a mile outside the village.

The beautiful old homestead, like buildings in the cities, had assumed a wartime plumage. The smoke-room now admitted no daylight, all its windows being obstructed by sandbags. The magnificent herbaceous border which separated the two lawns had given up many of its prize blooms to accommodate an air-raid shelter in its midst. Bulbs had been removed from all the outside lights and blackout boards rested below the upstairs windows – the ground-floor rooms being luckily fitted with their original wooden shutters.

Two weeks later, having done the round of all the family friends and relatives, dutifully allowing my mother to show me off, I headed for Whitby and the 22nd Dragoons.

Whitby is a small fishing town of considerable antiquity at the mouth of the River Esk. It faces due north and lies in what might be a small crucible tucked into the coastline. Inland it is completely surrounded by a horseshoe of high ground – the North Yorkshire Moors National Park. It has three approaches only; from Teesside in the west, from Scarborough in the east, and from York in the south-west. From all three of these approaches the view of the town and its harbour, with its two, now defunct, lighthouses beyond which project a pair of whalebone-shaped pier extensions, is spectacular. Approaching it by night, the sight of the lights of the town twinkling far below can only be compared to coming in to land at an airport. The dominant feature of the landscape, however, is the sizeable ruin of its sixth-century abbey which, as a result of the constant erosion of the coastline over the years, now teeters on the edge of the cliff overlooking the harbour and the sea.

In a sense, time seems to have stood still in Whitby. The Victorian photographer Frank Meadows Sutcliffe spent a lifetime with his huge and cumbersome plate camera recording the town and its inhabitants, and the backgrounds have changed little from that day to this. The harbour full of tall ships, the fishermen in their sou'-westers and high boots and their wives in full-length skirts and head shawls are the only anachronisms in photographs which could otherwise have been taken yesterday. For me, from the moment of my arrival, Whitby and its people have always spelt pure enchantment.

Whitby today, photographed by the author

In March 1941 the 22nd Dragoons were stationed in the requisitioned Royal Hotel, a pre-war luxury hotel situated on the West Cliff overlooking the harbour and looking straight across at the abbey on the other side. I reported to the adjutant and the first question that I was asked was what the hell was I wearing? Not a good start, I thought. The question not only hurt my pride but it was also, it transpired, about to hurt my pocket.

Apparently the outfitter at Camberley had got it all wrong. With the exception of my British Warm not one single item of my uniform was correct. I had to start all over again. The correct regimental tailors, Messrs Jones, Chalk & Dawson of Sackville Street, W.1., it transpired, were sending a representative up to Whitby during the following week to take orders, and I just had to face the fact that I had to re-equip myself right down to my socks. In the administrative offices of my new unit, I felt I had good grounds to reflect that 'someone had blundered'.

The 22nd Dragoons were formed from a small nucleus of senior officers and men taken from two long-established cavalry regiments: the 4/7th Royal Dragoon Guards, and the 5/6th Royal Inniskilling Dragoon Guards, both of which had their own quite distinctive uniforms. An outstanding feature of each was that the 'Skins' wore bottle-green trousers, very racy, and the 4/7th sported a shirt which was almost saffron in colour, and the most elegant silk crocheted tie. Well, some skilful designer in the bowels of Whitehall, the Cavalry Club or Savile Row, I know not which, had put together for us a very tasteful ensemble which was an amalgamation of the uniform worn by each of our parent regiments and which, when it was all finished and paid for, was, I must admit, a great deal more eye-catching than the one in which I had arrived.

The officers' mess was at the other end of the half-mile-long North Promenade to the Royal, and was established in a smaller private hotel called the Monkshaven; now Moorlands. It faced straight out to sea with only the road between it and the cliff edge.

My first night in the mess was a bit awe-inspiring. Most of the senior officers wore 'blues', clanked about in spurs, referred to girls as 'fillies', drank 'large pinks' and kept saying, 'Don'tcha know?' with monotonous regularity. All of which, like my time at Catterick, was to provide me with great background material for later life.

The colonel was a regular soldier. He had served in India with his regiment, the 4/7th, pre-war, had been their second-in-command in France in 1940 and had been evacuated with them through Dunkirk a year previously. The 22nd Dragoons was his first command. His name was Craig

Lt Col. G. L. Craig – my commanding officer in the 22nd Dragoons

– Lieutenant-Colonel G. L. Craig. He was in his early forties, of medium height, dapper, possessed sandy hair which was slightly receding, walked with a suggestion of a limp and he sported a spruce little cavalry moustache. He was an aloof man, difficult to talk to, had a sense of humour of the most obvious kind and was a ruthless disciplinarian; few people were allowed to make more than one mistake. In wartime, when everyone wore battledress throughout the daytime hours, he was, except on military exercises, always seen in service dress. He was, by his own admission, lazy. He always had a lie-down on his bed after lunch – but he was also astute enough to realise that if he didn't want to work hard, to retain his rank and regiment, someone else was going to have to. Consequently he developed decentralisation practically to an art form. He was an infuriating and, to me – certainly initially – not a very likeable man.

'Craigie' and I had nothing whatever in common; yet for some quite unaccountable reason he took to me. He also bullied me, derided me, belittled and, at times, humiliated me – though to give him the benefit of the doubt, he may not have realised he was humiliating me – but one thing he never did was ignore me.

I was, I think, never cut out to become a regimental officer. There *was* a place for me in the scheme of things but this was not to manifest itself until the last two or three years of my service. Here and now Craigie, probing and unsure of my potential, went on moving me round and round his regiment trying, with the most infinite care and patience, to find the square hole into which my seemingly square peg would fit, and each time, each move until the ultimate one, brought me nearer and nearer his personal sphere of influence. Opposites are, I believe, supposed to attract.

Well, there could have been no two more diametrically opposed people than Craigie and me and, let it be clear, until the last year of the war when I am convinced that he was responsible for saving my life, the attraction was all on one side. He drove me wild with frustration and anger.

To start with, I was allocated to 'C' Squadron, one of the three fighting squadrons of the regiment, and I soon found myself bivouacking in a wood a few miles out of the town, learning how to handle a troop of three tanks.

On the social scene, three nights after I had arrived in Whitby a fellow officer, a Second Lieutenant Haddock, known fairly obviously as 'Fish', after dinner took me down to the Spa, which was set in the side of the cliff between the Monkshaven and the Royal, to an all-ranks dance. These functions seemed to take place about twice a week. A local band used to bash it out up on the stage, the floor was packed with seething humanity and a small bar upstairs, in which it was practically impossible to move, swilled ankle deep in beer. The predominant colour was khaki, there being three complete armoured regiments – the 1st Lothian and Border Yeomanry, the Westminster Dragoons and ourselves – all stationed within a quarter-of-a-mile walking distance of the top of the cliff, but odd splashes of colour were provided by a limited amount of local talent that had paid its admission. Shortly before the end of the evening, Fish and I spotted two attractive young 'fillies' (I must get the nomenclature right) at the other side of the floor, and we made a beeline for them. I grabbed the taller of the two, who was wearing a salmon-pink dress, and wheeled her off into a quick-step to the strains of 'Amapola'. Her name was Pym, she was blonde, just eighteen, five feet six, sensationally pretty and a beautiful dancer. Fish's half of the deal was apparently her cousin. They were of an age and having both recently left school were occupying their time as telephonists at the local Civil Defence Report Centre. At the end of the evening we were driven back to the mess, all of five hundred yards, by Pym in her mother's Morris Eight and, after a brief and decorous 'snog', went in.

'An interesting evening,' Fish said as we had a final nightcap. 'What was yours like?' And with an arrogance that has embarrassed me throughout every one of the thirty-eight years since, I replied, 'I intend to marry mine.'

And I did.

From that day forward, until we left Whitby some five months later, my entire off-duty hours were spent with Pym. I had taken to her immediately. She was young and fresh, blue-eyed, wore her hair on her shoulders and her vital statistics, I was to learn later, were 34–24–36. She was Yorkshire through and through – born, bred and educated in the tiny Whitby area – yet she carried not a trace of a regional accent. She was warm, she was 'game', she was genuine. There was an innocence about her, an unsophistication that disarmed even the most worldly; it would have been impossible for anyone to patronise her. She was instantly likeable. She was also patient, considerate, tolerant, totally unselfish and, fortunately for me, a good listener. During those early weeks she never once yawned throughout my incessant chatter about the theatre and its personalities, all of which meant no more to her than a ball of chalk. She also, bless her, for several weeks accepted my wooing while simultaneously having to absorb the tales of my heartbreaking love for Dilys without batting an eye.

There was so much about Pym Maclean that appealed to me. At heart she was a country girl. She handled animals (including *homo sapiens*) with the utmost tenderness. She knew the name of every flower in the garden and also those in the hedgerows which we used to ramble past on our long country walks together. She had ridden throughout her childhood but was never 'horsey'. Pym's whole personality and approach to life was as clear and refreshing as a mountain stream.

Pym – a diminutive for a family surname, Pyman – was, and has remained, a chameleon. She is at home in any company (although she will rarely admit it) and all around her seem to love her. I wouldn't mind a fiver for every time someone has said to me, 'You're a very lucky boy, Ian. You honestly don't know how lucky you are.' But Ian does, you know. I assure you, Ian does.

In 1941 she lived alone with her mother in a charming detached four-bedroomed stone house called 'Penarth', which stood in the middle of its own small garden up a non-adopted, unmetalled, perfectly fiendish road in a village called Sleights, four miles inland. It was also next door to the one in which she was born. Her father, in peacetime, kept a poultry farm which he worked himself with the help of only one other man, and which was situated on a sun-drenched forward slope three hundred yards further up the lane. At the time I met Pym he was a captain in the Duke of Wellington's Regiment and was stationed 'somewhere in England'. The family Maclean also had a second and younger daughter who was away at boarding-school, so mother, who now physically ran the whole of the poultry farm on her own, and Pym, who was a vital link between the marauding Luftwaffe and the Royal Air Force and Civil Defence units and, for all I knew, Whitehall, were the sole representatives of the family living at home.

That summer was a most glorious one in more ways than one. The skies were blue, the sun shone, the air was balmy and 'shirt-sleeve order' was all we ever seemed to wear. The countryside was one of the most beautiful I had ever seen in my life: the rolling fields of the Esk Valley separated one from another by local dry-stone walls; the endless vistas provided by the heather-strewn North Yorkshire Moors; the little becks and waterfalls in the valleys and dales; the tiny villages with their stone cottages and sheep-cropped communal grass verges and greens, and the moorland sheep themselves wandering free-range amongst the cottages, snuggling up amongst the walls of the church, the pub, the little war memorial, tame and friendly as domestic cats. Then there was the sea and beach, though that was only to look at, all approaches to it being blocked with huge concrete cubes, 'dragons' teeth', tubular scaffolding walls and mile upon mile of barbed-wire fencing. The area was peppered with innumerable little country pubs where one could go into the back room and have the most delicious ham-and-eggs with real Yorkshire ham. Where it all came from in 1941 heaven knows, but there it was. That summer I fell in love, not only with Pym, but with the whole area and I am delighted to say that all three of us are still together.

I was the first officer in that barely six-month-old regiment to actually find a girl during that time and start to woo her regularly, and this warmed some sort of cockle in Craigie's heart. Every evening in mess nobody was allowed to leave the table without special dispensation until after the port had been round. Somewhere round about eight-thirty, on every night that she wasn't on duty herself, Pym would come round in that little Morris Eight (extra petrol because of her Civil Defence duties, no doubt) and sit outside the mess until I could get out and join her. The dining-room was at the front of the building and the moment she arrived Craigie would see her, make some ribald remark and then hurry the port up so that I could get away. He very much took to Pym, as indeed did every officer in the mess. On one occasion he insisted that we should take him and his adjutant out with us for a ham-and-eggs meal at one of our favourite pubs. He struck an incongruous figure – regimental 'blues' with their chain-mail, tight trousers and spurs going jingle-jangle-jingle in the bar parlour of a tiny village local inhabited only by farm-hands. The whole scene was an anathema to me; a gross and unforgivable intrusion on our privacy. I boiled with indignation. Later in the war such anti-Craigie fury was reported to Pym in my letters with a sudden switch to red ink. But Pym was my girl. She let me sound off on such occasions, or rather when such occasions were over, and always appeared sympathetic and understanding. When questioning her the other day, however, on the subject of my late CO for inclusion in these pages, it must be reported that she had never, she said, all the time she knew him, found him anything but kind and attentive. It was news to me, but I understood.

Somewhere about the middle of our five months in Whitby, Craigie's enigmatic affection for me started to manifest itself. The first signs appeared in the mess. At dinner the CO always took the head of the very long table and the senior officers settled around him. The junior officers gravitated to the other end as far away from authority as was possible.

One evening, after the mess sergeant had entered the anteroom and announced, 'Dinner is served,' we all trooped into the dining-room, led by the colonel. We were just about to sit down in accordance with the usual pattern when Craigie's voice was raised above the general 'rhubarb' of the others: 'Come and sit beside me, Ian.'

Hiatus. The 'frame' momentarily froze like it does at the end of so many TV commercials just before the final slogan is superimposed over the top. Did I, we, everybody, hear correctly?

'Come and sit beside me, Ian.'

We did – the action continued.

This was the first but by no means the last occasion that I received the Royal Command. Whether it was because I amused him, whether it was a desire to have youth about him, I know not, but apparently he found my company congenial – I can't for the life of me think why.

'Come and sit beside me,' needless to say, became a sort of catch-phrase to be used by my fellow subalterns every time they wanted to take a rise out of me.

In addition to the social side of regimental life, Craigie now decided that he wanted me nearer to him during working hours as well, and it was because of this he sent for me one day and informed me that he was taking me out of 'C' Squadron and attaching me to HQ Squadron, the administrative squadron of the regiment, and that he wished me to become his assistant adjutant. Now this pleased me no end. Administration, I was about to discover, I was going to take to like a duck to water. The post I had been allotted was a brand-new one created especially for me by Craigie. We had never had an assistant adjutant before and during my time with the regiment we never did again.

My mentor now was to be the adjutant who had never stopped giving me rockets since my arrival for not having my hat on straight. His name was Hine – his family somewhere along the line were the brandy people – and one of my first bits of advice from him was that I must never on any account pass on orders received from above unless I fully understood every detail about them myself. With these instructions ringing in my ears I found myself one morning at a third and recently added desk (trestle table covered with an army blanket) in the colonel's office under his permanent gaze. That is, of course, except when he was having his lie-down after lunch.

My second day in office – literally – I found myself alone for the afternoon. The chief clerk had brought me some bumph to read amongst which was a current Army Council Instruction. These were direct orders from the War Office to the whole service and were issued from time to time. The first paragraph in this particular ACI was an instruction concerning the storing of Two-Pounder, Armour-Piercing Ammunition, and it commenced something like this:

Ammunition, 2 Pdr, AP.
All units whose holding of the above ammunition is not stored in accordance with ACI 169/2b dated 9 December 1940, must indent forthwith for the necessary racks, steel, fireproof, these having been made available by the Ministry of Supply, on a pari passu basis as laid down in ACI 152/2b dated 23 November 1940, and ACI 153/2b dated 30 November 1940.

'Never, on any account, pass on orders ...' The adjutant's sonorous tones rang in my ears.

I picked up the telephone to the orderly room.

'Chief clerk here.'

'Ah, could I have ACIs 169/2b dated 9 December 1940, 152/2b dated 23 November 1940, and 153/2b dated 30 November 1940, please, sergeant-major?'

A pause. 'Can I help in any way, sir?'

'Well, it's about the storage of this 2 Pdr AP Ammunition—'

'Ah yes, sir, you don't want to worry your head about that, that's the quartermaster's responsibility, he's got a copy of the current ACI and he'll take care of it all.'

'Yes, but all the same, I think I ought to know all about what's going on.'

Another pause. 'Very good, sir.'

A few moments later the chief clerk entered the office with the necessary documents which had been bound, thirty at a time, into volumes between two bits of cardboard. The first one I looked up was simply cancelling an order given in a previous ACI, the second one cancelled that one and the third one simply said, 'See ACIs 111/44a dated 14 May 1940, and ACI 121/44a dated 27 May 1940.'

Telephone again.

'Chief clerk.'

'Ah, sorry to bother you again, sergeant-major, but could I have ACIs' – and I reeled off the references of the last three mentioned.

A longer pause and I think I detected a long-drawn-in sigh.

These duly arrived on my desk and they, of course, referred to even further ACIs. Half an hour later, when anybody entering the office wouldn't have been able to see me for the mountain of those volumes which was by then hemming me in, I decided to admit defeat and leave it to the quartermaster as advised by the chief clerk in the first place.

It was long after the war, when I met Sidney Hine again, that he recounted the incident, and apparently the following morning, when he returned to the office, the chief clerk had asked him respectfully if he could find Mr Carmichael something more productive to do as my earnest desire to get to the bottom of the Two-Pounder AP Ammunition Storage situation on the previous afternoon had held up the orderly room staff so completely that he and a typist had to work an hour's overtime to catch up with the backlog of form-filling and return-rendering.

Anyway, the time was drawing nigh when we were all due to leave Whitby. Luckily for Pym and me we were only moving some thirty miles inland to the small market-town of Helmsley, on the other side of the moors. We said our lingering and agonising goodbyes on the hearthrug in front of the sitting-room fire at 'Penarth', way into the small hours of the morning of the fateful day, and were both so emotionally torn that we agreed that when we finally separated, for the time being, that was to be it – there was to be no coming down to see us depart at midday.

When the sun came up it was to provide a most beautiful day. All our vehicles were lining the Esplanade and West Terrace, fully packed and ready for the off. During those last twenty minutes, if Pym circled the block in her mother's Morris Eight once, she circled it ten times. She was wearing a pale-blue angora wool bolero jacket and her eyes were full of tears. But she kept to our agreement; there were no waves, no kisses thrown – we both stoically pretended that neither of us had seen the other.

And then the 22nd Dragoons moved out.

CHAPTER TEN

HELMSLEY

Tanks, Theatres and Wartime Trains

Helmsley is a jolly little village-sized market-town clean and stone-built with a small market-square containing an ancient cross, which is over-looked on various sides by an old town hall and four licensed residential hotels. Just round the corner from the market-place is the imposing entrance and lodge to Duncombe Park. The Park itself, with its eighteenth-century mansion, has been the seat of the Duncombe family since it was built in 1713, but in 1941 it was already leased to an evacuated girls' school. Further into the park, and facing the house at its open end, is a large horseshoe-shaped wood, and it was this wood that was to be our home for two long, bitter winters and a total of nineteen months. A camp of brand-new Nissen huts, far from complete and ready for occupation, was our new accommodation, and as if to reflect my depression on leaving Pym and Whitby the scene and lighting changed accordingly. That August the rain poured down incessantly. The entire camp became a slimy morass. The new-laid or unfinished roads ran deep with a yellow glue of mud. Dampness wrapped itself about us like a blanket. In the mornings clothes were stiff with it and at night beds were as chill and cheerless as a grave. The following winter, in its severity, turned out to be one unparalleled in local memory. Duncombe Park was shrouded in a counterpane of white from before Christmas until mid-March. Rare moments of thaw loosened the snow in the trees above us, causing it to thunder down on to the tin roofs of the Nissen huts with the noise of distant gunfire. Within hours the resultant mud was frozen solid once again as frost and blizzard enveloped everything.

Despite the elements and discomforts, however, luck seemed to be on my side. Not only did Pym have an uncle and aunt living in the town, but her old supervisor at the Whitby report centre was married to the manager of the local branch of Barclays Bank, so whenever she could get over for an evening or a weekend there was always guaranteed accom-

Nissenland in Duncombe Park

modation; furthermore, accommodation in which we could stay alone together just sitting by the light of the fire until dawn, without some dressing-gowned hotel official coming in round about 1 a.m. to kick me out because he wanted to lock up and go to bed.

I managed to get back to Whitby quite frequently too. My squadron leader had also left an 'amour' behind in the town and his comparatively exalted rank gave him an access to transport that I did not possess. So, all in all, things could have been a great deal worse.

Shortly after our arrival at Helmsley the colonel decided to consolidate my position under his immediate sphere of influence; my appointment as assistant adjutant was quite unofficial and if we'd had to go to war at that moment I would have been jettisoned. He now legalised me, as it were, by making me leader of the regimental HQ troop of four tanks. The RHQ troop leader was to the colonel what the captain of a battleship (if anyone can remember such a thing) was to the admiral in whose ship he, the admiral, had decided to hoist his flag; this troop carried the colonel and his immediate staff whose responsibility it was to command the whole regiment. I was now on, and no longer surplus to, War Establishment.

In the mess I began to assume a new role too. One evening after dinner, under the influence of several too many, I extemporised what I can only describe as an 'entertainment'. Bending down to pick up a dropped napkin or some such, I reappeared from underneath the dining table assuming the role of a cinema organist rising from the bowels of the earth on his mighty Wurlitzer playing 'I do like to be beside the seaside' the while. On settling in to my chair again, I brought the number to a flamboyant finish and swung round on the seat to announce to an imaginary packed auditorium what I was next about to play. My voice I made practically inaudible as I always found most of those gentlemen were when not provided with a microphone; I then swung back to begin the concert with such verve that I vanished off my stool down under the table once again, becoming inextricably mixed up with all the bass pedals. From here on, amid paroxysms of laughter from the whole mess, I was away. I was sloshed, of course, and so, fairly obviously from the reception I was accorded, was the majority of my audience. Nevertheless, this splurge of high spirits and alcohol-inspired fooling proved to be my undoing. I became in demand. I, along with one Buzz Burrows, who before the war had been a cartoonist for the *Daily Sketch*, became a court jester and whenever Craigie wanted amusing, and particularly when VIP guests were being dined in, I had to repeat the performance. This, of course, was the thin end of the wedge, and ultimately I had to think up other 'entertainments'. Galling though it was on many occasions to be called upon to amuse at the drop of a hat, it seemed to reinforce Craigie's desire to retain my services and to try and integrate me into his war machine at all costs.

In November of that year the whole regiment, tanks and all, entrained for Castlemartin, which is situated in the south-western corner of Pembrokeshire. Here, on Linney Head, there was a tank firing-range. This was the only range in the country at that time where a half squadron of tanks could manœuvre as a complete unit and have a go willy-nilly, if you get my meaning. It was an eventful trip for me personally and one from which I would return never to be the same man again.

The weather was foul down there too. There was persistent rain, and when you get rain and tanks together you also get mud; that fortnight was to provide us all with as much of both as we were ever likely to want to experience again.

For me the most memorable moment of our visit occurred at the beginning of the second week. I had been out on the range with my troop all day. It was about 7.30 in the evening, bitterly cold and very dark. We had finished cleaning the guns, done the routine maintenance and were 'sheeting up' – that is to say, covering up the vehicles with a tarpaulin sheet. For some reason that the sands of time have obliterated, we were the only people out there. Everybody else had finished, been dismissed, and gone back to their respective messes or quarters. That, in itself, was not abnormal: all my life I seem to have been that much slower than everyone else.

I was on top of my tank, heaving away trying to close the lid of the turret which was being held fast by the tarpaulin sheet lying across one corner. Suddenly it 'gave'. It whipped across with unexpected speed and ferocity. And it happened.

I remember vividly my first words. I didn't scream, holler, yell or anything like that. I simply said, '*Christ!* I've lost a finger.'

I picked up a torch which was lying on the turret, shone it on to my wounded hand and found my assessment was dead accurate. I had, or to be correct the turret lid had, amputated the top of the second finger of my left hand as clean as a whistle.

It's interesting to note how a man behaves in times of personal crisis. I make no bones about it – I behaved admirably. In fact, the sheer bravado of my behaviour amazes me to this day because I am not a brave man; not to put too fine a point on it, I am a devout coward.

All my men fussed around to see if I was all right. 'Come on,' I said, with an air of command and authority that had always escaped me before, 'I'm all right. Get them sheeted up.' I stuck my wounded fist into the top of my overalls and looking for all the world like the traditional pictures of Napoleon, as solicitous as a mother hen, I ensured that every last detail was completed before finally dismissing the troop.

Then my sergeant suggested he should walk me back to the mess. 'I'm perfectly all right,' I lied. 'Don't worry, I can manage.' However, he insisted. We walked the half-mile or so back. He wanted to hand me over personally to the MO but I refused his offer graciously, bade him goodnight, opened the front door, entered, closed the door behind me and fainted on the mat.

When I came to, the MO poured a couple of stiff whiskies down me, applied a loose temporary dressing and said that I would have to go to the infirmary in a town some fifteen miles away the following morning to have it properly tidied up.

It was a filthy day when I arrived at the infirmary. It appeared to be visiting hours as there was a heck of a lot of coming and going. I reported to the reception desk and told my story. The receptionist, a man in shirtsleeves who turned out later to be a doctor, said, 'Let's have a look at it.' There and then he undid the temporary dressing and examined my topless, bone-projecting finger – and so did many of the visitors who were wandering in and out at the time. He slapped the dressing back on again in a rough and ready way and instructed me to proceed down a certain corridor until I found a certain room and there to get into bed. I followed his instructions and found a small ward with four beds in it. I got into one of them and waited.

An hour or so later the same man, still in his shirt-sleeves, came in. He might have had an open white coat on, I can't swear to the fact, but the overriding picture in my mind has always been that he was in his shirt-sleeves. Anyway, he threw a dressing-gown on my bed and told me to go along to the operating theatre with some vague instructions how to find it, and then vanished.

Of course, I got lost. It still seemed to be visiting hours (there were so many odd people wandering around with shopping baskets) and I found myself in the ludicrous situation of having to stop total strangers and, in my pyjamas and dressing-gown, enquire: 'Excuse me, could you tell me the way to the operating theatre?'

Eventually I found it. Both sets of doors were wide open and quite a crowd of these visiting types had gathered round to look in: you know, the same sort of people who gather round road accidents just to watch. 'Excuse me, excuse me,' I said as I edged my way through this mini-crowd; and then to a second man, also in shirt-sleeves who was leaning up against a door-jamb and who appeared to be completely uninterested in my presence, I said, 'I believe I'm next.'

'Get on the table,' he said.

It was wartime, of course; we were all short of many things but I hadn't realised until then that manners were also running a bit low. As I looked for somewhere to put my dressing-gown, the first man in the shirt-sleeves appeared again (he turned out to be the anaesthetist). He took it from me and I got on the table. The man leaning on the door-jamb then approached me. He took the cigarette out of his mouth, stubbed it out on the underside of the table, took hold of my wounded hand and said, 'Right, let's have a look at it.' He was the surgeon.

The fact that the whole thing went wrong a few months later wasn't surprising. However, I am prepared to admit that since I told the surgeon I was an actor and that I would be grateful if he would leave me as much finger as possible, it might have affected his subsequent bungling of the job. For the next few weeks, however, I soldiered on, somewhat incapacitated and intermittently in a certain amount of pain. To those who may ask, like a hundred others I have met since, why I hadn't picked up the amputated portion and had it stitched back on again, I can only say that obviously none of them have ever been inside a tank turret, let alone tried to find anything so small on the floor of one. In daylight, fully fit, it wouldn't be easy; in pitch dark and maimed – well, let's just say, 'I didn't think of it.'

And so 1941 drew to a close. An eventful year for me, what with one thing and another. I had passed proudly through Sandhurst, obtained the King's Commission, fallen in love – not for the first time but for what looked like being the most enduring one – developed a strange love/hate relationship with my commanding officer and sustained my one and only war-wound, albeit a self-inflicted one.

Back in Helmsley, 1942 opened with considerable boredom in the camp, occasioned not only by the weather but also by the spartan quality of the billets. We also began to feel more and more isolated because of tighter petrol rationing, and a general air of depression resulted from a growing impression that the Whitehall brass had forgotten all about us. The latter was not felt by me, or, I suspect, by many of the more imaginative amongst us, but the 'up and at 'em' brigade were ever impatient to get to grips with the Boche. To relieve this boredom a 'passion wagon' was run one evening a week to York, our nearest oasis. The wagon used to pick us up for the return journey shortly after closing-time outside a pub called, if I remember correctly, the Castle, whose main attraction was not its beer but the fact that it had a clock over the bar with a naked girl lying on her back in the centre. Her head was at twelve o'clock, her hips in the middle of the face and her legs provided the hands – if you follow me. The roar of approval she received at twenty-five past seven was nothing to the one accorded to her just after closing time at five past eleven.

All-ranks dances were held in Helmsley town hall and rather grand officers' ones in various large country houses in the area. 'Blues', chain-mail and clanking spurs were well to the fore, as also were girls in long evening dresses, the regimental band and groups sitting on stairways in the manner of those so frequently photographed and published in pre-war *Tatlers* bearing captions such as – 'Brigadier Somethington-Twit enjoying a joke with Lady Diana Gushington.'

But when summer arrived everything started happening again. The vagaries of the British climate were never more clearly demonstrated than when the 1942 summer followed the '41–'42 winter. Heat and drought predominated. Mud turned to dust. The shovelling away of snow was now replaced by the fighting of heath fires. This was not only a thankless task but also an unpleasant one. Smoke and flying particles of peat and heather swirled around in the air and filled the eyes until they were red-raw. The peat would burn two to three feet down and without several days of torrential rain the fires just had to be laboriously beaten out. Round-the-clock fire-fighting pickets were therefore provided and it was exhausting and seemingly fruitless work.

I escaped this chore for about ten days during which time other officers and men had managed, if not to actually extinguish the fires, at least to keep them in check. Eventually, however, my turn came round and at about four o'clock one afternoon I set out for the moors with twenty men in a three-ton truck. We relieved the previous squad and set to work beating.

Now this was my first experience of fighting moorland fires, and all that I have explained about them so far is knowledge gained by hindsight; at this particular moment I was green to their potential. After about an hour of beating the living daylights out of good non-productive Yorkshire earth, we appeared to have the whole thing under control; in fact, in my view we'd put it out. So not wishing to remain a minute longer than was necessary with streaming eyes, black faces and red-hot boots, I piled the lads back into the lorry and returned to camp. As we were de-bussing, the adjutant passed by.

'I thought you were on fire-fighting, Carmichael,' he said.

'We've put it out, sir,' I replied.

He looked at me sceptically and passed on his way.

In the middle of dinner that night the mess sergeant entered the dining-room, went up to the adjutant and whispered something in his ear. The adjutant then excused himself with the colonel and walked out.

Ten minutes later the mess sergeant came up to me and said the adjutant wanted to see me in his office. I, too, excused myself and did as I was bid.

'I thought you said you'd put that fire out,' said the adjutant.

'That's right,' I said.

'Just come with me a moment, would you?'

He then led me to the perimeter of the camp – the skyline beyond was ablaze as far as the eye could see. From the extreme right to the extreme left of the panorama there were flames searching high into the sky; furthermore, the whole inferno seemed to be advancing rapidly towards Duncombe Park.

That night one Light Field Ambulance unit and three armoured regiments, a force which comprised 126 tanks and 300 wheeled vehicles, had to abandon camp.

By dint of some good fortune, the nature of which escapes me, the fire was brought under control and we all returned the following morning.

In May our whole division was laid on the War Office operating table and dissected.

Experience gained by armoured formations in the desert war had resulted in the complete reorganisation and composition of the armoured division *per se*. One of the effects this had down at our regimental level was that a hitherto small troop of Daimler scout-cars under the command of a sergeant in HQ Squadron was to be increased to ten cars and was now to be commanded by a subaltern. The troop was to be designated the Recce Troop and it was to be the eyes and ears of the regiment in battle. Pushed well forward in front of everybody else, it was to seek out the enemy and report back direct to the colonel. It was to be an élite troop, which in fact it already was under the command of Sergeant Huse, one of the most likeable, efficient and enthusiastic sergeants in the regiment. The new troop leader had to be an officer of initiative and panache.

Whether it was something to do with the initiative and panache with which I had extinguished that heath fire or not, I shall never know, but inexplicably the colonel now decided to move me once again and give me command of the Recce Troop. It was possibly the biggest piece of miscasting that has ever happened to me before or since.

However, they were a grand bunch of lads and to my profound relief Sergeant Huse stayed on to be my guide, comforter and friend – though sadly for so short a time. Later that summer during a night exercise when I had to remain in camp as duty officer and he was commanding the troop in my absence, he was crushed and killed between his car and a tank in a moorland village that was shrouded in mist. It was a tragic and wasteful accident. He was one of those calm and gentle men whom nothing can shake. I and all his troop were devoted to him. I attended both his wedding and his funeral in St Hilda's Church in Whitby within about three months of each other.

But to happier things. Also in May, during a few days' leave at Elloughton Garth, Pym decided that we should become engaged. The moment of reckoning had arrived. One thing that has always scared the pants off me is burning my boats – or should it be bridges? Either way, the result is the same, and the thought of doing so now pulled me up sharp and scared the life out of me. Was my jealously guarded freedom suddenly to be flung irrevocably out of the window? One of the troubles with me is that I have always wanted to be able to have my cake and to be able to eat it as well. An outrageously selfish if not impossible attitude to adopt, I freely admit. However, after the initial fright at such a suggestion and some delaying tactics on my part – like laying on the line fairly heavily the insecurity of my chosen calling – wheedling, and, no doubt, a few tears finally broke me down. What I suppose clinched the matter was the thought that I might lose the girl, so by the end of our leave all was agreed and our engagement was announced on 30 May.

A week later Pym, now nineteen years old, in a surge of patriotism (people had them in those days) decided to volunteer for the WAAF, and only two weeks after that had to report to a training centre in Gloucester. So for the first time since we had met fifteen months previously, comparatively long stretches of separation were to follow, separation not only in time but also in distance, which always made it seem worse. But just as I was about to start fretting, I was awarded my second pip, which added a metaphorical cubit to my stature, and a timely and unexpected distraction entered my life in the form of Nigel Patrick.

Nigel was at that time a captain in the 12th KRRC (King's Royal Rifle Corps), which in the early days of the war became known as the King's Royal Repertory Company on account of the number of actors who joined its ranks; but in July 1942 he was our brigade entertainments officer, and Brigade HQ was stationed in a country house about a mile outside the town. I visited him regularly during my off-duty moments. We were kindred spirits and his office became our green room. Nigel was senior to me in the acting profession. He had several years' experience behind him as a leading West End player before the war. He had a fund of stories that emanated from the Green Room Club and, to me, the exciting world of pre-war Shaftesbury Avenue – stories of actors, authors and producers, the hem of whose garments I would have been happy just to touch. I would sit there in the manner of 'The Boyhood of Raleigh', lapping it up for hours.

I doubt very much if the actor in the services was any more vulnerable than any other civilian soldier, but we always felt we were. We always received the impression that 'acting' in the professional soldier's eyes was not an occupation at all. It was just mindless skylarking executed by a lot of effeminate layabouts. Consequently, whenever one found a fellow Thespian during those years a huge affinity and togetherness was nurtured. The jokes and the chat were very much of a 'them against us' variety. But actors rarely allow themselves to be oppressed for long. The lighter side of the most daunting situations are the ones that they will always ensure predominate. Let me tell you a parable – a true story.

Several years ago, a great friend of mine who was an actor made all the arrangements for a fellow actor's funeral on behalf of the over-wrought widow. The deceased was a Scot, and my friend had arranged with great taste and dignity a most moving service at the crematorium.

The coffin was draped in his plaid of the family tartan and his dirk and other regalia were laid on the top. White heather flown down from Scotland decorated the chapel. At the end of the service the small congregation sat quietly while a piece of the deceased's favourite music was played on tape, and finally as the coffin moved away a lone piper in full dress played a lament. It was all very moving and respectful and there wasn't a dry eye in the house.

When it was over, walking back down the aisle, my friend, with the widow on his arm, felt a hand on his opposite shoulder and another actor, whose name he has never disclosed, whispered quietly in his ear: 'I think you've got a success.'

A digression, but maybe it illustrates a point.

Anyway, Nigel Patrick, always ebullient, extrovert and the most congenial of company back in Helmsley in 1942, was both a friend in need and a friend indeed. We shared lots of laughs.

One day after we'd all been sitting on our bottoms in Duncombe Park for a year alternately clearing snow and fighting fires, he thought that the time might be opportune to persuade the brigadier to allow the two of us to put on a play. A new garrison theatre had just been built in the park. It was in an extra-large Nissen hut but it had, nevertheless, been custom-built as a theatre and was just waiting for someone to tread its boards.

The idea was to present a comedy by Ben Levy called *Springtime for Henry*, which had had considerable success both in London and New York in the early thirties. It posed few production problems – one set and four characters, two of each sex. So off went Nigel at a moment he thought propitious to chat up the brigade commander.

There was a scenic artist at Brigade HQ so the set would be his responsibility; two professional actresses should, according to our package, be engaged at the expense of army funds, the two of us would play the male roles and Nigel would direct. Two weeks' rehearsal would be required and the play would run for four performances. Admission would be charged and the proceeds donated to the KRRC and Lothians' Prisoner of War Funds. The latter point gave the project a respectable *raison d'être*

*With Benita Booth,
Anne Bibby and
Nigel Patrick in*
Springtime for Henry

beyond being just an exercise of enjoyment and exhibitionism for Patrick and Carmichael.

The brigadier took the bait and swallowed the hook. The Misses Anne Bibby and Benita Booth were engaged. Nigel and I were placed on light duties for two weeks and a fortnight later *Springtime for Henry* played to four capacity houses. A first-night party was given in the Brigade Head-quarters officers' mess and it had all the glamour of many that I attended in later life. Well, perhaps not *all* the glamour, but Nigel and I were elated with our reception and the approbation we received was caviar and champagne to our egos. Suddenly we had stature as we moved around Helmsley and the effect was not unpleasing.

Flushed with success, we next started to plan a revue, which was to be called *Acting Unpaid*. This, however, never materialised as Nigel received promotion and was posted overseas.

Meeting Nigel provided an oasis in my service life at that time. I was to learn a lot from him. Our paths have crossed several times since but never professionally. It was not, however, to be the last I was to see of *Springtime for Henry*.

Later that year Scarborough, the town to which in 1933 I had sworn never to return, entered my life once again – and this time its effect on me was like unto a child experiencing its first pantomime transformation scene.

Now, it must be appreciated that anywhere with four brick walls and normal civilised household amenities was bound to be El Dorado after a year sleeping in a camp-bed in a tin hut containing only a solitary cast-iron, hard-fuel central stove for heating and on which water was boiled in old petrol tins for the filling up of canvas washbasins. But Scarborough provided much more than a comfortable billet. It was a City of Light, if that is not a misnomer in the era of the blackout. And it was there I was to find myself, at the latter end of 1942, on a six-week driving and maintenance course.

Scarborough has two bays which are divided by a natural headland on top of which and dominating the coastline is the ruin of its twelfth-century castle.

In pre-war days Scarborough was really two resorts. The North Bay was Blackpool and Yarmouth, and the South Bay was Bournemouth and Torquay. In the years that concern this narrative, all the big hotels on the South Cliff, the ones with commanding positions overlooking ornamental gardens and the sea, were requisitioned by the services; but there were two in the centre of the town, the Pavilion and the Royal, both the properties of Charles Laughton's brothers, Tom and Frank, which remained open to the public. The Pavilion was unrequisitioned throughout the war but the Royal, though closed as a hotel, rented its ballroom and bar to the Royal Air Force, and there large service swing bands of the Dorsey/Miller/Squadronaires variety belted out 'Polka Dots and Moonbeams', 'I'll be seeing you', 'A Sinner kissed an Angel' and the like. But if the Royal provided really excellent all-rank dances the class stuff came at the Pavilion.

The Pavilion Hotel retained as much of its pre-war style, elegance and service as was possible in the austerity of wartime England. Its dining-room, even with rationing, retained a tremendously high standard and Henderson, the head waiter, and all his staff were ever polite and obliging. Dinner-dances were frequent and the little bar, designed and muralled with such taste by John Armstrong, was the social centre of the town and it was there that every evening seemed to start. The Laughtons were renowned family hoteliers and throughout the entire war there was no place like the Pavilion Hotel in Scarborough on the whole of the north-east coast.

The town also had five or six cinemas, good shops and a general air of opulence. In fact, in the wartime forties Scarborough was a very good place to be and to a twenty-two-year-old, fun-seeking subaltern it was a far cry from the one experienced nine years previously by a twelve-year-old imprisoned schoolboy.

The officers' mess in which I was billeted for the six weeks in question was housed just off the Esplanade in the Carlton Hotel, and in it I shared a double, bay-windowed bedroom with another 22nd Dragoon colleague, one Peter McLaren.

So it was into this rarefied atmosphere and these highly civilised surroundings that I was to move and spend six weeks with the most congenial of company. We drank, we danced, we dated, and generally behaved as if there was going to be no tomorrow – and who knew if there was? It was 'bonnet over the windmill' time.

It was during my stay in Scarborough that my finger, which had never healed up properly, started playing up rather badly and I decided that something really had to be done about it. Over the months I had consulted various doctors on the subject and none of the advice that I had received had appealed to me. This had varied from having the whole finger off (I had only lost the top joint) to, believe it or not, having a slit cut in my tummy into which the end of the finger would be inserted and kept for an unspecified period of time until eventually the skin from the former would be grafted on to the latter.

Well, being in Scarborough my mind went back to my schooldays, when one Sunday during which my family came over to take me out for the afternoon one of my small sisters had had her thumb crushed in the door of our Morris Isis. Digit-wise we have obviously been a bit careless, we Carmichaels. However, when it happened my father drove off like a bat out of hell looking for the nearest brass plate. At the first one he found, he leapt out of the car like the proverbial 'dose of' and began ringing the bell and banging on the door both at the same time with total disregard of anyone's post-prandial nap. The doctor was kind and helpful and did a splendid piece of first aid. By chance, it transpired the same doctor had recently done a successful cartilage operation on my divisional commander, so what with one thing and another, if he was still at the same address, a call on him seemed to be propitious. Was he still there? A quick glance in the phone book told me that he was, so off I toddled to see him. The first thing he said after examining me was, 'I can, of course, tell you nothing until you've had an X-ray.'

That was the first time those magic words had been uttered during my entire case history. I can understand how I, a layman, had overlooked this astonishingly elementary piece of advice, but all those highly imaginative medicos, I thought, had less excuse.

Needless to say, when it was taken the subsequent photograph showed that two bits of loose bone had been left in the wound by the original surgeon in Wales. His name, to this day, I remember very well indeed.

Dr Debenham of Scarborough eventually took me into the town hospital, did a first-class repair job, and as I managed to arrange for it to be done a few weeks after I had finished my course and returned to Helmsley, he was also instrumental in affording me another carefree week of pleasure and irresponsibility in the Queen of Watering Places, as its prewar publicity dubbed it. I had a private room, two gorgeous young nurses, with one of whom I had been at RADA, and the other, a redhead, thought nothing of allowing me, strictly against doctor's orders, to sneak out at night down to the Pavilion to dine and dance, provided I took her with me. *Quelle fortune!*

When it was all over, I felt that I owed Dr Debenham a great deal. Silver cigarette-boxes and the like were unfortunately rather beyond the pay-packet of a young subaltern, so two years later I persuaded my other sister to go to him and have a hammer-toe amputated. She has been grateful to me ever since. It was my intention that Dr Debenham should be too.

Our time at Helmsley, however, was drawing to a close. Pym, having opted for driving as a trade in the WAAF, had been moved from her basic training centre in Gloucester to Pwllheli where the WAAF MT school was located.

She had managed to get a few days' leave to visit me while I was in Scarborough, but like so many of our meetings at that time it was very much a 'hello and goodbye' forty-eight hours. For the next three years our lives seemed to be spent on funereal, blacked-out, smokey and draughty station platforms and in crowded corridors of trains – there were seldom any seats – or in hotel rooms that varied from the opulent to the tawdry. But like so many others, we grabbed each and every opportunity of being together, sometimes travelling hundreds of uncomfortable, exhausting miles in order to spend a few fleeting hours in each other's company. Just before my regiment left Helmsley I had one memorable forty-eight-hour pass. I went to visit her in Pwllheli, which is situated practically on the tip of the Lleyn Peninsula in North Wales.

I set off from Helmsley at about 4.30 on a Friday afternoon. Round about midday on the day of my departure, the excitement building up in my loins at the anticipation of seeing Pym again was becoming tempered with the suspicions of a thick head and a tendency to shiver. I quickly swallowed a couple of aspirins and set off for the station and all points west. As I made the second of my six changes in York station – a location which throughout the remaining years of the war became our spiritual home – there was no doubt whatever that I had contracted something far worse than a cold: it had to be 'flu. The journey progressed, the night got darker, the weather outside fouler, the temperature inside colder and I sat there huddled in the corner of the carriage with my British Warm wrapped round me like an inadequate bath towel.

By the time I made my fourth change – at Crewe I suspect – I was running a temperature of about 104°.

At 2.30 a.m. on Saturday morning I changed yet again at Bangor. I took my gas-mask off the rack, or to be more accurate my gas-mask haversack, which contained my overnight kit – the mask itself was back at Helmsley (a commonplace subterfuge at that time) – and I stepped out of the train on to an empty, pitch-black, freezing-cold station in torrential rain. I staggered up to the guard, the only other living soul I could see, and asked him if he knew what time my connection for Pwllheli was due in.

'Five fifteen,' he replied, blew his whistle, stepped back on to the train and was drawn away into the night. With what few feelings I had left in my shivering, aching body I stumbled down the open platform in search of some form of cover. Groping my way along from seat to seat and slot-machine to slot-machine, I eventually located the waiting-room. It was locked. At that point I decided I would die. No point in lingering on. I would pass away quietly in this small corner of a foreign railway station never to see my loved one again. Just as I was about to give up the ghost, I heard approaching footsteps. Quite a long way away at first, but they were coming closer. Up the platform, in fact, towards me. Suddenly through the darkness I was able to make out the silhouette of a man in a sinister long mackintosh and slouch hat, brim turned down and dripping with rain.

'Are you waiting for the Pwllheli train?' he asked.

'I am,' I managed to croak out through chattering teeth.

'You've two and three-quarter hours to wait,' he said. 'Come with me. I am from the YMCA hostel just across the street.'

Never before or since have I been so thankful to see anyone. He took me into the hostel, gave me a pint of piping-hot tea, and then showed me into a room containing half a dozen steel beds.

'Get your head down for a bit,' he said. 'I know what time your train is, I'll wake you in plenty of time to catch it.'

Sure enough, he woke me with a bacon sandwich and another piping-hot pint of tea just before five and then escorted me back to the station and put me on my train.

Feeling marginally better as the result of hot tea, a sleep and the warmth of the YMCA hostel, I travelled on as dawn broke to make my last change at a wayside halt called Afon Wen. When I eventually got to Pwllheli I dragged my creaking body along to the hotel in which I had booked a room and went straight to bed. When Pym arrived, shortly after nine o'clock, I was not to be found, as she had expected, digging into a hearty breakfast in the dining-room, but upstairs in bed shaking like a leaf with a raging temperature and only my nose showing over the top of the blankets. After the greetings, explanations and expressed concern, off she went into the town and returned as per Florence Nightingale with a variety of pills, potions and half a bottle of brandy. Dosed to the eyebrows and warmed through with ever-comforting animal heat, I eventually fell asleep. I awoke at midday a new man. I seemed to have shaken off the fever as quickly as I had contracted it. The day was sunny and we took some form of transport to Criccieth a few miles down the coast which she said was very beautiful and which she wanted me to see. We watched some French Commandos, in their matelot hats with little red pompoms on top, assaulting the cliffs, and returned to Pwllheli after tea in an Olde Worlde Tea Shoppe and went to see *The Jolson Story* in the evening.

At the end of a blissful Sunday, all too soon we had to say our tortuous goodbyes and I set off once again on the long and lonely trek back to Helmsley.

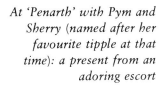

At 'Penarth' with Pym and Sherry (named after her favourite tipple at that time): a present from an adoring escort

And so to late February 1943, when our time came to move on. Eighteen months we had spent in Duncombe Park, through two of the severest winters and one and a half summers of sweltering heat. When we arrived the camp was barely inhabitable, but when we left the place looked like a new pin; Craigie had insisted on that. By the time we moved out practically every Nissen hut was surrounded by its spruce little garden. Some favoured vegetables, some grass, and some roses round the door, but everyone had had a go. The interiors of the huts were furnished with bookshelves and even improvised chests of drawers adapted from expendable petrol tins. Seats salvaged from old vehicles provided upholstered chairs, even the odd sofa, and Buzz Burrows and a couple of pre-war bricklayers had built two huge open fireplaces in the officers' mess huts which were fed throughout the winter with mammoth-sized logs from the surrounding woods.

We had made our own comforts and despite the weather, despite the isolation, despite the basic spartan quality of life in general we grew, maybe in retrospect, to love Helmsley.

As a regiment we were gypsies. We were formed in 1940 and disbanded in 1945. We had no peacetime home or depot and it is possibly indicative of our feeling for the little town of Helmsley that we chose its church to house our war memorial and it is there that we hold an ever-diminishing all-ranks reunion once every five years.

To walk through the Duncombe Park wood today, not a shred of evidence can be found of its inhabitants thirty-six years ago. How it ever managed to squeeze in three complete armoured regiments and all their vehicles passes belief.

But back in 1943 the battle was still some way away, and as we moved south to Warminster in Wiltshire we had ahead of us our largest and as yet unknown metamorphosis still to experience.

CHAPTER ELEVEN

WARMINSTER

A Show Must Go On

It was too soon to assess Helmsley dispassionately, such sentiments of affection are entirely retrospective: in February 1943 we were delighted to be out of it and the move that the authorities had planned for us was like rewarding a well-behaved child who had just experienced a period of deprivation and misfortune with a large toffee-apple. We were stepping out into the sunshine, both metaphorically and literally.

You may take it from an experienced and devoted northerner that there is a distinct climatic line across the centre of England from east to west, south of which the air starts to get warmer and, somehow or other, the plumage and natural habitats of *homo sapiens* seem to alter with it. The greys of stone and slate are replaced by the russets of brick and tile, and white and pink stucco. The wares in the High Street shops, too, seem to be more varied and exotic. The villages seem to have more of a traditional Old England appearance and in the spring – without any question in the spring – all nature is a good three to four weeks further advanced than in the north. And so it was when we arrived in Warminster on 12 March, having taken two weeks to get there, delayed by some large-scale army manoeuvres.

As if to welcome us after our privations in Yorkshire, spring, unlike in the popular song, arrived a little early that year, and as a result, and in comparison with what we had left behind, the whole town seemed to be *en fête*. Hedgerows were bursting with bright-green shoots, forsythia was exploding everywhere in yellow profusion, and the almond and cherry blossoms were soon to follow. The air was balmy, and 'shirt-sleeve order' and girls in gay, revealing summer frocks were not far behind.

But it was more than a change of climate that warmed our cockles. It was the accommodation that was to provide the most noticeable contrast. We were to be billeted not in the barracks just outside Warminster with the rest of the brigade, but in the town itself in civilian billets. We were back in a living, breathing, heart-throbbing community once again; shops, cinemas, pubs, a thunderingly hospitable civilian population and we were to be dumped right in the middle of it.

The officers' mess, which did not, in Warminster, include sleeping accommodation, occupied the extension wing of the Olde Bell Inn, in the heart of the main street – the great advantage being that if one wanted to get away from senior authority one could take one's aperitifs in the saloon bar below and yet, when dinner was announced, be up in time to sit down with the rest of them in thirty seconds flat. If, of course, after dinner one wanted a jar with one's cronies the reverse procedure applied. All highly convenient. I was billeted over a small milliner's shop in the main street. The proprietor was a lady who seemed to live alone, above the shop, with her nubile daughter, a fact that produced ribald and suggestive remarks from my brother officers, but they could have saved their breath. What my dear landlady did provide me with, however, was a bed with real springs and a bathroom containing a bath and, God be praised, permanently running, efficiently plumbed H. and C. My room also contained a wardrobe and a chest of drawers. Not much to write home about, you may think, but to be able to put one's clothes away in a bone-dry piece of wooden furniture after they had lived so long in sawn-off petrol tins was a luxury difficult to overstate.

In many ways our life in Warminster began to appear purposeless and dull. After the rigours of the last two years a general feeling of resignation and lethargy seemed to fill the air. There grew a feeling that we were now fully trained, fully equipped and ready for the fray but that it was all being dissipated by the authorities in 'the War House'. So with apparent time on our hands, our brigade commander issued a decree that each of the regiments in his brigade should put on a show in the garrison theatre up at the barracks.

Lieutenant-Colonel G. L. Craig, 22nd Dragoons, was nothing if not a regular soldier of the old school. An order was an order, and in addition a spirit of inter-unit competition was bred in his bones. If time *had* to be wasted on this sort of frippery, there was no question that the 22nd Dragoons' contribution had to be the best. I was sent for, briefed and told to get on with it.

I had very grand ideas in those days concerning the presentation of theatrical entertainments. These I had to revise considerably when I reached Germany two years later, but in 1943 my horizons were very

West End – very C. B. Cochran – and I left Craigie's office that morning feeling as light and inflated as a piece of puff pastry.

After a couple of days ruminating I returned to the regimental entertainments officer who had been appointed my overseer and made my outrageous demands. I would require the following:

1. *Carte blanche* to recruit my cast regardless of rank.
2. The entire cast, when assembled, to be completely free of all regimental duties for three whole weeks during the period of rehearsal.
3. The hire of all costumes from London and I could, at that time, give no guarantee as to how many or what sort they would be.
4. The unfettered use of the regimental carpenter and painter which, unless there was a sudden invasion of southern England, would take priority over all other demands on their services.
5. The hire of two grand pianos with the accent on the 'grand'. I would have no truck with any upright jobs, no matter how well they were tuned. My production had, in presentation, if nothing else, to be lifted above the plebeian level of a NAAFI concert.

The entertainments officer blanched.

'Are you out of your mind?' he asked.

'Never been saner in my life,' I replied. 'If Craigie wants the best, that's the cost of the bill. Go and tell him.'

He did, and the following day I was summoned to Craigie's office. The same question was asked, and with uncharacteristic courage and bravado I gave him the same answer. My demands were met and I started work.

Rehearsals were held in a large church hall. I sent for my 'civvies' to wear – a highly unorthodox practice in wartime – and the entire cast, comprising officers, NCOs and men, got down to some pretty hard graft.

During those weeks the demands I made on that poor, demented entertainments officer were prodigious. A few years after the war I read in a newspaper that the poor man had committed suicide by shooting himself in his car on a lonely car-park. I have had a conscience ever since that I may, in some way, have been a contributory factor in driving him to such precipitate action. Nevertheless, he bore my insatiable demands with fortitude.

Amongst the five skips of costumes I had ordered from London were seven complete suits of full evening dress for the production number which was to open the second half. I had envisaged a big spectacular Ziegfeld-type opening with oodles of beautiful, long-legged, statuesque girls and a row of potential Fred Astaires, all dressed in immaculate white ties and tails. This, understandably, proved a bit of a problem, not only

because the 22nd Dragoons didn't run to any long-legged, statuesque
Ziegfeld lovelies but also because it was a bit short of potential Fred
Astaires too. However, in my prevailing ebullient mood these obstacles
were mere bagatelles. I selected a basic number called 'You're the One'
from a current Hulbert show, and I decided that by doing a Busby Berkeley – i.e., choreographing fairly simple unison movements instead of complicated dance steps – I would achieve something like the same results.
One of the members of the cast, one of the officers actually, who said
he had been in revue before the war and at least looked reasonable in
a suit of tails, I selected to be the central character of the number. Whether
he had actually been a thespian prior to hostilities was, in my view, questionable. However, he carried around with him in a rather grand frame
a large portrait of a girl-friend : just the sort of bird with whom one would
have peopled the stage had a few of them been available. This was obviously the answer. In the absence of real live girls he would sing to the
photograph. Not exactly original but under the circumstances convenient
and, I hoped, acceptable. So I devised a simple revue setting in pearl-
grey drapes, comprising a white sofa slightly off-centre, a vase of arum
lilies on a sort of altarpiece somewhere up-stage and the photograph itself
isolated on a Grecian plinth down-stage right. Then in support of the leading man and to complete the Fred Astaire bit, I had six other blokes,
presumably his bachelor cronies, also in the full soup and fish.

I think it was the only number in the whole show which, though not
actually 'sent up', was certainly misunderstood. The fact that the six
members of the male chorus looked more at home in tank overalls than
in full evening dress would have mattered little, the fact that they eventually joined in the chorus :

> You're the one
> That makes my heart beat like a hammer,
> You're the one
> That makes my life so full of glamour,

mattered a lot. The reason being that the art of Busby Berkeley is not
quite as easy as it looks and under my less than experienced direction
the object of their affection appeared not to be the beautiful lady in the
photograph but the leading man himself. Not one of my brighter pieces
of invention. Well, you can't win them all.

After three weeks flogging our guts out in that church hall, we moved
into the garrison theatre up in the barracks to hold our dress rehearsal
on the evening prior to the one on which we were to open. Now it is

inadvisable for any backer ever to attend the dress rehearsal of a show in which he has a financial interest. For those not actively employed it can be a hair-raising, nail-biting experience and their resultant anxieties can only fluster those who have been paid to recognise the mistakes and catastrophes and whose sole responsibility it is to rectify them. I entered the garrison theatre on that evening in no way underestimating the task ahead of me. I had a large and inexperienced cast both on stage and backstage, and in addition to directing the show I was also taking quite a prominent part in it. Though the task was a daunting one, I had nevertheless all night and the next day ahead of me and I was fully confident that we would win through by eight o'clock the following evening.

I suppose we finally got the curtain up at about nine and as I made my entrance in the opening number I was horrified to see the lone and uninvited figure of Craigie sitting out in the stalls. He was in his customary 'blues' and was, no doubt, feeling mellow after a good dinner and several glasses of port.

The show itself was well rehearsed and went fairly smoothly, but the stage management was nothing short of chaotic. Everyone was bumping into everyone else and nobody could move backstage for the disorganised and growing pile of impedimenta comprising items that were either just about to go on stage or those that had just come off. This was nobody's fault (except possibly mine); it just hadn't been rehearsed.

When it was all over I hurried down into the stalls to confront an exhausted and white-faced commanding officer. I was rather hoping that what he had just witnessed would have left him speechless. It was wishful thinking. He went off like a maroon from a distressed ship – which was not inappropriate really, as I could see that was exactly what he considered us to be. What he had witnessed during the past four hours, he exploded, was a shambles, a farrago, bedlam and a disgrace, firstly to him, then to the regiment and finally to me. What the blazes had I been doing during the past three weeks? And what was more important, what the blazes did I intend doing about rectifying the mish-mash by eight o'clock the next evening? When he had run out of steam, I told him that there was little I could do at that stage about the content of the show, if he disapproved of that, but if, as I suspected, it was the shambolic stage-management that was bugging him, he could go home to bed and sleep peacefully. I was now about to dismiss the cast but retain all the stage staff and we were then going to go through the entire show again from start to finish, topping and tailing each item so that the technical side of the production would be as slick and polished as I, personally,

Acting Unpaid (left) *'Cricket Vignettes' by Herbert Farjeon. Lt John Allen, killed on D-Day, and Peter McLaren.* (right) *'Winter in Torquay' by Herbert Farjeon. Self in centre, Peter McLaren on left*

considered the rest of the performance to be. Mumbling something like, 'It'd better be,' he turned on his heels, clanked his way down the centre aisle and vanished through the swing doors at the back of the stalls.

Poor man – I fully sympathised with him. It was, of course, frustration. For the first time since I had met him I realised, as he did, that he was completely out of his depth. But then, like I said, backers should never attend their own dress rehearsals.

Not feeling over-ebullient myself, I went back on stage, thanked everyone for their hard work and patience, sent the cast back to their billets and bed, and after coffee and sandwiches the stage staff and I set to work to go through the whole thing once again. We finally finished at 7.30 a.m., and feeling much more confident about the evening ahead of us, we locked up the theatre and went back for breakfast.

There is an old theatrical saw which proclaims that a bad dress rehearsal always produces a spanking first night, and, God be praised, so it was with us. The 'house' was full, and if the reception was anything to go by we were warmly approved of by all and sundry; and the sundry, I am delighted to say, included Craigie.

Acting Unpaid – the title I retained from the revue Nigel and I had planned back in Helmsley – followed its opening performance in the camp theatre with a Sunday matinée in the Regal cinema in the centre of the town for the civilian population and one more performance in the camp theatre three evenings later to which Craigie, by now as proud as a peacock, brought both our brigade and divisional commanders.

For two weeks after that we toured the show round several outlying units. It took five three-ton lorries to move us – one for the grand pianos alone. That was the last occasion connected with troop entertainment that I was allowed such a luxury.

So, my fall from grace with Craigie was but momentary: I was back on top again, my star well and truly in the ascendant. Under which circumstances – it was ironic in its timing – he chose only a few weeks later to change my job once again. A change, moreover, which many of my fellow officers would have considered as dismissal with ignominy. To me it was quite the reverse. After months of patient trial and error, dear Craigie had at last found the square hole into which to insert my square peg. From that moment on, my military career never looked back.

It was one evening after dinner in the mess, the table had broken up and I was just withdrawing from the bar with a tankard of beer in my hand when he came up to me, laid a hand gently on my elbow and said, 'Come and sit down, Ian. I want to talk to you.' He led me back into the dining-room and sat down with me at the long mess table which still wore its white tablecloth and called for another glass of port. After it had been set in front of him, he looked me straight in the eyes and said, 'Ian, how would you like to be my liaison officer with Brigade HQ?'

Now I must explain exactly what this meant. In an armoured brigade at that time there were four regiments and each one provided a subaltern who went to live at Brigade HQ. He was there to carry all important verbal messages and orders from the brigadier to his own commanding officer. In addition, and between times, he acted as one of the brigade commander's staff officers. Fringe benefits were a strong chance that living conditions would be better than those at regimental or squadron level, and also the *cachet* of dealing with even grander hierarchy at Divisional HQ, thus giving one more status and a general feeling of greater importance. All this appealed to me very much. I had always felt that my forte might be in administration rather than in regimental soldiering; desk work was not, to me, the anathema it was to many of my colleagues to whom to be deprived of leading their men into battle wielding a metaphorical sabre was the nearest thing to death than actually doing it. I knew instantly for the first time since I joined the army that from that moment on I would actually start to enjoy soldiering.

'I'd love to be, sir,' I replied, without a moment's hesitation.

By mid-1943 the international situation had changed considerably from the dark days of 1940–1. The war was slowly being won. The annihilation of the German armies opposite Stalingrad was already history and in Africa another vast army was on the point of destruction and surrender. The air over England was heavy by day as well as night with the thunder of Allied bombers making steadily for Germany. The whole momentum of the war effort in Britain was moving towards the inevitable second front which everyone knew could not now be far away; the only closely guarded secret was where and when. It was against this background that I packed up my belongings above the little milliner's shop in Warminster High Street, and moved up to the barracks to join Brigade HQ. There I reported to the Brigade Major – the Chief of Staff at a Brigade HQ – Major the Lord (Michael) Killanin; the same who in 1972 became President of the International Olympic Committee. With Michael – another member of 'The King's Royal Repertory Company' and a pre-war journalist – I got on well. He was a hard task-master, but he worked hard and played hard and had no 'side'. We understood each other and talked the same language. He remained my immediate boss until the end of hostilities in north-west Europe.

Within a few weeks of my joining Brigade HQ, however, something happened which caused the spirits of the whole formation to slump to the very nadir of their existence. In August news was received from those who controlled our destiny far away in Whitehall that our entire division was to be disbanded. We were to move out of our comfortable billets in Warminster pronto to make room for a newly arrived American armoured division (one of the first arrivals of the US pre-invasion build-up) and in the meanwhile we would have to accept temporary accommodation in the Cotswold area until such a time as our future had been decided upon.

It is difficult to explain to anyone who has never experienced a similar break-up exactly how shattering such news could be. Whether one possessed a keen and offensive nature and couldn't wait to get to grips with the enemy, or whether one was of a more placid temperament and dreaded the day of the first confrontation, the effect was very similar. If one is a member of one of the armed forces in wartime, to go into battle, sooner or later, is more or less inevitable, and under such circumstances it is preferable to live, fight and die with those with whom one has trained, rather than be drafted to undergo the same experience with total strangers. So it was with morale at a very low ebb indeed that in September, after a round of dewy-eyed goodbye parties, we slowly and reluctantly accepted the inevitable and headed north for the Cotswolds.

The possibility of Brigade HQ having the edge on the regiments when it came to accommodation was immediately apparent on our arrival in the new area. My regiment's new address was an impressive one – Maughersbury Manor, Stow-on-the-Wold. In effect, however, they had returned to Nissenland again. We, on the other hand, settled into a fine country house a few miles outside Banbury, which, if my memory serves me right, was a pre-war home of a much hyphenated family, who, popular rumour had it, were 'in jam'. I made a mental note to get into jam the moment the war was over. The property had, as an immediate vista outside its tall ground-floor windows, a rather grand blue-tiled and chromium-accessoried swimming-pool with an adjacent structure in white stucco containing a high-stooled bar; all rather more Hollywood than England in 1943, and which was, anyway, no use to anyone in October and November. The inside of the house, however, boasted its own private squash-court which was a lot of use to all of us.

But all this Cotswold business was, had we known it, but a brief breathing-space before we were to be rearmed, retrained and reformed into a new and highly secret division in which we would, all too soon, go to war. Those whose sole amibtion it was to 'get to grips with the Boche' and whose spirits had so recently been dampened practically to extinction were about to get their opportunity in full measure.

CHAPTER TWELVE

EAST ANGLIA

Waiting for the Off

A few days before leaving Warminster, I arranged two weeks' leave to go back up to Whitby and get married and I took Peter McLaren with me as my best man. Peter, who had accompanied me on that wild six weeks in Scarborough, was my best buddy in the regiment. He was short and dark and sported a small, debonair moustache. He was also cultured, soft-spoken, impeccably mannered, oozed charm and, whatever else he was, he was essentially and always a ladies' man – every diminutive inch of him. Peter was, in fact, a smoothie.

Pre-war he had been in the tobacco industry to which he returned at the end of hostilities, and during the following twenty-five years he and his subsequent family moved around the Middle East from trouble spot to trouble spot as coup followed coup, losing all they possessed in successive countries. It's a sad tale. He is now back in England, retired, and the close friendship that we established in Helmsley and Scarborough still remains.

Pym had by now left Pwllheli and was stationed at an RAF station which operated Wellington bombers out of Burn in South Yorkshire. Amongst other MT duties she drove the aircrews to and from their nightly dispersal points and the sudden absence of familiar faces around the camp the day after a raid became a heartrending fact of life to which she had to become hardened.

We were married in Sleights village church on 6 October. It was a white wedding, sparsely attended on a very grey day and had austerity stamped all over it. All clothing at that time was rationed and our respective mothers and various aunts rallied round, unselfishly sacrificial, to equip the bride and her three bridesmaids.

There was no photographer. There could have been only a couple of them in Whitby at the best of times and they were both in the services. For a pictorial record of the event we were entirely reliant on the amateur

Wedding day

talents of various friends with their box Brownies.

There were two fashionable cafés in Whitby at that time. We had the reception at James's (now a builders' merchants). It was run by friends of my in-laws and we all sat down in their small ballroom to a knife-and-fork, cold meat and fruit-salad nosh-up in the middle of the afternoon. Food was also, of course, heavily rationed, so we were reliant solely on the ingenuity and scrounging capacity of Pym's mother. She managed splendidly, though the meal was of necessity unimaginative. A ham had been donated by some friends who owned a pig, and my future mother-in-law had herself spent the best part of the previous week wringing, plucking and drawing chickens over on the farm to augment it. Eggs, another rarity for the salad, were also provided from the same source.

At the end of the feast we left by taxi for Scarborough to start our honeymoon. Scarborough is barely twenty miles from Whitby but even so we were still shackled by wartime restrictions. Because of petrol rationing, taxis were not allowed to undertake a journey that exceeded a round trip of twenty miles. So to reach our destination we had to hire two of them. We left in one from Whitby which took us to the Falcon Inn, an isolated hostelry exactly equidistant between the two towns, where we were met by another one from Scarborough. Following on behind a discreet one hour later with similar transport arrangements were Peter McLaren and a perfectly enchanting fair-haired lass called Betty Cree who was serving with Pym in the WAAF. Betty we have sadly never seen since the war ended. She is now married and lives in Canada with her husband and five children, which doesn't surprise me a bit. I refer to the five children. She had a smile as illuminating as the sun on midsummer's day, which could, I had no doubt, charm the pants off any man – and obviously it had done. What a difference thirty-three years make in accepted standards of behaviour. The fact that we wanted Peter and Betty with us to celebrate on the first night of our honeymoon was so unorthodox a practice at that time that to save our relatives any embarrassment their ultimate departure from the reception was a very cloak-and-dagger operation.

We had wanted to spend two nights at the Pavilion in Scarborough and the rest of the honeymoon in London. Unhappily the Pavilion was fully booked so we had to make do with a smaller and less grand establishment a hundred yards away called the Victoria. The Victoria was the original hotel owned by the Laughton family, the one in which Charles himself had been born. Fortunately, however, we were still able to use Mr Henderson's dining-room in the Pavilion so, as usual, all our meals were served and supervised with his customary courtesy and solicitous attention. We dined and danced on our wedding night replete with whole lobsters and champagne. After a couple of days in Scarborough we set off for the capital by train, changing, as ever, in our spiritual home of York station.

This was the first time we had been in the metropolis together and more than anything I wanted to show my bride who, like myself before coming south in 1938, was an insular northerner all the places and if possible the people that I had told her about during our period of courtship. I took her to meet Marjorie Fox in Roland Gardens, Joan Sterndale Bennett who was working (as ever) at the Players Theatre, then in Albemarle Street, and Geoffrey Hibbert, by now a signalman in the Royal Corps of Signals and stationed somewhere near Town. Nigel Patrick happened to be on leave at the time too and we also met him for a drink in a small dive in Covent Garden called the Kümmel Club. We dined at Hatchett's in Piccadilly where George Shearing was playing and which became our favourite dine-and-dance restaurant, and we did a round of the small drinking clubs where Geoffrey and I had once done the odd 'songs at the piano' act. We also took the occasional glass in rather grander watering holes like the Berkeley Hotel – the old Berkeley Hotel in Piccadilly – at that time the statutory rendezvous for cavalry officers on leave in London.

We also paid what was for both of us our first ever visit to a film studio. While I was in Warminster Carol Reed was directing a movie concerning the war in the desert called *The Way Ahead* and for a week a second unit visited us to shoot location shots of tanks on Salisbury Plain. I was attached to them during the period to ensure that they got all they wanted and when they left the production manager invited me to visit the main unit in Denham Studios should I ever be free to do so. We watched a morning's shooting on the picture, had lunch starry-eyed in the studio restaurant and then took in Olivier working on *Henry V* in the afternoon.

After five days we returned home to my parents in Elloughton for forty-eight hours and finally back to 'Penarth' for forty-eight hours more, on our knees with exhaustion. In an insurance against the failure of our amateur photographers' efforts on the day of the ceremony, on our return to Sleights, Pym's mother insisted that Pym don her wedding dress again, pick up her ten-day-old faded and drooping bridal bouquet and that together we proceed into the garden to be immortalised once more in her own box Brownie – the results of which are a pictorial record of what would appear to have been the most debauched honeymoon on record.

I returned from honeymoon to the regiment's new home in Banbury to find great excitement in the air. Rumours were rife that we were about to join a new and very secret division commanded by Major-General Percy Hobart. 'Hobo', later to receive a knighthood, was a man of the most astonishing drive and diversity of interests. We had already had a taste of him in the Whitby days when we had been part of another division that he then commanded. He was a product of the Royal Tank Corps, had served in the First World War and was considered to be the doyen of armoured formation commanders. All his subordinate senior officers and particularly the members of his staff quailed before him. When asked a question you had to have the answer instantly. It need not necessarily be of a military nature either. He had an ever-enquiring mind. I never served on his immediate staff but I knew many who did and their lives were permanently insecure. I remember one poor fellow accompanying him in his staff car shortly after the Normandy invasion when the beach-head was but a few miles deep, having a question fired at him out of the blue concerning the location of a small town in West Germany. Unable to answer he suffered a characteristically blistering tirade. 'Damn it!' explained the distraught man to me afterwards, 'I thought I was pretty well covered. After all, I'd taken sufficient maps

The GOC – Major-General Percy Hobart

to cover us all the way to Flushing!'

Anyway, to Hobo's command, it was rumoured, we were now about to return and the rumour, it transpired, was not a false one. In November it was confirmed that we were to come under command of the 79th Armoured Division – the Bull's Head Division. It was a division which as a result of the singular vehicles and weapons with which it was equipped became known throughout north-west Europe as 'The Funnies'; and Hobo and our complete formation came directly under the personal command of Montgomery himself.

The 79th Armoured Division, we soon discovered, was a very large and complex formation indeed. Its various brigades were stationed as unusually far apart as Cumberland, Suffolk, the Kyles of Bute and Stokes Bay near Gosport in Hampshire. Its equipment was highly secret and in November 1943 still largely experimental and to learn about it we all had to go back to school again. New vehicles, new weapons, new techniques of fighting. Eight months later Monty was to write in a foreword to *The History of The 9th Armoured Division*:

The Division has been, and is, unique among all the Divisions in the Allied Armies.... [It] is composed of units and equipment which have no parallel in any other Army in the world, and the skilful use of this equipment enabled us to obtain surprise in the tactical battle.

We were, in short, being trained first and foremost to bash our way through the minefields and massive concrete and iron obstacles of Hitler's Atlantic wall, thus to enable the Allied armies to advance up the Normandy beaches. Thereafter we were to continue doing a similar job on the mainland. It was to be our task to spearhead the attacks on all the major prepared enemy defence works – and several major natural obstacles – that obstructed the Allies' advance into Germany.

The division as a whole was equipped with the following:

DD tanks – Amphibious Sherman tanks which were launched at sea and approached the shore looking for all the world like outsized rubber dinghies until they touched down and drove up the beaches.
CDL tanks, which mounted a large searchlight.
AVREs: Churchill tanks manned by Royal Engineers which mounted an assortment of accessories for filling in or spanning anti-tank obstacles and blasting their way through reinforced concrete at close range.
CROCODILES: flame-throwing Churchill tanks.
KANGAROOS: tracked armoured personnel carriers.
BUFFALOS: amphibious tracked personnel carriers.
CRABS: flail tanks – minesweepers.

The latter were Sherman tanks fitted with a projecting boom which in turn supported a horizontal metal drum spanning the full width of the vehicle. This, to which were attached a lot of heavy chains, revolved at high speed thus causing the chains to beat the ground in front of the tank as it advanced and explode all the mines in its path. It was with CRABS that our brigade was now to be equipped.

Our stay in Banbury was a short one. By the beginning of December we had moved into a requisitioned Victorian manse in the tiny village of Theberton three miles from the sea in Suffolk. At the same time our three armoured regiments, having handed over all their Covenanter tanks, many of them to the scrapyards in Birmingham, moved into the surrounding countryside. Soon the first of the new machines started to arrive, all of them shrouded in tarpaulin sheets in front of the driver's cabin to conceal their Top Secret equipment during the journey from the factory.

In the course of training for our new role a cloak of security descended on all our activities with impenetrable blackness. A vast area on the coast of Suffolk in the vicinity of the little town of Orford had been evacuated of all civilian personnel, and within a perimenter of barbed wire whose few entrances were closely guarded day and night, hundreds of Suffolk acres with their prosperous farms and villages had been made over to the machines of 79th Armoured Division. Over the open stretches of heather, among the pine trees, about the farms and in the gardens of the deserted villages the rabbit alone remained to compete with the tank in its role of destruction. It was a scene of horrifying desolation.

In the centre of this area, whose sandy soil was very similar to that of the beaches and inland dunes of the Normandy coast, had been built a series of replicas of German coastal defences with deep ditches, concrete walls, 'dragons' teeth' and similar anti-tank obstacles. Except that they contained no hostile gunners, these defence works bristled as effectively as though they had been erected in Suffolk by Rommel's own engineers. They possessed their perimeters of minefields and barbed wire and they were equipped with trenches, concrete gun-emplacements, block-houses and command posts. When, on 6 June of that year, it fell to squadrons of the 79th Armoured Division to lead the Allied armies up the beaches of Normandy, it was as if they had been there before; and in many respects, thanks to the Orford training area, they had.

Even to those not as closely associated with preparations for the invasion as we were, it was becoming increasingly obvious that the inevitable second front couldn't be all that far away. It was also obvious to the entire population of England that when that day dawned the majority of the troops now assembling in our island, inflating it almost to bursting

Pym Carmichael – but only just

point, were going to be involved in it. Pym and I therefore saw little point in allowing our lack of proximity to continue a day longer than was necessary. Consequently she now applied for what was known as a compassionate posting. Magically, within a matter of weeks, she was moved to an American fighter station at Martlesham Heath just north of Ipswich and within ten miles of Theberton.

I now entered six months of feverish activity and hard work interlaced with off-duty moments of memorable happiness and relaxation. Pym's nearness now enabled us to spend many hastily arranged weekends together; in the Crown at Woodbridge, the Bell at Saxmundham and our particular favourite, the Dolphin at Thorpeness. Thorpeness, a tiny holiday village on the coast a few miles north of Aldeburgh, in the winter of 1943–4 appeared to be, with the exception of the Dolphin, totally unpopulated. Situated but a stone's throw from the heavily mined and barbed-wired beach, this small hotel was a story-book haven for young lovers. Warm open fires, low ceilings, dark oak beams and furniture, with cosy chintz curtains and covers all bathed in the soft light of table-lamps. We spent many blissful weekends there, often accompanied for dinner by friends from the 22nd Dragoons or Brigade Headquarters.

It was in Suffolk that once again Craigie the enigma (or could it all the time have been Ian the enigma?) was to demonstrate his strange contradictory character.

My regiment was stationed at Rendlesham Hall, a vast, unhandsome, Edwardian mansion six miles from Woodbridge. One day, having learned that Pym – who had by then risen to the dizzy heights of LACW – was now stationed in the area, he said to me, 'You must bring her round to the mess one evening for a drink, Ian.'

I couldn't believe my ears. No female, to my knowledge, not even his own or any of the senior officers' wives, had ever been allowed in such a sacrosanct male stronghold. In peacetime such things might happen, but they had never done so in the 22nd Dragoons. Not only that but Pym was not even of commissioned rank.

'Make it tomorrow evening,' he continued.

'Er – I've no transport, sir,' I burbled, 'and anyway, I don't know whether or not she's on duty.'

'Then find out,' he said. 'There's the telephone. I'll supply the transport.'

Had he had a seizure, or was I going mad?

'Well, go on, boy; don't stand there gaping.'

I managed to locate her.

'She's off duty at six, sir,' I said while asking Pym to hold on.

'Then tell her we'll send transport for her at six-thirty,' he said.

At half past six the following evening Craigie's personal staff car and corporal driver pulled up outside Pym's semi-detached billet in Martlesham Heath. She was then driven in state to Rendlesham Hall where she was made a great fuss of by all. Finally, after being escorted back to the car by both the owner and me, she was returned to her camp with the same pomp and circumstance.

No, it was obviously I who was the enigma.

But the race for mastery of our new weapons and the invention of a technique with which to assault the apparently impregnable German defences was now on with a vengeance. Nobody knew exactly when the balloon would go up but nobody doubted that this mammoth task, absolutely vital to the success of Operation Overlord, would take all our waking hours and probably a few more besides.

From the comparatively dashing role of a fast-moving, marauding armoured division, which even in an age of mechanisation still reflected the swashbuckling spirit of former cavalry glories, we were now reduced to advancing head-on at a seemingly invincibly protected enemy armed to the teeth with the most lethal of weapons, in front of which a tank was just about as immune as a grouse in front of buckshot, at the suicidal speed of 1 mph – to go faster would be to risk missing mines the explosion of which was our primary task. Furthermore, the flail tanks were destined to be the forefront of the assault team and the only protection on which they could pin their hopes was saturation bombing and shelling of the target area for as long a period as possible immediately prior to the attack. Our chances, it appeared, were going to be just about as healthy as those of the Light Brigade advancing at a stately trot; but the very novelty and challenge of the task, plus the pressure of the time factor, prevented defeatist thoughts and kept morale high.

The arrival of spring in 1944 found the whole of the Allied invasion force gradually moving south to concentration areas preparatory to actually embarking and setting sail for France, and our time had come too. We, that is Brigade HQ, moved into a sizeable house called Corbie Wood in the St George's Hill area of Weybridge. Training was now complete so there was little to do but wait.

Pym had managed to obtain another compassionate posting and was now in London. Billeted in Loudon Road, St John's Wood, her MT office was in Hamilton Terrace and the vehicle park on the Nursery End of Lord's Cricket Ground. Her many waiting hours were spent sunbathing on the top balcony of the gracious MCC pavilion while no doubt the ghost of many a long deceased blimp shuddered at the thought of women in such a hallowed male preserve. Corbie Wood was only fifteen minutes' walk from Weybridge main-line station and the trains to and from Waterloo were every half-hour, so we grabbed as many days and nights together as we could, each one of which we imagined would be our last.

CHAPTER THIRTEEN

NORMANDY AND POINTS EAST

Into Battle

At H-Hour on D-Day – 6 June 1944 – squadrons of the 22nd Dragoons and Westminster Dragoons landed on the coast of France. We at Brigade HQ back in Corbie Wood were to hear about it at breakfast on the same day. In Weybridge it was a magnificent midsummer morning and with the aid of large diagrams the brigadier immediately briefed his staff with the details of the battle plan, for so secure had been the web of secrecy woven around D-Day that only he, and possibly Michael Killanin, his chief of staff, knew the actual details of the assault.

To understand the remainder of this wartime narrative it is now necessary to explain the relationship that, in the new order of things, existed between the brigadier and his three regiments. Our conversion to flail tanks meant that not only would 30th Armoured Brigade never fight as a brigade, it also meant that no regiment in it would ever fight as a regiment. Now the all important formation, the only really autonomous one as far as a battle command was concerned, was the squadron. For every battle that required assault troops, and most of them did, squadrons of our brigade were allotted out and placed under command of other formations who were actually carrying out the assault *in toto*. Consequently, both Brigade HQ and the three Regimental HQs were largely reduced to, on the one hand, administrative bodies who serviced their subordinate formations, and on the other, advisers to senior commanders who were allotted specific 'Funnies' and were perhaps not fully *au fait* with their capabilities and techniques. All of which explains why we were to be found in Weybridge on that sunny morning while four of our squadrons were flailing their way up the Normandy beaches.

On 16 June – D + 10 – Tactical Brigade HQ crossed the Channel in an American tank landing ship – one of the larger craft that sailed right into the shore, opened two huge doors like the jaws of a whale lying on its side and spewed out its contents on to the beach. Its contents on this occasion included myself and my driver in a Humber scout car which was to be my personal vehicle for the remainder of the campaign. It was a lousy crossing, and I am not, I was to discover, a good sailor. We landed opposite Courseulles-sur-Mer. I was two days off my twenty-fourth birth-day and I had never been out of the UK in my life. The approach to the shore I found hypnotic and when I actually stepped out of the vehicle on to French soil I felt, no doubt, as Neil Armstrong must have done on a rather more momentous occasion twenty-five years later.

The beaches, which by D + 10 were completely clear of the enemy, seemed to be busier than Epsom Downs on Derby Day and the sea as crowded as the Solent during Cowes Week. We drove up the beach between white tapes marking lanes through the minefields, and headed for a small farm in a village called Villiers-le-Sec on the lateral Caen–Bayeux road. Here we established our Tactical HQ which was to be joined in due course by the remainder of our strength, and here we were to stay for the best part of two months until the Allied armies finally broke out of Normandy.

The early days in the beach-head were very noisy indeed, particularly at night. We slept in holes in the ground for a good week until our main body arrived with tents and the remainder of our vehicles. Rations were plentiful but it was some considerable time before we saw a loaf of bread. The substitute was hard-tack biscuits which didn't worry the younger of us overmuch but those who wore dentures had a problem or two. The local produce was Camembert, cider and Calvados. Nobody had seen a Camembert in the UK for four years, consequently the immediate local supply, though no doubt in normal circumstances sufficient to meet demands, very soon developed into a shortage. Of cider, however, there always seemed to be a plentiful supply. Shortly after our arrival I managed to buy several dozen Courseulles oysters which I took back to the mess and offered up with all the pomp of Herod presenting Salomé with John the Baptist's head on the charger. Sadly my offer was spurned. Not a soul would touch them as it was the month of June.

The pattern of my life on the mainland of Europe was soon to establish itself and from that pattern it seldom varied until VE-Day ten months later. I've already indicated that, as a youth, I was inclined to be idle, but the moment I joined the headquarters of 30th Armoured Brigade I started to enjoy work and I buckled down to it with enormous enthusi-asm. I was deluged with it; the routine stuff that I'd been used to in Eng-land largely remained, but now there was all the additional administra-tion occasioned by the constant planning of new offensives. I was on the

'G' or 'Operations' side of the staff, and our squadrons were constantly in action. Whenever a concerted thrust to break out of our tight little perimeter in Normandy failed, the troops involved probably settled down to a holding position affording them a moment of respite. On such occasions the respite rarely extended to ourselves. Our specialist machines, techniques and knowledge were immediately required for a new offensive elsewhere. And so it was to be throughout the entire campaign in north-west Europe.

One of the duties that filled me with less than normal enthusiasm was accompanying my brigadier on visits to his forward squadrons. I think his inability to actually 'fight' his regiments had left him frustrated and had invested him with a feeling of redundancy which he now tried to combat with acts of, in my view, reckless bravado. These manifested themselves in a burning desire to show his flag as often as possible and as far forward as possible to as many of his troops as he could. As one of the minions who had to accompany him on these daily trips, I was tempted at times to query the purpose of many of them. Frequently, after completing a visit, instead of returning home, which would have beneficially cleared the congested roads for more essential traffic, he would 'swan' (a verb of the time which meant to drive about aimlessly) around

'Cooking' the Brigadier's map in the information tent prior to setting out on a 'swan'

the forward areas purely as an inquisitive spectator. Danger seemed to draw him like iron filings to a magnet. My fellow LOs and I developed a drill to counteract this craving for adventure. Before setting out on one of these expeditions, we would always go to the information room to ascertain the exact position of all the troops that he wished to visit and to generally mark up his map with the current tactical situation. The standard way of marking the enemy's position on a map at that time was to use a blue pencil. We would therefore, quite deliberately, mark in the position of the German front line with a heavy blue contour extending right across the map a good three-quarters of a mile nearer to the home goal than it actually was: subterfuge that might, we hoped, if he felt in need of a little stimulation, have a restraining influence on his curiosity. Nevertheless, on more than one occasion such influence was supplied by a pugnacious, though luckily inaccurate, riposte from an 88 mm gun.

In the middle of our six months' training in Sufflok, my old mentor and tormentor Craigie, amongst scenes both emotional and boisterous, had left his 22nd Dragoons for promotion. The regiment which he had nurtured from its birth until the moment it called upon to give account of itself in battle he was destined never to command in hot blood, a sad disappointment for a professional soldier. Nevertheless, his departure was paradoxically a cause for celebration and congratulations and he was seen off with due pomp and circumstance. After he left we lost all hair and hide of him until five weeks after D-Day, when, certainly to my surprise, he turned up in Villiers-le-Sec sporting an OBE ribbon and the insignia of a full colonel, complete with red tabs and hat-band. He had arrived to take up the appointment of second-in-command of the brigade. Over the years Craigie had in turn driven me mad with rage and done me great services. He was now about to do me the greatest of the lot.

A new 'push' was being mounted in the centre of the British sector, squadrons of ours were to be involved and Craigie was packed off to the HQ of a senior participant formation to act as adviser. He asked if I could go with him as his aide. This was agreed and we set off in my scout car to remain with the HQ concerned until the battle was over. The troops to be employed were massing in the forward areas and we joined them in what had got to be the noisiest few fields in the whole of Normandy. We were in the middle of a twenty-five-pounder gun area, the occupants of which seemed throughout the entire day to be shelling the Hun who, understandably disgruntled, retaliated gamely with low-flying bombing raids at night. We dug in and throughout the darkness tried to grab what sleep we could at the bottom of our respective slit-trenches. On our third sleepless night one of the German bombers was hit by ack-ack fire and crashed but twenty yards from our temporary accommodation. The approaching hysterical scream of its twin engines as it hurtled earthwards had, I was convinced, my number written all over it. It erupted with a mighty roar as it hit the ground, bursting into a raging inferno which lit up the entire area, thus providing a king-sized flare for the following waves. It wasn't long before a remaining stick of bombs still housed in its belly exploded and the small-arms ammunition destined for its machine-guns started to go off like firecrackers on 5 November. My bed-roll, barely dried out after torrential rain during our first day, was, by the time the last flame flickered out from that burning aircraft, sopping wet again. The following morning two charred corpses were removed from the machine and buried respectfully slap next door to our 'bedrooms'.

The night before our attack was due to go in a final briefing was given by our host brigade commander, and under the cover of darkness his troops were to move into position. Craigie left the briefing conference looking a very pale and worried man. He came and sat down in our car and stared in silence at his map for about ten minutes. He then spoke. 'If that man puts his HQ where he intends to put it, there'll be nothing left of any of us by an hour after dawn tomorrow morning,' he said. It matters little now what the position was, but you may take it from me that it was one which Craigie considered, 'come the dawn', as he kept repeating, would be tactically untenable.

Now, my dear colonel had no authority whatsoever over the conduct of the forthcoming battle. He was responsible for advising on the handling of our own troops only, who made up but a small percentage of a sizeable attacking force. Nevertheless, such was his concern and firm conviction that the senior officer to whom he had been attached was wrong that he could not sit back and accept the situation as inevitable. He ruminated for another twenty minutes, drank a mug of tea that I'd brewed up for him on our Primus stove, then with a look of determination on his face he climbed out of the car, put his hat on and, clutching his map, strolled over to the brigadier's caravan. He was gone for half an hour. Eventually he emerged with the colour back in his cheeks. He had managed, somehow or other, to persuade one of the more hot-headed armoured brigade commanders in the beach-head to change his mind and as a result the dawn came and we all lived on.

Towards the end of July the Allies finally broke out of the restricting Normandy beach-head. On the right flank the American armies burst into Brittany – at one time the troops of General Patton's army covering twenty-five miles in thirty-six hours. On the left flank the British and Canadians drove south from Caen creating, with other American armies, unbelievable scenes of carnage and destruction in the Falaise pocket. From where on, side by side, the combined forces of the Allied war machine marched due east slowly rolling up the German carpet which had been laid down wall to wall in 1940.

For us in the flail brigade there was to be no let-up. We were continually on the move; tents and camouflage-netted vehicles dispersed in orchards and farmyards, monasteries, village schools and the occasional grand house or château providing our temporary resting places. The pace and pressure of work never waned and no one, I think, would have had it any other way.

In mid-September I was given my first day off since we landed three months previously to the day, and I spent it in the recently liberated city of Rouen with a pal of mine called John Moore. John was a subaltern in the Royal Tank Regiment and our intelligence officer with whom I shared accommodation throughout the entire campaign and with whom I established a long and lasting friendship. Rouen was the first town with inhabitable shops, cafés and bars that we had been in since leaving Weybridge in June. We had a lot of booze in a number of the latter, one of which I seem to remember was furnished entirely in bamboo, but the main kick was to be able to tidy up, put on my dress forage cap and walk down the streets of a town populated with urban civilians once again. Hitherto the only natives with whom we had been in contact were farmers, peasants and those essentially of the land. I hastened to the shopping area to buy presents for Pym. Scent (Lucien Lelong, 'N'), silk stockings (£7 a pair), kirbygrips and a Thermos flask – all items practically extinct in wartime England; the latter actually requiring a permit to purchase. Such a spending spree no doubt made a bit of a hole in my exchequer. The last few weeks, however, had provided little opportunity for extravagance so with luck I might, by now, have accumulated a small reserve in my name. Which was just as well, really, as when I embarked for France my entire worldly assets were contained in a current account which showed a total credit of £14 4s 6d. At the end of the day we drove back to our ever-mobile HQ, tired, slightly inebriated and ready for the next move at 6.30 the following morning.

Shortly after this trip the liberation of Fécamp, the home of the liqueur Benedictine, provided another pleasant interlude. Benedictine, like silk stockings, kirbygrips and Thermos flasks, was a commodity that had not been seen in England since the German occupation of France in 1940. The sudden sight of the distinctive DOM bottles once again had an astonishing, if not obfuscating, effect on its liberators. We drank it solidly and practically solely in our mess for a whole week. There was one particularly wild evening when gentility was thrown to the winds and we were quaffing it out of tumblers.

Soon France and most of Belgium, both of which we crossed at a fairly breathless pace, were behind us; but Holland and northern Belgium were an entirely different matter. Between September and the end of the year we were buffeted backwards and forwards across the Dutch/Flemish border like a shuttlecock. At the beginning of October, however, we had our first real taste of comfort since our arrival on the Continent. We moved lock, stock and barrel into a requisitioned hotel in the centre of Bruges, where we stayed for five weeks planning the invasion of Walcheren and other operations to clear the Scheldt estuary and open up the vital port of Antwerp. One week after Antwerp had been declared clear of the enemy the first flails thrashed their way over German soil opposite the industrial town of Geilenkirchen. Three weeks after that Hitler, through the agency of Field-Marshal von Rundstedt, temporarily put the cat amongst the pigeons by summoning all his fast-diminishing resources in a desperate attempt to cut the Allied armies in half in the Ardennes. The weather had by then become bleak, wet and very cold and it was in conditions of ice and snow that we had to pick up our skirts and hurry back into southern Holland and industrial Belgium to meet the contingency. The offensive eventually repulsed, we settled down in Eisden, a small town on the most southerly tip of the Dutch–Belgian border, and operations generally ground to a halt as winter set in with a vengeance. Ice and snow spread across the Dutch landscape making one reflect that not much seemed to have changed in rural Holland since similar scenes were immortalised on canvas by the seventeenth-century Dutch masters. In the lull that followed we had the opportunity to develop new assault techniques for the forthcoming crossing of the Rhine, the last formidable obstacle that lay before us.

It was about now that my personal soul-searching began. Until this lull, apart from a brief forty-eight hours' leave in Brussels in mid-November, there had been little time to think of anything but the job in hand. Until I joined the army I had spent my entire life day-dreaming about a successful future for myself somewhere in the realms of show business. From the age of about seventeen this had crystallised itself into an unwavering resolution to become an actor, and never, since then, had I considered any other career. Between the ages of eighteen and twenty I had had practical experience of the life which confirmed that my decision had been the right one. I could conceive of no other way of earning my living. I adored it. I lived and breathed 'theatre'.

I had, nevertheless, left this world shortly after my twentieth birthday when I was still really an adolescent. Four and a half years had passed since then and I was now a man. My horizons had widened. Interests that I never knew existed had been awakened. Abilities that I never knew I possessed had made themselves evident. Responsibilities that nobody had ever trusted me with before had been thrust on me and I was thriving on them. The money, though small, was regular, and with the services, at least *pro tem*, looking after the food and lodgings side of both my own and my wife's life I never had to give finance a second thought. In short, with the exception of the killing side of it and the separation from Pym, the job I was doing filled me with adrenalin.

So what of the future? The battle was still raging, and even when Germany had been licked, for those young enough, and I was one, Burma and the Far Eastern conflict loomed ominously ahead, so maybe it was premature to start worrying yet; nevertheless, in more contemplative moments the dilemma reared its ugly head. The smell of the greasepaint, the roar of the crowd had begun to recede into soft focus. When eventually I was demobbed I would return to civilian life now having to provide for two, not one, and we had always had amibitions to start raising a family while we were young. Both Pym and I had had young parents and we had foreseen the advantage of children in their late teens having parents who were still young enough to understand and share their problems. When I returned to my old life I would be twenty-five, twenty-six, twenty-seven – who knew? I would have to start again from scratch, banging on agents' and producers' doors. I had no real connections; Herbert Farjeon, by whom I had set so much store, was now dead. It looked an ominous prospect. What was I to do? I was born under the sign of Gemini and Geminians are notorious for their inability to make decisions. I have made many in my life, many of them important, but always for others and with these I have never had any problem. Decisions regarding myself I have always found much more difficult to make.

So it was that I found myself ruminating in Eisden chilled by a bitter Dutch winter round about Christmas in 1944.

The New Year duly arrived and time for such thoughts was soon extinguished. After a brief respite the battle started up again with renewed vigour. The Allies on the northern sector of the front had been held on a line roughly ten miles short of the Rhine and this ground had now to be taken before the river itself could be crossed. The area was strongly defended by the renowned Siegfried Line, a man-made obstacle, and the

Reichwald Forest, which was not. It was a foregone conclusion that the enemy would fight like a tiger to hold this ground as, once across the Rhine, the whole of Germany was wide open before the Allied steam roller.

On our sector a huge attack involving five divisions was mounted, in which we ourselves were heavily involved. During the two weeks of planning Operation Veritable, the majority of our small staff had practically no sleep at all. Eventually, however, when all was ready, at five o'clock on the morning of 8 February, a barrage of over a thousand guns burst forth and continued for five hours and then the leading troops crossed the start line.

Resistance was as tough as had been expected and to occupy all the ground that had been Montgomery's objective took a month to the day, but on 9 March the Allied armies stood poised on the Rhine ready to cross and deploy across the plains of Germany proper.

The staff work involved in planning Operation Veritable was, however, a mere shadow of that which had been required to get myself home on leave about ten days after its kick-off.

Towards the end of 1944 a grateful General Staff had decreed that the tactical situation was now secure enough to entertain the commencement of UK leave for all ranks. A system of priorities was worked out and everybody began to consult calendars and do higher mathematical sums to try and calculate when his would fall due.

For me, however, the pinpointing of my own leave date was only a beginning. Pym, being a serving woman, had to arrange her leave to coincide with mine, and even when both dates were satisfactorily nailed down the capricious behaviour of the North Sea could cause cancellations of sailings which would throw the whole intricately planned timetable into confusion. Such delays were taken into account when calculating the length of stay of a returning soldier, but Pym's allotted span was fixed and any extensions caused by such misfortunes were far more complicated to arrange.

On the last day of January Pym received a letter from me saying that seven days' UK leave looked like coming my way sometime in February. The agonising personal staff work now began. No detailed preparations could be made as yet but I suggested that the time was ripe for her to start making noises in the right quarter about requiring leave herself sometime during the month in question.

All through the build-up for Veritable one half of me was sweating on the top line that we would get all our troops moved and assembled without any major mishap, and the other half was reacting in a similar fashion over my personal move back to the UK. The former task, I am delighted to report, went off well; the latter went something like this:

Letter dated 19 Jan., 1.30 a.m. (No. 98)
Self to Pym
At last it's official! My leave starts and I arrive in England *all being well* on 15th Feb.... Better go ahead *now* and book a room at the Cumberland [the hotel in which we had stayed on honeymoon] for the nights of both 15th and 16th just in case of cancellations.
P.S. A new 'must' record – Dinah Shore's 'My Guy's Come Back'. Have you heard it? I love you V much.

Letter dated 21 Jan. (No. 99)
Self to Pym
Darling, we must dance an awful lot when I get home. Hatchett's on the first night and we must try and spend one night in Scarborough. Where would you like darling – the Pavilion or the Victoria?

Letter dated 26 Jan.
Pym to Self
Whoops of joy! Leave all arranged and room booked at the Cumberland for 15th and 16th. I love you darling. Please make it soon.
P.

Letter dated 30 Jan., 1.15 a.m. (No. 103)
Self to Pym
About meeting the train at Victoria – I don't think that's on. There might be more than one leave train each day and anyway I don't know which of two ports I shall be docking at. Go straight to the hotel and wait until I arrive which I think should be somewhere between midday and midnight. It will be a miserable wait for you darling, I know, but I'm afraid it can't be helped....

Ring up and book a table at Hatchett's for both the 15th and 16th. The 16th is only a precaution but I think we should book well ahead.

Darling, if by any remote chance some hitch prevents me arriving on 15th, wait in Town one more day and if I still haven't arrived by the morning of 17th, go up north to Elloughton and I'll join you there.
P.S. Just received £20 income tax refund. We now have a total bank balance of £130!

Letter dated 1 Feb., 1.35 a.m. (No. 104)
Self to Pym
Angel, just had a letter from home telling me everything is laid on regarding the car [a reference to the transfer of ownership from my mother to myself so that I could obtain special leave petrol ration] so we can go 'swanning' round all the pubs between Elloughton and Sleights with impunity – isn't it marvellous?
P.S. Oh, darling – won't it be heaven to see York Station again!

Letter dated 2 Feb., 1 a.m. (No. 105)
Self to Pym
Hell, damn, blast and bugger! All leave has been put back one day – so now I shall be arriving on 16th not 15th. Would you do all the necessary cancellations darling and re-book for 16th and 17th?
P.S. What would you like for a 21st birthday present?

Letter dated 6 Feb., 2.10 a.m. (No. 107)
Self to Pym
Darling, leave has been postponed yet another 24 hours. The old North Sea playing up again. I shall now arrive, all being well, on 17th so once again darling I'm afraid you'll have to go and sweeten your officer and try and push all our bookings back one more day.

Letter dated 7 Feb. (No. 108)
Self to Pym
Darling, just in case my last letter went astray – everything has been postponed another 24 hours and I shall now be arriving on 17th. On reflection, and if you don't mind, I now think it would be better if you remained in Town until I arrive even if by any misfortune I'm 48 hours or more late.... Oh God, isn't it all so complicated?
P.S. His Lordship has just informed me that the Brigadier has approved my appointment as SLO [Senior Liaison Officer] which means another pip as soon as it is promulgated. Can't be bad, eh?

In the event, at the eleventh hour, I somehow or other managed to wangle a flight (the first time I had ever been off the ground) in an RAF Dakota from Brussels to Northolt early on the morning of 17 February and I was on English soil by 11 a.m. Some form of service transport was provided to run the passengers into London, but such was my impatience to get in touch with Pym that I stopped the driver and de-bussed at the first GPO telephone-box that I saw *en route*. By chance, it was on the corner of a crossroads on Western Avenue just behind where the BBC Television Rehearsal Rooms' building now stands. It is still there and over all the years that I have rehearsed at the 'Acton Hilton', as it is commonly known in the profession, I have passed that box on every visit and waves of nostalgia envelop me. I rather wish I had been able to buy it. But on the day in question I was on to Madam in a flash. Rockets took off – rainbows glowed, brass bands played and tears of joy flowed at both ends of the line.

She could knock off immediately. 'See you at the hotel in an hour – kiss, kiss, kiss.'

When I emerged from the phone-box and removed my rose-coloured spectacles, I realised that in my frenetic dash to talk to my bride I had completely omitted to ask the transport to wait for me; it had gone. How

I eventually reached London I still have no recollection. I was on Cloud 9 and nothing whatever could bring me down to earth until we finally fell into each other's arms in our hotel room an hour and a half later.

That night we dined and danced to Chappie d'Amato and George Shearing at Hatchett's and the following day boarded a train at King's Cross for Hull and my parents' home at Elloughton.

It must have been a marvellous leave, though many of the details have by now been smudged and washed away. One fact, however, has been documented. In view of my new-found wealth, or rather what was left

With Pym
on leave at Elloughton

of it after seventeen days' leave (this time the unpredictable North Sea responded in our favour), we decided we would push the boat out on the last night of it and stay at the Mayfair – a hotel which had perhaps rather more style than the Cumberland. That evening we were joined by a fellow 22nd Dragoons officer and his fiancée at the Bagatelle and we danced our hearts out to Edmundo Ros in a vain attempt to forget that on the morrow we would all have to part again, for who knew how long?

At seven o'clock the following morning, after the most agonising goodbyes, I left Pym in bed, walked down to Reception with a lump in my throat the size of a water melon and asked for my bill. Now when it comes to 'style', as everybody knows, you don't get it for nothing. That one night at the Mayfair hotel in a double room with private bath, always extra because not every room had one, with fully cooked breakfast in our room which was wheeled in on an enormous trolley, the sides of which when raised became a table, cost me all of £2 11s 9d – so you see.

In due course, having travelled by train, boat and transit camp, I arrived back at my HQ three days and twelve hours after walking out of the Mayfair Hotel. The jet set would have found life very tedious back in 1945.

During my absence the Veritable fighting had been hard and bitter, but by now General Brian Horrocks's 30 Corps, which comprised the five divisions involved, was almost established on its final objectives. HQ 30th Armoured Brigade was on German soil for the first time. To reach them I had driven through both Goch and Cleves and the sight that greeted me was unbelievable. I had witnessed the devastation at Caen in the Normandy beach-head and the carnage in the Falaise Gap, but never, it seemed to me, had I seen such destruction as this. Hardly a building was left standing in either town – historic Cleves one bled for. Salvaged items of furniture that householders had attempted to rescue from what remained of their houses lay littered incongruously in front gardens and on roadsides. In the fields dead cattle were everywhere and the air was thick with the sweet stench that such carcases exude. Brick dust from the acres of rubble clogged the nostrils and cordite fumes still clung to the shattered masonry. In addition, the atmosphere was heavily charged with the blatant hostility of the civilian population. The good news, however, was that during my absence my promotion had come through and I could now put up my third pip and call myself captain. Such news was, nevertheless, tempered by the fact that, also during my absence, the system of release from the services on the cessation of hostilities in Europe was just beginning to filter through and all the signs were that after VE-Day I would be a dead cert for Burma – a happy thought!

Within three days of my return the west bank of the Rhine was cleared of the enemy and the next two weeks were spent in planning the assault across the river itself. Our job, later assessed by our divisional commander as the most important operation undertaken by his division since D-Day, was, apart from fighting DD tanks swimming the river, largely one of ferrying troops across it and lighting the night scene with CDL tanks. On the evening of 23 February, at nine o'clock on the nail, immediately following a three-hour barrage of 1,700 guns, the assault was launched.

Captain I. G. Carmichael, SLO

At ten o'clock the following morning I stood on the west bank of the Rhine and watched with awe the immense armada of the 18th Airborne Corps flying west to deliver its troops behind the German lines. 541 parachute-dropping Dakotas, 1,250 Stirlings and Halifaxes towing 1,230 gliders plus 100 fighter escorts blackened the sky for as far as the eye could see. It was the most prodigious sight that I witnessed during the entire campaign. Slowly, stately and magnificently they came – a steady, relentless, heavily laden, ponderously moving stream – wave after wave of them. For one whole hour they passed directly overhead, dropped their para-boys, cast off their gliders, turned round and returned the way they had come. It was like an endless conveyor belt. In addition, 1,200 supporting fighters, including rocket-firing Typhoons, made successive sweeps over enemy ground targets and 2,200 heavy bombers, a figure which excludes the medium bombers of the Second Tactical Air Force which always moved in support of the armies in the field, were also employed. 'Until this day,' I wrote to Pym afterwards, 'I never really comprehended the meaning of the word "air-power".'

Two days later I crossed the Rhine briefly with my brigadier and the day after that the whole HQ crossed at Rees and we entered hostile Germany proper. Forty-eight hours later our HQ and its attendant 'Funnies' were divorced from the Second British Army and became married to the

First Canadian Army which turned back into Holland. There we were to clear out the large pockets of enemy which had been left behind and still remained bottled up in that country.

By now we were within six weeks of VE-Day. The 'hoovering-out' of the remainder of Holland took little time and by the end of April we had settled under canvas and in our lorried offices and command vehicles in a spruce little park in the centre of Deventer, a town about twenty miles north of Arnhem. Spring was almost upon us and late on 4 May the text of the following message was received from HQ 21 Army Group which I, as duty officer, signed and passed on immediately to all units under our command at 0115 hours the following morning. This, remembering my original brief from Sidney Hine about passing on orders, was one that I did understand.

MESSAGE FORM

Date & Time of Origin
050115B

FROM:- 30 ARMD BDE
TO:- I Lothians   W Dgns   1 N Yeo   141 RAC
1 CAC Regt   5 Armd Engr Regt RE
30 Armd Bde Sigs   502 Coy RASC
'A' Bde Sec 16 Lt Fd Amb   30 Bde Wksps REME
Adm Offr

G 3730 (.) RESTRICTED (.) Following text EXFOR MAIN GO 411A of 042050B quote all offensive ops will cease from receipt this sig (.) orders will be given to all tps to cease fire 0800 hrs tomorrow SAT 5 MAY (.) Full terms of local German surrender arranged today for 21 Army Gp Front follow (.) Emphasise these provisions apply solely to 21 Army Gp Fronts and are for the moment exclusive of DUNKIRK unquote (.) ACK

AS WRITTEN   CIPHER   PRIORITY
                                                       IMMEDIATE
(Signed) I. G. CARMICHAEL., CAPT.

It is difficult to describe to anyone who has not lived through six years of total war the immediate feelings of euphoria that burst when the news arrives that the final whistle has been blown; a tight cork exploding from a warm bottle of champagne would produce nothing in comparison with such effervescence. For six long years the people of Europe had never seen a light of any sort or description in the streets after dusk unless

HQ 30th Armoured Brigade Staff at Deventer on VE-Day. John Moore standing second from the right, Michael Killanin in peaked hat sixth from the left, self sitting cross-legged centre

it had been either a blue one, the slim pencil-light of a masked-down torch carried by a pedestrian, or the narrow – extremely narrow – letter-box slits to which the lights on all vehicles had been reduced. The fact that the maiming and killing had stopped; the fact that one had come through unscathed; the fact that that night every light in the town could be put on and the curtains left wide open, were all causes for unconfined ecstasy. Deventer now went mad. Lights were switched on everywhere and street after street was mobbed with Dutchmen of all ages carrying bright orange lanterns illuminated by candles. It was a warm May night and windows and doors were thrown wide open. Music blared from radios placed on window sills and dancing in the streets was wild and abandoned. On one normally busy crossroads the traffic had stopped completely. The area had been floodlit with unmasked headlights and dancing was in full swing to music pouring out of a large amplifier that had been rigged up on the side of one of the houses. Then the processions started and every house was 'open house'.

Sometime in the early hours of the morning, in a family home that John Moore and I visited quite often, the lady of the house tucked us both up on a camp-bed and a sofa (we were far gone) with tears pouring down her cheeks. Earlier that evening I had had no ears for a maudlin and, at the time I thought, cynical local journalist who told me to enjoy it all while I could because, mark his words, 'In fewer years than you can imagine, you will have to go through the whole thing again with Russia. They are the real menace, Ian, believe me.' But after the euphoria there was time for reflection. Despite the suicidal nature of their task, the casualties in my regiment over a year of hard fighting had been astonishingly light. Six officers and 26 other ranks killed, and 13 and 108, respectively, wounded. But included in those figures were many of my friends.

Neither John nor I had had a single day off duty since we had each returned off leave in early March. Life had been hectic at HQ 30th Armoured Brigade during the intervening two months and we were all dog-tired. It was therefore with some relief, and even incredulity, that an apparently grateful brigade major came up to both of us later that day, Sunday, and said he thought we had earned a rest and that we were to take a staff car the following morning, go to Brussels, and that he didn't want to see either of us again until the staff conference on Friday morning.

The next morning neither of us moved out of his bed-roll until eleven o'clock. VE-Day, we then discovered, had been officially announced for 8 May – the following day – and the thought of spending it in Brussels made us purr more than somewhat over an extremely leisurely late break-fast. Astonishingly, it is the mundane pleasures that linger. As on our brief trip to Rouen back in the previous September, the biggest and initial thrill was to be able to put on clean service-dress once again and step out with creased trousers, brass buttons newly polished, a Sam Browne belt and, in my case, the 22nd Dragoons' gold-piped, black and cream forage cap. The mildew had been duly shaken out of them all by Mus-grave, the Lothian and Border Yeomanry batman who had looked after me so solicitously throughout the whole campaign, and our battledresses were left, almost literally, standing up in the corner of our tent. Shortly after midday we stepped into a staff car (a great privilege for the likes of us) and set off for the, by now, bright lights of Belgium.

On our arrival in Brussels we checked into our hotel in the boulevard Adolphe Max and went up to our room. As we entered it, the first com-fortable room in a smart hotel that we had experienced for what seemed like eons, we both stood for a moment in silence. It was John who spoke first.

'This rings a bell,' he said.

For 'starters' we decided to soak for about an hour in a hot bath.

In the early evening, refreshed and ready for the fray, we went out on the town and the whole thing started again. Two days previously we had witnessed and shared the elation of a small town with its street parties and orange lanterns; now we were in a big capital city with the lights of shop windows, neons, floodlit squares and even fireworks being sent heavenwards off the top of its trams. The streets were packed. Everybody loved everybody and rockets and thunderflashes were being ignited on every street corner.

After visits to innumerable bars, we wandered into Maxim's to watch the cabaret. There we joined the company of two half-cut but friendly GIs with their ATS escorts and after several bottles of champagne we emerged an hour or so later feeling in pretty much the same condition ourselves. Nevertheless, no time for bed yet we decided, so we sampled a few more cafés, in one of which we got tangled up with two young Belgian married couples who shared a flat and who insisted that we went back to it for further celebratory glasses. Somewhere about 1 a.m., unable to keep up with John's fluent French, I finally passed out on the sofa. He, several cups of coffee and one bottle of cognac later, ultimately woke me at 7 a.m. We then embraced our hosts and, swearing eternal friendship and intentions of meeting for a yearly anniversary from then until the end of time (which, needless to say, we have never done), staggered back to our hotel where we fell into bed and slept until lunch-time.

We felt surprisingly good when we woke up and after another bath – they had been such a rarity during the past few weeks – we made our plans for the day. If yesterday had been VE-1, we reflected, what might the Belgian capital have in store for us on the big day itself? We were, to be honest, beginning to feel the accumulated effects of the Deventer 'thrash' on Saturday, our own mess celebrations throughout Sunday and yesterday beating up Brussels, so under the circumstances we decided that a twenty-four-hour recuperation period might be both prudent and beneficial. Bruges, we reasoned, was but fifty-five miles away – why not let's have a spot of lunch and then drive up there to see Dédé and Mimi, a charming young couple who had befriended us during our five weeks' stay in the town? Unanimously agreed; so after a spot of lunch we hit the road.

It was a nostalgic journey. The countryside was resplendent in the afternoon sunshine. The last time we had travelled in those parts a pall of gunsmoke had been overhead and alternately ice and mud under foot. When we arrived we were received with open arms. A bottle of the best cognac came out and after innumerable toasts had been drunk we were quite easily persuaded to stay for dinner and bunk down there for the night. The following morning we slept in again – we had so much of that to catch up with – and came down at midday feeling on top of the world. Everything, we concluded, even though Jule Styne hadn't written it yet, was 'Coming up Roses'. Eventually we said our fond and grateful fare-wells and round about 3 p.m. set out on our return journey.

When we arrived back in Brussels the impression we got was that no one had been to bed since we left it. The streets were still packed with a jollificating populace, they were still letting off rockets from the tops of trams and no doubt if we had returned to Maxim's those two GIs would still have been sitting there with their ATS escorts.

Well, if you can't beat 'em, join 'em. So we did.

Brussels, like many cities in war zones all over the world, was fes-tooned with large painted signs indicating the direction to follow in order to find this unit or that unit, or this HQ or that HQ; even this Prophylactic Centre or that Prophylactic Centre. They were affixed to every lamp-post and every bollard. That night John and I, full of ebullient high spirits, some of which had no doubt come out of a bottle, decided that we would relieve Brussels of a few of them. Such was the preoccupation of the average man in the street that, over a period of two hours, we managed to shin up lamp-posts, crawl over traffic islands and generally remove fourteen of them, which, without so much as attracting a raised eyebrow, we smuggled back to our car parked in some square or other several blocks away. Infantile, you may think. Yes, I suppose it was really: but our collection of signs that night was, to us, what policemen's helmets had been to Gussie Finknottle on far-off boat-race nights. Would we do it again? You bet your life we would.

Thursday morning duly dawned but we never saw it. Again we were out to the world – this time in our hotel room. Again we rose at midday, bathed and after lunch went to see Cary Grant in *Arsenic and Old Lace*. That evening we had an early dinner, and then set off back to Holland. Five and a half hours later we arrived in Deventer. The following morning there was no bath and no sleeping in, but we were on parade at Michael's staff conference at 8.30, doing our best to look bright-eyed and bushy-tailed.

In Deventer the heat that May was sweltering, and our little park looked as pretty as a picture. It contained a small lake which was bordered on one side by a chorus-line of weeping-willow trees interspersed with chest-nuts and hawthorns, both of which were in full bloom. Two days after our return from Brussels our lads had arranged an alfresco concert for the local civilians. For a stage, a sizeable raft supporting a mini piano had been launched on to the centre of the lake and the background of trees had been festooned with fairy-lights. The audience sat on the opposite bank and on that idyllic Sunday evening it was difficult to recall that total war was only one week behind us.

I saw a lot of Holland during the following months. There was little else to do now except to enjoy oneself – and worry; I could see the Far East looming up in front of me like an approaching storm. But Burma or no Burma, at the age of twenty-four I reckoned I still had a further two years to serve His Majesty, so, adopting a policy of 'live for today', I decided that it was time I got home to see my loved one once again. I succeeded. With very little trouble I soon wangled myself on to an aerial photograph interpretation course in Matlock. In Matlock, a few weeks later, our first-born was conceived.

CHAPTER FOURTEEN

GERMANY

Back to Square One

And so I entered the last round of my life as a soldier.

On returning from England I found 30th Armoured Brigade with the greatest difficulty. After another period of protracted travelling, I finally ran them to earth at a place called Gifhorn, about eighty miles north of Brunswick. Gifhorn, I soon realised, was probably going to be, if not our final destination, at least one in which we were likely to be entrenched for some considerable time. The war in Europe had finished. The future for me looked ominous. It was time for a personal stock-take. Time to ask 'Whither Carmichael?' Had I any choice in the matter? Well, miraculously, it so transpired that I had.

About ten days after my return, a letter from the senior welfare officer of General Brian Horrocks's 30 Corps arrived at our HQ. It stated that, as the fighting was now over and we had to settle down and become an occupation force, the corps commander had decreed that the welfare and entertainment of his troops was to be a number one priority. In pursuance of this policy he had authorised his welfare staff to assemble a central pool of artistes to be recruited from all the units under his command regardless of rank. From this pool, it went on, it was hoped to form a corps repertory company, several concert parties and perhaps even the odd orchestra. Commanding officers were asked to give the scheme publicity in their unit orders and to forward the names of those wishing to attend auditions.

This letter hit me with all the impact that that beefy gentleman imparts to J. Arthur Rank's gong. Was this the answer to my problems? I don't think I ever for a second considered not forwarding my name, but my letters home to Pym were couched cautiously in terms full of self-justification. While on leave we had discussed our future together and I had expressed to her my nagging doubts about going back to the acting profession. A gap of five years now separated me from my last professional

engagement and if I was to sever my ties with the theatre I obviously
had to do so immediately after demob. The problem now posed was on
a par with that of giving up smoking. I had, I thought, if I was strong
enough, conquered my addiction for the theatre – even though it had
been occasioned by force of circumstance – but if I had just one more
'puff' now, would I find myself hooked again? I didn't know. I didn't
even know if I wanted to be cured. My mind was a welter of indecision.

A day or two later I unearthed some intelligence that was to affect
the situation considerably. I discovered, as a result of a chance encounter
with a knowledgeable friend, that a brigadier chum of my own brigade
commander was heading for the Far East and he was trying to persuade
him to release me to go with him as his GSO 3 – a staff appointment
of more permanence and stature than SLO. This had to be avoided at
all costs. Whatever my post-war future was to be, I did want to have
one to come back to; having come through one campaign, I had no desire
to flirt with providence by launching myself into another. On the other
hand, I always knew that my rank as captain went with the job I was
now doing. If I left it, unless another captain's vacancy could be found
for me at Corps HQ, which was highly unlikely, I would have to drop
a pip and revert to lieutenant. If librium had been as readily available
in 1945 as it is today, I would have lived on it that week.

After several sleepless nights the fog began to clear. My rank, I decided,
could go hang; Burma or 'back to the boards' was really the only decision
I had to make. It wasn't a very difficult one. The next morning I filed
up to my brigadier and asked him if he would be kind enough to allow
me to forward my name for an audition.

A little over a week later I was summoned to give an audition in the
garrison theatre at Nienburg. Nienburg is about thirty miles north-west
of Hanover and was the town in which HQ 30 Corps was situated. I arrived
with my music tucked down my battledress blouse, as terrified as I have
ever been before or since on such occasions. The back of the stalls was
peopled with soldiers awaiting their turn to do their piece before a young
Royal Horse Artillery major who was sitting with a clipboard in the sixth
row.

Eventually my name was called and I mounted the stage. The number
I intended performing was one I had written myself for our regimental
revue in Warminster and for which, until a week ago, I had had no music.
I had spent hours singing it to a pianist at our HQ who had written it
down and then laboriously penned a full piano transcription for me. I
needn't have bothered. The accompanist, a lance-corporal sitting at his

piano on the stage, was a pre-war cinema organist and one of that enviable breed of audition accompanists whose skills are uncanny. You can approach them without a dot of music to your name and say 'Do you know "Moonlight on the Waterfall" ?' – and if they don't, their invariable reply is 'No, but you sing it and I'll follow' – and, unbelievably, they do. Astonishingly gifted men they are. Anyway, as I handed my music to Lance-Corporal Clark and was explaining what I wanted, the major's voice rang out from the stalls: 'Don't I know you ?'

Major Richard Stone, MC

I turned, looked, and indeed he did. It was one Richard Stone, who had been at the RADA during my time, albeit he had been a couple of terms senior to me.

'You probably do,' I said. 'We were at the RADA together.'

'Good gracious me!' he said. 'Never mind all that, come and sit beside me.'

Where had I heard that before?

My meeting with Richard Stone was to be the start of a very close business relationship and personal friendship which was to last for twenty years.

Richard was a driving force – that was and always has been his forte. The whole '30 Corps Theatrical Pool' project, as it eventually came to be known, was his. He was a human dynamo. Though good company, he was at times exhausting to be with. He lived and breathed his job and consequently assumed that all his minions did the same. He never relaxed; he was on the go the whole time. His plan was always the grand one, the broad strategy, and like so many other men with similar abilities he found it difficult to consider detail; that was for someone else to take care of – and for another year that someone was destined to be me. There and then he told me to return to Gifhorn, that he would definitely give me a job in the Pool and that eventually a posting order would be sent out for me, which in about ten days it was.

On my last night with 30th Armoured Brigade I had a sad and sentimental farewell party in the mess and on the following morning I packed all my belongings into a car and set sail for Corps HQ and my new life.

On arrival I found Richard once again in the garrison theatre. He was sitting in the same seat in the same row of the stalls with the same clipboard on his knee passing judgement on a different selection of service talent which, as previously, was scattered all around the auditorium. As I approached him down the aisle, I noticed that he had an RAF squadron leader with him. When it was too late to turn and run away, he had already seen me.

'Ah, Ian; welcome. Come and join us. Do you know Felix de Wolfe?'

I certainly did know Felix de Wolfe. Furthermore, I still owed him my final week's commission for the 1940 tour of *Nine Sharp* – four full shillings and sixpence. Squadron Leader de Wolfe, however, either had a bad memory or was prepared to let bygones be bygones; he recalled our pre-war relationship graciously, shook me warmly by the hand and no further reference was made to the matter. It really is an inconveniently small world at times.

Come lunchtime we repaired to the officers' club where, over a hasty repast (all meals with Richard were hasty at that time), he outlined the plans that he had for me. A play called *Desert Rats*, which had been both directed and presented by the late Henry Sherek, had just finished its run at the Adelphi Theatre in the Strand, and while on leave Richard had persuaded him to come over to Germany to direct one of his companies in it. It was to open for two weeks in Berlin and then tour the corps area. I was to play the young subaltern. It was, however, going to take a week or so to obtain permission for Sherek, a civilian, to come out and join us and so until his arrival it was to be my lot to act as Major Stone's assistant and general dogsbody – a temporary occupation which was to prove a great deal more arduous than if I had been able to go straight into rehearsals.

As we had broken for lunch and were leaving the garrison theatre a doleful-looking corporal had accosted Richard and asked if he could give him an audition. Richard asked him if he was on his list. He said that he wasn't; the sole reason for his presence in the theatre was that he was in charge of one or two other lads from his unit who *were* on the list.

'What do you do?' asked Richard.

'I make 'em laugh a bit,' said the corporal.

In response to further questioning it transpired that he had no professional experience, but nevertheless, having watched a few others at it that morning, he considered that he hadn't really a great deal of competition.

'O.K.,' said Richard. 'See you this afternoon.'

After we returned from lunch his name was duly called and he went up on the stage to assay what I have always considered to be the most soul-destroying task that can be asked of an entertainer – a comedian's audition. Trying to make two lone figures laugh in the cold, cheerless atmosphere of an empty theatre – well, it just shouldn't be allowed. Anyway, on this occasion it was his own choice and after a brief conference with Lance-Corporal Len Clark he launched into 'A-tisket a-tasket – I lost my yellow basket,' which if memory serves me right, and it is a long time ago, he interspersed with various jokes. He smoked the stub end of a cigarette throughout, which he periodically laid down on a chair behind him and was, I thought, very gauche. When the poor man had finished, Richard said to me, 'What do you think?'

'No,' I replied. 'Too undisciplined and not very funny either. Very much the amateur.'

'You're wrong,' said Richard. 'I'm going to book him and send him to "The Waggoners" [the 435 GT Company RASC Concert Party] as principal comic.'

We all have our crosses to bear in life, and that one was destined to be mine. If I had had my way Frankie Howerd would have slipped through our fingers and would never have given pleasure to countless soldiers before his eventual demob, and, no doubt, millions of people after it.

That night Richard took me back to his personal flat in which he said I was welcome to doss down *pro tem*. The *pro tem* was to last for a whole year.

The following morning we drove down to greet the initial intake of about eighty bods with assorted talents who had been assembled in the small village of Hoya, about half an hour's drive away. Were there any complaints, Richard enquired on arrival? There were, it transpired, plenty, all to do with initial teething troubles concerning the accommodation, but as all the assembled company had just left the army discipline of their units to join what promised to be a bit of a Fred Karno's outfit where parades and 'bull' were going to be a thing of the past, the voices of dissent were not raised too loudly. There and then, with this motley collection of soldiery sitting around him and with the aid of a nominal role which also indicated the particular talent of each individual, Richard proceeded to assemble five companies. One big band show, two mobile concert parties, one small string ensemble to give light music concerts and one play. The straight actors he immediately sent on leave pending the arrival of a few ENSA girls who he had arranged to be attached to us personally – well, when I say 'us' I mean to 30 Corps Theatrical Pool. The remainder he put straight into rehearsal and we returned to Nienburg. There I was to get my first glimpse of the Stone office suite.

His own office was a small one but next door to it was a larger room where Lance-Corporal Len Clark, that exemplary audition pianist, reigned with his superior, Corporal Craven. Beyond that was a larger room still which resembled an amalgamation of the showrooms of Messrs Chappell, Boosey & Hawkes, the HMV record shop in Oxford Street and Frizell's, the Leicester Square chemist. Records, sheet music, musical instruments, make-up, copies of plays and sketches, all of which were available to the units under General Horrocks's command. All the time I knew that suite of offices it was never less populated than a department store on the first day of the January sales. The two tolerant and phlegmatic corporal clerks were more akin to sales assistants than products of the trade for which they had been trained. If you wanted a letter traced you were in for trouble, but if you wanted the band parts of 'Someone's Rocking My Dreamboat' they were on your desk in a flash. My introduction to this Aladdin's cave immediately stirred up all the old adrenalin that had for five years lain dormant. It was exciting, it was stimulating and I was well on the way to being hooked again.

During the next few weeks I travelled hundreds of miles in search of civilian variety acts which I was then called upon to assemble into additional shows to augment our service output. If, during those early days, I ever found myself in Nienburg for a night with a chance to put my feet up, I was always bundled into Richard's jeep as the office closed and, after calling briefly at the mess for some very dry sandwiches, I was driven off by him (something which in itself I always felt deserved a medal for bravery) a distance of anything up to seventy miles to see some show

Producing one of the German variety shows

or other; furthermore, we always returned to Nienburg the same night without so much as a cup of coffee afterwards. During my first few weeks as Richard Stone's unofficial PA and resident producer, as I appeared to have become, I doubt if I ever got to bed before 2 a.m. and I always had to be in the office at nine o'clock the following morning.

It was at the end of the third week, when there was still no sign of Henry Sherek, that Richard asked me if I would be prepared to abandon my wish to join one of his companies as an actor and become his staff captain for which there was an immediate vacancy. This was a bit of a blow. Primarily I wanted to act, that was my sole reason for joining the pool, but if I accepted his offer it would solve the problem of my inevitable reversion to the rank of lieutenant. This, pride and my bank balance finally persuaded me, was of vital importance and as a result I accepted the offer gratefully. A few weeks later my appointment as SCAWS (Staff Captain Army Welfare Services) was officially promulgated.

Now that my position was regularised I decided to strike a blow for freedom. One morning, after a particularly late night in pursuance of our duties, Richard left the flat for the mess at 8.15 and I was still in bed.

'Aren't you coming to breakfast?' he said.

'No,' I replied, 'if you can be bothered, maybe you would be kind enough to bring it to me in the office.'

'In the office?' he expostulated.

'If you wouldn't mind,' I said. 'A bacon roll and a fried egg roll would do fine.'

He left the flat not really sure whether he'd heard correctly or not.

I was in the office prompt on nine, and so was Richard – with my breakfast.

This pattern then continued regularly.

Richard has always maintained that he was the only major in the British army to bring his captain's breakfast to him in the office.

Soon our ENSA actresses started to arrive. We appropriated ten in all, so we were then able to cast a number of plays. I was very anxious to direct Terence Rattigan's *While the Sun Shines* which I had seen in the West End on my last leave. The leading part of Able Seaman the Earl of Harpenden required a light comedy performer of some stature. It was an ideal role for my old chum Geoffrey Hibbert whom I knew was now soldiering somewhere on the Continent and would, no doubt, be delighted to lay down his rifle and finish his army career with us if I could only locate him. After a week's blood-hounding I ran him to earth. He was now a sergeant in charge of a theatre somewhere in the Ruhr area; within a fortnight I had managed to get him transferred to us and *While the Sun Shines* went into rehearsal.

After about three months we had thirty shows on the road which we routed at a weekly conference every Thursday morning in our office in Nienburg.

The office itself was now permanently besieged by an endless stream of foreign artistes and their requirements. A conjurer who worked entirely on his own when we originally booked him suddenly acquired a girl assistant – no extra charge, but she would now qualify for British rations; an illegal 'carrot' that tempted many to work for us at reduced rates. An aerial act wanted additional petrol coupons because the car in which they had once travelled had been sold and their new acquisition had a greatly increased petrol consumption. Could we supply a permit for a new set of tyres for the 'Continental Express' company coach – if not they could not possibly get to Wolfenbüttel to open next Monday? Most of the requests were bogus but they nearly all finished up getting what they wanted. One female juggler actually arrived in the office one morning requesting that we should supply her with sanitary towels.

'Certainly, dear, I always keep a handy supply in the bottom drawer of my desk.'

The saga of the circuses was a jolly little headache too. Apart from having to supply fodder for the horses and elephants, there was also a routing problem that reared its ugly head; Germany is a land of circuses, as we were very soon to find out.

We started out with one – Circus Althoff. For its opening fortnight we sent it to Osnabrück. On the first Wednesday morning the lady proprietor arrived in our office.

'Herr Kapitän,' she started, 'in Osnabrück this week is also Circus Heimsoth. Is not possible two circuses can do good business in one town. What you do for us, please?'

I apologised for the double booking but until her arrival, I explained, I had had no knowledge of Circus Heimsoth's existence. Only one solution seemed possible. I got into a car and set off for Osnabrück. There I interviewed the proprietor of Circus Heimsoth and suggested that, in his own interests, maybe in future we should route his circus too to avoid another clash. He readily agreed and in two weeks' time we sent Circus Heimsoth to Hanover and Circus Althoff to Hamlin.

On arriving in the office on Tuesday morning, Effi Plotz of Circus Althoff was waiting for me once again.

'Herr Kapitän,' she began dolefully, 'in Hamlin this week is Circus Charlie. Is not possible two circuses can do good business in Hamlin. What you do for us, please?'

Practically before she had finished, Herr Heimsoth also arrived in the office.

'Herr Kapitän. In Hanover this week is also Circus Brückenbeck—' etc, etc, etc.

I had little choice but to visit the circuses Charlie and Brückenbeck and make to them the same suggestion that I had made two weeks previously to Circus Heimsoth.

By the end of six weeks we were routing eight circuses. It was a nightmare. More elephants, more horses, more sea-lions to feed. When I finally left Germany I prayed fervently that I should never see another circus as long as I lived.

In July 1945 the frog, the mouse or whatever poor innocent animal was deputed to do the doctors' work for them gave a positive response to its injection and in late August Pym was demobilised on the grounds of pregnancy. We had of course no home of our own as yet, so she went back to live with her mother at Sleights.

In December Richard, I found, was beginning to have itchy feet to tread the boards once again. Two new girls, the Misses Elizabeth Ewbank and Patricia Norman, were due to arrive in Nienburg any day and as we had no immediate production for them he started thinking out loud; thinking aloud such thoughts as, did I know any play that would be suitable for

With Elizabeth Ewbank in the Pool's production of Springtime for Henry

the four of us? 'We could run it for one week in Nienburg,' he said, 'which would not interfere unduly with our daily office work.'

This grabbed me immediately; after all, it was what I had joined his organisation to do. I hurriedly suggested that *Springtime for Henry* would be an ideal piece and started to look round for a copy. I found my original one back at the flat and it appealed to him instantly. His tireless brain then started to get it all together. A company that had been playing *French Without Tears* was due to finish its tour in three weeks' time and their set would be ideal – well, almost ideal. The fact that Rattigan's play took place in a villa on the Côte d'Azur and *Springtime* in a flat in Belgravia worried us little. All the doors and windows were in the right places and with a little judicious 'dressing' it would suit our purpose well. So *French Without Tears* was to be routed into the Nienburg theatre for its final week at the end of which its set would remain *in situ* and we would move straight into it on the following morning.

I, it was agreed, would play the part that Nigel had played in Helmsley and I would also direct. Richard would assail the other slightly smaller role. In the event we played for three nights in the garrison theatre, Nienburg, one in a theatre at our corps commander's personal HQ a few miles away and a 3.30 matinée at the Herrenhausen Theatre in Hanover on the following Sunday so that members of our other companies could come and see it if they so wished. The last performance we used as an excuse to give them all a party on the stage afterwards, at which the ghost of *French Without Tears* made its presence felt and turned the whole evening into Mardi Gras. *Springtime* had again proved to be a grand, foolproof, rip-roaring comedy.

Having tasted the wine, we were all for opening more bottles at the first available opportunity. A new assistant had recently joined us in the office, another pre-war actor called James Ottaway, and he wanted to have a bit of a go too, so three months later, augmented with one other actor from the pool, we entered the Nienburg theatre with our second production. This time, under the banner of 'HQ 30 Corps Repertory Company', we presented a double bill of Noël Coward's *Fumed Oak* and George Bernard Shaw's play about Napoleon, *The Man of Destiny*. The latter was directed by John Benson, George's brother, who was also a member of our ranks, and the former by Lieutenant-Colonel Cecil Clarke. Cecil, now Head of Special Drama at Associated Television, was then a senior officer on the administration side of General Horrocks's staff and provided a touch of class to our production.

A few months later we had one more go – a few scenes from Shakespeare that we played in the most enchanting theatre I have ever appeared in in my life. It was a perfect opera house in miniature – 190 seats only – which had been built on the top floor of the Schloss in Celle in 1674. I played Romeo in a powder-blue ensemble which had perhaps better be forgotten.

April 1946 was an eventful month in my life. On the fourth I was working on my own in our office in Nienburg when a rather overweight corporal with a face like a blood-orange arrived from Hamburg. He had come apparently to deliver a box of twelve alarm-clocks that I was neither expecting nor, now they had arrived, did I know what to do with. In the middle of his explanation as to why they had been sent, Corporal Craven came in with a telegram for me. Forgetting the clocks, I ripped open the envelope and read: DAUGHTER ARRIVED APRIL 2ND BOTH WELL. (You will note that the GPO didn't seem to work any faster in 1946 than it does today.) From that moment my original visitor got pretty short shrift.

'I'm a father,' I whooped.

'Congratulations, sir,' he said as I bundled him out of the office with a summary dismissal in order to go and spread the good news from 'Ghent to Aix'; well, all over the outer office anyway. The next time I saw that face (once seen never forgotten) was when we worked together on the film *The Colditz Story* at Shepperton in 1954. His name was Denis Shaw.

Later that afternoon my colonel, the head of our department, put his head into our office and said, – 'Ian – did Captain Jess by any chance send a case of alarm-clocks down from Hamburg for me today?'

Woe was me; in my elation I had omitted to listen to Corporal Shaw's instructions regarding the clocks. They had been, it transpired, a personal present for my senior officer from his opposite number in Hamburg. Within the hour I had given every one of them away. Americans express their exuberance by handing out cigars. No cigars being available on that day, I had expressed mine by generously dispensing the first thing that came to hand.

'Congratulations, Herr Kapitän.'

'Thank you very much, old chap. Have an alarm-clock.'

Finally, in April the whole system of providing entertainment for His Majesty's Forces world-wide began to undergo a complete reorganisation and this, unfortunately, was to introduce regulations that would considerably restrict the hitherto unfettered running of our highly successful and efficient little organisation. Ah well, it had to happen sooner or later; luckily, however, by the time it did, my service was over and I was out of it all.

ENSA, now in its last days, was about to be replaced by an organisation which was in the process of being formed in what had once been gracious 'Upstairs, Downstairs' mansions in Eaton Square. I say once, because that graciousness was not immediately apparent on entering them in 1946. These, however, housed the Welfare Department of the War Office which was now accepting the responsibility of supplying all the entertainment for HM Forces throughout the world. The new organisation was to be called the Combined Services Entertainment Unit, and Richard Stone was about to receive promotion to lieutenant-colonel and be returned to the UK to command it.

Some people had a better war than others and I'm certainly not complaining about mine, but nobody, I think, could have fallen on his feet like Richard did in his appointment to Eaton Square. First of all, the flat in which he lived with his actress wife, Sara Gregory, and their baby son was in Ebury Street but two minutes' walk round the corner from his office; secondly, as he had by then decided to give up acting and become a theatrical agent after his demob, while seeing out his time with CSEU, he was on the spot to set the whole thing up.

The immediate effect all this had on me was a happy one. On 29 April

I was promoted to major and I took over his old job at HQ 30 Corps.

For another two and a half months I soldiered on, very proud of my new rank at the age of twenty-five, and continued the policy of a regular production of new shows. I was by now, of course, fully hooked once again on that pernicious, addict-forming drug called show business. There was now no doubt whatsoever that I would return to it all when my release number came up in July.

8 July 1946 found me in a demob centre in Leeds. I left it an hour later with a certificate stating that I was granted eighty days' leave from 8 July, and that with effect from 26 September I was 'released from Military Duty'. I also left with a plain brown cardboard dress-box tied up with string which contained my demob suit, a hat, a mackintosh, a pair of brown shoes and one shirt with three matching collars. I made for Leeds station, took a train for Brough and within a couple of hours I was reunited at Elloughton Garth with my wife, daughter and parents. I had been away five years and ten months all but four days.

Like thousands of others – I make no claim to being unique – I have never known what it is like to be between twenty and twenty-six years of age in a normal peacetime atmosphere. Have I missed anything? I don't know – I think, perhaps, I became a man quicker. But now the test was to come. It was a great feeling to be out – there was no denying that; but I was frightened. In fact, I think I was very frightened indeed.

Lee with her parents, Major and Mrs Ian Carmichael

PART III
From 1946

Citizen Carmichael, as immortalised by Anthony Buckley, immediately following demobilisation

CHAPTER FIFTEEN

CIVVY STREET

A Study in Survival

Overnight, Major I. G. Carmichael, an officer who had been responsible for providing entertainment for an area the size of Wales, with a sizeable staff, his own flat and car, neither of which cost him a penny, and with a regular salary, suddenly became plain Mr Carmichael, with no job, no home, no car and precious little money. A feeling of being cut down to size I suppose just about sums it up. All this was, of course, tempered with the relief of being out and reunited with Pym and our baby daughter Lee, but an all-pervading feeling of insecurity hung over me like a threatening cloud. Where do I go from here? How do I start?

Well, to begin with, I made one self-disciplining and inviolate plan: it was my avowed intention to work as hard as I possibly could for five solid years during which time I would take no holiday at all. It was essential that I should build up some sort of bank balance, because apart from my army gratuity, which would hardly keep Lee in orange juice and gripe water for a couple of months, we had just about enough in the bank to set me up with the minimum of essential tools of my trade; professional photographs, some sort of wardrobe, make-up and a year's subscription to the *Spotlight Casting Directory* and British Actors' Equity. In the event, that five years proved to be a considerable underestimation of what the fates were to allow me: we were not able to take a proper holiday *en famille* for fifteen years.

After a couple of weeks at Elloughton, therefore (I had completely abandoned any idea of taking eighty days' leave), I took Pym and Lee up to Sleights and then, like Dick Whittington – and with not much more luggage – set off for London town to seek my fame and fortune.

After the close relationship I had had with Richard Stone during the past year, it seemed inevitable that I should put the managing of my future career into his hands. He had asked me to, and, at the risk of sounding ungracious, not only did I not know of a better 'ole, I didn't know of any other 'ole at all. So on my arrival in the big city it was to him that I flew for succour and this I received in full measure. In addition to handling me professionally, he and his wife looked after me and my small family during those early months with a kindness and generosity that it is difficult to exaggerate. They had a most charming studio flat in the back wing of the Ebury Street property and, while arranging for me to rent a small bedroom in the main part of the house, they insisted that, apart from when I hit the sack, I should live and eat with them at all times.

A base established, something to wear seemed to be the next essential. The suits provided by His Majesty's Government, though serviceable, were hardly, in either cut or material, what I would have chosen to impress leading West End impresarios. In fact, the choice offered had been so depressing that I had deliberately chosen the one that I considered to be the most useful prop for playing, with the greatest respect to their esteemed callings, either impecunious City clerks or third-grade civil servants. I had, however, anticipated the wardrobe problem and brought back with me from Germany four cream silk shirts, three ties and a suit, all of which had been what the Americans call 'custom built' for me for our Pool production of *Springtime for Henry*, but rather like some wines, I'm afraid they didn't travel well. Over there on the stage, and after five years in uniform, I felt as if I had been turned out by Huntsman and Turnbull and Asser. Over here in Civvy Street, however, the same articles seemed to lose a certain chic. I also brought across with me two suit lengths of cloth out of the Pool wardrobe. These I rushed to my father's tailor whom I instructed to run me up a couple of tasteful ensembles as soon as he liked. Having measured me, he gave what I thought was a somewhat sceptical look at the material I had just laid laid on his workbench and, after rubbing it critically between his thumb and first finger, he uttered one of those opening gambits which are always so amusing when delivered in a derisory tone by Al Read.

'Where did you get this, then?'

The implication behind his remark didn't become fully apparent until a few weeks later when I took the finished articles away and started to wear them. The materials themselves, though a fine-looking herringbone, one grey and one brown, could only, I felt (literally), have been woven in a saw-mill rather than the sort usually associated with the weaving of cloth. However, as long as I didn't sit down in them too hard, the chance of my being splintered was only about fifty–fifty.

While waiting for these to roll off the production line, my next requirement was some up-to-date professional photographs and the obvious person to take them for me was an old 30 Corps colleague, one Major Anthony Buckley RA. Tony, also recently released, had been the officer in charge of the Army Kinema Service in Nienburg and he, Richard and I had been close buddies. Now, having got all his equipment out of mothballs, he had set up shop once again in a studio at the back of the Carlton Cinema in the Haymarket. A sitting was duly arranged and after a good old reunion session he took some quite splendid snaps, one of which I immediately bunged into *Spotlight*. I then declared myself ready to go and see any prospective employer to whom Richard wished to send me.

Now, there had been formed at that time an organisation known as the Sunday Services Society. Its object was to put on plays for one performance only – on a Sunday evening – to afford returning authors and performers a shop-window for their talents. Everybody gave their services free in the hope that the end-product would be seen and bought by a commercial management and given a subsequent West End run.

Within three weeks of my return to London I found myself going into rehearsals for a new revue which was being presented by that society. It was called *Between Ourselves* and was written by, amongst others, Alan Melville and Eric Maschwitz, with music by Norman Hackforth. Norman, by one of those strange quirks of fate, was eventually to become known to millions as the Mystery Voice on the radio panel-game *Twenty Questions*, though his main stock-in-trade was that of a musician. Before, during and after the war he was the personal accompanist to such luminaries as Noël Coward, Beatrice Lillie and Douglas Byng. Hedley Briggs, a highly experienced pre-war revue performer and director, was to direct, Bill Fraser was to be leading man and the production was to be presented at the Playhouse Theatre on the night of Sunday, 1 September.

I was very much a member of the Wines and Spirits, as those of a cast who do not warrant any special size or feature billing are known; it was, nevertheless, great to be back in revue once again.

Between Ourselves was eventually purchased and presented in the West End but the negotiations seemed interminable. For many weeks its fate hung in the balance. I struck up a good friendship with Bill Fraser who had himself only recently returned from serving with the RAF in Germany and, while waiting for someone to decide on our future, we lunched together almost daily at the cold table of many pubs in the Belgravia and

Chelsea area. The delay for me, however, was becoming crucial; my money was running out fast. In addition, there was no guarantee that, if the negotiations were successful, all the members of the original Sunday night cast would be employed in it. For Bill, as leading man, the prospect was worth waiting for, but in my position the gamble was of more questionable merit. It was with great relief, therefore, that just as I was reaching desperation stakes, help came from a most unexpected quarter.

Geoffrey Hibbert's father, having heard on the Hull grapevine that I was now demobilised and looking for a job, suddenly became my patron and benefactor; his own son, I should add, was still serving in Germany.

Through his connection with the Hull Repertory Theatre, Arnold Hibbert had a friend of long standing. His name was A. R. Whatmore. 'Whattie', as he was known to everyone, had over the years been both an actor and a director at the Little Theatre in Hull and was, in 1946, running his own company in Dundee. He also wrote plays and his most recent offering had just been purchased by a London management. Dear Arnold Hibbert, with the thoughtfulness characteristic of all his family, now, quite unbeknown to me, wrote to Whattie on my behalf. Would he, Arnold requested, see me?

'Certainly, old chap. Get him to write in,' was Whattie's immediate response.

A few weeks later, by appointment, I duly arrived at an office in St Martin's Lane, where Whattie and the producers who were to present the piece were seeing actors and actresses conveniently spaced at ten-minute intervals. For whose convenience these ten-minute periods really apply is always a mystery. After the first half-hour of such casting sessions there is invariably such a log-jam in the outer office that to clear it efficiently would require half-a-dozen highly experienced Canadian lumberjacks. The wretched victims just collect there, smoking, combing their hair or pretending to read a newspaper that they have just bought on the last street corner expressly to hide behind, until such time as their name is called and they pass out of the fetid atmosphere of the inadequately seated 'waiting-room' into the sub-zero temperature of the inner sanctum. It isn't, of course, sub-zero – it just feels like it when confronting the author, director and producer who, more like than not, at that moment, alone stand between the interviewee and starvation.

On this occasion the cast of the play was a large one and as the candidates were being asked to read for Whattie, who was also directing, the wait was a long one. As it turned out, his faith in Arnold Hibbert was

She Wanted a Cream Front Door. *Left to right, Sidney Vivian, self, Robertson Hare, Peter Haddon, Constance Lorne*

astonishing. Apart from the stars of the piece – Robertson Hare and Peter Haddon – and possibly the leading lady, Constance Lorne, I must have been the only member of the cast of *She Wanted a Cream Front Door* who was not called upon to 'sing for his supper'. After the briefest of introductions I was immediately engaged to play two small character parts – a precious hotel receptionist in Act II and a BBC roving-mike reporter in Act III – for which I was offered (and accepted) £12 a week; a seven-and-a-half-pound rise on my last professional salary which at an increase of not much under 200%, I didn't think was too bad.

Both 'Bunny' Hare and Peter Haddon were dears. Peter, himself only recently demobbed, had prior to that been running some sort of radio programme in Cairo. He was a jolly man, very tall, fair turning to grey, and he sported what used to be called a toothbrush moustache. He was an excellent foil and contrast to the small, urbane Robertson Hare. He was also one of many people who showed immense kindness to me and my family over the next few years.

We opened a twelve-week tour of the provinces at Whattie's own theatre in Dundee at the beginning of a chilly October, and though I was still separated from Pym, who remained at home with her parents, I was at least back in the professional theatre earning a regular salary and receiving a certain amount of approbation for my work, so life was beginning to look up.

I left my loved ones in Sleights for three reasons. First of all, I had not yet found a home of our own in which to leave them; secondly, though digs were cheap – on an average three guineas a week each for a bedroom, shared sitting-room with an open fire and three hot meals a day including one after the show in the evening – I did want to emerge from the tour with a refurbished bank account; and finally, I was quite adamant that any children of mine would be brought up in the normal environment of a stable home. I did not subscribe to the Hollywood romanticism of being born in a trunk, a different home every week and a dressing-room festooned with 'diapers'.

The nearest we had to a character on that tour was our company manager and stage director who, in massacring the English language, ran Mrs Malaprop a very close second. One Monday night after the show Bunny hauled him over the coals because the Act I set (we had three completely different ones – how times have changed!) had not been erected properly and gaps had been evident between the side and back walls. This, said our company manager, was not his fault – there was a rake (a forward slope) on the stage in that particular theatre which put the whole set out of 'prospectus'.

I offered him a drink in a bar one day.

'What would you like?' I said.

'A whisky please, Ian.'

'Any particular sort?' I asked.

'No, no – any priority brand will do,' he replied.

Another little gem was an admonishment at an understudy rehearsal that was not going too well.

'Now, come on, come on, come on,' he said. 'This is no good at all. You must all pull your socks together.'

During a week in my home town of Hull, I achieved a certain notoriety by receiving a notice in the local paper which contained both the adjectives that to an actor are derisory.

Giving a competent and capable performance at the New Theatre this week is twenty-six-year-old Ian Carmichael, son of....

Oh, well – a prophet in his own country and all that. As a local friend of mine pointed out (Geoffrey Hibbert's brother, actually), 'You're in good company, Ian. Jesus didn't do too well in Nazareth, you may recall.'

In early February, the tour over, we opened in London at the Apollo Theatre in Shaftesbury Avenue to mixed notices, but, nevertheless, we settled down for my first appearance in the West End to a four-month run during which I had a dressing-room of my own on the second floor. Now I began what was to become an increasingly depressing search for a home for us all.

On our return to London Richard and Sara kindly took me in again for a while until Geoffrey was demobbed, after which we became reunited on our old stamping ground in South Kensington. This time Marjorie Fox, to whom we naturally returned, was unhappily full, so we settled in Wetherby Gardens not far away. It was from there that I started my seemingly endless quest.

First-home buyers invariably encounter one insuperable problem – money. We, at that time, had none and, cautious and frugal as I had now disciplined myself to become, what savings I was managing to accrue would only be sufficient to provide us with a meagre subsistence for a few weeks when my play eventually came off. Flats were the only properties that I could entertain; I had no capital whatever to put down on a mortgage for a house. Yet flats were equally taboo, since landlords offering leasehold flats at that time were all demanding several hundreds of pounds' 'key money' in addition to a weekly rent.

After several demoralising weeks I eventually found an attic flat, five flights up with no lift, in a newly converted Victorian property in Cranley Gardens just off the Fulham Road. It contained one small, gas-fired living-room, one small double bedroom and a tiny single ditto off the former. It also contained a sink and draining-board in the minutest corridor which joined the two larger rooms together, but no cooker and no room whatever for a work-bench or store-cupboard of any sort or description. In addition, there was a bathroom/loo which, unless one person was in the bath, it was impossible for two people to occupy at the same time. For this accommodation the landlord required no 'key money' (a miracle) and five pounds a week – a sum which I suppose is the equivalent of about thirty pounds in today's money. If I was out of work for two weeks, God knows where I was going to find the rent, but at least I didn't have to put down any deposit. It was a monumental millstone to hang around my neck but it was also Hobson's choice. I leapt at it and even convinced myself that it was a 'cabin in the sky' dream home – which, as it was our first, in some ways it was.

Having secured the property, we then had to find the wherewithal to furnish it. Our wedding, taking place when it did, produced few practical presents. With the hundred pounds which was my parents' contribution, we had, thanks to a good discount at R. P. Carmichael's of Hull, already purchased a Regency dining table and three charming chairs of the same period (a bargain because they were an odd number), also a very attractive eighteenth-century circular, tripod-legged occasional table which went well with them. Pym, during the war, had had the foresight to buy a couple of Utility beds with their mattresses and fitted bedspreads made of a cherry-coloured hessian which were going cheap, but apart from that we were as bereft of mod. cons. as a couple of ancient Britons. The only practical thing to do, therefore, was to discuss the situation with my father, which I then did. His response was very much in accordance with Polonius's advice to Laertes. He offered me nothing from his own coffers but suggested that he should arrange with the bank (we fortunately shared the same branch manager) a two hundred-and-fifty pound overdraft for me which he would guarantee. This suited me fine. The following week Pym came down for a few days and off we went to spend it. It was a wild spree at the end of which we were left with exactly eight shillings. With this we entered the nearest off-licence, spent six-and-six-pence on a bottle of British sherry and then returned, happy as grigs, to Wetherby Gardens to share it with Geoffrey.

The following morning Pym returned to the north of England and within three weeks we were all installed together in our first home.

Cream Door came off at the end of May, but for the next two years Richard, to his eternal credit, kept me working fairly regularly in a variety of jobs, which was better than not working at all, though the salaries fell far short of what I needed. The first employment I undertook after the play closed, however, was one which I owed entirely to Geoffrey Hibbert. It was also to be, on and off, a long, happy and fruitful one.

The Late Joys, the old Victorian music-hall entertainment provided by the perennial Players Theatre Company, I had first visited in 1940 in its original home in King Street, Covent Garden, where I had gone as a guest of Joan Sterndale Bennett who was one of their regular artistes. I had also called in to see her on several occasions during my leave from the army, but by then it had moved to its wartime home of Albemarle Street. By 1947 it had moved again, this time to its present premises – underneath the arches below Charing Cross Station. Geoffrey had worked there occasionally during the war when, as a signalman at General Montgomery's headquarters, he had been stationed in London. He had also returned to them since his demob and was, at the time in question, back on the bill once again.

Leonard Sachs, who for years now has done the same job in the long-running television show *The Good Old Days*, was, throughout this period, its incomparable chairman – I speak in the Victorian music-hall sense. He was also its general administrator and leading light. In fact, Leonard Sachs *was* the Players Theatre.

'Get yourself a number and go and see him,' counselled Geoffrey. 'I've had a word with him and he's agreed to give you an audition.'

So – Geoffrey, with access to the Players Theatre music library, took me down to the theatre one afternoon and we selected a light, George Grossmith, Hayden Coffin type number – I forget who performed it originally – called 'I Must Go Home Tonight'.

With Geoffrey as my accompanist I learnt it, arranged a little routine with hat and cane and duly turned up to show it to Leonard Sachs. It appealed and I was on the bill three weeks later. It was to be the first of many numbers that I was to perform at the Players Theatre during the next four or five years.

From the actor's point of view, the joy of the Players in those days was that each bill ran for a fortnight, each contained about ten to twelve numbers and they never seemed to be put together very far in advance. Consequently, with the prevailing amiability of Leonard and his excellent staff, whenever one looked like being out of work, one could go up to them at very short notice and say, 'Can you pop me into the bill in three weeks' time?' and they would always bend over backwards to do so. Another advantage was that the show didn't start until quite late in the evening and, once again, this accommodating management would, if requested, slot one into the last part of the programme so that, if one was working in a play elsewhere in London, there was still time to go on to the Players and make an appearance there as well later.

My long connection with the Players Theatre was a very happy one. The salary was eight pounds a week for all, as well as reduced prices at the bar and in the supper-room. Everyone connected with the Players was the salt of the earth and I shall be ever grateful for the kindness and the way they looked after me during those early years of dire need.

A few weeks later I landed a job in a play written by an elderly female analytical psychologist. It was an eternal-triangle piece – husband, wife and mistress – but the novel twist, if such it can be called, was that each of the three characters was played by more than one person; one to each side of his or her character. Apart from thunderingly confusing the audience this also had the effect of packing the tiny little stage of the Mercury Theatre in Notting Hill Gate with so many actors that it was practically impossible to move. I played the male side of the wife, if you follow me – and if you do I'm delighted because I don't think many of the paying customers did. It wasn't surprising, really; I wore a contemporary dark suit over the top of which was placed a medieval tabard and a chain-mail cowl. I also carried a sword of the same period in a belt around my waist and sported a pair of trendy, brown-leather driving gauntlets. To complement this bizarre ensemble I had to wear my hair in a fetching roll at the front. To obtain this effect, Pym put it into rollers for me in the middle of every afternoon, which meant, of course, that I couldn't go out from four o'clock onwards. In the evening I travelled to the theatre by tube with my demob hat (a navy-blue pork-pie) balanced precariously on top of it all, and on arrival an actress called Ruth Lodge very kindly removed the rollers and combed it out for me.

The set, if such it could be called, had on one wall an enormous, heavy, empty, Victorian picture frame. At the dress rehearsal I asked our director, an immigrant American, what picture he was going to put in it. 'None,' was the answer I received, 'then everyone can imagine his own picture.' It was one of *those* productions and, somewhat understandably, at the end of its three week run it was never heard of again.

Five months later the same director showed himself in a more commercial vein. He sent me a copy of an American play called *Out of the Frying Pan*. It concerned the fortunes of six student actors – a word, in these days of the Sex Discrimination Act, I use in its all-embracing sense – who share an apartment in New York City. From a situation point of view it was really a transatlantic 12 Roland Gardens. The play, which had had a short run in New York, was, I thought, a funny one and the role offered to me was the lead. It was also one which, I was informed, had done great things over there for the young Alfred Drake. It was now to be performed for one week at the 'Q' Theatre, which at that time stood on the north bank of the Thames a stone's throw from Kew Bridge.

Our cast included two members of the original American company but the remainder were English.

Now, there is a phenomenon that often occurs amongst players while performing which is known in the profession as 'corpsing'. The outward manifestation of corpsing is that the players concerned become hysterical with laughter as a result of something, invariably undetected by those outside the frame, that has occurred on stage. The situation is then exacerbated by the fact that they have, by hook or by crook, to stifle their hysteria as it rarely fits in with the situation being presented. This in turn causes faces to turn the colour of a Post Office van, tears to roll down cheeks and blood to spout from bottom lips which have been viciously punctured by piercing eye-teeth in an attempt to maintain self-control. There is never any other reason for it all except that the participants have, even though no one else may share the joke, found something funny.

One day during our rehearsals for *Out of the Frying Pan*, while per-

forming a scene that involved about half-a-dozen of us, Alexander Arch-
dale, another Players Theatre artiste, and I could never get past a certain
line without 'corpsing'. Each time we reached it the rehearsal came to
a grinding halt. There was then a pause while we pulled our socks
together, after which we would all go back and start again. All went
swimmingly until we arrived once more at the same point, when disaster
struck again. After assailing the section three or four times, each with
the same result, the director broke the rehearsal and suggested that we
should both go outside and get some air for a few minutes. During the
break he took his two compatriots on one side and explained to them
quietly that he had been working over here for some time and he had
experienced this strange phenomenon with English actors before.

'You've gotta be patient, understanding and sympathetic,' he said. 'It's
not their fault. There is still rationing in this country, you know, and
it's all caused by a lack of red meat.'

I had pinned great hopes on *Out of the Frying Pan*. We opened on
Tuesday, 6 December. On the following morning a real Thames valley
'pea-souper' descended on the entire area from Hammersmith to Kew
and stayed there for six whole days. We played for the entire week to
practically empty houses, and not a soul who might have been in a position to offer me future employment and further my career came near the
place.

1947 was also notable for me personally as it provided two 'firsts' in my
life: my first appearances before both the television and the movie
cameras.

Television at that time was the exclusive prerogative of the BBC, which
possessed two studios only and both were located, back to back, in the
same building as the transmitter in Alexandra Palace. The reception area
was very local indeed and stretched no further than London and a limited
area of the Home Counties. This meant that many TV performances that
I was to give during the next few years were never seen by my family
up in Yorkshire.

My first ever television production was another revue and once again
I found myself working with Bill Fraser. It was an edited version of an
Eric Maschwitz show called *New Faces* which had run successfully at
the Comedy Theatre in 1940, and in which Bill had made his West End
debut as its leading man. It was also the show in which that celebrated
nightingale started singing in Berkeley Square and from which, regardless
of traffic jams and petrol fumes, it seems to have been warbling ever since.

Several other members of the original cast were in the production. Charles Hawtrey, now a stalwart of the *Carry On* films, John Bentley, for many years the leading man in *Crossroads,* and the vivacious red-headed Zoë Gail who had during the war years repeatedly declared her intention to get lit up when the lights went on in London.

My first impression of working in a television studio was that above all else it was nerve-racking. The small studio itself was always jam-packed with lights, cameras, microphone booms, technical staff, artistes and, in a musical, Eric Robinson and his entire orchestra which was no chamber ensemble; all of which made finding one's way around it akin to negotiating a commando assault course. Added to the horror was the fact that such negotiating, always done at the double during a revue because of the quick changes involved, included the added hazard of the whole thing being transmitted 'live'.

My first experience of working in a film studio, on the other hand, was the complete antithesis. Whereas at Alexandra Palace everything had been go, go, go, a feverish, frenetic few hours devoted to getting through the show as many times as possible before it went on the air that very evening, at Welwyn, where my talent was to be immortalised on 35 mm film for the first time, there appeared, by comparison, to be an inertia usually associated with mausoleums – much more, I am bound to say, my pace of working. Deadlines have always scared the life out of me. They are stimulating to those who find them necessary, but to me they are apt to produce panic and are, consequently, counter-productive. The film studio, therefore, immediately held more appeal for me than its television counterpart.

Anyway, as a result of my performance as the effeminate hotel receptionist in *Cream Door,* I landed a job as a *maître d'hôtel* in a swank restaurant in a film called *Bond Street.* Now, in 1947, in order to get to Welwyn for an early call, I had to set my alarm clock for 4.30 a.m. I had no car and there were no Tubes running at that hour, so I had ordered a taxi the night before. An early train out of King's Cross got me to my destination while it was still dark. I checked in, was given a dressing-room key and, after being made up, I climbed into my tail jacket and striped trousers and was on the set by 8.30 sharp. It was a large set, and also lounging around on it at the same inappropriate hour were about sixty extras all in full evening dress.

It is at moments like these that I have always admired the film actor. Next time you're at the cinema, or watching an old one at home on the box for that matter, stop for a moment to consider that passionate embrace between the leading man, in immaculate dinner jacket, and his leading lady, who, in the most revealing of Givenchy creations, stands with him on a moonlit terrace outside the Villa Bianco on the Italian riviera. More like than not it was performed in a freezing studio at 8.30 on a Monday morning in midwinter when both of them were half asleep; but don't let me spoil it for you.

In 1973, in the course of recording *Murder Must Advertise* for BBC television, I spent one whole night chasing poor Bridget Armstrong, who wore nothing but a dress of diaphanous tomato-coloured chiffon, through Burnham Beeches when the temperature was sub-zero and the ground-frost was sparkling like diamanté. Her face was blue and every time she opened her mouth to speak her breath condensed like steam from a boiling kettle. It was, of course, supposed to be midsummer. Not the least galling thing on such occasions is the fact that the director and all the technicians behind the camera are always muffled up to the eyebrows in scarves, anoraks, woolly caps, fur-lined gloves and several chunky sweaters; but, as I say, don't let me spoil it for you.

On this particular morning in the late autumn of 1947, however, I was very new to it all and as a result I was not only cold and tired but nervous to boot. The part, as I remember it, had but two lines: 'Good evening, sir' and 'Would you come this way, sir?' One shot – maybe two.

As is the way of things in film studios, the director decided to shoot the scene at the table between the two principal characters before he shot their entrance. This resulted in the arrival of 5.30 p.m., when filming finished for the day, without my having done a hand's turn. I removed my props and make-up and wearily set out on the journey back to Cranley Gardens where I arrived tired and hungry somewhere about nine.

The following morning at five o'clock I left home once again on the long haul back to Welwyn. The scene was eventually committed to celluloid somewhere about the same time, post meridian. When I returned to town that night the early rising and the tedium had, I decided, been well worth it – I was £40 richer than I had been forty-eight hours previously. But movies are a funny old world and the reasoning behind some of the executive decisions are, on occasions, hard to follow. I had been cast, the Lord be praised, for that part in *Bond Street* directly as a result of my performance in *She Wanted a Cream Front Door*. It could have been played for considerably less money by any 'extra' who would have jumped at both the opportunity and the additional 'bubble'.

Many years later, when I was playing the leading role in a film at Pinewood, I was sitting in the make-up chair one morning when the producer came into the room to talk to the make-up man about the minute part of a tramp who appeared in a scene due to be shot on the following day. He was carrying a copy of *Spotlight Casting Directory* – a vast tome containing glossy photographs of practically every performer in the profession. He had two fingers inserted in the volume, each marking a separate page. He opened it at the first one and, indicating the photograph of a clean-shaven, middle-aged actor, said to the make-up man, 'This is the guy that's going to play the tramp tomorrow' – he then flipped the pages over to the place marked by his second finger. There he indicated the photograph of another actor in a beard and heavy character make-up: 'And I want you to make him look like that one,' he continued.

They move in a mysterious way their wonders to perform.

Also in 1947 I appeared for four weeks with a distinguished cast of players at the Arts Theatre in a good modern comedy written by Rodney Ackland called *Cupid and Mars*, and Richard Stone, wearing his CSEU hat, had also employed me to produce two shows for Germany. But by Christmas of that year, though I had been demobilised for fifteen months, during which time it must appear that I was seldom out of work, the financial side of my life was proving a disaster. At the end of the last quarter of 1947 I had to pocket my pride and beg a loan from my father to pay the landlord, otherwise we would have been out in the street. The following year Pym had to sell a family heirloom – a three-stone diamond ring that was left to her by her great-aunt – to enable us to make ends meet. It was a worrying and disheartening two years. We had no car, no fridge, no TV and only a hired radio. Whenever I appeared on television during those months Pym had three options if she wished to see me: she could go round to Richard and Sara's and watch it with them, do likewise with an old 30 Corps Theatrical Pool friend who had settled not far from us in Chelsea, or she could go and catch it in a soulless viewing-room in Broadcasting House. It was several years before we owned our first set and even then it was only made possible by my mother-in-law being kind enough to put down the necessary deposit for us.

It was an even longer time before we owned our first motor-car and the lack of one added considerably to my depression at that time. After the wide open spaces of north-west Europe, around which I had gallivanted footloose and fancy free during the previous two years, I was now suffering badly from claustrophobia. I paced around that tiny garret flat like a tiger in a cage. It was, I suppose, all part of the adjusting to Civvy Street once again. Many men of my age, I think, suffered it, but that didn't make it any easier to come to terms with. There were, however, small mercies to be thankful for and these were all provided by the warmth, loyalty and affection of a bunch of very dear friends, some of whom were suffering the same traumas and all of whom, plus coincidence and a small world, had deposited within a few streets of each other after His Gracious Majesty had disposed of their services.

Bill d'Arcey, whose television Pym used to go and watch, was a kind, soft-spoken Irishman. He had been an officer in the Royal Artillery and for the final year of his service life had been an actor touring Germany in one of our Pool productions. Before moving to Chelsea, he and his pretty little wife, Sue, had had a flat only round the corner from us in the Old Brompton Road. Geoffrey, who had now settled in Wetherby Gardens, had a girl-friend in the final play in which he had appeared for me in Germany, an attractive, dark-haired ENSA lass called Prudence Rennick, and she, whom he eventually married, had returned to live with her parents in a basement flat practically next door to him. John Moore, my constant companion during the campaign in north-west Europe and with whom I had temporarily lost touch, had, on demobilisation, joined the Foreign Office and then taken a flat in Sydney Place a mere five minutes' walk away.

Also in Cranley Gardens were Patrick McNee and his wife, both pre-war Webber–Douglas students and old friends, and Donald Houston, another chum with whom I had only recently appeared on that crowded stage at the Mercury Theatre, was soon to move into the area with his effervescent and diminutive red-headed wife, Brenda. The Houstons set their stall out in Drayton Gardens, two streets away, and almost next door to the Drayton Arms where most of us would meet for apéritifs on a Sunday morning. We were all struggling, we all had little money, but the bond of friendship bound us together and kept us ebullient.

In early 1948 Peter Haddon wrote a play in partnership with a journalist, for which he went into management himself in order to produce. Peter had been very kind and encouraging to me ever since *Cream Door*. He was many years my senior, but he offered me his friendship and advice in the most generous manner. On several occasions he came down to the Players to catch my act and give me pointers as to how I could improve it.

Peter was a widower. He had been married to Cicely Courtneidge's sister who died when their immensely talented daughter Rosaline was born; thereafter he became devoted to his sister-in-law.

Peter had been a light comedian of considerable stature between the wars, having graduated from the Cambridge Footlights to the demanding schools of Charlot and Robert Courtneidge in which he learned his trade. The sort of roles in which he excelled were those of the silly-ass Englishman, a type which had become rather *démodé* after the Second World War, and as a result I think he experienced a bit of a problem finding a new *métier* for himself. He tried everything, even the music-hall, with an application and tenacity which was typical of him. Towards the end of his life he took a lease on the Wimbledon Theatre which he ran successfully for several years.

Peter, I think, could be fairly described as an endearing eccentric. He would frequently turn up at the theatre for an evening performance wearing a pair of none too well pressed cavalry twill trousers, down-at-heel suede desert boots, a blue and black open-necked hockey shirt, a jacket of battledress blouse design and a very battered, chocolate-brown felt hat worn far forward over his eyes and forehead.

His voice was 'blah', his vowels tending to be distorted, but except in very serious moments everything he said was underscored with infectious bubbles of laughter. He galumphed a bit too – he was a very tall man. He was also a great gesticulator and all in all he had no difficulty in holding an audience either on stage or in a drawing-room.

In the late '40s Peter lived with his daughter in a ground-floor studio flat in Stratford Road on the border of Earls Court and Kensington, an area well within the range of our Sunday afternoon walks and we used to call on him regularly. His flat was light and roomy and in many ways it reflected his life and personality. The large, all-purpose living-room, which boasted two huge studio-light windows, had a wall-to-wall floor covering made by joining together three carpets from his pre-war home, none of which was large enough to do the job on its own. One was a rich burgundy and the other two were the individual blues of the Oxbridge universities. It had no fire, but a huge hard-fuel boiler around which was gathered his sofa and chairs. One end of the room housed a light wood dining-room suite of a trendy 1930s design and the wall over his desk at the opposite end was packed tight, from floor to high ceiling, with framed 10 × 8 inch glossy photographs which provided a pictorial record of his not inconsiderable career. He also had a fine collection of ivory animals and with these he would play with Lee on the floor for hours on end.

Peter's play, *Tomorrow Is A Lovely Day*, was not, I'm afraid, really good enough and after five weeks of touring, during which the rewriting that went on was prodigious, he finally decided to close it on the road. I was engaged to play the part of an English public school journalist and was generously granted a weekly salary that exceeded any other that I had hitherto received in the theatre by six pounds. Peter was a generous man and the extra loot gave me a considerable psychological boost. I felt that I had at last arrived as a properly paid, middle-grade, potential West End actor. Unhappily it was for so short a time.

As a result of the premature demise of *Tomorrow Is A Lovely Day*, I returned to town little richer and no less befuddled than I had been at the beginning of the year. My future was still as uncertain. I was still rent with the inner turmoil as to whether or not I was treading the right path for myself and my family, and I was still searching for something to fill the gaping void that had been left in my vitals as the result of the loss of the huge responsibilities that I had carried during the last three years. Frequently since those early years people have paid me the most undeserved compliments about my steadfastness of purpose. I never possessed any such thing. It was all cowardice. I hadn't the guts to tackle the alternative – or perhaps just the guts to make a decision. But then, you see, I am a Gemini – and if nobody else does, I know other Geminians will understand.

For the moment, therefore, I weakly allowed the dicta about the ploughman and his plough and the cobbler and his last to predominate in my thinking, and, closing my eyes to the dangers ahead, I put my foot hard down and on we all roared.

That said, however, a pattern was beginning to emerge and it seemed to be a musical one. My talents, such as they were, seemed to lie in the mould of the light-comedy juvenile song-and-dance man and I was, ironically, destined, for the time being anyway, to follow almost exactly in the footprints left behind by Peter Haddon fifteen to twenty years previously.

CHAPTER SIXTEEN

ALLY PALLY AND THE SEA

Enter MICHAEL MILLS – *a benefactor*

Shortly before I joined Peter Haddon's company, someone entered my professional life who was going to have a profound and recurring influence upon it for the next twenty-three years. His name was – indeed, still is – Michael Mills.

Michael, a short, pipe-smoking product of Westminster School and the Royal Navy, is marginally older than me and at that time he was a light entertainment producer for BBC Television. All the time I have known Michael he has worn a dark goatee which, like his hair, not before time, has finally conceded a smattering of 'pepper and salt'. Until only a few years ago he was a confirmed bachelor and, like many such, sartorially he was always a bit of a scruff. Dark, unvaleted suits (rarely can I remember seeing him in anything less formal), collars and ties slightly creased, black shoes of a decidedly masculine design, and, if it was winter, over the top of it all, a biscuit-coloured duffel coat. Occasionally he would surprise everyone by sporting under his suit (invariably navy blue – natch) a Tyrolean waistcoat that he had picked up in his travels. In the TV studio, when he removed his jacket and waistcoat, his trousers were more often than not supported by a pair of either bright scarlet or bright orange braces. These had, in a crowded TV studio, the same practical and beneficial effect that workmen on our roads now obtain from 'Dayglow' jerkins of the same hues: you could see him a mile off.

Michael has an abundance of energy and is also articulate and well read. Another enviable quality he possessed, at that time, was that, despite his lack of foppery, he always had the most super-looking birds in tow. He is now married to that corking girl Valerie Leon who came to the fore (yes, I think that's the right word) a few years ago by trying to persuade a gullible television public that it wasn't the male animal but the aftershave that was turning her on.

Today Michael is still performing the same job as a freelance and 'twixt then and now there is very little that he hasn't done in his own particular field. In January 1948, however, he was one of the pioneers of the medium and he was in the process of producing and directing three half-hour TV revues starring, written and composed by a young Welshman called Cliff Gordon. Cliff died young; a tragically wasted and dissipated talent. The revues were called, each independently, *Once*, *Twice* and *Thrice Upon A Time*. Michael employed me in the second of them. Now he was about to launch himself on an epic one-hour spectacular called *The Passing Show*.

The Passing Show was to be a parade of numbers out of musical shows that spanned 1900–1920. It was to have a narrator and was to include scrapbook film clips of world events which took place during the years concerned. It was the sort of show at which Michael excels. His sense of period is always observant and one-hundred-per-cent respectful. He engaged Freddie Carpenter, another dab hand with period material, to arrange the numbers and do the choreography, a small company to perform them and Geraldo and his Orchestra to provide the music. In this splendid package he invited me to be the song and dance juvenile. I had, without knowing it, at last slipped into a niche which was eventually to be both enjoyable and profitable for me.

I think probably the biggest kick I got out of *The Passing Show* was arriving at the Band Call to go over my numbers with Geraldo. Gerry had emerged from the war as just about the biggest thing there was on the British dance music scene and my only previous experience of the great man was when, at the age of fourteen, during a holiday at Llandudno, I had asked him for his autograph after a Sunday concert with his Gaucho Tango Orchestra. Here was fulfilment in full measure.

One day towards the end of rehearsals for *The Passing Show*, after we had finished for the day in a large hall at the back of the Cumberland Hotel, Michael asked me to go and have a cup of tea with him in a greasy spoon 'caff' just across the road. He told me that as soon as *The Passing Show* was finished he was going straight into rehearsals with a pre-war musical comedy called *Tell Her The Truth*; would I, he asked, play the Peter Haddon part?

'Here it is,' he said. 'Take it away and read it.'

I swallowed my tea, dashed home and three hours later I had finished it. Peter had originally played it sixteen years previously at the Saville Theatre and the piece itself, though slightly dated, was, nevertheless, still highly serviceable for television in 1948. Anyway, I had neither the heart nor the head for altruism. It was a zonking great light-comedian's role complete with a love interest and musical numbers – in every way the sort of part I had always dreamed about playing; the sort I felt in my bones I should be playing and which, so far, nobody but Michael had ever offered me. I was over the moon.

The following morning I returned the book to him feeling like I hadn't felt since Sir Kenneth Barnes had offered me Flute in *A Midsummer Night's Dream* back in my student days. Was this to be the breakthrough? Well, not quite – but it was most certainly the first step in the right direction. *The Passing Show* and *Tell Her The Truth* were only the first of ten musical shows in which I was to appear for Michael during the next two years.

Tell Her The Truth was followed by *Lady Luck*, another pre-war musical comedy, and in that I worked for the first time with a most engaging comedian called Desmond Walter-Ellis. Desmond could never have been anything else in our profession other than a comedian. He is tall and gangling and the possessor of a horse-like mouthful of teeth and a nose of almost Cyrano proportions. He is a gentle, soft-spoken, unaggressive comedian and I was not the only one to find him very funny indeed.

There were three male roles of stature in *Lady Luck*. The principal one was played by a leading comedian of the day called George Gee, I played the light-comedy juvenile and Desmond was cast in the one that slotted in somewhere between the two. We established an immediate rapport which Michael was quick to spot. The moment *Lady Luck* was over he engaged us both to appear together once again.

This time we were to supply the linking comedy in an original show which he was devising for transmission at the end of the year. It was another Michael Mills special. His idea, spawned perhaps by his *Passing Show* production, was again steeped in nostalgia. Instead of spanning twenty years, however, this one was to take place on one evening only – New Year's Eve 1909. During it two young Edwardian 'cards' – Desmond and I – decked out in full evening dress, top hats, cloaks and canes would undertake a carefree, and, as the evening wore on, a slightly inebriated tour of London's theatres and music-halls. We were, of course, purely a peg on which to hang a number of musical items which, indeed, had played in those theatres on that date. It was a splendid idea and an engaging entertainment it made too. It was called *Give My Regards to Leicester Square*.

In any form of the performing arts, when a certain indefinable rapport between two people ignites iridescent sparks – a state of union now referred to as 'chemistry' – it is foolhardy and commercially stupid not to exploit it to the full. When it occurs in the field of comedy it is especially to be nurtured, for such a union is a blessed one. I believe that Desmond and I had such chemistry. I certainly found enormous pleasure and fulfilment in our work together. Some performers are loners and prefer merely to have supporting players around them who will act as their ciphers. That has never supplied me with anything like the magical levitation that is induced by working in harness with a kindred spirit. Such an attainment is rare. It has happened to me maybe three or four times throughout my career and on those occasions the playing of scenes together has provided an exhilaration seldom experienced outside orgasm. Michael Mills must have shared my views as he was soon to cast us together again in yet another pre-war musical play – *Jill Darling*.

Jill Darling was another product of the Saville Theatre which had originally starred a comedian called Arthur Riscoe and an up-and-coming young actor called John Mills. This time Desmond and I were to play their respective roles. Vivian Ellis's charming score was rearranged by Paul Fenoulhet (leader of the wartime Skyrockets Orchestra) for a modern combination of six saxophones and eight brass, and we were also joined in the vocal department by the Keynotes – the 'in' vocal group of the day. Freddie Carpenter was roped in once again to arrange the dances which made the whole thing feel like 'old home week'.

Michael employed another daring innovation in his production of *Jill Darling*. As already explained, there were only two studios in Alexandra Palace; for *Jill Darling* he used both of them. This introduced several new hazards into a 'live' performance of television, as if the ones already inherent were not enough. For the first time the musical numbers were performed with the orchestra in one studio, while the artistes, receiving the accompaniment through loudspeakers, were in another. The extra acting area thus provided was a welcomed boon but not to be able to see one's conductor was initially the most hair-raising experience, particularly as the show was going out 'live'. Hazard number two was the possibility of arriving to play a scene completely out of breath as a result of having just belted, pell-mell, down the corridor from one studio to the other in the middle of transmission. Finally, Becher's Brook was represented by the large scene-door of one of the studios having to be left wide open throughout the entire show to accommodate a section of the set. This last necessity meant that if any uninformed supernumerary not connected with the production happened to stray into the vicinity whistling, say, the waltz song from *Tom Jones*, it would, unless he was in the same key, be a bit discordant with Marie Seller and I who were giving out with 'I'm on a see-saw'. No, Michael was nothing if not a trail-blazer

Television from
Alexandra Palace

LEFT Give My Regards to
Leicester Square – *with
Desmond Walter-Ellis*

BELOW The Passing Show –
*doing the 'Tickle Toe' with
Lois Green*

RIGHT Tell Her The Truth
– *with Frances Marsden,
Edward Rigby Jnr, Diana
Decker and Charles
Hawtrey*

BELOW RIGHT Lady Luck –
*with George Gee and
Michael Balfour*

BELOW FAR RIGHT Jill Darling
– *with Marie Sellar*

and living dangerously seemed to attract him with the same magnetism that had drawn my brigadier to it in 30th Armoured Brigade.

For the moment, however, we must leave Ally Pally because running concurrently with all that television activity was a whole mountain of work that I was to undertake for Richard Stone, who seemed determined to extract the maximum amount of recompense out of me in return for all those months of bringing my breakfast to me in our office in Germany.

Richard is difficult to describe physically because he is very much the man in the street. If you were told to meet him at Victoria Station off the 8.10 a.m. commuter train from Purley, you'd be hard pressed to find him. He is about a year my senior but, because his hair started to recede quite early in life, he has possibly always looked that much older.

He is a product of Charterhouse School, saw war service in North Africa and Italy in addition to north-west Europe, was awarded the Military Cross and speaks with round, clipped, elocution-trained diction. His conversation at that time was always one-hundred-per-cent shop and, apart from a bit of shrimping when he was at the seaside, he had no other interest outside his work. Whether Richard would have made a good actor is purely academic because from the word 'go' he only really wanted to be involved with the business side of the theatre. His first job out of RADA was to enter management. He took a small theatre in Saltburn on the north-east coast for the summer season and into it he put his own concert party in which he also appeared as an actor-manager. It was no surprise therefore when he now, in addition to holding down his job at the War Office (one he was soon to relinquish) and running his theatrical agency in partnership with Felix de Wolfe, decided to go into the production of his own summer shows – and that is where I was to come in.

In the summer of 1948 he obtained a lease of the Jolly Roger Theatre at Clacton. The Jolly Roger, more of a floral hall without the flora really, was situated at the very end of a quite unique pier – probably the only freehold, privately owned pier in the country – and it was the property of an indomitable, elderly power-house of a lady called Mrs Kingsman. Her son was her henchman and adjutant but, make no mistake, Mrs Kingsman was the one in charge and the sight of her small dowdy figure – which was to be seen daily, walking-stick in hand, hobbling up and down her domain – disguised the authority of an admiral bestriding the bridge of his battleship. In addition to the Jolly Roger at the seaboard extremity of her empire, there was another theatre at the land end. This was a more modern and better-equipped fun palace known as the Ocean Theatre, and in the summer of 1948 Tony Hancock was leading the company that was appearing there. Other attractions included a vast figure-of-eight roller-coaster and a large open-air swimming-pool. It was practically impossible to move, or even sit down or go to the loo, on Mrs Kingsman's pier without spending money, and her mind was a good match for Richard's. She thought of everything. When, in due course, we opened *The Lagoon Follies* in the Jolly Roger, she sought me out on the morning of our first night to enquire exactly what time our curtain would come down. Her concern was not for us or anything to do with the show, it was purely so that she could issue concise instructions to her son which would ensure that the public lavatories would not be locked up until twenty minutes after the theatre had been emptied. She was a remarkable lady.

Richard's first post-war essay into management, which he asked me to produce for him, was a very modest affair indeed. It was nothing more or less than a six-handed concert party – three boys, three girls and a pianist. By trade, as it were, they answered as follows: the men – principal comedian, light-comedian and baritone; the girls – comedienne, soprano and general purpose girl who was also wife and feed to the principal comedian. The producer's job with such a company was an all-embracing one. The budget was minimal – almost non-existent, in fact – so he was responsible for finding all the material, finding the costumes, finding the props, even constructing and painting the very limited items of scenery which were essential to the sketches and then generally sewing it all together and getting it on to the stage.

The company carried two programmes which alternated every Thursday, thus ensuring that holidaymakers who visited the resort for one week only had the opportunity of seeing two different shows during their stay. The artistes concerned in the enterprise, while doing a splendid job at the Jolly Roger, have since faded from the theatrical scene, so no names, no pack drill, but two years later in the same theatre we gave the principal comedian's job to a young man making his first appearance in this capacity called Terry Scott – and the experience doesn't seem to have held him back in any way.

I was to develop a potent love–hate relationship with this whole form of entertainment. It was, however, one with which I was to become increasingly involved during the next few years.

For the last of the present round of productions for Richard (I had immediately followed Clacton with four more at the Dolphin Theatre, Brighton) he once again asked me to produce a show to tour Germany. The usual sort of offering: song and dance, comedy and the odd variety act. He had the whole show cast with the exception of the principal comedian.

Now it so happened that at that time Donald Houston had just landed the most sought-after job that was currently being offered to a young actor in British movies. For some while the studio concerned had been searching around for a young man to play opposite Jean Simmons in *The Blue Lagoon*. To put the situation in a more modern context, it was a search as long and seemingly endless as the one that was to be mounted several years later for an actor to play '007'. It was a great coup for the unknown Donald and a few days later, jubilant and exhilarated, before departing for Fiji to start location work, he bought several new items for his wardrobe and then invited a small and select band of friends to have a celebratory dinner with him at the Landsdowne Restaurant, now the International Sporting Club, in Berkeley Square. Frank Weir, his clarinet and small orchestra occupied the bandstand, and it was a great dine and dance evening. Few, if any of us, could have afforded such a spree ourselves (the previous week, for that matter, neither could Donald) and it was a most kind and exuberant splurge of generosity.

As if he hadn't already done us more than proud at the Lansdowne, he then piled us all into taxis and took the entire party to a night-club in Regent Street called the Windermere. Bottles were placed on the table and we were well into both the gin and the whisky when somewhere about 1 a.m. the cabaret started. By 1.15 we were all hysterical with laughter. Humour is a great divider, but on this occasion there was no dissenter; we were all convulsed. Out on the dance floor was a comedian new to us all. He was a huge man – six-feet-plus tall and practically the same across the shoulders. He wore a dinner jacket and had the audience eating out of the palm of his hand with conjuring tricks, all of which ended in disaster. He had an enormous chin and long, lank locks of hair which protruded below a fez. He was excruciatingly funny and he was, of course, Tommy Cooper.

The next morning I telephoned Richard and said I thought I had found our principal comedian. That night we returned to the Windermere together; Richard went 'snap' and during the following week, after somewhat protracted negotiations with his manager, he was ours.

Rehearsals required all my understanding and tact and I think I was probably lacking in both; but I am not really sure what else I could have done. Tommy, after his act at the club every night, never got to bed before 4 a.m. We started rehearsals in Eaton Square, a long way from his home, at 10 a.m. He pleaded that he couldn't be with us until the afternoon which, though concerned, I understood. There was a lot of ensemble work in the show – sketches, comedy routines, musical scenas – and Tommy, as principal comedian, was obviously required in most of them. His own act was, as always, a winner, but he was at that time inexperienced in production work and I don't think he was very happy in it either – a situation which was exacerbated by my concern at valuable rehearsal time going begging and Tommy's increasing tiredness as the days went by.

I am sure the final result was successful when it arrived in Germany – it would be difficult to imagine Tommy not being a success – but I can't speak as an eyewitness. As with all my work for CSEU, my job finished with the final dress rehearsal in this country – I never travelled overseas with a single show, not even to see it through the first week.

As 1948 drew to a close I again started my soul-searching. I was anxious. I was tormented with self-doubt and I was still in a welter of indecision. My life, at that time, I kept seeing in the form of an express train that was careering at breakneck speed towards the edge of a precipice and in it I, the driver, stood stupefied, totally incapable of doing anything to stop it. It was a nightmare. This incapability was at total variance with the resolution and industry that I applied to my work. I was mystified. Why could I be so rocklike and decisive about so many things, and so weak and vacillating about others? I don't know; it has been the enigma of my life. I am convinced that those perishing Geminian twins are mostly responsible but that never helps me to conquer their divisive influences. So then as now, I had to learn to live with them.

An additional responsibility now entered our lives. Pym had just been declared pregnant again and our Cranley Gardens attic was no place for an expectant mother. Climbing up and down seventy-eight stairs at least twice a day carrying a two-year-old baby and a heavy shopping basket was exhausting enough on its own, to continue doing it while pregnant was, we both agreed, imprudent to say the least. It was fortunate, therefore, that my first big break – a break which was to provide me with the training on which my whole career as a light-comedian owed its success – was just around the corner, and before the end of the year we would be moving out of Cranley Gardens for ever.

CHAPTER SEVENTEEN

PALM BEACH AND HELVETIA

Enter LEO FRANKLYN – *a comedian*

In 1949 a sprightly Lancastrian octogenarian cinema owner, who some referred to as a millionaire, decided that his life was becoming dull and mundane. Bolton, the heart of his empire, had presumably ceased to stimulate his belated craving for adventure, so he resolved to diversify into something that would provide him with either additional verve – or alternatively, no doubt, a heart attack.

Despite his apparent exuberance, John Buckley looked frail. He was of medium height, skeletal in frame and moved slowly with a stick. Sartorially his appearance was the epitome of that other millionaire figure; the one who does not wear silk shirts, diamond tie-pins and vicuna overcoats. John Buckley obviously didn't believe in spending a lot of money on his personal wardrobe – not regularly, at any rate – and because of this he was not always the best advertisement for his outfitters. His clothes generally, though no doubt of excellent quality, seemed to be decades out of date and they hung on his undernourished figure in folds like the skin on a baby rhinoceros. An almost perfect impersonation of John Buckley is given by the actor who plays the chairman of Grace Bros – the store in the BBC TV series *Are You Being Served?* – and as David Croft, the producer and co-author of it, also worked for Mr Buckley at this time, I would be surprised if the fact was a coincidence. Nevertheless John Buckley was a kind and friendly man, as I was soon to find out.

The diversification he now sought took him into the realms of theatrical management and in March of that year he opened two productions – one, *Belinda Fair*, a musical in partnership with Leslie Henson, at the Saville Theatre, and the other, a provincial tour of a beautiful thirty-year-old operetta called *The Lilac Domino* by the Frenchman Charles Cuvillier. The latter piece, set in glamorous Palm Beach, had an enchanting score and a romantic, fairytale plot – i.e., nothing so distracting that it would interfere with the music or be sufficient to tax the grey matter of the most undemanding theatre-goer. It was also obligatory in the many similar musical shows that proliferated in the first half of this century that there should be comic relief. Such relief was invariably only tenuously connected with the plot and nobody minded very much if it was, in fact, totally extraneous to it. The comic relief in *The Lilac Domino* was supplied by one principal comedian and one light comedian, who also served as feed to his better half. The two characters were inseparable; whenever one was on the stage so was the other – they ran side by side through the entire evening.

Jack Hylton had presented a revival of *The Lilac Domino* at His Majesty's Theatre in 1944 and in it the principal comedian had been a highly experienced performer called Leo Franklyn. John Buckley now acquired the touring rights of the piece, I suspect Jack Hylton's sets and costumes, and certainly his principal comedian. Freddie Carpenter was then engaged to direct it and with Freddie's influence, coupled with a certain amount of push from Arnold Taylor, John Buckley's production manager, who had always been a fan of my work at the Players, I was contracted to play the part of Norman – the foil to Leo Franklyn's Prosper. The production was to tour the provinces for twenty-four weeks and from the outset the whole tenor of my life changed. My nagging doubts as to my future finally vanished and the optimism that replaced them was also, I am delighted to say, shared by my hitherto anxious bank manager. It was to be the emergence of Ian Carmichael, light comedian, for the very first time in full-sized commercial theatres, and the credit goes in its entirety to the training, coaxing and encouragement of one man – Leo Franklyn.

The whole company assembled for the first time one Monday morning on the stage at the Victoria Palace. My first meeting with Leo was very much a 'hello and good-bye' affair, but he struck me immediately as being friendly. He was, at that time, playing 'dame' in pantomime at the Palace Theatre, Manchester, and consequently was unable to attend regular rehearsals in London. The plan was, therefore, that when the pantomime closed on Saturday, 12 March, *The Lilac Domino* would open in the same theatre on the following Monday. To achieve this, Leo, who knew the part anyway, was excused the majority of the London rehearsals and for the final week the entire company would assemble in Manchester and complete them there. In a way this was fortunate for me as without Leo there was little, if anything, that I could personally rehearse, which enabled me to concentrate on our immediate domestic affairs.

The tour was to be a long one; Cranley Gardens had now become more of a liability than an asset, so the only sensible thing to do seemed to be to give two weeks' notice, store what little furniture we possessed and for Pym and Lee, for the time being, to return to live with her parents in Sleights. This would, at one fell swoop, both ensure the expectant mother's good health and also relieve us of the millstone of the weekly rent in London. In addition, it would also mean that, with an increased salary of £25 a week, I might now, at long last, have an opportunity to accumulate some tangible savings. So this plan we now adopted.

Pym's mother came down to stay for our last two nights in the flat in order to help pack up, and then to escort mother, child and cat back up to Yorkshire. On the last Saturday morning the removal men arrived early and after the place had been gutted I accompanied the three girls to King's Cross and put them on a train for the north. If the truth be known, the whole manœuvre was, though a sad parting, a blessing in disguise because we were down to our last farthing. I didn't even have the money for their rail fares; my dear mother-in-law financed the entire move.

That week the whole of north-east England was shrouded in a mantle of deep, crisp snow and the local postman who had, by private arrangement, driven to York to pick up my tired and cold family had had considerable difficulty in traversing the heights of the normally majestic North Yorkshire Moors between Whitby and Pickering. This stretch of the English countryside, for most of the year, is breathtakingly beautiful. In winter, however, it can be cruel. It is one of the first places in England to get snow when it is in the air and winds, sweeping its bleak expanses, can cause mountainous drifts which make the roads impassable and many of its villages become cut off for days. On the return journey, therefore, before negotiating the final twenty-mile stretch to Whitby, the driver thought it prudent to call at the Pickering police station, the last place of civilisation before reaching Sleights on the other side of the moors, to enquire 'the prospects of play' as it were. His worst fears were realised – the road was blocked and would not be passable until the snow ploughs could be got to work the following morning. That night my mother-in-law, my wife, my two-year-old daughter and our coal-black cat, which seemed to be failing dismally in its traditional role of talisman, all slept fully clothed in one double bed in a pub in Pickering market-place; the postman, with a commendable sense of propriety, opted to shake down on a sofa in the bar parlour.

The following day the road was temporarily cleared and they all arrived home to be greeted by my relieved father-in-law. There both my wife and daughter were to remain for the next twelve months, and when eventually they were to travel south again, there would be three of them.

Having seen them all off at King's Cross, I then set out for Euston and the train for Manchester, and that night I went to see Leo's pantomime at the Palace.

It was a beautifully mounted production. The comedy, as always with Leo involved, was infectiously funny and as pure as driven snow. Here was glamour: a big show in a big theatre and in one week's time I too would be up there doing it myself in a similarly mounted production. All of which made considerable amends for the concurrent collapse of my personal family life.

In March 1949 I was twenty-eight and Leo Franklyn was two weeks off his fifty-third birthday. He was on the short side – stumpy might be a good way of describing him – and by the time I knew him he was going very thin on top. His voice was a bit gravel-boxy – an occupational afflic-tion that seemed to affect many comedians before the days of theatre amplification. He loved his work, at which he was very expert, having spent many years in musical comedies and pantomimes in this country, Australia and South Africa. He also loved his golf and cricket, both of which he played for most of his long life. He was always a remarkably fit and agile man. He loved life – I can never remember seeing Leo down in the dumps. He married one Mary Rigby, a most strikingly attractive woman who hailed from a longstanding theatrical family; she was his constant companion. Between them they spawned one son – William – who has inherited both his father's flair for comedy and his love of sport.

After having caught the performance on that Saturday night, I went round to see him in his dressing-room. I found him, as always two minutes after curtain-down, stark naked except for a jock-strap with a tumbler of gin and water in his hand.

'Come in, dear boy, come in.' Mary was sitting there looking radiant. 'Mummy' – he always called her 'Mummy' – 'Mummy, pour the boy a "Gunga" – he probably needs one.'

A moment later I was handed a large Gordon's gin and told to sit down. Gordon's gin I like but I never took to his habit of diluting it with plain water.

'Now then,' he said, starting to remove his predominantly pink dame's make-up – the figure he cut at that moment was hysterical. 'What are you doing for supper?'

'The landlady's leaving me something cold,' I replied.

'That's no good for a growing lad, is it, Mummy? You're coming back with us to the Midland. From now until we open you and I have got to live in each other's pockets. We've got to learn everything we can about each other – what makes us tick, what makes us laugh, what makes us cry, our individual quirks and foibles – we've got to learn to think as one man. All right?'

'Fine,' I replied.

'Good. Then, when we've opened, we can relax a bit. Do you chase the elusive pill?'

I was already beginning to see the wisdom of our getting to know each other as soon as possible; Leo talked a language of his own.

'Do I what?' I asked.

'Do you chase the elusive pill?' Then in answer to my blank expression, 'Golf, old lad, golf. Do you play golf?'

'Frequently, but not very well.'

'That doesn't matter, does it, Mummy? Get some good fresh air into your lungs, that's what matters. You can't work in this business unless you're fit. Anyway, we're going to enjoy the next few months, you and I. I can't wait to get out of these skirts and into a pair of trousers again. Give him another "Gunga", Mummy.' And so it went on.

The Lilac Domino opened to packed houses, a credit to Leo's popularity, and that week, my salary being on a sliding scale dependent upon the box office receipts, I earned an extra ten pounds.

Our first entrance together was about six minutes after curtain-up. The setting was the lounge of the casino at Palm Beach and the two of us were, supposedly, being ejected from a gambling saloon situated off-stage. Leo couldn't bear standing in the wings. His dressing-room was nearly always the one nearest the stage but it could, nevertheless, still be some distance away; on some occasions even on the next floor. I had to get used, very early on, to having to stand waiting alone night after night as our entrance drew nearer and nearer with no sign whatever of my partner. He would leave his dressing-room at the very last possible moment and, slap on cue, he would burst through the swing doors at the back of the stage – banging, shouting, stamping, 'rhubarbing' past me and all the chorus who were also standing in the wings and were encouraged to join in the cacophony – tear up off-stage steps on to a rostrum at the back of the set and shoot straight out on to the stage with me trailing in his wake. He never once missed an entrance. If the audience had been dozing before his arrival, they were certainly wide awake by the time he reached the footlights.

'Still We Smile' – *with Leo Franklyn in* The Lilac Domino

The first scene we had together he used as a thermometer. If the house was receptive – no problem. If they were sluggish and slow to respond, when he came off he'd say, 'They're tough tonight, Ian, old lad – tough. We've got to go out and get 'em, me old china. Wake 'em up.' Our next scene he would take at such a cracking pace the audience didn't know what had hit them. He never gave them time to laugh. If ever they tried to he cut them short. Then gradually, bit by bit, as if giving a horse its head in the final furlong, he'd gradually loosen the rein. He'd let them laugh a bit more and a bit longer each time, until finally we were past the post and we'd leave the stage to a roar of approbation and a round of applause.

'They're all right now, Ian,' he'd say as we returned to our dressing-rooms. 'We've got 'em, boy. We've got 'em.' It was an object lesson in the art of stagecraft.

Another lesson I used to receive was on most Saturday nights. After weeks of touring, several members of the cast would wish to catch the last train to London to spend the weekend with their loved ones. This was frequently a very close call. The curtain would probably come down at about 10.55 and the train would be due out at 11.05. There were props to be got out of, make-up to be removed and packed away, and the distance from the theatre to the station to be covered in ten minutes flat.

On such occasions, Leo would arrive on stage for our first entrance of the second house fractionally earlier than normal.

'Right, "train version", Ian – "train version",' he'd instruct. 'No time for double-takes. No mucking about. Bing, bang, wallop – straight through. We've only ten minutes in which to catch that puffer. Got to get home to Mummy.'

The musical side of the show was an immovable feast that would take the same time every night. The only slack that could be taken up, therefore, was in the comedy which had little to do with the plot anyway. During 'train version' performances pages used to go. I never knew where the cuts were coming – they were never rehearsed – I just had to be right on the ball the whole time ready to pick up a quick pass whenever it came. It was an exhilarating experience. The curtain could come down on those occasions as much as five minutes early and because of the tightness of the performance it was often the best of the week.

Leo was never a selfish comic. I was always allowed my own laughs (except in the 'train version'). Very early on in the run he suggested a bit of business for me to do with my hat at a moment of acute embarrassment. This I built up over the weeks until eventually the whole thing took about a minute. He would just stand there beside me, patiently watching, letting me get on with it until the laugh began to fade and then, at precisely the right moment, he'd come in, clip it off and we'd carry on with the scene.

Off-stage he was something of a practical joker, though never cruel. I remember an occasion during the forty-minute wait between the houses one Saturday. Two of the kids from the chorus – both of them about eighteen years old – were going out for a quick cuppa. Leo saw them as they passed his door. He called them in.

'Are you going out, girls?'

'Yes, Mr Franklyn.'

'Do me a favour, would you?' he said, handing one of them a £1 note. 'Pop into the chemist on the corner and get me a packet of Chava Pegs?'

'Pardon?'

'On second thoughts, better make it two – two packets. Better be on the safe side.'

Mystification. 'What were they, Mr Franklyn?'

'Chava Pegs, dear, Chava Pegs. Don't worry, they'll know.'

Bewildered looks exchanged between the girls. In unison – 'Chava Pegs?'

'That's right, but if they're out of them, and they may be, come to think of it – it's Saturday – get me a large pot of Rumpo ointment instead.'

Whereupon he shut his dressing-room door leaving the two girls standing in the corridor, pound note in hand, stupefied.

The last week of the *Domino* tour we played at the People's Palace in the Mile End Road – the theatre in which I had made my first professional appearance.

On the last day of that week, 9 September, a day on which London was bathed in sunshine, in Chubb Hill Nursing Home in Whitby Pym gave birth to our second beautiful daughter – Sally Maclean. Whereas Lee had been born three years previously in Pym's own bed at 'Penarth', Sally's arrival had been planned to take place elsewhere so as to relieve Mrs Maclean of the additional administrative burden.

That afternoon I arrived at the theatre at half-past three for the four o'clock matinée bursting with the news. Before the final curtain fell that evening the entire theatre-going public of Stepney was in on it. Leo, sharing my jubilation, somehow or other managed to work the information into the text of *The Lilac Domino* certainly once, if not twice or three times, during the course of those two final performances. The principle was nothing new – we'd had the current Test scores worked into the text on more than one occasion. It was, however, a day of mixed emotions for me. While over the moon about my family news, I had that night to say goodbye to a man of whom I thought the world. For twenty-four weeks Leo had been my friend and tutor and I had come to love him dearly; he had taught me so much. I was never to work with him again, but we had many more years of friendship ahead of us. It is perhaps interesting to ponder that the star with which all Geminis are supposed to be in accord is Leo.

The following morning, sad and affectionate farewells behind me, I was at King's Cross by nine and with Pym and Sally by mid-afternoon. Apart from the fact that Sal was a bit bruised around the face, in Dad's eyes they were both of them looking radiant. Not for the last time in my life a momentous event had taken place on the last night of a run.

❖

I had now but two weeks before starting rehearsals for yet another musical comedy tour. My professional stock had suddenly become high and, although we were still without our own home, I was at last beginning to feel more secure financially and the future was looking even brighter still. I spent most of those two weeks with my family at Sleights but took a few days away to visit my parents whom I hadn't seen since we played Hull in June.

During the last few weeks of *The Lilac Domino* I was being wooed by one of the most powerful men in the English theatre – Prince Littler. He was at that time chairman of the Stoll Theatre Corporation, chairman of Moss Empires Ltd, and a director of Howard and Wyndhams Ltd, three companies which, between them, controlled a good half-dozen theatres in the West End and a vast chain of them in the provinces. He was also a theatrical producer on his own account, and in 1949 he decided to put out a tour of the big 1932 Drury Lane success *Wild Violets*.

Wild Violets has the most beautiful score by Robert Stoltz, the Austrian composer of *White Horse Inn*, and for my money it is the more tuneful of the two. Perhaps the best known of its melodies is 'Don't Say Goodbye', no doubt because it has been used as a signing-off tune by the Victor Sylvester Orchestra for as long as I can remember. In 1932 it had been a big spectacular production with a revolving stage and several huge sets built on mobile trucks.

The story, set in the year 1902, concerns the amorous adventures of the students at the Château Violette, a girls' finishing school in Switzerland, and the boys of the adjacent Helvetia College. 'A Muscial Comedy of Romance and Youth' it was billed as and the production boasted a cast of sixty.

Prince Littler's revival was being done on a grand scale. The sets and costumes were all brand spanking new and exact replicas of the originals. In addition, because of the problems of touring such a vast production, it was to play two weeks in each town instead of one and it would open on a Tuesday instead of a Monday to give the staff the necessary time to build the sets and hang all the extra lighting. The tour was also to embrace a five-week Christmas season in the enchanting Lyceum Theatre in Edinburgh, a city I adored. I was now being offered a part in it and my salary was to be the same as that which I had been receiving in *The Lilac Domino*.

From a personal point of view there was only one blot on the whole glittering landscape – the part. The main comedy in *Wild Violets* is carried by a girl – the keeper of a local hostelry – a role that had been played

Wild Violets – 'A Girl Has Got My Heart'. Centre
left to right David Croft, Alan Christie and self

in the original production by the American comedienne Charlotte Greenwood. The other central characters are three girls at the Château Violette
and their three suitors from the Helvetia College, of which I was to be
one. A certain amount of the light comedy was carried by this sextet but
after *The Lilac Domino* it all struck me as being decidedly insipid. To
raise laughs with such weak material would, I decided, be a question of
making bricks without straw. To move, therefore, from a show where
I had, with Leo, been responsible for the entire comedy for a complete
evening's entertainment to one in which the material was poor and the
part subservient seemed to me to be a step in the wrong direction. In
addition, it was to be another tour and after twenty-four weeks away
from my family I thought it was time that we started to find a home of
our own and the only way to achieve that was to seek employment in
the metropolis for a while. As a result of all this I gritted my teeth, summoned all the nerve I could muster and as graciously as possible declined
the offer. Within days it returned with an added inducement of another
five pounds a week. Unfortunately, it wasn't a question of money – I
just didn't want to play the part. I declined again. Three days later Frank
Marshall, Prince Littler's production manager, who was going to direct
the revival, rang my agent 'upping the ante' by yet another fiver. This
was getting embarrassing. Again I thanked them and declined. It was after
they had returned for the third time with the offer of another fiver that
I had to stop and think. Suddenly, whether I liked the part or not, it had
become one that I couldn't afford to refuse. I was, however, saddened
to find myself living proof of the adage 'everyone has his price'. I opened
in *Wild Violets* at the Bristol Hippodrome on 25 October 1949.

The prospect of five weeks in Edinburgh over Christmas and Hog-
manay meant that, for the first time in seven months, it would be worth

while having my family up to live with me for a period. I immediately wrote off to book digs with a landlady of excellent reputation – I had no intention of taking Pym, Lee and a three-month-old baby in a carry-cot into anywhere that had not been personally recommended. I was delighted, therefore, when in due course I received a reply saying that she could accommodate us all.

The week before we were due in Edinburgh, however, we were playing in Newcastle and a vocal group who were appearing at the local Empire imparted to me the disturbing news that under no circumstances were we to stay with the lady in question – they themselves had lodged there two weeks previously; the place had changed hands and the new proprietor, an elderly poof if I remember correctly, was still trading under the original owner's name and his ministrations bore no resemblance whatever to the excellent but departed Mrs McSomebody. Panic. Five days to go and Edinburgh a town with four big theatres, all of which at Christmas time would be housing shows with unusually large casts. What accommodation still remained available, I ruminated, was bound to be, if not the dregs, at least of Fourth Division standard. By now totally desperate, I rang the stage-doorkeeper of the Lyceum Theatre and was given the number of a Mrs Carruthers of No 10 Grove Street. I rang Mrs Carruthers – yes, she could take us. I had no option but to accept and just pray.

In addition to accommodating my own family she also had rooms for two of my chums in the company, and on arriving in Edinburgh on a bitter cold Sunday morning (my family were arriving on the following day) the three of us piled into a taxi and headed for – who knew what? My heart was in my mouth during the entire journey – what were we going to find? The taxi turned into Grove Street. It was a street of terraced houses built of dark, forbidding Scottish stone, the front doors of which opened straight out on to the pavement. My heart sank. We paid off the taxi, picked up our cases and with my spirits at rock bottom I rang the bell.

A few minutes later we stepped into the most beautiful light and airy hall. Everything was spotlessly clean, and from the moment we entered I knew the crisis was over. We were received with the most welcoming of smiles and after being shown up to our rooms we were ushered into a large first-floor sitting-room that all six of us were to share. It was cosy, comfortably furnished and there was a roaring coal fire burning in the grate. I was now about to spend five weeks in the best theatrical digs I have ever stayed in before or since.

My two friends who were to be our living companions were Stella Moray – an attractive, slim, dark-haired young lass who was playing the Charlotte Greenwood part – and a lad of my own age called David Croft.

David was the younger son of highly successful theatrical parents, both of whom had achieved stardom in musical comedy in the '20s. He was of medium height, had fair crinkly hair, wore spectacles and was the possessor of a good singing voice and an astringent, dry wit. He played the third of the trio of male students. After several years as a performer he was later to turn to lyric writing and eventually to television production. He has since been responsible for producing, directing and also for being part author of such TV successes as *Dad's Army, Are You Being Served?* and *It Ain't 'Alf 'Ot Mum.* We were to become close friends.

The following day Pym and the children arrived and we all settled in for our first happy family Christmas and New Year together as a foursome.

While we were in Edinburgh we received news that at the conclusion of our Christmas season we were to play two more weeks in Glasgow and then the entire production was to return to London where we were to open at the Stoll Opera House in Kingsway. This was most welcome news. The Stoll Opera House contained a vast auditorium. On the site today is an office block of considerable proportions and in addition the entire new Royalty Theatre.

We were received coolly by the London critics. While colourful and lavish in its presentation, against the new American invasion – *Oklahoma, Annie Get Your Gun* and *Brigadoon* had all opened by then – we appeared sadly dated. Nevertheless, we got a sixteen-week West End run out of it which gave me the required time to look around for a new home for my family.

As always, Richard and Sara took me in once again. They had, during the intervening months, moved to a large, white terraced house with a most enviable southern aspect and an uninterrupted view over Primrose Hill. This time these two dear and loyal friends allotted me a small but comfortable room at the top of their house into which the sun streamed during the day and at night I fell asleep to the accompaniment of the roaring of the lions in the zoo.

No sooner had I moved in than I started to search. With two young children to rear, the open air and greenery of Primrose Hill and Regent's Park appealed to me. So too did the fact that it would be nice to settle somewhere near Richard and Sara and their own growing family. Alas, the area was full of the most beautiful and desirable properties all marked at the most hideous and undesirable prices.

After a few weeks I unearthed – an apt choice of word – a freehold Victorian property which was up for sale but a stone's throw (no pun intended) from Richard and Sara. It had a basement, ground and two other floors and was situated in quite the most unsalubrious, not to say slummy, street in the entire area. The houses in it were terraced, squalid, rundown and largely occupied either by council tenants or those of some irresponsible landlord who refused to put a penny piece back into his decaying investments. The properties on the opposite side of the street backed straight on to the main lines in and out of Euston Station and the trains using them in 1950 were powered exclusively by steam. To add to the general grime of the area, a coaling plant at which the engines used to 'coal up' was so adjacent it could have done no more damage had it been sited slap-bang in the middle of the street.

It is endemic to London that such areas can be found only round the corner from ones that are prepossessing and highly sought after. It is also endemic to London that Gloucester Avenue, NW1, has now – the railway having been electrified and the offending properties sold and renovated – become a most desirable address housing a number of celebrities. In 1950, however, the main appeal of No 173 was its price – £3,000. Added attractions were that it was positioned on a gentle banana-shaped bend in the road which allowed it and its two neighbouring properties to be staggered, each slightly in front of the others, thus providing them with a pillared porch apiece – a marginal individuality distinguishing them from the remainder of the long row. It also possessed a small back garden. The first thing, however, was to seek Pym's approval of the property. Obviously it was going to either turn her on or alternatively – after a quick 'shufti' at the surrounding environs – right off in a very big way. To me, as with Cranley Gardens, the decision rested solely in its financial viability, but over the years not everyone has seen things my way.

In due course Pym came down to London on a fleeting visit of inspection. I had a matinée on the day in question and she arrived at the Stoll in the middle of the evening performance. After the show we took a 68 bus from right opposite the theatre to Chalk Farm. 173 Gloucester Avenue was but a three minutes' walk from the terminus – we had to pass it on our way to Richard and Sara's; how fortunate it was that my loved one's first glimpse of our proposed new home was to be in the dark.

The following morning we had an appointment with the owner, a Miss Oliphant, who was to show us round. Pym's spirits had, it transpired,

started to fall the previous night the moment the bus had left the main
Camden Town Station crossroads and started to proceed up Chalk Farm
Road. Furthermore, her nocturnal view of the property and its immediate
neighbours had succeeded in pulling the wool over nobody's eyes and
they had promptly plummeted even further. Miss Oliphant's conducted
tour, sadly, did nothing to alleviate the situation – madam was undoubtedly full of deep disappointment. Pym Carmichael, however, has
always possessed a practical nature, an adaptability with which few are
blessed and always the highest and most unselfish consideration for
others. She did not, as a result, show me her true feelings. There was
also, fortunately, one other factor that affected her assessment of the
situation. She had now been living with her most tolerant of parents for
a whole year and was beginning to feel that we never would be reunited
as a family. It was therefore very much a matter of any port in a storm.
So, in the final analysis, there was no question but that we should try
to raise the cash.

We bought 173 and within six weeks we were all reassembled under
its roof. The place was a shambles. The basement floor and staircase were
riddled with just about every form of rot that can get into wood, the
bathroom had been a bathroom/kitchen and housed in addition to the
usual bathroom furniture an ancient gas stove, the decorations left more
than a great deal to be desired and the garden was a wilderness – but
it was home. The first and biggest thrill was to be able to actually walk
down stairs for breakfast on our first morning – albeit to a mice-infested
basement kitchen. The second was taking tea out into the garden in early
spring sunshine – albeit spread on a patch of heavily overgrown grass
and with not a plant or a flower in sight to enrich the dun-coloured surrounding masonry and the tall, windowless back wall of a warehouse
that provided its bottom boundary.

It was some time before we could get builders in to start renovations
but eventually it all started to take shape and by the time *Violets* closed
at the Stoll we were as shipshape as we could afford to be and very proud
and comfortable in our new home.

The uneventful West End run of *Wild Violets* drew to a peaceful close
on 27 May. Uneventful, that is, except for an unexpected visit from Noël
Coward and a small party one distressingly empty matinée which was to
have repercussions twelve months later. But by now summer was upon
us and Richard Stone was sitting like a vulture atop the Stoll 'front of
house' marquee, waiting for the corpse to utter its final death rattle.

CHAPTER EIGHTEEN

THE SEA AND ALLY PALLY

Enter RONALD WALDMAN – *a tempter*

Four years had now passed since my demobilisation and I was well within my self-allotted five-year span of work with no holiday. I could, needless to say, by now well have done with one, but in my profession, particularly when young, an actor's bred-in-the-bone sense of insecurity prevents him from turning down work when it is offered. Even if he can afford to do so – which isn't often – the fear of never being asked again, or at best an interminable period before the next offer materialises, activates a forbidding warning buzzer like the one in some cars that sounds off until you have fastened your seat belt. So when Richard Stone swooped down off his perch in Kingsway with a daunting programme of summer shows to be directed, there was never any question but that I should take off my coat and get down to them.

That year, the summer of 1950, in addition to filling the Jolly Roger Theatre at Clacton once again, he had also undertaken to put shows into the Butlin's holiday camps at Clacton, Pwllheli and Skegness; each of which had to carry four complete changes of programme.

My next few weeks were spent gathering material and routining the musical numbers. I was also sent far and wide to scour for costumes; from the upper reaches of the Edgware Road in which, over an insignificant grocer's shop, was stored the wardrobe from a recently failed West End revue, to the ice-rink at Bournemouth where they were selling off items from the previous season's ice-show, and all to be bargained for and secured at the minimum possible cost. This process, which was prescribed by the budget, was an irritating and frustrating 'cart before the horse' order of things for the director – the available costumes, not his creative ability, invariably dictating what the production numbers were to be.

In due course, however, after hours of burning the midnight oil and days spent in trying to blend harmoniously the frequently divergent wishes of the artistes, the camp entertainments officers and Richard Stone, I finally got it all together. The following weeks, in pursuance of my duties, I spent living in chalets in various Butlin's holiday camps and I can't say that I personally found them a commensurate replacement for either Whitby or Le Lavandou. They were, nevertheless, packed to capacity with satisfied customers, so it must have been I who was wrong.

Richard's shows at the seaside opened; before I had even had time to shake the sand out of my shoes another old friend moved in and claimed my services – Michael Mills.

Michael was about to present four hour-long spectaculars up at Ally Pally called *Floor Show at the Regency Room*. They were a typical Mills product and had a great deal of class. The setting, as the title indicates, was a sort of 'Talk of the Town' theatre restaurant. Each programme featured one, perhaps two, big international stars – Rose Murphy, Kay Thompson or whoever – and a resident company of eighteen provided the remainder of the entertainment. Each programme, in the middle, featured a musical production scena built round the works of one composer – Berlin, Porter, Gershwin, *et al*. The dances were again arranged by Freddie Carpenter and the orchestra – in vision. (In those tiny Ally Pally studios it was simpler to have them in rather than out of it. There had, of course, been occasions when they appeared in when they should have been out – but that's another story.) Anyway, said orchestra was directed, as usual, by Eric Robinson.

Of *Regency Room* one reviewer wrote:

The production numbers by Freddie Carpenter and special orchestrations by Arthur Wilkinson [a most unlikely musical figure – he looked exactly like the late Raymond Glendenning] are the best and most imaginative that television has so far provided, and in Ian Carmichael, Michael (Cecil B. de) Mills has an artist who merits better prominence in the credit titles.

Ian Carmichael had been awarded the role of song and dance juvenile in the resident company, in which capacity he had a ball.

Regency Room was presented every alternate week and during each week that intervened I was also appearing in another TV series – *Don't Look Now*. This was a half-hour comedy show which starred Alfred Marks in which I was providing comedy and character work in the sketches. The two shows running concurrently provided me with a wonderful contrast in performance and, within the limited reception area, two months of first-class television exposure.

For *Regency Room* we rehearsed in the old Holborn Restaurant which

'Thou Swell' in a Rogers and Hart scena from an episode of Regency Room

stood on the corner of Kingsway and New Oxford Street opposite the Holborn tube station. One morning during our first week Michael didn't arrive until after lunch; he had been attending a producers' meeting up at Alexandra Palace. During tea-break he told me that at that meeting Ronnie Waldman, the current head of TV Light Entertainment, had announced that he wished to employ the odd freelance director and that he had then called upon the assembled company for suggestions concerning likely candidates. Michael apparently had put forward Freddie Carpenter's name and my own.

'How do you feel about it?' he asked.

For a moment I was speechless. When I eventually found my tongue, I said, 'You're joking, of course.'

'Never been more serious in my life.'

'But—' I stammered, and then petered out.

'I think you're the ideal man,' Michael continued. 'You've produced all those shows for Richard; you know how to put one together. You've done several shows for me – you know what goes on on the floor of a

TV studio. Why so chicken-hearted?'

'I may know what goes on on the *floor* of a TV studio,' I replied, 'but I've never been up in the producer's box – the control room – in my life.'

'That's nothing to worry about,' said Michael (he, you understand, is one of those irritatingly cool, unrufflable men before whom life's little crises seem to flatten out like walnuts before a steam roller). 'There are technicians up there. They'll see you through that side of it. Anyway, we'll do the first show together. Fifteen minutes with one artiste; pick whoever you want. You work it out and rehearse it and I'll watch over your shoulder, vet your camera script – all that sort of thing. Then, on transmission, I'll sit in the box-seat up in the control room while you plonk yourself behind me and see what happens. Second show you're in charge and I'll sit behind you; third show you're on your own. How about it?'

As I have mentioned before, young actors rarely turn work down; there's also the bit about fools rushing in. There was a long pause.

'Will it really be like that?' I said. 'Do you promise to hold my hand through the first couple?'

'Of course I will.'

I took a deep breath. 'O.K., then – I'll have a shot.'

'Good man,' he said. 'I'll tell Ronnie.'

The following morning he came down to rehearsals his usual ebullient self.

'Ronnie's delighted. Your first show is in three weeks' time – 8.45 p.m., 11 August. Think about it tonight. Pick yourself an artiste, let me know tomorrow and Yvonne (Yvonne Littlewood, his secretary and PA throughout all those early years, now a BBC Light Entertainment director in her own right) will put in a booking for you.'

The suddenness of the whole thing was stunning. What had I, for John Logie Baird's sake, agreed to do? I must have been out of my mind. And now, just to exacerbate the situation I had been allotted my first show bang in the middle of a period when I was already appearing in two television series at once. I had to have taken leave of my senses. In time, however, the feeling of panic was partially, though only partially, tempered by one of stimulation and challenge.

I didn't have to think long about my artiste – in fact I had already made up my mind the previous night.

'I'd like Petula Clark, if we can get her,' I said.

'An excellent choice,' said Michael.

These fifteen-minute spots with one artiste were used frequently at that time to fill in awkward gaps in the evening's viewing and they were presented under the umbrella title of *Starlight*. Because of my existing commitments, the planning and rehearsals of ours were done on Sundays – as indeed was the transmission itself.

I first met Pet, then a teenager, with her father and accompanist Joe Henderson. The programme was arranged, the theme of which was to be 'something old, something new, something borrowed and something blue'. It was an idea of their own and they had the song suggestions to back it up.

Now, at this point I must explain that, for any show, rehearsals in the actual studio with cameras was always at a premium. One never – even with the big musicals that I had been doing for Michael – ever got into the studio before the day of transmission. Even when in the studio, the technicians' union hours were restricted, so every minute of camera time was like gold dust.

On the morning of 11 August 1950, I arrived in Studio B at Alexandra Palace with time to spare. When I entered it I had never been inside a producer's control room in my life. Gradually the technicians started to arrive. Pet and Joe turned up and when the clock got round 'to 10.30, or whatever time I was allowed to blow the starting whistle, everyone was in his or her place waiting for the off. Everyone, that is, except one man – there was not a sign of Michael Mills.

I waited. Ten minutes – fifteen minutes – half an hour. The studio was at an infamous standstill. As the clock moved into the second half-hour of inertia I was only too aware that every eye in the whole crew was on me. There was only one thing for it. Inwardly a dithering wreck occasioned by a mixture of terror and fury, I started to mount the vertical steel ladder to the control room.

'Where do I sit, please? Ah, thank you.'

The 1950 producer's control room bore about as much resemblance to today's model as the cockpit of a Sopwith Camel to the flight deck of Concorde. It was, however, nonetheless frightening for that. Patiently and courteously, those more qualified than I then kindly gave me a quick crash course in the surrounding impedimenta.

We started.

Maybe an hour later, through the grace of God and the patience of the technicians and the artistes alike, we completed a 'struggle through'. I went down on to the 'floor' to give notes. Fifteen minutes later, there still being no sign of Michael, I again mounted the dizzy heights of that ladder to go through the whole thing once more. Thereafter we broke for lunch.

After lunch, when we were all reassembled in the studio, Michael breezed in.

'Where the blazes have you been?' I exploded.

'How are you getting on?' he countered blandly, totally ignoring my question.

'Where the hell have you been?' I repeated. 'You said you'd take the show over once we got into the studio. All I'd have to do, you said, was watch.'

'Cool down, cool down,' he said in the most irritatingly smug tone of voice. 'I repeat, how are you getting on? Been through it yet?'

'Twice,' I said through clenched teeth.

'Good, let's go upstairs and have a look at it.'

After my third ascent up that ladder without oxygen, I motioned him to the director's seat and made to move round behind.

'No, you do it,' he said. 'I'll watch.'

For the third time we completed a run through. When it was over Michael rose, said, 'Fine,' and made for the door. As he opened it he turned and said, 'I'll give you a ring tonight and let you know how it looked. Good luck.'

I caught my breath. 'Where are you going?' I exclaimed in anguish.

'Home,' he said. 'You're perfectly capable of handling it yourself,' and vanished.

At 8.45 that evening we went on the air 'live'. At 9.05 I had a complimentary call from Michael and the following morning Ronnie Waldman also made nice noises in my direction.

I made my nice noises immediately we were off the air to my tolerant and accommodating crew; also to dear, talented Petula Clark. I had, as Michael had said at the time, made an excellent choice; even then she was a highly professional young lady. I could have wished for no one else with whom to share my baptism of fire. Whether she felt similarly disposed towards me, I doubt if I shall ever know.

While all this had been going on, Prince Littler had decided to put out an extensive post-London tour of *Wild Violets* and all the members of the original cast were offered their old jobs back. Ninety-nine per cent of them, including myself, accepted.

We completed the tour just prior to Christmas and I returned to town, a loving and lonely wife and my ever-loyal, fairy godfather figure – Michael Mills.

Rehearsing

Michael's next show was another of his original brain-children. The occasion was the opening of the new, bigger, better and more luxurious light entertainment studio in the BBC's recently acquired premises in Lime Grove – the old home of Gainsborough Films in Shepherd's Bush. It was a tremendous advance from the comparative chicken-coops up in Alexandra Palace and to be invited to appear in the show that actually opened the new studio gave one a feeling of making history.

The show itself was worthy of the occasion. It was called *Here's Television*. It was written by Muir and Norden and was an hour's take-off, send-up, call it what you will, of all the most popular television programmes of the day. The items were tied together by Clive Morton who, playing the director-general, sat behind a vast desk in his plushy, panelled, book-lined office. At the end of the programme he rose, crossed to the door to pick up his hat, umbrella and briefcase preparatory to going home, and as he spoke the line '... but we at the BBC will continue to bring you the best in visual entertainment. We are building, building, building all the time', the camera then pulled back to show for the first time that the office was only partially completed. His exit was then made by stepping over the hitherto undisclosed wall in the foreground – only four courses of bricks high – on to the exterior scaffolding and finally down a ladder and out at the bottom of the 'frame'.

Immediately I completed *Here's Television*, Ronnie Waldman sent for me again and asked if I was interested in continuing to direct for television. I had nothing else in the book so I asked him what he had in mind. It turned out to be a series of six programmes with Richard Hearne which were to be called *Mr Pastry's Progress*.

Dickie Hearne was a star when I was still at school. He had been on the stage since he was a baby. His father was an acrobat and between the ages of nine and eleven he appeared with him in the circus. He later toured in variety, touring revues and entered pantomime. In the 1930s he graduated to, and became a great success in, many West End musical comedies in which he almost always appeared in the guise of a lovable, old, white-haired, walrus-moustached, bespectacled character whom he had eventually christened Mr Pastry. Mr Pastry became to him what the Tramp had been to Charlie Chaplin.

Dickie is a clown really and a very athletic one at that. It now became my job to direct him in six fifteen-minute situation comedies – a job which I did not assess an enviable one – a bit cheeky, in fact. It was, I felt, going to be very much a case of the lance-corporal leading the general. But Dickie is a nice man, we got on well together and the partnership, I like to think, was a successful one.

He was, at that time, a paradoxical figure in many ways. Although Mr Pastry was many years older than his portrayer, Dickie himself always appeared many years younger than he actually was. He abounded with energy and seemed to possess the secret of eternal youth. He was also kind, considerate and an extremely generous man. At the time in question he was appearing with Fred Emney in a musical at His Majesty's Theatre called *Blue For A Boy*.

The first problem that faced me with *Mr Pastry's Progress* was the scripts. Dickie himself had many ideas for story lines, all of which embraced a maximum amount of broad, slapstick comedy at which he excelled. But the skeleton required flesh on its bones; the participant characters did have to have lines to speak and no writer had been engaged. Dickie didn't seem to think one was necessary, words to him were unimportant, 'business' was the only thing that mattered, so in the event we did the job ourselves. On some occasions he would come to the theatre early and we would tackle it in the large No. 2 Dressing Room at His Majesty's which I was to occupy myself during two successful plays several years later, and on others I would travel down by train (we still had no car) to his enchanting old-world oasthouse cottage in Kent on Sunday afternoons where we would put the rest of it together, each of us throwing in alternate lines all of which I then wrote down in longhand.

The results of our labours were transmitted live, with no audience, from Alexandra Palace on six consecutive Sundays and not the least of my problems was deciding whether to either duplicate sections of the set so that the more extravagant items of comedy business could be tried out first – or, alternatively, to trust to luck that if we did it first time on transmission everything would go according to plan. I refer to such subtleties as two plumbers working on the house next door inadvertently breaking through the party wall complete with burst water-pipe.

One of the happier by-products of *Mr Pastry's Progress* was the opportunity the job afforded me to offer employment to several of my out-of-work actor chums.

My friendship with Dickie has lasted for many years.

I followed the *Mr Pastry* series with three different 'one-off' light entertainment half-hours and then became lumbered with a dead duck. Well, it wasn't actually dead when it was handed to me but it was in a parlous state and all I was really expected to do was to administer the last rites as discreetly as possible and finally lay it quietly to rest.

The 'invalid' came in the form of the last two programmes of a series which had, for several weeks, been presented by another director. He, no doubt breathing a sigh of relief, had been assigned to another job and was out of the hot seat before you could say 'Gilbert Harding'. Which was appropriate, really, as the show was the television version of the radio panel game *We Beg To Differ* in which Gilbert was joined by Joyce Grenfell, the Bradens and two other distinguished broadcasters with Roy Plomley in the chair. The show had proved unequal to the transfer from Portland Place to Shepherd's Bush, but, refusing to believe that its malady was terminal, I was determined to give it a reviving blood transfusion.

First of all, I took the whole team out of its clinical setting – the sort of shop-counter-like construction which today has become *de rigueur* for panel games – and moved them into deep, plush, Dickensian armchairs and a sofa which were themselves set in a replica of what might have been the library in Woburn Abbey. A low table was placed in the middle of them all on which rested a coffee service.

'Relax,' were my instructions, 'and help yourselves as and when the spirit moves you.'

Next, as politely and graciously as possible, I dispensed with the services of the 'other two distinguished broadcasters'. I decided that, as the programme was nothing more or less than a debate on various trite topics, a man and woman 'from the street' might provide colour. For the man I went straight round to my old army chum John Moore – ex-schoolmaster, Foreign Office official, good listener, articulate and personable

– an ideal choice. Fortunately he agreed without too much persuasion. For his partner, at John's suggestion I approached the American-born Jocelyn Corbett, a young lady who had lived in England since she was eighteen. At the time she entered my life she was a buyer for a London store. So, the setting refurbished and the team reinforced, I then selected an appropriate piece of music to back the credit titles and get the whole thing away to a good punchy start; a choice which had in fact been my very first bright idea for the programme the moment Ronnie had handed it over to me. For a debate programme called *We Beg to Differ*, what could possibly be better than the Gershwin brothers' oldie written for the Astaire–Rogers film *Shall We Dance?* –

> 'You say eether and I say either,
> You say neether and I say neither' etc.

So, the kiss of life duly administered, I became reasonably confident about the patient's chances of survival.

The first of the two new-look *We Beg To Differs* was transmitted, like my previous three 'one-offs', from Lime Grove.

The following morning I flew to the papers to see how it had been received by the Press. They'd watched it all right and all my innovations had been noted – particularly the signature tune. In fact it was its title that one of the nationals had used as a headline – 'Let's Call the Whole Thing Off' was emblazoned in heavy block capitals right across the top of the column.

'Yes, I thought they'd pick that one up,' was Ronnie Waldman's comment. Well, he might have told me.

Regardless of my failing to save the life of *We Beg To Differ*, it was immediately following it that Ronnie asked me if I would become a full-time director on his staff. That, of course, would mean that I would have to quit acting altogether. It was another murderous decision to have to make. At last security within my own chosen calling was being dangled in front of my nose like the carrot in front of the donkey. This time, however, I found it an easier one to make.

We had, by now, just entered 1951, the year of the Festival of Britain. It was also to be the year in which I was to fully consolidate myself as a West End actor and a year which was to provide me with the biggest success I had been associated with to date. It was to be a unique, exhilarating and, to those who participated in it, a never-to-be-forgotten experience. 1951 was the year of *The Lyric Revue*.

CHAPTER NINETEEN

HAMMERSMITH AND POINTS WEST

Enter WILLIAM CHAPPELL – *a wise counsellor*

In 1951 the whole of Britain was *en fête* and spring and summer produced weather to match it. H. M. Tennent Ltd, London's leading theatrical management, decided to put a modest intimate revue into the Lyric Theatre in Hammersmith. The theatre itself, now sadly demolished, was a charming little playhouse dating from 1890, and it was situated just off King Street only spitting distance from Hammersmith Tube station. The show was to have six boys and six girls, all of whom would share equal 'billing'; there were to be no stellar 'names'.

Auditions were to be held in April and Richard at once rang up John Perry – the H. M. Tennent executive producer of the show – to ask if I could be included. John Perry had, most unfortunately, been a member of Noël Coward's small party at that disastrous matinée of *Wild Violets*. I was never very proud of my performance in *Violets* at the best of times – in an effort to get laughs in the face of such a paucity of comedy material, I had tended to overplay outrageously – but on that particular afternoon the tiny handful of people who had attended the matinée had been so depressing it had, I am afraid, made several of us fall into the unforgivable but tempting trap of playing to amuse ourselves intead of the audience. It wasn't until the curtain came down that we heard there had been distinguished patrons in the house; we were ashamed and mortified. Just retribution was now to fall upon my head.

'Ian Carmichael?' said Mr Perry to Richard. 'Don't waste my time – I saw him in *Wild Violets* and he is quite dreadful.'

'But it won't cost you anything to see him,' pleaded Richard.

'I've told you, I have seen him and he's dreadful. I've got better things to do – don't waste my time.'

Richard persisted manfully and John Perry weakened.

'All right, send him along,' he said. 'But he's wasting his own time as well as mine – I shan't employ him.'

I went to the auditions and to a cold auditorium bare except for John Perry and the director, William Chappell, I gave my Players Theatre routine for 'I Do Like To Be Beside The Seaside'. Well, I don't know who or what worked the oracle – Billy Chappell, I suspect – but, miraculously, I was in.

In view of what was to follow it is probably worth listing the entire cast of *The Lyric Revue*; Graham Payn and George Benson, the two most senior members of the company, were joined by Myles Eason, Jeremy Hawk, Tommy Linden and myself, and the girls were Dora Bryan, Joan Heal, Irlin Hall, Pamela Marmont, Hilary Allen and Roberta Huby. In 1951, with the exception of Graham Payn and George Benson, not one member of the cast meant a thing at the box office. Such 'names' as the show could boast were to be found exclusively amongst the writers and composers – Noël Coward, Michael Flanders, Donald Swann, Kay Thompson, Richard Addinsell, Norman Hackforth (who was also to lead the small orchestra in the pit) and several others. When we all met on the first day of rehearsals it was dinned into us very firmly that the show was being mounted on a shoe-string and that we were to have no aspirations about eventually transferring to the West End. We were to tour for four weeks and then open at the Lyric, Hammersmith, for four weeks only.

The main bulk of the material for *The Lyric Revue* was written by the actor Arthur Macrae. It was excellent stuff but Arthur's gifts lay principally in writing for the girls and in particular for Dora Bryan. The main hankering of all revue performers, however, is to have his or her own solo number: without this, there is a feeling – which does contain a grain of truth – that one cannot make one's own personal mark. It is, nevertheless, seldom possible for an entire cast to be so accommodated, a fact that can at times lead to petty jealousies and nail-biting frustrations during rehearsals.

I was fortunate. I was given a number called 'The Hangman's Son' – probably better remembered by those who saw it as 'Darling Boy'. It was written and composed by two Frenchmen and was translated by Michael Flanders. I say I was fortunate, but at the time all my male colleagues, and in particular those who had not been given a solo number themselves, seemed to do their best to undermine my morale with lines like: 'You can't sing that, Ian, it is in the worst possible taste,' and 'You'll never get away with it,' and 'Well – rather you than me.'

It *was* a strange number, they were quite right. The first verse and chorus set the small boy's character perfectly.

'*Darling Boy*' – The Lyric Revue

He loved to swing on the garden gate,
Play for hours with the neighbour's cat,
He loved to read: but more than that
Out in the garden, early or late,
He'd bowl his hoop along the paving
Good as gold 'til day was done,
He'd not be found misbehaving....
He was the Hangman's small son.

He *was* a darling boy!
Obedient, quiet and charming –
Never was rude or alarming,
He would smile and say, 'Yes, Papa':
As fair as Fauntleroy,
Oh, how could you find any harm in
Someone so kind and disarming?
He would smile and say, 'Yes, Papa'.

As the song progressed his father, hoping that his son would eventually
succeed him in his calling, became increasingly alarmed at his docility

and apparent disinclination to do so. Ultimately, fed up with his parent's persistent efforts to drum up in him a sense of pride in the family craft, the small boy, with a seraphic smile on his face, strangled his dear papa with his skipping rope and then continued with his favourite game of bowling his hoop.

Billy Chappell, an ex-dancer, choreographed an intricate, busy and exacting routine for me with a hoop and the number achieved an astonishing popularity. I, in fact, never really enjoyed it very much, but not for any reasons of propriety. I performed it in a very hot knickerbocker suit of heavy Lovat tweed and it took a lot of 'working' – I would have infinitely preferred to have had one containing a lot of funny lines which required less energy.

I was also lucky enough to be awarded, arguably, the best bit of comedy material that was ever written for an intimate revue. It was called 'Sweet Belinda' and was ostensibly a duet that I performed with Joan Heal immediately before the finale – the prime spot in the show. It was written by Arthur Macrae and Richard Addinsell and at the outset gave the impression that it was going to be a charming period ballad. I, in full periwig, elegant white brocade, knee-length, flared jacket of the period, breeches, white silk stockings, black tricorne hat, quizzing-glass in one hand and lace handkerchief in the other, played a gallant at the court of King James I. Joan, a demure young lady in full skirt, bonnet, ringlets and fluttering a fan, was carried on to the stage in a sedan chair. The two chairmen and her escort of three other young ladies then left the two of us together. The scene was St James's Park and I started to serenade her. When it became Joan's turn to sing, I moved to open the door of the chair so that she could step out and join me. It wouldn't budge. Try as I might, I couldn't shift it. Giving a final heave as decorously as possible without stepping out of character, the handle came off in my hand – sweet Belinda was a captive. The duet continued throughout while we both made valiant efforts to retrieve the situation. We tried the window – that was stuck. Eventually one final exertion on my part forced it open only to have the song rent by a piercing shriek from Joan as her hand became trapped between the cross-brace of the window and the sill. Heave, heave, heave – finally we freed it and it flew up again with a resounding bang. As I moved away I became ensnared, and very nearly throttled into the bargain, by the ribbon round my neck on the end of which was my quizzing-glass; during the earlier mêlée the latter had become trapped inside the chair by the window. This eventually released, the window flew up once more, this time trapping Joan's head between it and the top of the frame

– and so it continued. It was a magnificent piece of material and the laughs built and built and built. They were still continuing long after we had started the finale.

The list of comedians and comediennes that have since played 'Belinda' in one show or another is as long as my arm, but I don't think it has ever worked as well as it did in *The Lyric Revue* and for a very simple reason. In revue every member of the cast does everything – comedy numbers, straight numbers, sometimes even dramatic sketches – consequently, the audience is attuned to, as it were, one man in his time playing many parts. It was essential with 'Belinda' that at the outset they should believe that it was going to be a pretty number – a 'straight' number. When a well-known comedy figure is carried on in the chair, there is never any doubt that it will develop into a comic number and hence the essence of surprise when things start to go wrong is never achieved.

I am a meticulous performer – it is the only way I know how to work – the extempore is never for me. In 'Belinda' I knew exactly on what note of music and on what word in the line the window had to be opened or the door-knob had to come off. Joan worked the same way, which made for a harmonious relationship and, I like to think, a well-honed and highly polished end-product. A year or so later when Joan had a baby daughter, she christened her Belinda.

We opened *The Lyric Revue* at the Prince of Wales Theatre in Cardiff towards the end of April. My main memory of the first night was that we were considerably over-length, and the following morning – as always in the opening weeks of a new revue – the heartbreaks started. Four items came out immediately. Two of them were certainly 'singles' and for the poor sufferers life overnight ceased to be worth the candle. Over the next four weeks the 'running order' of the show was juggled with until the right mix was discovered, and on 26 May we opened for our limited few weeks in Hammersmith.

The next morning when we all woke up we didn't know what had hit us. The previous night's reception had been echoed in full by the critics. 'It's a Grand Lark ...', 'A Banquet of Wit', 'Brighter Than Coward', 'Happy Revue', 'This Revue has Zip', 'This is Brilliant', 'West London, not West End has Festival's Best Revue', were just a few of the headlines. We played for eighteen capacity weeks at the Lyric, Hammersmith, after which we transferred to the Globe Theatre in Shaftesbury Avenue where we ran for a further nine months.

The period at Hammersmith was as exciting as anything I have ever experienced in the theatre. Every night we drew fashionable London to the dubious attractions of W.6. Every night we were 'standing room only'. Every night as we all came down to the stage a few minutes before 'curtain up' the question 'Who is in front tonight?' was asked by each in turn as we hastened to the spyhole in the corner to see for ourselves. Royalty came, Cabinet ministers, international VIPs and it became the thing for visiting American film stars to sample *The Lyric Revue* their very first night in town. We were the toast of London.

One night Frankie Howerd visited us (our first meeting since demob) and invited the entire company back to his flat in Holland Park for a party. On transferring to the Globe, the glamour, the triumphs and the entertaining continued. We were invited to party after party – frequently as guests of honour. Always after the show, always black tie, always a delicious cold buffet and always the 'in' drink of the day – pink champagne. Noël Coward invited us to his studio flat in Gerald Road, Terence Rattigan to his house in Chester Square, Emlyn Williams to his in Pelham Crescent and 'Binkie' Beaumont, the managing director of H. M. Tennent, to his in Lord North Street. It was tremendously heady stuff. Such acclaim accorded to us as a complete cast bonded us together with a cameraderie that is rare. In our quieter moments, however, maybe as a result, we became in many ways introverted. We wanted our moments of togetherness which we were unwilling to share with others. We each of us in turn gave parties for the express enjoyment of ourselves. On such occasions, husbands and wives were tolerated but beyond that no guests outside the company were invited. At one of these insular junkets that Pym and I hosted at 173 the rule was broken, but we could do nothing about it. Most of the company had assembled after the show and we were well into a round of fairly lethal dry martinis when the front door bell rang. Pym, still in an apron, wooden spoon in hand, left the kitchen where she had been sweltering over a hot stove and a vast bowl of spaghetti bolognese in order to answer it. There on the doorstep was Graham Payn and standing beside him was Noël Coward.

'Pym, darling,' said Graham, 'you don't mind if I bring a friend, do you?'

Mrs C., meeting The Master for the first time – particularly when she was in such a state of *déshabillée* – very nearly swooned on the mat. For my part, I could only, for the second time in recent years, thank the Lord that when someone important had arrived in Gloucester Avenue, it had been pitch dark.

❖

In the early summer of 1952 my old sparring partner David Croft decided to get married. The night before his wedding, which was a Sunday, he, his elder brother Peter – another actor now turned television director – Cyril Ornadel and I went out on a stag-night Hampstead pub crawl. Cyril was at that time a struggling pianist with aspirations to become a musical director and composer. He had been my accompanist at several auditions, was talented, dark, wore horn-rimmed spectacles and his face was permanently lit up with the most infectious of grins; he would, in fact, have been perfect casting for the Cheshire Cat. David and he I had introduced to each other at the time of *Wild Violets* and for several years they were to write songs together. Eventually, Cyril, at a very tender age, became the number one choice as musical director for a succession of imported American musicals until finally he took to record producing, freelance conducting and composing. He was also an incurable Casanova.

Anyway, it was this quartet that started out at the Flask Inn, Well Walk, shortly after opening time on the Sunday in question, to spend a convivial evening seeing off our colleague's bachelorhood.

Later that same evening we decided to return to Cyril's flat in Weymouth Street to conclude our wassailing there. Right outside Great Portland Street station the driver of our vehicle, who shall be nameless but who was grinning like a Cheshire Cat at the time, failed to see a taxi which was approaching us on our starboard quarter. Either that or the taxi driver failed to see us approaching him on his – I refuse to take sides, although I eventually had to in Marlborough Street Magistrates' Court. However, the immediate outcome of this slipshod navigation was that a taxi hit us with some force amidships. I in the front passenger seat received a crippling blow on my left shin from the volume knob of the radio and a cut across the right eye from the corner of the driver's rearview mirror. An adjacent pub was emptying at the time and several people quickly gathered round to help me out. This they achieved with difficulty but on completion I was laid on a small central reservation in the middle of the road. Somebody forced some brandy down my throat and soon I heard the approaching sound of an ambulance bell. By the time it arrived I was surrounded by quite a throng of concerned individuals all anxious to relieve my suffering. It was then that the most considerate of them all pushed her way through to the front. She was middle-aged and carried a small notebook and pencil. Kneeling down beside me as close to my ear as possible she said, 'Quickly, quickly – give me your name and address. I get messages through from the other side.'

Eventually we disposed of the ambulance and all of us staggered back

A characteristic study of Cyril Ornadel 'carving' at The London Palladium

to Cyril's flat a good three-quarters of a mile away where, when pressed to sign the visitors' book, a large drop of blood fell from my eyebrow on to the page. I ringed it in ink and duly signed it. After half an hour or so I was bundled into a taxi and returned to Gloucester Avenue. I had gone out without my latch-key so had to ring the bell. I had, until then, hardly bothered to take stock of my appearance. I should have been more considerate. The shock of opening the door to a husband whose shirt and jacket, to say nothing of his forehead, were covered in blood, for the first and, to date, the last time in her life made Pym feel faint. While I tried to explain what had happened, she attempted to clean up my eyebrow with a handkerchief. As she touched it a piece of glass fell out on to the kitchen floor which administered the *coup de grâce*.

The following day at the wedding ceremony Peter was the only one not affected. I hobbled slowly and agonisingly into our pew, my head swathed in a bandage; the bridegroom escorted his bride down the aisle with a stick in his other hand and three ribs bound tightly together with some sort of plastered adhesive, and Cyril never turned up at all.

Poor Mrs Croft: but the injury seems to have been in no way permanently incapacitating. They still live happily together and have, at the last count, produced a modest family of seven children.

The following day my leg seized up properly and I was off from the show for a week. The actor who had the job of understudying me in 'Darling Boy', from that moment on, looked upon me with enlightened admiration. No one was more delighted to see me return to the company than he was.

During the last few months of *The Lyric Revue* the management decided that they would keep the entire cast together (which they did with the exception of Diana Decker replacing 'Bobbie' Huby) and invite the whole creative team to prepare a new revue to continue in the same theatre. It would be called *The Globe Revue*, a title which, under the circumstances, was altogether more appropriate. Since our move to Shaftesbury Avenue the fact that *The Lyric Revue* was appearing at the Globe Theatre but two doors away from the West End Lyric Theatre had, understandably, caused a certain amount of confusion amongst patrons.

We rehearsed the new show while still performing its predecessor. Finally we closed *The Lyric* on Saturday, 29 June, and opened *The Globe* at the Theatre Royal, Brighton, the following Monday. With the dress rehearsal taking place on the intervening Sunday we none of us had so much as a day's holiday in between.

After one week in Brighton we returned to our old home where we opened on the following Friday. Miraculously we did it again. 'It's Electric and so the Globe Shines', 'Globe Revue succeeds again', 'Just What a Good Revue Should Be', 'Here's ONE Blue Riband We Keep' ran the following day's headlines.

There was, however, one dissenter. His contribution ran something like:

The new revue arrived on the stage of the Globe Theatre last night with all the chic of an elegant Parisian bandbox tied up with ribbon. As the bow was untied, and the lid removed, however, out fluttered a collection of aged moths.

This notice prompted Noël Coward to send a telegram to the company. It was affixed to the stage-door notice-board and awaited our arrival for the second performance. It read:

DEAR AGED MOTHS CONGRATULATIONS BUT WATCH OUT OR I SHALL BE AFTER YOU WITH SOME BALLS LOVE NOEL

Once again, in *The Globe Revue*, I was lucky enough to draw an ace out of the pack. One day during rehearsals Gerry Bryant went up to Billy Chappell with an idea for a piece of mime. It was no more than an idea. Billy Chappell thought about it and then tentatively presented it to me.

'The idea is,' he said, 'that of a shy, modest, more-sinned-against-than-sinning, suburban gent arriving on a crowded beach in mid-summer, and attempting to undress and don his swimming costume with propriety beneath the protective cover of his newspaper and voluminous mackintosh. What do you think?'

The first thing that struck me was that initially it was going to require a lot of invention and subsequently a great deal of hard work. How I craved for a good, well-written number with funny lines where the author had done the work and all I had to do was interpret them.

'Where do we get the crowd from?' I enquired.

'There won't be any,' said Billy. 'You will have to establish all that in mime.'

My Gemini twins asserted themselves characteristically. 'I don't know,' I said indecisively. 'I'm no Marcel Marceau, surely this is a job for a specialist performer. What do *you* think?'

'I think we can have some fun with it,' said Billy. 'Why not have a go?'

I thought for a few moments. My mind became a dull, unenthusiastic blank.

'All right,' I replied. 'If you think it's worth it.'

'Good,' said Billy. 'I'll get Donald Swann to write a little tune and we'll get down to work.'

Billy was marvellous; again his choreographic skills were to prove invaluable. The removal of each item of clothing was done to a specific number of bars in the music which, though skilful, nevertheless brought its own problems. The fact that everything was done under the mackintosh meant that if, as occasionally happened, I couldn't undo a particular button or bootlace, Norman Hackforth would have no idea since, unfortunately, he didn't have X-ray eyes. This could result in my getting bars behind with the music. Eventually he became adept at distinguishing between expressions of genuine desperation and those that, as the character, I was acting out in response to the simulated situation. It was never easy and in hot weather, when all the clothes stuck to me, it became a nightmare. I have never had a truer thought than my initial one – 'It's going to be damned hard work.' But Billy had again picked a winner for me. In reception 'Bank Holiday' outdid anything that I had received for 'Darling Boy' and the critics too were generous in their approbation. In addition, in the following weekend's *Sunday Express*, Giles devoted his entire cartoon to eight separate 'frames' showing my complete routine, step by step, under the heading: 'UNDRESSING ON THE BEACH.

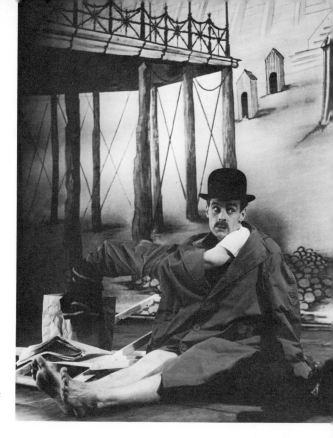

'Bank Holiday' –
The Globe Revue

Bold new satirist interprets classic English custom.' Finally, in a feature
article in *Theatre World* two months later, the author wrote:

Though Mr Carmichael appeared in *The Globe Revue*'s predecessor, none of
the items gave him the chance to make such a deep and favourable impression.
Now he has set the seal of success upon his career and for years hence the
mere mention of his name will be the cue for someone to ask, 'Do you remember
him undressing under his raincoat in that revue at the Globe?'

The originals of both the Giles cartoon and the talented Loudon Saint-
hill's design for the backcloth in front of which I performed 'Bank Holiday' have, warmly inscribed and signed by their creators, hung proudly
in my home ever since. And the irony of the whole thing is that Gerry
Bryant's original idea had been suggested to Billy Chappell for a girl.

The Globe Revue ran for six months. The company that had been
formed at the beginning of March 1951 for such a limited period had
remained together triumphantly for a year and ten months. We established a very close and special relationship with each other – like the
members of an exclusive club. Even today, though we have all gone our
separate ways and may not see each other for years on end, between those
of us that are still left there remains a deep-rooted friendship and loyalty.

CHAPTER TWENTY

THE WEST CONSOLIDATED

Enter MGM *– an eye-opener*

In London in the early 1950s there were three flourishing schools of intimate revue. The Tennent school – *The Lyric* and *The Globe*; the Laurier
Lister school – *Tuppence Coloured* (although this had Tennent's
financial backing) and *Penny Plain* which featured Joyce Grenfell, Max
Adrian and Elizabeth Welch; and a small but talented group of young
writers and performers who had operated a succession of highly successful
late-night offerings in the many fringe, club theatres that proliferated all
the way from the Watergate to Notting Hill Gate. These fringe revues
were written, in the main, by Peter Myers and Alec Grahame with music
by Ronald Cass. Opinion on the relative merits of the three schools is
very much a matter of taste. My own view is that Tennent's and Laurier
Lister vied with each other to be the leader in style, but the former I would
adjudge to take the laurels for topicality and wit. Laurier's shows, I think,
showed a fear of offending and were consequently much gentler. The
Myers–Grahame–Cass school, which was occasionally augmented by
David Climie and John Pritchett, were, in addition to being topical
and witty, astringent and totally irreverent. They were a considerable,
rising force which neither Tennent's nor Laurier Lister could afford to
ignore.

At the beginning of 1953 a London management decided to give this
latter school its first commercial West End showing. Billy Chappell was
engaged to direct it and he asked me to join him, which I did the moment
The Globe closed on Shaftesbury Avenue.

High Spirits, which was to be its name, had a very strong 'book' indeed.
It contained all the plums that these writers had tried out in their fringe
revues over several years and it was to star Cyril Ritchard and the lovely
Diana Churchill.

Cyril Ritchard was an Australian and for many years in the twenties
and thirties he and his wife, Madge Elliott, had been stars of musical

comedy both 'down under' and in London. Just prior to the war he became the leading man in Herbert Farjeon's revues at the Little Theatre and was, during my time and in my view, the finest exponent of the genre in the country; I was now thrilled to be working with him.

The main body of the cast were those that had been with the group in the club theatre circuit, several of whom have since made considerable names for themselves – Leslie Crowther, Joan Sims and Dilys Laye, for instance; Patrick Cargill was also a member of the 'Wines and Spirits'. I, for the first time in my life, was to be given first feature billing – a line on my own immediately below the title and larger than anyone else apart from the two stars.

One of the great boons of the Myers–Grahame–Climie team was that they could all write equally well for either sex and I came away with a fund of good material.

As a result of a commitment in the United States, Cyril arrived one week late for rehearsals but, when he did so, such was his talent that he immediately made all the rest of us feel totally inadequate. He was, in addition to being gifted, a very nice man and we got on famously together. One item in the show, however, in which we were both to appear, had its teething troubles.

It was a cruel burlesque of an ENSA concert party called *Something For The Boys*. There was, at the outset, no part in it for me, but Billy had the idea that I should play a lady pianist who would be on stage throughout the entire skit accompanying the concert on a mini piano. At rehearsals, there being no piano available, I simply sat there on a chair doing nothing while the others went through their paces. After a week of this Cyril, who was playing the principal comedian of the troupe, stopped in mid-song and said to Billy Chappell, 'What's Ian doing there?'

'What's Ian doing where?' said Billy.

'Well, he just sits there on that chair throughout the entire proceedings doing nothing every time we rehearse it.'

'Oh, I see,' replied Billy. 'He's playing the pianist, the accompanist, only we haven't got a piano for him yet.'

'I see,' said Cyril. 'But what's he got that handbag on the floor beside him for?'

'He's a woman pianist,' exclaimed Billy. 'He's in drag.'

'Is he?' replied Cyril, handing his script to Leslie Crowther. 'Right – you can play this part, not me,' he said and smartly stepped down.

After a short provincial tour, *High Spirits* opened at the London Hippodrome – now the Talk of the Town – and on its first night I had a

*As Esther de Groot in
'Something For The Boys'
from* High Spirits, *the lady
with whom Cyril Ritchard
refused to appear*

very nasty experience indeed. One of the last notes we had been given by our director after the dress rehearsal on the previous evening was that no one was to walk behind the sky-cloth at the back of the stage during the actual performance as there was little room and such action caused it to waft in the breeze. If anyone wished to get from one side of the stage to the other 'he or she', said Billy, 'must get there by crossing underneath it', a common enough route in most theatres.

I was constantly on the move in *High Spirits*, with quick change after quick change. I was in ten items throughout the evening. One particular quick change I had immediately prior to my 'single' as the guardsman who always faints on parade. It was the only occasion that I had to cross in one heck of a hurry) from one side of the stage to the other. On the previous evening I had used the forbidden route. At this point on the opening night I flew down the steps to the stage basement. On arrival there appeared to be no door or opening through which to pass leading in the right direction. The only available route to follow was one heading towards, for all I knew, the box office; it was certainly far off course for my required destination. I had no choice; I took it. I belted along realising with horror that every step was taking me farther and farther away from the stage. Somewhere above me I could hear the item before mine drawing nearer and nearer to its conclusion. Ten seconds later I calculated that I was somewhere underneath one of those second-hand bookshops in the Charing Cross Road. Panic set in with a vengeance. It was then I met Ronnie Stevens travelling in the opposite direction having just completed his number.

'Where the hell's the stage?' I cried, nearly demented.

'Keep straight on,' he said. 'Have faith – you'll come to it eventually.'

After what seemed to be another mile and a half in that unending subterranean labyrinth I finally arrived at the other side just in time to grab my rifle from a prop man and dash out on stage with hardly a breath left in my lungs and a heartbeat that must have been heard in Wyndhams.

The London Hippodrome, I must explain, had been built in 1899 and what eventually became the stalls was originally a huge circular water tank in which were staged aquashows. The route from one side of the stage to the other did not, therefore, as is customary, traverse directly underneath it but completely circumnavigated the site of the tank, going all the way round the back of the auditorium in a horseshoe until it finally fetched up on the opposite side. From that night onwards, if ever I had to make a similar journey in a strange theatre, I never failed to reconnoitre the route prior to the first performance.

One evening during the run of *High Spirits* I was most unexpectedly to meet one of my schoolboy idols; it was on the evening that he visited the show and came round backstage to call on Cyril afterwards. Cyril and I had the only two dressing-rooms on a mezzanine floor and my door was directly opposite his. I had removed my make-up, changed and was just about to leave when there was a knock on my door. I said, 'Come in,' and in he walked. He was, as always, immaculate. He was wearing a dinner jacket with a clove carnation in the lapel. He extended his hand warmly for me to shake and said, 'Hello, old boy, my name's Jack Buchanan.' Everything about Jack Buchanan was immaculate. It was one of the most courteous, charming and totally superfluous introductions that I have ever received in my life. He then complimented me on my performance and left as suddenly and as charmingly as he had arrived. No one else could have made me feel as I did when he closed the door behind him. Ten feet tall doesn't describe it. We were never to meet again.

Four years later, in tragic circumstances, I was to attend a cocktail party which was held in the Lord Chamberlain's apartments in St James's Palace. It was convened to inaugurate an appeal to raise money to endow

With Cyril Ritchard in High Spirits

a Jack Buchanan memorial ward in the Cancer Research Hospital in Lincoln's Inn Fields after his untimely death. The gap he left in our theatre has never been filled.

High Spirits had a sixteen-week run at the London Hippodrome. It was a good and elegant show (it had been designed by Osbert Lancaster) and was always well received. Basically, however, we were in the wrong theatre for an intimate revue – it was a huge house which, I am afraid, didn't help us.

When *High Spirits* closed at the end of August I had been in constant work for a period of seven years, during which I had had no proper holiday and for vast stretches of the time I had been doing several jobs at once. I had, in fact, simultaneous with my appearances in the West End, directed *another* round of summer shows for Richard (though I could never leave town to actually stage them in the resorts), a revue at the Irving Theatre – a small club theatre just off Leicester Square – and several more television shows for Ronnie Waldman. I was, however, a fairly fit young man, wiry and with an abundance of energy. Throughout those years and for many to come, despite the fact that I downed a fair ration of beer, ate three cooked meals a day including a massive two-course affair plus cheese and biscuits which, on arrival home after the theatre at night I took up to bed on a tray, I somehow managed to retain a sylph-like figure and never weighed a pound over nine stone. Stripped I was ideal casting for an undernourished inmate of a prisoner-of-war camp. Nevertheless, when I left the stage-door of the Hippodrome on the last Saturday night, I was very tired. I badly needed a break. We had, there- fore, decided to go up to Sleights for three weeks' holiday. I had been looking forward to it for a long time and I left a strict brief with Richard that I didn't want disturbing for anything or anybody.

On the Monday morning we all piled into the train at King's Cross and in the most beautiful sunshine steamed off for the north. The English countryside was looking a picture, the woods and hedgerows in full and lush leaf and the cornfields golden and ready for harvesting. After so long in the Smoke it couldn't have been more inviting. When we reached 'Penarth' we all wandered over to my father-in-law's farm and the children helped to collect the eggs and feed the hens. That night, after supper, I accompanied him down to Whitby for a few pints – an inviolate habit of his which he undertook every single night of his life in all weathers. The whole scene was idyllic and I started to relax the moment I breathed the clear, fresh air of the moors, the Esk valley and the salty tang of the sea.

The following morning my tranquillity was shattered immediately after breakfast just as we were about to set off for a picnic. The telephone rang – it was Richard.

'Look, I know you don't want disturbing, old boy, but the juvenile lead in a new MGM movie that starts shooting with four weeks' location in Holland in a month's time is on offer and the director wants to see you right away. The stars of the picture are Clark Gable, Lana Turner and Victor Mature.'

Even so rosy an offer failed to stir an iota of enthusiasm in my vitals.

'Are you there?' said Richard.

'Yes,' I replied.

'Did you hear all that?'

'Yes, I did,' I mumbled.

'Well, what about it? The director's called Godfrey Reinhart and he's staying at Claridge's. How quickly can you get back?'

'Oh God,' I said. 'I don't particularly want to see him at all.'

'Don't be a fool,' said Richard, unable to believe his ears. 'You've got to, you can't afford not to.'

'Oh God,' I repeated. 'I'm bloody tired, Richard, all I want is to be left alone.'

'Look, mate, you've only got to come down to see the fellow. You can go back again the next day.'

Finally I was persuaded yet again to pull my socks together and an appointment was made for me to see him in his suite at three o'clock the following afternoon. That evening I changed my mind and decided that I wasn't going to go – and if it hadn't been for Pym, I wouldn't have done, either. She looked up the trains and discovered that I could, in fact, do the round trip in a day; I wouldn't have to stay a single night away from Sleights. Nevertheless, right up to the moment of departure, I was all for calling it off.

The following morning she woke me at 6.30, made my breakfast, ran me to the station and, as I was still in a fiendish pet, literally had to push me on to the 7.30 to King's Cross.

I got to London about mid-day, went to Gloucester Avenue to don a respectable suit and showed up at Claridge's on time. Mr Reinhart was affable, smiled a lot and, after about fifteen minutes, no wiser about my suitability for the role than I had been on my arrival, I left him.

Somewhere about 9 p.m. I stepped out of a train at York. Pym met me with her father's car and we were back at 'Penarth' in time for me to accompany him for his late evening libation.

The following day Richard telephoned to say that I had got the part which, of course, made our three-week holiday for us.

The picture started out by being called *The True and the Brave* but finished up with the title *Betrayed*. The subject concerned the Dutch Resistance movement at the time of the Battle of Arnhem. I played the part of a captain in the Grenadier Guards and I left for Holland to start the location work towards the end of September. It was an interesting and nostalgic four weeks as the main locations we used were ones that I had frequented during the battle seven years previously.

The making of *Betrayed*, apart from earning me quite a lot of money, was to prove a frustrating disappointment. Initially I had an excellent part which, though it was an action picture, contained a lot of good comedy. It had been scripted by the English playwright Ronald Millar, but by the time it reached the cinema nine months later it, and much of the original story, was practically unrecognisable.

The American actors I found a model of self-discipline. Clark Gable, a quiet and retiring man – or so he appeared to me – was always the first on the set every morning. Always there, sitting in his chair, ready for a prompt 8.30 start, and during the entire period of shooting I never once saw a copy of the script in his hand.

Victor Mature, a larger than life, flamboyant extrovert, one night asked

Pym and me to have dinner with him and his wife at the Savoy where they were staying. Neither of us was on call the following day so it was a relaxed evening. We started with several shakers of dry martinis in his riverside suite; then, somewhere around 10 p.m., we repaired (maybe 'lurched' would be a better word) downstairs to the Grill Room. During the coffee stage a waiter brought a written message to him at the table.

'Blast,' said Mature. 'They've switched things. I'm on call at 7.30 in the morning.'

'Oh, look,' I said, 'it's already getting late. Pym and I will down this and leave you.'

'What the hell for?' said our host.

'Well, you'll want to get to bed, and you've got your lines to learn for tomorrow's scenes.'

'In the first place, I'm not tired,' he said, 'and in the second, I know my lines.'

'You know them?' I said. 'How come? You've only just had your call.'

'I learned the whole film before I left Los Angeles,' he replied.

I felt and no doubt looked incredulous.

'That's amazing,' I said.

'What's amazing?' he replied. 'What other way is there of doing it?'

Nine out of ten English actors, unless the scene is a 'pill', rarely learn their lines until the night before they're called upon to shoot it. Apart from anything else, in many films new, rewritten pages to the original script are issued with such monotonous regularity that to undertake too much advanced study is frequently a waste of time. Such, in fact, was the case with *Betrayed*.

But life was not to be all dry martinis and dinners at the Savoy Grill. Back at the studios I had, at the beginning anyway, a sizeable role and yet in scenes with any of the principals, rarely can I remember being favoured by the camera. The shots were nearly always taken over my shoulder towards the star and, if ever the director decided to shoot the complementary reverse angle on me, it was a red-letter day in my life. I don't think I ever had a close-up. In addition, many of my scenes, regretfully, ended up on the cutting-room floor.

When *Betrayed* was eventually premiered at the Empire, Leicester Square, I was astounded to find that the posters and advertising gave co-star billing to an actor called Louis Calhern. I had been on the picture throughout the entire production – in Holland and in the MGM studios at Borehamwood in Hertfordshire – and Louis Calhern had never been anywhere near us. It transpired that after the shooting was completed and the stars and director had returned to America, an entirely new character had been written into the story and his sequences had been shot in Hollywood and slotted into the finished product at various intervals.

The whole experience, however, had been both interesting and enlightening and, despite the many disappointments, life in movies appealed to me. I liked the hours, I liked the less claustrophobic atmosphere as compared with the theatre, I liked the actual work itself, and I liked the pay. But no sooner had I finished at MGM than I was back in revue once again and this time, for the first time in my life, with star billing.

It was Christmas week 1953 and the thrill of being so exalted was amplified by the fact that I was also renewing acquaintanceship with many old friends.

First and foremost, the two ladies with whom I was to share top billing were Hermione Baddeley and Dora Bryan. 'Toté' Baddeley, apart from a chance encounter during the war, I don't think I had met since I was her assistant stage-manager and small-part player in the *Nine Sharp* tour some thirteen years previously. Dora and I, of course, had been parted for only about ten months.

'That Versatile Trio' from At The Lyric *and* Going to Town *with Dora Bryan and Hermione Baddeley. A 'send up' of one of those hideously talented (?) family variety acts whose turn includes everything from playing all conceivable instruments to dancing, plate-balancing and paper-tearing*

The director was, once again, to be Billy Chappell, the management my *Lyric* and *Globe* employers, H. M. Tennent, and finally we were back at the scene of former triumphs – the Lyric, Hammersmith.

The revue was called *At The Lyric* and was written mainly by Alan Melville. Alan I had not worked with before. He had, of course, had enormous success with his *Sweet and Low* series of revues at the Ambassadors Theatre during the war years and was soon to show that he had lost none of his old flair.

We opened 'cold' on 23 December to an excellent reception both in the theatre and in the following morning's Press and we ran happily through to Easter and into the beginning of May. Somewhere around March, it was decided that several of the items would be replaced and that we would, when ready, move into the West End with a second edition. This we did, opening in the St Martin's Theatre during the week following our closure in Hammersmith under the new title of *Going to Town*. Again we were received well but this time we only managed to run for a further couple of months. It is a sobering thought that the stage-door right opposite our own at the St Martin's was that of the Ambassadors Theatre where, at that time, *The Mousetrap* had been running for a mere year and a half and was still with its original leading man, Richard Attenborough. It is now in its twenty-seventh year.

During the run of *Going to Town* I also spent a lot of time at Shepperton Studios appearing in the second worthwhile part that I had been offered in movies. The film was *The Colditz Story* and once again I impersonated an officer in the Grenadier Guards. It was a most enjoyable experience, even though I was getting to bed at midnight and up again at 6.30 the following morning for several weeks. It also did much to wash the nasty taste out of my mouth that had been left by my previous experience of movie-making.

During the making of *The Colditz Story* I struck up a close and enduring friendship with the late Richard Wattis. He too played a Guards officer and we appeared throughout the film together as a sort of insouciant double act. Dickie and I shared a hire-car to the studios every morning and once again in my life a friendship was established on the solid and, to me, infallible foundation of concordant senses of humour.

Richard was several years older than I and it was after many months of working and playing together that we discovered that we had both been educated at Bromsgrove. Occasionally, he saw fit to pass on this piece of information to others: 'Do you realise that both Ian and I went to the same school?' – a line I always followed hastily with one that we eventually came to recite in unison, 'But not at the same time!'

I had by mid 1954 spent most of my professional life doing musical work and the last three and a half years of it almost exclusively in revue. I was now beginning to get tired of it. I was running out of ideas for characters. I was even running out of moustaches and I wanted very much to get out of it before my performances started to deteriorate. I was also getting physically tired. Revue is an exhausting medium, essentially one for the young. Whenever the revue performer is not on the stage he is charging back to his dressing-room two steps at a time to change, not only his costume but also his make-up. Frequently he hasn't got time to reach his dressing-room and has to use a hastily constructed quick-change room on the side of the stage. I was, by now, dearly wanting a nice part in a good comedy play in which I had to create one character only during an evening instead of six or seven, and also one that would allow me to walk down for my entrances and change, if I had to, leisurely between the acts. There was also another purely technical hazard to performing too regularly in revue which could seriously impede the advancement of an actor's career. The majority of performers in intimate revue – sadly now an entertainment which has become *démodé* – were primarily straight actors who could sing and dance a bit. Nevertheless, casting directors, invariably and unimaginatively, pigeon-holed such performers as 'revue artistes' – a category which, in their eyes, was not to be considered seriously when casting plays or films.

All these thoughts had been passing through my mind during the run of the two Alan Melville revues and it was at the first-night party after the opening of *Going to Town* that I tackled Binkie Beaumont and pleaded that he should now try to find me a nice part in a good play.

'All in good time, Ian,' he said. 'All in good time. Have some more cold salmon.'

I had been fobbed off. I knew it.

I maligned him. Binkie was as good as his word, and when the part came it was a beauty.

CHAPTER TWENTY-ONE

PLAYTIME

Enter HUGH (BINKIE) BEAUMONT – *a keeper of promises*

During the intervening years extensive renovations had been carried out in Gloucester Avenue. The property had been redecorated inside and out, the basement gutted, refurbished and let off separately and a lot of modernisation and structural improvements undertaken. In addition, we had laid a new lawn at the back and planted flowerbeds to brighten us up during the summer. In the front the area had been crazy-paved, a privet hedge established and a tall wrought-iron gate of classic design hung between the two masonry gateposts that stood lone and silent sentinels to the day when Mr Churchill commandeered all the original iron-work in the street to make guns in the early days of the war. My earning power might have increased since we moved into 173 but my crumbling castle was rapidly absorbing most of the extra loot.

We also had other problems. Since coming south Lee had started to develop a bronchial complaint and the Gloucester Avenue environment was not helping the situation. It was fortuitous, therefore, that, shortly after *Going to Town* had opened, I bumped into one of the chorus-boys from the cast of *Wild Violets*. His name was Bill and he had a small house in a charming little enclave called Eton Villas but half a mile away from us on the other side of Adelaide Road. We had frequently walked round the area pushing prams on a Sunday afternoon and had envied the locals and coveted their homes. They too were of the Victorian semi-basement variety but they were more *bijou* than the standard model. In addition, they all faced due south and possessed both front and back gardens. They were owned by Eton College and the rents were unbelievable. Bill was on the bitter end of a ninety-nine-year lease at something quite ridiculous like thirty shillings a week. The new rents, however, were being raised to three pounds and Bill wanted to move. Would we, he enquired, like to apply for the new lease? Wouldn't we just? We immediately made the necessary application and, in due course, after having secured a long tenure, put Gloucester Avenue on the market the following day.

During the run of *The Globe Revue* I had got to know an extremely good-looking, young and charming Australian who was a friend of Myles Eason. He had recently arrived in England with little money and was managing to keep his head above water by playing the piano nightly in a club almost opposite our stage-door. He also had a talent for interior decoration and had recently helped Myles to redecorate his flat in Jermyn Street.

One night shortly after we had acquired Eton Villas he came into the theatre during a break in his piano playing and I told him our good news. 'Would you', I then asked him very tentatively, 'be prepared to design us a new bathroom?'

'I'd love to,' he said.

Two weeks later he returned with an immaculate model painted in the minutest detail and Pym and I both flipped. He had used white bathroom furniture and also white paint for all the woodwork and the ceiling. On two opposing walls he had applied a black marble paper and on the other two one of the Royal Stuart hunting tartan – which, for the Sassenachs, is predominantly post office red. The window he had invested with a white Venetian blind and curtains of lemon glazed chintz. The floor-covering was also lemon and he had arranged a pattern of four Victorian prints on one of the marble walls. We were thrilled and in due course we went ahead and built it.

Before he left that day we both thanked him profusely and asked him what he wanted as a fee.

'Oh, don't be silly,' he said, 'we're friends, aren't we? I was delighted to do it for you.'

He was, I knew, fairly hard up, and he had a wife to support. 'Nonsense,' I replied. 'You can't do that – come on, what do I owe you?'

'Nothing,' he said adamantly.

After a further attempt to break him down he finally made a small concession. 'I'll tell you what,' he said, 'just pay me for the materials for the model. That's all I want.'

'How much is that then?' I asked.

'Call it a fiver,' he said.

I think I insisted on his accepting £20, but I can't be sure.

Were I to employ Jon Bannenberg today, I estimate that I would have to pay him somewhere in the region of twenty times that amount.

Soon he opened up a small interior decorating business in a tiny shop off the Brompton Road which he called 'Marble and Lemon' and, with the success that he achieved, eventually moved into Bond Street. During the last two decades he has designed homes for the wealthy all over Europe and also much of the interior of the *QE II*.

But a new house was not the only thing to come my way at this time. Quicker than I could ever have imagined, Binkie Beaumont came back to honour his word. One day towards the end of the run of *Going to Town* he telephoned me to say that he had just sent the script of a new play down to the theatre for me by hand. It was, he said, going into rehearsal immediately the revue finished. Would I take it home that night, read it and see if I would like to play the part of David? I was elated.

On my arrival at the theatre the stage-door keeper handed me a large envelope along with my mail and I took it up to my dressing-room and ripped it open. The manuscript was red with a yellow binding and on the label on the top right-hand corner of the cover, I read '*Simon and Laura*, a new comedy by Alan Melville.'

Dora too, it transpired, had received a copy by the same 'post'; Binkie's idea was that we should play opposite each other.

The play appealed to both of us instantly. Simon and Laura of the title, who were to be played by Roland Culver and Coral Browne, were a celebrated married actor and actress team who had fallen on hardish times. They were also of individual fiery temperaments, and 'at rise', as American playwrights say, a flaming row was in progress as Simon, not for the first time during their tempestuous marriage, was preparing to 'go home to mother'. At this point a young and wildly enthusiastic BBC TV producer – one David Prentice (self) – arrives on their doorstep to sell them the idea of appearing in a daily soap-opera which would mirror the lives of an ideally happily married couple. In view of their recent vicissitude, they have little alternative but to agree, and it is from the juxtaposition of their personal relationship and the one that they are to play that the comedy arose. Dora was to play the script-writer of the series who, after the obvious amatorial mix-up between the four central characters, winds up with David, her first love.

The whole package was an ideal one for me. Two distinguished leading players, a funny play, a marvellous part, and Dora, whom I knew well, to play opposite. Binkie had come up trumps.

Going to Town closed at the end of July and after a month's rehearsal we opened *Simon and Laura* at the Opera House, Manchester, at the beginning of September. We were received well and the morning after the first night, it being 1 September, the author took his four principals out for an oyster luncheon.

We toured *Simon and Laura* for twelve weeks before opening in the West End, during which time I enjoyed myself enormously. 'Roly' and Coral, who were new to me, were a joy to work with. One word only is required to describe their respective abilities – 'expert' – and when playing comedy, all I have ever asked to be associated with is expertise.

With Coral Browne and Roland Culver in Simon and Laura. *Dora Bryan back to camera*

During those weeks, when we weren't able to return to London at the weekends, we travelled from town to town in Roly's Daimler, and one particular legacy that I inherited from the tour I treasure to this day. It was to be donated by Miss Browne.

Coral Browne, who has now married the American actor Vincent Price, is a great loss to the English theatre. She is a paradoxical figure in many ways. She is Australian and is infused with a certain brashness which is characteristic of many of her countrymen. She also possesses so many qualities that make great leading ladies. She has style; panache; bravura. She can wear clothes, has taste, poise and stature and she has the most striking of good looks. She is also a fine actress. In addition to all these sterling qualities she has, when she wishes to lash it, a renownedly stinging, but nonetheless amusing, tongue. I learned a lot from Coral – an improved vocabulary of expletives, to mention but one (those chaps in the Hull City dressing-room didn't begin) – but the thing for which I shall ever remain in her debt is that it was she who first taught me how to eat. Until meeting Coral, food to me was mere fodder. Coral taught me the pleasures of eating, and not in grand restaurants either – in the humblest of digs. For most meals she brought home a bottle of wine to accompany it and in her presence, however unpretentious, every meal seemed like High Mass. She knew her landladies and she picked discriminatingly. There was one Irish lady in Liverpool who would come in after the main course and say, 'What would you like for afters?'

'What have you got to offer us?' asked Coral.

'Would you like a nice apple pie?' she enquired.

We concurred.

It took rather longer than customary in normal digs for the pie to arrive, but when it did it was piping hot and the crust was almost invisible under what had got to be the entire contents of a 1 lb packet of caster sugar. The reason for the delay, of course, was that she had ascertained what we would like first, then gone out and baked it. We were also mystified for a few days as to how she always seemed to have whatever cheese we fancied already in the house.

'What sort of cheese would you like, me dear?'

'Have you any gorgonzola?'

'I have that,' and in ten minutes it would be on the table. It was on about the Thursday we discovered that she never had any cheese in the house. What ever it was we asked for, she would then put on her hat and coat and slip round the corner to buy.

One thing we never did discover was when and where the good lady went to bed. She was always still up when we retired and was still about when we came down to breakfast in the morning. Every room in the house we could account for and none was hers. We finally came to the conclusion that when everyone else had retired, she dossed down under the stairs.

Simon and Laura opened at the Strand Theatre in late November and for the first time I had my name up in lights. The critics approved of our offering and we settled down to a four-month run at the Strand, after which we transferred to the Apollo Theatre in Shaftesbury Avenue where we ran for a further three.

The most memorable anecdote that emerged from the run of *Simon and Laura* has long since passed into the annals of theatrical folklore. Towards the end of Act I Coral and I had a scene together, dead centre

stage, during which a celebrated elderly character actor who was playing
the butler was laying a table for dinner in a bay window alcove up at the
back. This was subservient to our dialogue and should have been executed in a decorous and undistracting manner which occasionally it
wasn't. During one particular performance Coral, who had a line which
was always a sure-fire laugh, was astonished to find it being received in
stony silence. As it had been delivered in the manner in which she always
delivered it, the fault could only lie in the fact that something distracting
had been going on behind her back. A few moments later the curtain
fell and as we were climbing the stairs to our dressing-rooms Coral said
to me, 'I hope you get on all right with my understudy next week, Ian.'

I was dumbfounded. 'Understudy?' I said. 'Why? What's happening
to you?'

'I'm going into hospital to have an operation,' she replied.

I was even more dumbfounded. 'I had no idea,' I said. 'I am sorry.
What are you going to have done?' – and, half turning to the elderly
character actor who was following behind us, she said, 'I'm going to have
eyes put in the back of my bloody head.'

Ever chivalrous, I have, of course, cleaned up Miss Browne's language
somewhat.

Another Coral Browne-ism occurred on a night when she was giving
a supper party after the show and during the performance her mind was
obviously more on that than on the immediate situation.

It occurred early on in the play when Simon was packing to leave Laura
and she had come down the stairs with an armful of his clothes to assist
him to do so. The scene was interrupted by the arrival of David Prentice,
and after his long sales spiel the couple agreed to remain together but
for professional reasons only. Whereupon Laura threw her armful of
Simon's clothes back at him and said, 'All right then, go and put these
back in the wardrobe.'

On the night in question, two suits, some shirts and a few ties flung
back at Roly were accompanied by the immortal line, 'All right then,
go and put these back in the oven.'

Roly was not without his moments of mental aberration either. His
purler came one night in Act III. Act II finished with a punch-up and the
third act opened with him on the stage alone the following morning with
a black eye which could hardly have been improved on by Muham-
med Ali. As the act progressed, joke piled upon joke as each successive
member of the cast came on and referred to it in graphic detail. After
which they, each in turn, proceeded to give him varied remedies for

relieving both the pain and the discoloration. The audience responded politely, which is all they could have been expected to do under the circumstances, as Roly had forgotten to paint it on during the act interval.

In due course, I was to play *Simon and Laura* in every medium except radio. The last occasion was on television in 1964 when I appeared as Simon to Moira Lister's Laura with Richard Briers in my original role.

During our run at the Apollo, as if to keep me out of mischief during the daytime, someone came along and offered me the part of Tom Willoughby, one of the four young officers in the third remake of the classic A. E. W. Mason novel *The Four Feathers*. The one before ours was probably the definitive version; it was made in the mid-thirties and starred Ralph Richardson and John Clements. Ours featured Anthony Steele and Laurence Harvey and was in Cinemascope. The third and fourth members of the male quartet, though useful parts from the point of view of making money – plenty of days' shooting – really scored no runs at all; the two leads were, intrinsically, the only ones worth having.

We were directed by Zoltan Korda, who had directed the Richardson-Clements version, and every scene in ours had to be a replica of the one in his original production. Each night he repaired to the cutting-rooms to view the 1930s version of the scenes that he was due to shoot on the following day. It was a restricting experience to be so irrevocably tied to some other fellow's performance, even if, as in my case, I was having to emulate the admirable Roger Livesey.

'Zolie', in many ways, was a sadistic director. He always carried a stick and at massacring the English language he had to run Sam Goldwyn a close second. ('You must see ze part as a mild man. All ze time he is like butter won't melt on his head.') Yet there are very few people from whom one cannot learn something; one sentence from Zolie Korda I found more articulate than any other director had succeeded in being when trying to teach me the secret of performing to the camera.

'Stop ecting, Ian,' he said. 'Stop ecting. You do not have to ect in front of a camera. Just behave.'

It was an uncomfortable film to make. For the scenes towards the end of it, when we had been locked in the sweltering heat of an Omdurman dungeon for several months, we had to get to the studios at 6.30 a.m. The make-up – a Rip van Winkle affair with long hair, an unkempt beard and a long-drawn appearance indicating undernourishment, plus overall body suntan, sweat and general grime – required two hours to put on. The scenes themselves were shot in a claustrophobic set which was

In Storm Over The Nile *with, left to right, Ronald Lewis, Christopher Lee and Anthony Steele*

packed to Black Hole of Calcutta proportions with a vast posse of practically naked and sweating humanity recruited from, presumably, the London docks. Such unskilled labour handling rifles and stampeding to order made one feel, at times, that it might have been wise to take out some form of personal insurance at the beginning of the picture.

The vast crowd and battle scenes shot on location in Africa in the thirties version were, having been stretched by some alchemy known only to the boffins of photography, used once again in 1955. This resulted in one actor, Jack Lambert, appearing in the picture twice. A shot of him in the previous film in which he portrayed a drummer boy was included in the new remake in which he appeared as the colonel of the regiment.

Our version was retitled *Storm Over The Nile* and keeps turning up at off-peak hours on television with monotonous regularity. Any viewer having caught such a showing could, however, be excused for not having realised that I was in it. I was, more often than not, consigned to the edge of the frame, and as Cinemascope was not designed for the proportions of a cathode ray tube, when viewed on television I hardly ever am.

The Four Feathers story, however, seems to be indestructible; only recently yet another version has been made, this time with Robert Powell and Simon Ward.

While all this was going on, we had, as a family, become happily ensconced in our new home. If we had been happy in Gloucester Avenue, in Eton Villas we were in Elysium. Gone was the grime and pollution, gone the squalor and heavy traffic that used Gloucester Avenue as a by-pass to Camden Town during the rush hour; and in their places were fresh air, greenery and a quiet backwater.

Simon and Laura closed on Shaftesbury Avenue at the end of May 1955 and overlapping its closure by one week there began a whole new era of my life. Having by then achieved a 'name in lights' status in the West End theatre, the big and exciting doors of the film studios were now about to open for me with unforeseen haste.

CHAPTER TWENTY-TWO

FROM PINEWOOD TO BOREHAMWOOD

Enter THE BOULTING BROTHERS – *Starmakers*

At a luncheon in March 1956 the Variety Club of Great Britain awarded me a Silver Heart. It says on it: 'The Actor Who Made the Most Progress in 1955'. It is, believe it or not, only as I write, some twenty-years later, that it has struck me that the wording on the award could have been a deliberate pun on the title of a film I had made during the second half of that year.

In the spring of 1955, however, I was approached by the Rank Organisation and asked to repeat my performance as David Prentice in the film of *Simon and Laura*. This was tremendous news. It was to be made at Pinewood, in colour – an accolade in 1955 – and was to star Peter Finch and Kay Kendall. Playing opposite me was to be the petite and gamine Muriel Pavlow. Work on the film overlapped the play by one week and it was for me a week of mixed emotions. On location, which occupied the first week, I had a feeling of being an interloper. I knew the piece well – nobody else did. Consequently, I felt, I'm sure incorrectly, that I was an embarrassment to others, particularly to Peter and Kay – or Katie, as she was known to all and sundry. Returning to the theatre at night, the fact that I alone out of the cast had been engaged to play in the film also caused me embarrassment. This too I am sure was totally unnecessary as it is an unfortunate fact of life that film producers, when casting leading roles, always go for the big film names or their own contract artistes if they have any, and in this case they had. I am convinced, therefore, that neither Roly nor Coral expected to play in the movie, but the sensitivity was there nevertheless. At the studio this shyness was soon broken down, largely as a result of Katie's and Peter's innate warmth and friendliness.

Katie had a bounce, a vivacity, an ebullience that would be difficult to exaggerate. She sparkled like a roman candle from 7 a.m. to knocking-off time. She was warm, she was funny, she was tall and beautiful and

*With Peter Finch and
Kay Kendall in the film*
Simon and Laura

her effervescence permeated everyone around her. Everybody loved her
– it was impossible not to do so.

Peter, while full of fun and geniality, was perhaps more susceptible
and had his occasional moments of minor key introspection. I got to
know him and his mother and sister well, and many a convivial evening
we shared at their house off the Fulham Road. But nobody could be
introspective for long in the presence of the beguiling Miss Kendall. We
all basked in her aura of sunshine and champagne and it developed into
a hilarious ten weeks.

Friday night was the end of the working week – 'Squeak for joy night,
wifey,' in Katie's parlance – and when it was over we would all adjourn
to the bar and drink far too many Black Velvets.

Four years later I was in the middle of a heated conference in a private
room in the Midland Hotel, Manchester, during the opening week of
a new musical, when I was called to the telephone. It was a national newspaper informing me of Katie's death from leukaemia at the age of thirty-
two. I was stunned. I took the news back into the conference and so was
everyone else.

As things turned out, I was severely critical of my performance in the
film of *Simon and Laura*. It was fairly larger than life in the theatre and
in my view I failed to reduce it to the size required by a movie camera.
It is not difficult, when experienced and well directed, to initiate a performance for the screen, but to reduce one that has been played successfully in the theatre for many months poses problems.

The film of *Simon and Laura* was a milestone in our family lives too, as it was during it that we bought our first car. I was thirty-five years of age. It was a fairly modest chariot but it was brand new. A Ford Consul in a colour known for some unaccountable reason as Lychfield Green. The weather was glorious that summer and Pym took delivery of it one morning while I was at the studios. That evening the entire family drove down to Pinewood in blissful sunshine to pick me up when I had finished work. The thrill and the pride with which we drove home defies description; at that particular moment no state coach could have felt more opulent.

I carried away another souvenir from the film of *Simon and Laura* which I still treasure very much. 'Finchie' was, in his spare time, no inconsiderable painter and when it was all over he presented the two girls and me each with one of his water-colours mounted and framed. Mine is a black and white brush-wash of an old town in Spain and is always greatly admired by our guests. I am only sad that he neglected to sign it.

I was to return to Pinewood in nine months' time but my next visit was not to be such a happy affair.

I cannot for the life of me remember the exact order of events that first brought the Boulting brothers into my life, but the marriage of our respective talents was certainly momentous for me. The first I knew of their interest in me was during the making of *Simon and Laura*. Richard rang me up one day and proceeded to make one of the blandest statements that could ever have accompanied a pretty earth-shattering offer.

'I've just had the Boulting brothers on the telephone,' he said. 'They want to turn you into a film star.'

A pause. 'Pardon?'

He rattled on as if he had five other calls waiting. 'They have two subjects for you – two novels – the first will start shooting immediately you finish *Simon and Laura* and the second in mid-fifty-six. They want an option for five films. They are sending the books to you today. When you've read them they want you to go and have a chat with them. Give me a buzz when you're ready.'

Another pause.

'Hello? Are you there?'

'Are you serious?'

'Of course I'm serious. Read them quickly and I'll fix up for you to go and see them.'

And that was that. I put the telephone down speechless. I wandered downstairs to tell Pym who was in the kitchen.

'Guess what?' I said.

She looked at me as if it was forenoon on 1 April.

Twenty-four hours later a parcel arrived from Charter Films, the Boultings' company. I opened it and took out two brand-new books still in their dust jackets. One was called *Private's Progress* by Alan Hackney and the other *Brothers in Law* by Henry Cecil. Over the next few days I read them and found them both hilarious. The leading part in each was an absolute cracker. They were, in my view, and presumably in the Boulting brothers', tailor-made for me. The following day I went to see them in their office in Grosvenor Street.

John and Roy Boulting are identical twins. They are of average height, slim and aquiline-featured. In 1955 the one easy way of distinguishing one from the other was that John wore horn-rimmed spectacles. An additional identification at that time was that Roy smoked a pipe while John, on the set anyway, practically chain-smoked cigarettes – principally other people's. They are both imbued with considerable charm yet can summon up chilling forthrightness when they deem it necessary. They each have an abundant sense of humour which can at times be sardonic and they have, over the years, both been blessed with several fruitful marriages.

As film-makers they invariably switched producing and directing turn and turn about, and they were always involved in the writing of their own screen-plays. They are the most articulate of men, an attribute which, to an actor, made them directors of exceptional quality. They were also good listeners, analytical and decisive. I don't think during the course of the six films I made for them I ever reached a compromise over interpretation with either of the Boulting brothers. If we disagreed about anything, John, in particular, would go away for a walk round the back of the set humming tunelessly to himself to weigh the situation up. After a while he would return and say, 'You're right; it's a good idea – we'll do it your way.' Or alternatively, 'You're wrong, Ian, and I'll tell you why.' And he would; furthermore, he would be convincing. As a result, I don't think I was ever given anything to do for either John or Roy about which we were not in accord. Finally, they were both fanatical cricket fans which provided an immediate rapport between us the moment I was asked to sit down in their office. According to John my nervousness at the beginning of the interview was tempered by the distraction of an oil painting of W. G. Grace at the wicket which hung above his desk.

*With Ian Bannen
and Richard
Attenborough in*
Private's Progress

'You interested in cricket?' he asked.

'Very,' I replied, and we were away.

Private's Progress is the story of one Stanley Windrush, an underdog,
and it chronicled his catastrophic experiences in the army in the early
1940s. It was to be directed by John, and after several weeks' location
in August we moved into Shepperton Studios. Joining me in the cast were
Richard Attenborough, Terry-Thomas, Jill Adams and also Dennis Price
with whom I was to form a close relationship ten years later.

The making of both these initial films for the Boulting brothers gave
me more pleasure than anything I had done before. I adored film-studio
life, both the work and the play. During the making of all my films for
the Boultings, I think I came the nearest I have ever been to being a relaxed
person.

Professionally, I found them perfection. They were quiet men and they
liked to work in a peaceful atmosphere. Voices were never raised even
between shots; if the normal chatter of the studio exceeded a certain
number of decibels, whichever of them was directing would turn to his
assistant and say, 'Shush, shush, shush, Phil. There's too much noise,
old chap, too much noise. Quieten it, dear boy, quieten it.' And immediately a cathedral-like hush would descend once more. This was great
– I find it impossible to think when there is the distraction of noise. The
only exception to this inviolate rule of theirs was if there was a piano
on the set. On such occasions John would wander over to it periodically
and give us a tune while the next shot was being lit. Even then his performance was *piano* and his choice of melodies tuneful and tranquil.

Frequently he would call me over to sing 'Home Again' – the finale of both the *Lyric* and *Globe* revues – while he tried to pick it out. He never quite mastered it. Finally he would abandon the concert, close the lid and with a 'Got a cigarette, Ian?' light up and return to his chair and script.

On test match days a blackboard was erected beside the set and it was the prop boys' responsibility, with the aid of their transistor, to keep the score permanently up to date. On location the same prop boys, in addition to the props required for the day's shooting, always had to carry in their van a complete set of cricket gear. This, on arrival at our destination, would be set up on some adjacent patch of grass and the moment shooting was held up for lack of sun the entire unit would move over to play cricket.

Socially, during the summer I used to see a lot of the Boultings. Most weekends they were to be found in the centre of the sun-deck immediately below the scoreboard of the Father Time Stand at Lord's. They had, in their youth, been Sussex supporters and the Middlesex versus Sussex game, which used to take place over what was once called Whit weekend, was an annual pilgrimage. It was the Boultings who got me playing again. They were always responsible for a couple of charity games every year, and for these I and a number of their principal artistes were prevailed upon to dig out a set of whites and a pair of cricket boots.

John lived in Acacia Road, St John's Wood, which was no distance from Eton Villas (and Lord's), and I became a frequent visitor at his house.

The Boulting brothers' new series of comedies coincided with my arrival in their employ and together we shared the fruits of some tremendously successful ones.

I once put it to John that, but for Binkie casting me in *Simon and Laura*, I might never or certainly not so quickly, have bridged the gap into movies. 'Nonsense, dear boy, nonsense,' he replied, 'Our employing you had nothing whatever to do with *Simon and Laura*. It was your undressing on the beach in *The Globe Revue* that did it, and furthermore we couldn't even remember your name.'

When *Private's Progress* was eventually screened it hit the jackpot and almost overnight my name became a national one. It was a tremendous feeling. Suddenly my own name and photograph were being featured in those movie magazines that I used to buy and study so avidly as a boy. Begone dull care – why had I ever doubted myself – and to add to my euphoria, as a result of *Simon and Laura*, the Rank Organisation now came back and wanted to put me under contract for three further films.

My guardian angel was working overtime. The first of these films, which was to be shot at Pinewood, was, however, to be a sad disappointment, and, after working in such accord with John and Roy for twelve weeks, a frustrating and nail-biting experience.

The Big Money was a comedy about a family of pickpockets. The lead part was that of the elder son who was the black sheep of the family. That is to say, he was the most inept, cack-handed, accident-prone 'dip' who could be found on a crowded racetrack. When not plying his trade, he spent his time dreaming of the day when he would make the big strike and how he would spend it all on the blonde barmaid at his local, on whom he doted.

I was to play the ill-starred, love-lorn youth, the ravishing Belinda Lee who was soon to be killed so tragically in a car accident in the United States, was to be my amour and John Paddy Carstairs was to direct.

The original premise on which the story was based was a good one and the early sequences gave it a promising start. Such early promise, however, was not maintained and very soon it descended into the broadest comedy clichés. I filed up to my producer and director to express my fears and concern. Unfortunately, they did not share them, so I resolved to take the matter higher. This was a decision which, in the light of later events, could have proved highly beneficial for all concerned. Unhappily, it didn't.

Bryan Forbes, in those days a young actor with whom I had worked on *The Colditz Story*, had started augmenting his income by doing a spot of writing. The Rank Organisation, who on this occasion can be congratulated on realising his potential, were, at the time, employing his services as a staff writer and script doctor. On the penultimate Thursday before shooting was due to begin, Bryan rang me and said that he'd just had the script of *The Big Money* thrown at him by the head of production at Pinewood with instructions to give it his considered attention.

'As this is primarily a vehicle for you, old boy,' said Bryan, 'it would seem sensible if you came round and we had a chat about it.'

I spent the whole of Friday and Saturday at his house, during which time we roughed out a new treatment for vast sections of the more arid patches and we also, I think, managed to put a bit of flesh on to the bare bones of several of the more obvious and colourless characters. On the Sunday I left Bryan alone to bash away on his typewriter. The following morning he had a telephone call from Pinewood.

'Bryan?'

'Yes.' It was the executive producer.

'I hear you've been seeing Ian Carmichael over the weekend. Is that true?'

'Certainly it's true,' replied Bryan.

Then, in his infinite wisdom and with a sense of logic that we both found totally astonishing, he said, 'Right, forget it, kid. I'm taking you off it. Post the original back to me today.'

The Big Money went on the floor a week later with hardly a line of the original script altered. In due course, when it was finally assembled and ready for dubbing, the powers that be thought so little of it that they decided it should never be shown. As a result it remained locked away in a vault for several years.

Its ultimate emergence was fortuitous. John Paddy Carstairs was, at the time, making a Norman Wisdom movie which contained an Ascot sequence. Paddy always hated going on location and he spent a lot of time trying to persuade his producer that it could all be shot in the studio. His final throw was 'Look – I've already done it in *The Big Money*. Try and get permission to get it out of the vault and see for yourself.' His producer did exactly that and on returning the key to, no doubt, the managing director (the whole thing was practically a Watergate break-in), he said, it is reported, words to the effect, 'I can't think why you've kept *The Big Money* locked away all these years. It's not *that* bad. If you give me a bit of money to dub some music on to it, you stand a reasonable chance of, at least, getting your money back.'

His confidence was misplaced. *The Big Money* should have remained incarcerated or, better still, destroyed.

After that expensive little fracas, my contract with the Rank Organisation was terminated by mutual agreement. I didn't like factory farming, which was what I assessed the film production at Pinewood to be at that time, and they, no doubt, didn't like my argumentative interference in a side of the production which they probably considered to be none of my affair. The fact that all along I had been right about *The Big Money* could also only have rankled – and once again no pun is intended.

After *The Big Money* I had but three weeks to prepare myself for my return to John and Roy. These were fully occupied with winding up at Pinewood – 'still' sessions and the usual post-production chores – also fittings and visits to the Law Courts for my role of Roger Thursby, the young fledgling barrister in *Brothers in Law*.

In *Brothers in Law* I was to be directed by Roy Boulting for the first time and the production went on the floor at the British National Studios in Borehamwood, now a part of Lord Grade's ATV complex. It was exhilarating to be returning to work for two people with whom I had been so happy after the traumas of the previous four months.

The first day of shooting was my thirty-sixth birthday. The first shot was to be my entrance into the chambers of a senior barrister with whom I hoped to obtain experience. After the shot had been lined up and lit we rehearsed it several times until Roy was satisfied.

With Terry-Thomas in Brothers in Law

'Right, we'll go for a take,' he then announced to his assistant.

'O.K. Quiet, everybody, this is a take,' repeated Philip Shipway.

The shooting bell sounded; the large doors to the stage were bolted and the red light glowed outside them. I took up my place outside the door of the office. My heart fluttered with joy and excitement.

'Ready, Ian?' called Phil.

'Ready.'

'Right – turn over,' he instructed.

'Running,' announced the sound recordist.

'*Brothers in Law*. Scene One, Take One,' yelled the clapper-boy, as his clapper snapped down with a resounding crack. He then scooted out of shot and there was dead silence. After the briefest of moments it was broken by the voice of Roy Boulting.

'Many happy returns, Ian,' he called. '*Action.*'

I was home again.

At the conclusion of *Brothers in Law* in mid-September I was due to com-mence a new film in four weeks' time but a rather exciting, if at the same time frightening, turn of events intervened between the two dates which yet again prevented me from getting away for a holiday.

At the beginning of October or thereabouts, I received a letter inform-ing me that I had been included in the list of artistes who were to be presented to Her Majesty the Queen at the Royal Command Film Per-formance on the 29th of the month. After only two films of any pith and moment, this elicited from myself guttural noises of total disbelief and from Pym the sort of instantaneous reaction common to all women at such times: 'But what on earth am I going to wear?' The reaction of excitement was immediate; that of fright was to follow – when the organising authority sprung on me a request that I should act as compère to the presentation of the stars on the stage at the conclusion of the Royal Presentation in the dress-circle lounge. There were twenty of them in all including such luminaries as Joan Crawford, Marilyn Monroe, Victor Mature, Laurence Harvey, Anita Ekberg, Dana Andrews and Brigitte Bardot.

This struck terror into my vitals. The Empire Theatre, Leicester Square, where it was to be held, would be filled not only with the royal party but every conceivable dignitary in the entire British and many foreign film industries. A flattering but far from enviable task. Obviously I couldn't refuse but, on seeking an audience with the organisers to ascer-tain the exact nature of my duties, there was worse to follow. I discovered that my first task was to stand alone in the centre of the stage and give the Loyal Address to Her Majesty on behalf of the industry.

Somebody had undoubtedly had a rush of blood to the head. I begged the authorities to think again. What was all the top brass doing on that night? There had to be someone more suitable. The authorities were flattering and persuasive, beneath which pressure I weakened. I was, how-ever, insistent on one point – that someone should write the Loyal Address for me; a request with which they readily complied.

Several days later it arrived. I was far from happy about it. It struck me as being formal, stuffy, personalityless and more suitable for a red-coated toastmaster than a lightweight young actor. I immediately picked up the telephone and rang John Boulting.

'John? It's Ian. I'm in trouble, old lad. Can I come round and see you?'

'I'm in bed with a stinker, cockie, but if you're prepared to risk catching it, come round.'

'Now?' I said.

'Got a cigarette, Ian, old chap?' On location with John and Roy Boulting

'Now.'

I got into the car and was round at his house in three minutes flat. I showed him the speech.

'This is dreadful,' he said. 'You can't use this.'

'I know,' I said. 'Where do I go from here?'

'There's a pad of paper and a pencil on that table behind you. Take this down.'

He then dictated a speech to me practically without hesitation which I eventually delivered without altering a line. It had struck just the right note of respectful informality.

On the great night, as all the artistes assembled in the dress-circle lounge, everyone was eagerly awaiting a glimpse of the fabulous Marilyn Monroe – she hadn't attended the rehearsal on the previous day. She was, possibly characteristically, the last to arrive and the first sight of her was breath-catching rather than breath-taking. She arrived on the arm of her husband Arthur Miller, in an off-the-shoulder gown of unrelieved gold lamé and with what appeared to be no make-up at all. The pictures of her in the papers the following day *were* breathtaking; the lady knew exactly what she was about.

The Royal Presentation line was assembled in alphabetical order so I found myself standing between a pert little Brigitte Bardot on my right and the *grande dame* but quaking with fright figure of Joan Crawford on my left. Whether by cunning design or genuine fear I know not, but at the rehearsal of the stage presentation Miss Crawford expressed her terror of falling over while curtseying, so she requested that I should cross to meet her on her entrance and hold her left hand as she curtsied. This I did. She was the only one who received such an attention-attracting presentation. Two days later I received the most gracious and charming letter of thanks from her.

Pym, to return to earth, was dressed in an evening gown of crushed strawberry with long white gloves and a white fox fur, and all-in-all it was a most memorable night for both of us.

The offer of the film that I was to start at the beginning of November, when it was made to me, made me feel for all the world as if I had been presented with a big, rosy-red apple for having been a good boy. Stanley Windrush in *Private's Progress* was a gem of a part; Roger Thursby in *Brothers in Law* was as good if not better, and now I had been cast as Jim Dixon in Kingsley Amis's award-winning best-seller *Lucky Jim*, which was, to continue the metaphor, an absolute pip.

Lucky Jim unhappily did not get off to a good start. The project was the property of three experienced talents, a lady who by trade was a film publicist, a distinguished and successful writer who had done the screenplay and a director with an impressive list of achievements to his name. By dint of some contractual agreement about which I am not over-clear at this distance in time, the whole package eventually came under the Boultings, and they presided over it in the capacity of executive producers.

Shooting started one Monday morning on the largest stage at MGM Studios in Borehamwood in which a vast set depicting the huge quad-

With Maureen Connell in Lucky Jim

rangle of the university at which Jim Dixon was employed had been built. We were in the set for the whole of the first two weeks. From the word go there was a communications gap between the director and myself; not an auspicious beginning to a shooting schedule which was to last for ten weeks.

Entirely separate from my own problems, John and Roy had been viewing the daily rushes and had not been, I was to discover, over-enamoured with what they saw. Such disenchantment grew into concern and after two weeks' shooting a decision was made at executive level to relieve the original triumvirate of their command. On the Monday of the third week John took over as director and nobody was happier than I to see his comforting presence on the floor. The first day under his jurisdiction was not, however, to prove a panacea for all ills. My lack of rapport with the original director had not been shared by another member of the cast with whom, until that moment, I had had no quarrel. Unfortunately, the switch, he now seemed to consider, had been a deep-rooted and manic plot on my part to undermine his own performance. We got little done that morning, the atmosphere was super-charged. In due course, however, things started to settle down and ultimately I think a funny film resulted.

In February of the following year *Brothers in Law* was released. The Boulting brothers had done it again and their de-bunking of stable and sacred institutions was becoming a cult. First the army, now the bench – what was to be their next target? Well, their next was to be the bull's eye of them all and it is still shown today these twenty years later without a whit of its topicality being eroded. But that was still two years away and in the interim they provided me with a little domestic trifle of timeless charm. It was to be called *Happy Is The Bride* and was a remake of the original film of the 1938 Esther McCracken play *Quiet Wedding*.

Happy Is The Bride was made by an independent producer called Paul Soskin. Soskin was six feet tall, erect, aristocratic-looking, immaculately turned out, and a mid-European with a splendidly resonant voice who was always known to Kay Kendall affectionately as 'Prince Sanilav'. Roy Boulting was to be his director. Most of what had now become the Boulting Brothers' Repertory Company were employed in it and this time I was to play for the first of several occasions opposite Janette Scott and also with that splendid actor Cecil Parker whose sister was our local vet. Also in the cast was the beautiful, talented and tragic Virginia Maskell who was to die so young only a few years later.

It was during *Happy Is The Bride* that, flushed with the success of recent months, I decided it was time to improve my motoring image. All the Kenneth Mores and Laurence Harveys of this world were at that time driving around in Silver Clouds. With two children to educate, however, I still couldn't afford the Rolls-Royce status but it was certainly time that I did something to show the flag.

In 1957 Mercedes Benz had done practically nothing to open up their U.K. market and for many months I had had my eye on one of their 220s. One weekend I saw advertised in the *Sunday Times* what sounded like a very likely possibility. The moment I had a break from shooting the following morning I rang the advertiser, a firm in South Audley Street. The car, it transpired, was in Woking – fairly adjacent to Shepperton – could they send it over to the studios for me to see that very afternoon? Certainly they could.

'We also just happen to have a beautiful, eighteen-month-old 300 in stock,' continued the salesman (actually no one so lowly – he was a director of the firm). 'Can we bring that down to show you too?'

'That will be more than I wish to pay,' I replied without hesitation. 'Just bring the 220.'

Round about four o'clock *both* vehicles arrived at the studio. They looked opulent and they glistened in the afternoon sun. They were accompanied by the director from South Audley Street and another senior executive – both well dressed with a touch of the old school tie about them.

I had never seen a real live 300 before; in 1957 they were as rare in our island as bougainvillaea. I was dazzled.

'Tell me about it,' I said. 'Whose was, or is, it?'

I was supplied with the name of a quite senior peer.

'Why does he want to get rid of it?' I enquired.

'Doesn't really,' came the pat answer. 'It's primarily that Her Ladyship suffers badly from arthritis and finds her Bentley easier to get in and out of.'

'Is that the only reason?' I continued to probe.

'That, and the fact that he thinks it's a bit absurd having such a large barouche just to travel from his flat in Eaton Square to the House of Lords and back. A bit ostentatious, what?'

Inwardly I was hooked.

'Let me think about it,' I said. 'I'll come back to you within forty-eight hours.'

That evening I rang Dickie Wattis who lived smack in the middle of Belgravia and was very 'genned up' with Society info. With his help, I

*With Janette Scott
in* Happy Is The Bride

located the owner's country seat (it was a castle) and its telephone
number. I rang straight through to speak to the fountain's head.

'Hello. Little Twittington 123.' I thought I'd got on to Ian Wallace.

'Is that Birdlington Castle?'

'It is.' It had to be Ian Wallace.

'I wonder if I might have a word with Lord Thing.'

'Who is calling, please?'

I told him.

'If you will hold the line I will ascertain if His Lordship is in.' It *was*
Ian Wallace – either he or Paul Robeson and the latter was either in the
United States or dead.

After a lot of clicking and voices on 'distort' caused by the castle's inter-
nal communication system, His Lordship was located and informed that
there was a Mr Carmichael on the line who wished to speak with him.

His Lordship was most helpful. It *was* his car; there was, to his knowledge, no serious defect in its mechanical performance and during its lifetime with him it had always behaved immaculately. I thanked him and
replaced the handpiece. Two days later I bought it. That evening I drove
home from the studios feeling like a belted earl myself.

The moment *Happy Is The Bride* finished, the BBC sent me a splendid
comedy TV play by Philip Mackie. It contained a virtuoso part for myself
as a young man who couldn't stop falling in love but each time, just as

he was about to pop the question, another even more beautiful damsel would come along and off he would go with her instead. It was called *The Girl at the Next Table* and is worthy of note because of several of the people involved in it.

It was directed by Stuart Burge, a director of considerable distinction in the theatre, and I took with me Janette Scott and Virginia Maskell. In the part of my neighbour who lived in the flat opposite, I worked for the first time with Bill Franklyn – Leo's son. The last girl to enter my life in the story and with whom I eventually escaped the encircling tentacles of all the others was one who, on the last page of the script, rang my front door bell in error. The part, with all of its three lines, was played by the enchanting Jennifer Wilson, now an actress of considerable stature who became known to millions for her performance in the long-running TV series *The Brothers*.

After *The Girl*, the school holidays being in full swing, we again set off for the north *en famille* to spend a few weeks with each of our parents. On this occasion, for the first time, we arrived in grand style. If few people had seen a Mercedes 300 in the metropolis, nobody had in Hull and Whitby. In August 1957 I returned to Yorkshire something of a celebrity.

CHAPTER TWENTY-THREE

THE AMERICAN CONNECTION

Enter ROBERT MORLEY – *another comedian*

During the next four years I was to appear in three successful West End plays, in each of which I hardly ever left the stage during the entire evening, one musical and five movies, three of them on ten-week shooting schedules throughout the course of which I was on call practically every day. In addition to this there were appearances on television, charity shows and a variety of taxing promotional functions which took me all round the country. I was, towards the end of it all, to suffer as a result of an arrogant belief that, from a health point of view, I was Superman. I think the experience, when it arrived, altered my entire philosophy of life. For the moment, however, we had just arrived in Yorkshire for a holiday and, as usual, I was to be left alone for but one week.

It was during the week of the Scarborough Cricket Festival – the last week in August – that I was sent the script of a current, successful New York comedy, and it came from a recently formed management whose two partners were Robert Morley and his manager Robin Fox. I read it with interest. It was a funny play, there was no doubt about that, and it was a big star part, but the subject matter scared the life out of me.

Augie Poole, an unsuccessful cartoonist, lived with his wife, whom he adored, in an attractive, converted (though still mice-infested) barn in Westport, just outside New York. After five years of trying unsuccessfully to raise a family, they had finally decided to adopt one. This did not, however, prevent Mrs Poole from studiously grabbing her husband and dragging him off to bed regardless of the hour every time her temperature, which as instructed by her doctor she took at regular intervals, exceeded a certain degree. At a later date, Augie, while his wife is away and in a moment of weakness, is seduced by the glamorous investigator from the adoption society who, nine months later, is about to have his baby. When in due course the Pooles are informed that the adoption society will have a baby for them in only a few months' time, Augie is terrified that it will be his.

The Tunnel of Love was written by Joseph Fields and Peter de Vries and in the late 1970s sounds pretty innocuous stuff, but in 1957, in my view, it screamed bad taste on every page.

I played the whole thing very coolly and expressed my concern to my prospective employers via Richard Stone – nothing, at that moment, was going to take me away from the cricket. Within twenty-four hours I was informed that the mountain was coming to Mahomet and could I drag myself away from the ground for an hour to have lunch with it at the Pavilion Hotel the following day? When someone as important as Robin Fox comes two hundred and fifty miles to see you in a town not all that accessible on British Rail, you don't argue the toss.

The following day I turned up for lunch to find Robin already waiting for me. I had never met him before. He was a tall, dark-haired, fit-looking old Harrovian and oozed charm from every pore. He was also, incidentally, the father of both James and Edward Fox. Having ordered drinks, the next thing he did was to present me with the sort of bribe that he obviously realised I would find totally irresistible. It was a table-lighter (for lighting cigarettes, that is, not tables) which was mounted in the centre of a beautiful bright red cricket ball. He was two-thirds of the way home before we had gone into lunch.

Over lobster mayonnaise and champagne (another way to my heart) I explained my fears and he did his best to dispel them. Robert himself, apparently, intended to direct and though I had not yet agreed to appear in the play, by the time the coffee arrived we were discussing leading ladies. At 3.30 p.m. he left to return to London.

I forget the actual moment that my resistance caved in, but cave in it did, though I never, until after we had opened, lost that feeling of apprehension about the way that I, a performer who had acquired a reputation for being connected with clean, wholesome offerings, would be received in such a play. My face didn't fit 'blue' material and several weeks later, when we were in rehearsal, I remember full well travelling with my director down Shaftesbury Avenue in a taxi and begging that if, during the course of the tour, we discovered that such a permissive comedy did not prove acceptable to the audiences, it would be closed on the road and not brought into town. It was a plea on which he skilfully avoided commenting.

We started rehearsals on the last day of September in the Apollo Theatre and I had been fortunate enough to get the lovely Barbara Murray as my leading lady, Dilys Laye, an old friend from *High Spirits*, as the seducer from the adoption society and Bill Franklyn, who once again was to play my neighbour – a fertile wolf whose wife (Charlotte Mitchell) only had to look at his trousers to become pregnant; a fact which added a certain ironic twist to the plot.

Robert Morley, as everyone knows, is an outsize personality. He is also witty, garrulous and adores holding court. He is, in addition, an inveterate gambler and extremely generous; as a result of which, his management followed the grandiose style of those in bygone days.

On the first day of rehearsal he expressed a wish that we should start early each day, say 9.30-ish, work straight through with no lunch-break and finish somewhere around 3 or 3.30 p.m.

'If you're not "on", my darlings, you can peel off into the wings and have a cup of coffee and a sandwich which the management will provide.'

In the event, the cup of coffee and the sandwich was interpreted by Ros Chatto, the lady who was then his assistant and is now, since Robin's death, his manager, as the full Ascot cold buffet lunch with several bottles of *vin rosé* or hock to wash it down. This, of course, we soon found, regardless of Robert's intentions, we did break to consume; and all the while he personally provided the cabaret. After lunch we all had considerable difficulty in staying awake for the afternoon's session.

After a week of such generosity, the cast begged me to approach Robert and, while offending him as little as possible, request that, in the interest of getting the play ready for our opening in Liverpool three weeks later, we return to the more orthodox routine of 10.30–5.30 with a break for lunch when we could all get a bit of Archer Street's polluted air into our lungs. He reluctantly agreed.

Another quirk of dear Robert's was, during the first two of the four weeks' rehearsal period, a certain indecisiveness about the positioning of the furniture on the set. Each morning he would announce that he had, during the previous evening, thought about the general geography of his production and that he wasn't happy about it.

'Not happy about it at all, my darlings. We can't possibly have the bar that far up-stage, you're lost up there, all of you – can't see your beautiful eyes, Barbara dear. I'm going to bring it down to the front and that will necessitate moving the sofa to this side of the stage and that chair over into the corner.'

Towards the end of the second week I again had to approach him and ask if we could finally settle on one arrangement and stick to it as we were now ten days into rehearsals and still hadn't got past setting Act I.

Robert is an engaging man and these quirks just had to be lived with.

With Barbara Murray in The Tunnel of Love

Two years later, when he was directing another piece in which I was appearing, he turned to his actors, who, as a result of someone's entrance, now numbered four, and made the totally disarming statement, 'Now you must all be very patient with me, darlings; I'm not very good when I've got more than three people on the stage.'

The Tunnel's opening out of town was a triumph. My fears, it seemed, had been groundless. Though several papers pointed out early in their reviews that the play was '... unashamedly about sex', a statement which had a tinge of admonition about it, there followed passages such as:

There is a delicacy of touch in the writing, and particularly in the playing, that disarms and a subject that might have been offensive, vulgar and coarse, becomes a medley of sophisticated, frank conversation and outrageous situation.

and:

But this spicy revel is acted with such high spirits, good taste and sophistication that however near the bone it gets, it seldom chills the marrow.

The tour will always be indelibly marked in my memory for an incident that happened during the mid-week matinée in Leeds. At one point in the play Bill Franklyn, Dilys Laye and I had a scene together which culminated with the arrival on stage of the other two girls, Barbara and Charlotte. On the afternoon in question, we arrived at the end of the scene and there was no sign of the girls; in theatrical parlance they were 'off'. After a brief hiatus the three of us ad libbed for what seemed like three-quarters of an hour. In due course we had exhausted every possible topic we could think of that was remotely connected with the plot and they still hadn't arrived. I then, in a flash, hit on a new one that, with invention – and Bill had a wealth of it – we could keep going *ad infinitum*. I introduced a brand new character into the conversation who had nothing to do with the play whatsoever: 'Heard anything of George Warburton recently?' I asked him. Without a moment's hesitation my friend replied, 'He's dead.' That was the end of my contribution, I decided; let them get themselves out of the mess, and I promptly left the stage. I charged up two flights of stairs to Barbara's dressing-room. I burst in and there were the two of them sitting calmly over a couple of cigarettes, discussing the health of their children. In retrospect I suppose I could have asked Bill what George had died of, but as no other message seemed to be getting through to our two recalcitrant actresses I still feel that I took the right decision to dig them out myself.

After five weeks on the road we opened just before Christmas at Her Majesty's Theatre in the Haymarket. Unlike the tour, our critical reception was mixed. Most of the Press gave us rave notices but there were a few who chose to dub it as 'tasteless' or, even worse, 'a joke in bad taste'. The latter, I am delighted to say, made not a ha'porth of difference to the business at the box office.

The Tunnel of Love was a big hit and it ran for over a year in the West End. I had to leave the cast after nine months to fulfil a film commitment, after which Brian Reece took over my part and it subsequently moved to the Apollo.

The Morley–Fox partnership's generosity continued to the end. We were a cast of six and each of us had received a small silver cigarette-box from Asprey's as an opening-night present and on leaving they presented me with a large engraved silver salver. For me, however, there was to be, though perhaps of less intrinsic value, a much more moving present which, through their kindness, I was to receive from the company.

In the centre of the stage in *The Tunnel of Love* there was a large Windsor chair and on this chair I had, over the early weeks, built up a piece of comedy business which went on for rather a long time. It was at a moment of acute embarrassment and one way and another I got myself inextricably mixed up with, first of all, the fitted cushion on the seat and subsequently the rungs that supported the arms and back. No sooner had I freed one part of my anatomy than another became trapped somewhere else. The play was, I'm afraid, apt to come to a grinding halt until I had finished. We had a party in my dressing-room after my final performance and towards the end of it two of the cast vanished and came back with the most enormous parcel, gift-wrapped and tied up in red ribbon. It was set down in front of me.

'Go on, open it,' someone said.

I did, and as the paper fell away there was my chair. It had had a brass plate affixed to the headrest at the back which read, 'From those left in The Tunnel.' A similar but smaller plate – a Bill Franklyn inspiration – was affixed to the front of the seat itself: 'The Milking Stool' it pronounced. That chair has remained one of the most treasured possessions in our home ever since.

What nobody knew, as I didn't want to put the 'mockers' on the occasion for everyone else, was that the moment the final curtain had fallen Pym had telephoned to tell me that, during that afternoon, my father had died.

The following day we hastily packed a few things in a suitcase and all the Ian Carmichaels set off for Ferriby, my parents' new home a few miles away from Elloughton; the old family homestead having been sold in 1948. We went via York, quite a distance out of our way where, by arrangement, we met my in-laws in the Station Hotel car-park. With little ceremony and few words, the children transferred to their car and went back with them to Sleights. We then proceeded on our way to comfort my mother and make arrangements for the funeral.

My father had had repeated angina attacks for the best part of a year and knew he was dying. He had, however, never passed on his concern to any of his children and, if he had discussed it with my mother, she too had kept the secret to herself. Three days before he died, cancer of the lung was also diagnosed. My mother and his doctor then decided that he should be told. She knew him better than anyone else and I have never questioned their decision. He was a punctilious man and she felt that he would prefer to know so that he could spend what time he had left preparing himself spiritually and generally tidying up his affairs. He received the news with great courage. The first thing he told my mother he wanted to do was to make arrangements for the sale of his stamp collection. It was a spasmodic hobby and not a very big collection as philately goes; to this day I don't know what it was worth – nothing, I'm sure, that would have made much difference to his estate – but I have been for ever grateful that he didn't have time to carry out his plan. After his death I retained it and many years later I handed it over to his eldest grandson who had expressed a wish to own it.

During the final week of his life his eldest brother had telephoned me to say that the situation was becoming grave and that my place was up there in Ferriby. I explained my responsibilities to the show and said I would go at the weekend. I did go at the weekend, but it was too late. He would, I know, have understood.

He was sixty-four and although he was the youngest of his family by ten years, he was the first to go. It has always pleased me to know that he lived long enough to be proud of my achievements. Sadly, there was only one thing he missed seeing and that by but a whisker – it would have given him infinite pleasure.

In the spring of 1958 a letter arrived out of the blue, from the bursar of Eton College offering us the freehold of our rented home in Eton Villas for, believe it or not, three thousand pounds. Later in the day I discovered from several of my neighbours that similar offers had been received in the area. After consideration most people seemed in favour of not rising to the bait. There was some doubt about the future of Provost Road, one side of our little enclave; in future council plans, it was reported, it was earmarked for demolition.

Pym and I discussed the matter. With the girls growing up and one of them now away at boarding-school in Mill Hill, we had frequently talked about moving further out to where there was a bit more greenery. We decided to act unilaterally. I wrote back offering two thousand five hundred pounds. A few days later I received a reply accepting my offer. It was a gorgeous sunny morning on the day it arrived and, no time like the present, the moment we'd got young Sal off to school we piled into the car and drove off to start and search for a new home.

We knew exactly where we wanted to be – the Mill Hill village, Totteridge Manor green-belt area – so we pointed ourselves in that general direction and set off to seek out the local estate agents.

At 3 o'clock that afternoon we turned down a cul-de-sac lane just off the Mill Hill end of Totteridge Lane. In the first hundred yards we passed two or three charming little properties on one side of the lane; on the other side was a wood. Then suddenly we emerged into the most delightful and unexpected splurge of green countryside. Unbelievably we were still in the London postal area.

The lane – another two hundred yards of it – was umbrella'd under a bower of magnificent trees in full leaf. On the left were the grounds of a very grand house with several acres of garden and wild woodland, and on the right was a huge field filled with a herd of Friesian cattle.

Elysium – 'Moat Lodge'

At the bottom of the lane stood a white stuccoed house with green tiles which overlooked, firstly, part of its own modest plot, and then nothing but the field and the grazing cattle. This was called Moat Lodge and it was the property we had come to see. We were, as a Yorkshire friend of mine delicately puts it, 'gob-struck'. I knew immediately that unless the place was falling to pieces inside, this was it, we need look no further.

The study wing of the house had been the gardener's lodge to the original 'big house' of the area which lay behind it and was quite old. In the early 1930s the remainder, the largest part of the house, had been built on to turn it into a good-sized family home. The exterior architecture had a faintly Spanish air about it and the interior several classic features of 1930s design.

Moat Lodge became our dearly loved home for the next nineteen years and it had taken us but twenty-four hours to find. When we moved in Lee was twelve and Sally was just nine. When we left, they were both married and we already had three grandchildren. My father knew before he died that we had bought the property, but sadly he never saw it. If he had done so, I think he would have been thrilled to bits.

The privacy that the area afforded us was almost total. The hedge round our garden was only chest height, but during the summer any of us could, if we wished, run around in it stark naked without fear of being arrested. The field in front of us, over the years and consistent with the rotation of crops, either accommodated the dairy herd from Sydney Box's farm which was on the other side of it, or grain – the combine harvester being a sight that visitors from the more urban areas of London found difficult to believe they were actually seeing. Sydney Box, the film producer, had sold us Moat Lodge and he and his then wife, Muriel, who had directed me in the film of *Simon and Laura*, were our neighbours, in due course they were also to make available to us, for a peppercorn rent which would hardly have bought a peppercorn, an adjacent plot on which the children subsequently kept their ponies, rabbits, ducks and a variety of other livestock.

Over the next nineteen years, when driving home from the theatre after work – a journey of thirty-five minutes at that time of night – I would walk down the path from the garages to the house breathing in the clean fresh air (we were very high up there), counting our blessings and wondering at our good fortune. It was a magnificent spot.

After I pulled out of *The Tunnel of Love* the pace of my life hotted up with a vengeance. I had exercised my release clause to make a film for Messrs Launder and Gilliat. It was to be called *Left, Right and Centre* and was a comedy about a Tory candidate at a by-election who became romantically entangled with his opposite number, a female of the Labour party. She was played by an attractive young lady called Patricia Bredin who was new to films and who, by a curious coincidence, also hailed from Hull. The inimitable Alastair Sim – an actor who throughout his life resolutely refused to sign autographs – added his considerable talent to the cast, and the respective candidates' agents were played by Richard Wattis (mine) and Eric Barker (Patricia's).

On the first day of shooting, Dickie was the subject of what might, to some actors, have been a disturbing exchange of dialogue with the director. He, Sidney Gilliat – who was part-author and also the director of the piece – and I were sitting in our production chairs on the edge of the set chatting away amiably about nothing in particular while we were waiting for the first shot to be lit, when Dickie said, 'We haven't really had a chance to have a talk about my part yet, Sidney. Don't you think we ought to do so before we get under way?'

Sidney, a man with a considerable sense of humour, looked him in the eyes and without a flicker of a smile said, 'I hope you're not thinking of doing anything with it. I wrote the part for *you*.'

Another engaging snippet of conversation occurred when we spent several days on location at Woburn Abbey. The young Lord Russell – then a mere red-headed boy – spent a lot of time watching us accompanied by his tutor. I was nattering away to him one morning between shots, asking him general questions about his family. Knowing that his father, prior to becoming the thirteenth Duke of Bedford, had been farming in

With George Benson and Moira Fraser in Left, Right and Centre

South Africa, I asked the young man if he had been born out there; to which, with a slight stutter, I received the engaging reply, 'I was born – in the Ritz Hotel in London.' How very right and proper, I reflected.

We finished *Left, Right and Centre* just before Christmas and in early 1959 I started work on the Boulting brothers' blockbuster, *I'm All Right Jack*.

I'm All Right Jack is still seen so frequently on television it is unnecessary to outline its story. It was conceived, however, when John and Roy, who always prefer to write their own screen-plays, persuaded Alan Hackney to write another novel about the exploits of the principal characters that he had created in *Private's Progress*. This time he was to follow their exploits after their release from the army. The result was a book called *Private Life*, a story which took the most enormous swipe at both the unions and management.

As with *Private's Progress*, the sequel was directed by John and the original cast of principals was joined by Margaret Rutherford, Irene Handl and Liz Frazer who played Stanley's busty blonde girl-friend and the daughter of his tormentor, the Hitlerite shop steward Fred Kite – the role in which Peter Sellers made such an enormous impact.

There are certain mementoes that one carries away from all movies and the one I carried away from *I'm All Right Jack* was of a practical nature. I absconded with the suit of blue dungaree overalls that I wore while operating the fork-lift truck on the factory floor. I have used them

for home decorating and similar chores ever since. It does my ego good
to know that after twenty years I can still get into them.

The moment I had finished my fifth film for the Boultings – the last
of their options – I started work at the Associated British studios in Borehamwood on a film based on the *Lifemanship* books of Stephen Potter.

The producer was a dynamic and irrepressible American called Hal
E. Chester who, I would guess, was a man of about my own age. Hal
was small and possessed a face which, if it hadn't looked so youthful,
might have seen several years in a boxing ring. Hal had an undisclosed
and, I feel sure, a varied and colourful past in many fields of the entertainment industry. He was sharp and I think possibly the most effective
of his skills was his ability to put it all together. Throughout the time
I knew him he always managed to gather around him a package of considerable talent. Hal had a burning desire to be creative and, rather like

Once again as Stanley Windrush – this time with Peter Sellers in
I'm All Right, Jack

the one under the Arc de Triomphe, his flame never went out. His energy, his drive, his enthusiasm, even at times against formidable opposition, were indomitable. In adversity, I can't say he kept his cool – Hal was hot all the time – but he smiled throughout and appeared to remain totally unruffled and resolute. He was, however, not the best of delegators and was always apt to want to add his own talents to those of his extremely capable lieutenants. At times this made Hal Chester the most infuriating man to work for and yet one could never actually dislike him – I couldn't, anyway.

The original screenplay of *School for Scoundrels* had been written by Peter Ustinov, which wasn't a bad start. The director was to be Robert Hamer who had directed, amongst other successes, the Dennis Price/Alec Guinness classic *Kind Hearts and Coronets*. Joining me in the cast were some old friends: Terry-Thomas, my rival for the affections of the pretty little Janette Scott, the battle for which was to drive me to the School of Lifemanship at Yeovil, principal Stephen Potter (Alastair Sim), in an attempt to learn the ploys and gambits with which to outwit the bounder. Also in the parts of a couple of shady car salesmen were Peter Jones, and once again, Dennis Price.

Mr Ustinov's script was a beauty and I therefore showed quite natural concern when Hal, with his burning desire to be personally creative, tried to improve it by bringing in an American writer (albeit an excellent one) to provide amendments and write additional scenes. Many of our producer's ideas had jokes slanted towards an American audience which is something guaranteed to make me turn red, white and blue with anger when dealing with an essentially English subject. Apart from that, the continual arrival of new scenes after a film has started shooting from whoever's pen I have always found disconcerting to say the least; to say the most, they can result in considerably damaging a performance. If, for instance, one had known that one was going to have to play a newly presented scene, one might have played a previous one that had already been shot quite differently. New scenes, new pages always disturb me, and with Hal there were quite a lot of them. Apart from this, the film moved along steadily until the director fell ill three weeks before the end and had to be replaced by another. Luckily I knew his replacement well. He was a gentleman called Cyril Frankel who had been one of our entertainments officers in the 30 Corps set-up in Germany.

When *School for Scoundrels* was eventually shown, however, the cracks didn't seem to show and it enjoyed an enormous success on both sides of the Atlantic.

As work at Associated British was drawing to a close, I was approached by some more Americans; a consortium which, on the strength of its credits, was a fairly impressive one.

The composers Robert Wright and George Forrest are mainly famed for their adaptation of other people's music, *The Song of Norway* (Grieg), *Kismet* (Borodin), but somewhere around 1958 they had written, *in toto*, a brand new musical which they had based loosely on the medical plays of Jean Baptiste Poquelin Molière. It had been called *The Carefree Heart* and had toured the United States with little success, eventually folding without ever reaching New York. After it had closed they undertook considerable rewriting and now, together with a producer called Lynn Loesser and Albert Marre, the director of their highly successful *Kismet*, they had arrived in London in order to mount a new production of it in this country. It was now retitled *The Love Doctor*. Miss Loesser had been on to Richard Stone to arrange for Joan Heal and me to go round to see them at the Savoy Hotel where they were all staying, to hear the music.

A few days later the three of us showed up as requested and Messrs Wright and Forrest played and sang the entire score through for us. I forget what Joan's views were after hearing it, but my own were distinctly reserved; they were to remain so when, that evening, I read the book.

Being strangely, but in this case understandably, indecisive, Richard and I decided to take the whole project to Robin Fox and Robert Morley to get their views.

I remember little of the subsequent discussion except that Robert conducted most of it lying full length on his back on the floor of his office. To me, however, the overriding factor, which undoubtedly coloured my judgement, was a considerable respect for the past track record of the team involved. This was to prove a mistake.

In due course a decision was made; Joannie and I (who were ultimately joined by Douglas Byng) would do it and Robin and Robert were to join Lynn Loesser in partnership to present the piece.

The Love Doctor opened a three and a half weeks' run at the Manchester Opera House on 27 August to a cool reception. Scenically the show was a hazardous one and the first performance suffered some unfortunate stage waits and a couple of near disasters, but the general consensus of opinion was that the show was tuneful, easy on the eye and, though there was still a lot of work to be done, it was full of promise.

The work started in earnest the following morning and continued every day and all day during our stay in Manchester, Sundays included. New scenes, new numbers, new dances and, in some instances, new costumes. No two consecutive performances were the same. Try this tonight – learn it, rehearse it, put it in and unless it was an improvement it was ousted the following day and something else had to be written, learned and rehearsed to replace it. It was one of the most exhausting four weeks of my life. By the time we were due to leave Manchester to go to Oxford we'd all been at it every waking moment for eight solid weeks. The kids – the dancers in particular – were on their knees and as our final weekend in Manchester approached I had to go to Albie Marre and tell him that, unless we were given the Sunday off to get a bit of sleep, he was liable to have a rebellion on his hands.

Towards the end of the Manchester run Michael Stewart was flown in from the States to do considerable, but unfortunately not enough, re-writing. Michael, whose credits embrace such successes as the books for *Carnival* and *Hello Dolly*, could only stay one week.

During the final week in Manchester, worn to a frazzle and with my own spirits at their very lowest ebb, I begged Robin and Robert not to take the piece into London, a request they certainly appeared to look upon sympathetically.

Our last two weeks on the road were to be at the New Theatre, Oxford, and on arrival there, to add to my general debility, I developed an abcess on a wisdom tooth. I played one performance in excruciating agony and the following four, after surgery, with two stitches in my jaw. At Oxford the decision was made to bring in another director, or to be more accurate, two directors, as the job was to be shared by Robert Morley himself and Wendy Toye. This caused both Wright and Forrest to desert the, by then, fast sinking ship and to vanish in their vast American automobile that they had brought over with them on a tour of Scotland. We never saw them again.

At the beginning of the final week in Oxford, one night after the show a pale, tired and emotional Robin Fox came and sat down in my dressing-room. He seemed to have something to say which he was having difficulty getting off his chest. I looked at him and saw that his eyes were full of tears. In a flash I knew what he was trying to say.

'You want us to open in London next week, don't you?'

He nodded. 'I'm afraid we've no choice in the matter,' he said. 'There's been a massive new injection of cash into the show and we've just got to hope and pray we can get some of it back.'

We opened at the Piccadilly Theatre on 12 October to disastrous notices. 'Pass Me the Morphia' (the *Star*), 'Musical with a Note Missing' (the *Daily Telegraph*), 'Were Molière alive I think he'd sue' (*Evening Standard*), 'I Was Fortunate ... I Fell Asleep' (*Daily Express*).

The Love Doctor was really a light-hearted pantomime. It looked enchanting; the Frenchman Bernard Daydé had designed it as if for a children's story book. We never got it right, but there are many people (Pym amongst them) who, even in the state it finally achieved, found it full of simple and engaging charm. It ran for two weeks.

The critic in the following month's *Plays and Players* wrote a review which was discerning.

The first night critics sneered. The second night audience approved. The show lasted just two weeks. Who was right?

If we use a 'touchstone' system of criticism, then this deserved to fail. But should every musical be compared with *Oklahoma* or *West Side Story*? By such standards, what modern drama would survive after comparison with *Hamlet* or *Macbeth*?

The ethics of such criticism seem as unreasonable as to condemn the novels of Nevil Shute because they do not compare favourably with *War and Peace*. *The Love Doctor* was an unspectacular, unpretentious little musical which would have given pleasure to thousands had it not been killed by the hypersensitive critics.

The moment *The Love Doctor* closed I launched myself into another film. If you fall off a horse, theory has it that you should get right up there again. I did.

It was called *Light Up The Sky* and it concerned the antics of a squad of 'gunners' who manned a searchlight 'somewhere in England' during the Second World War. This time my role was essentially a supporting one, which was a blessing; the two leads were played by Tommy Steele and Benny Hill. *Light Up The Sky* was to act as a welcome buffer which allowed me to lick my wounds after the mauling we had all received at the Piccadilly, and prefaced the start of a brand-new partnership which was to prove one of the happiest of my entire career.

CHAPTER TWENTY-FOUR

THE SAVOY AND THE ALPS

Enter HAROLD FIELDING – *a philanthropist,*
accompanied by MOIRA LISTER – *a Leo*

In early 1960 I was informed by Richard that Harold Fielding was about
to send me a new comedy to read. The morning it arrived I stayed in
bed for three hours to read it. It was another American success, which
had, for a while, been played over there by Tom Ewell who had also
created Augie Poole in *The Tunnel of Love*. It had been written by Alec
Coppel and it was called *The Gazebo*. It was the second American
comedy to come my way and this too I found hysterically funny. The
machinations of the plot are far too complicated to go into here – sufficient to say that the leading part was that of a television script-writer
who lives with his beautiful actress wife on Long Island and during the
course of the first few minutes of the play, while all the lights are out,
he believes that he has killed an intruder into his home. In any event,
when the lights are put on there is a perfectly good corpse lying on his
living-room carpet. The question then is, what to do with it. That afternoon his wife, it transpires, has fortuitously bought an eighteenth-century
gazebo which she intends installing at the bottom of their garden. Ideal.
In a breathless panic twenty-four hours later, at dead of night, he dumps
the body into the foundations and then Bob's your uncle, along come
the builders the following day and cover it up with the gazebo. It was
essentially a comedy thriller – in my view a good one – and it contained
yet another super part for myself and also one for some lovely lady.

The moment I'd closed the end-cover I picked the telephone off the
bedside table and rang Barbara Murray.

'Darling?'

'Yes. I suppose.'

'Oh, sorry. It's Ian.'

'Oh, well, that's nice to know.'

'Darling, I've found a super new play for us both,' and I told her all
about it.

It was not long before I went round to meet Harold Fielding. I don't want this narrative to become repetitious, but it just so happens that around that period my life was becoming peopled by dynamic little men. Harold, like Hal Chester, is both dynamic and on the small side. He has sandy-coloured hair, the most infectious of grins which permanently lights up his face and he is the possessor of a rather high-pitched voice. But it is Harold's enthusiasm and indomitable theatrical courage which, in my view, raises him head and shoulders above all his contemporaries. His organisation has an almost Germanic efficiency about it; I decided then, and I have never had reason to change my mind since, that Harold Fielding is our most outstanding theatrical producer. Harold is an impresario in the mould of Cochran and Charlot. Harold promotes. Harold spends money to make money. Harold, when he doesn't wish to, will never take 'No' for an answer or let a bad Press review veer him off course. I personally have heard him say, 'I'm always at my best in a crisis' – I would never contradict that remark. It could never be anything less than exciting to work for a man in whom the adrenalin flows so freely.

Fielding House is in Bruton Street and most of its door handles are large and in the shape of violins. On arrival I was greeted warmly and after a cup of coffee had been thrust into my hands we sat down in the office of one of his executives, Ian Bevan, and started to put it all together.

The first director to be approached was one of the most successful and experienced light-comedy directors in the English theatre. He was strangely, however, the most paradoxical of men. His skill and lightness of touch with a comedy was totally belied by his permanent air of depression and pessimism, a quality which earned him the pseudonym of Jolly Jack. Dear Jack Minster was cadaverous-looking, wore a hat most of the time and, in view of the fact that he rarely took his inveterate cigarette out of his mouth while talking, he was, more often than not, extremely difficult to understand. It is true to say that at that time he was wanting me to appear in a stage version of *The Girl At The Next Table* for his own management, but regardless of that, he refused to entertain the offer to direct *The Gazebo*.

'Can't possibly make 'em laugh, old boy, with a corpse on the stage for most of Act One. Dreadful taste – absolutely dreadful'. (Cough, cough, cough.)

Our second choice was Anthony Sharp, an old friend who luckily shared our views on the play's comic possibilities, and agreed immediately. Barbara, everyone concurred, would be the ideal leading lady and I also managed to persuade them to employ Reece Pemberton, who had designed such an enchanting light and airy set for *The Tunnel*, and Michael Northern, who had lit it. Rehearsals were set to start in late January and a four-week tour was then booked for a good warm-up prior to our opening in London. Everything in the garden, in fact, was rosy – until two weeks before we were due to go into rehearsal. One morning my telephone rang and a plaintive Barbara Murray, no doubt with mixed emotions, quietly announced to me that she was pregnant. This was, from my point of view, the most distressing of news. Barbara and I got on famously together and the thought of having to find someone new with whom I could dovetail so amicably filled me with trepidation. However, 'one door closes' as the adage hath it, and sad though I was to lose the delightful Barbara, the other door that was about to open provided me with a long, happy and memorable partnership.

For a whole day Tony Sharp and I and Ian Bevan sat in the latter's office making short-list after short-list which eventually whittled itself down to Moira Lister. Moira I knew well by reputation, but I had never actually met her. Would we have the same rapport? How were we for height? (I could never bear the thought of playing opposite a lady as tall as myself.)

'Well, time is short,' said Tony. 'We'd better check her availability and then make a date to see her.'

The former was quickly done – she was available. The latter we decided we had better do straight away. I was apprehensive.

'What are we going to say to her?' I said. 'We can't just go up to an actress of Moira's standing and say "Excuse me, we've just called to see if you are smaller than Ian".'

What her colouring was also interested us. In actual fact, Moira has never been anything but bright blonde all the time I have known her, but I didn't know then that the shade was a standard fixture.

'I'll give her a ring,' said Tony. 'We could be with her in fifteen minutes. Let's see if she's in and if she can see us.'

She was and she could, so, into a taxi and we were ringing the bell of her Belgravia flat on about the stroke of 6 p.m.

'When she's standing up, I'll try and manœuvre myself around to be nearer her so that you can surreptitiously check us for height,' I said while we waited.

Moira is, by marriage, the Vicomtesse d'Orthez and the opulence of her apartment very much reflects the title. Tony and I were shown up a magnificent circular embassy staircase to a first-floor landing, which seemed to have pillars at every corner, and finally through a grand mahogany door into a huge first-floor reception room. We sat down and waited briefly on one of two settees and then Madame breezed in.

She was, if I remember correctly, wearing a headscarf, so bang went any hope of discovering the colour of her hair without a specific request for her to remove it. The important thing, however, was that from the moment we met I had no shadow of doubt that, if she would accept the job, here was my new leading lady. The chemistry mingled on sight. Sparks crackled and the rapport was instantaneous: and no wonder – she is, I was to find out later, a Leo. Once again an identical sense of humour was to prove the foundation for a successful partnership. But, in addition, Moira's and my whole approach to the playing of comedy was identical. I have recounted earlier in this story the feeling of levitation that the professional marriage of kindred spirits produces. Moira and I had it in full measure. It was not only on stage that our most extraordinary 'oneness' was to manifest itself either. Over the years the strangest of coincidences – almost as if we shared some inexplicable ESP – were also to pepper our lives. About our first meeting, Moira has already recounted elsewhere that Tony and I had arrived '... for a quick drink and ostensibly to look me over! They stayed for three hours.'*

After its four-week provincial tour during which it fared well, *The Gazebo* opened in late March at the Savoy Theatre to decidedly mixed notices, and in this case I would assess them as being about fifty–fifty pro and anti. Once again, I am delighted to say that the critics' judgement was not reflected at the box office and the play had a run of well over a year.

On the opening night of *The Gazebo* I presented Tony Sharp with a small cigarette-box similar to the one Robert and Robin had given me at the beginning of *The Tunnel*. Inside the lid I had had engraved 'Thanks to your expert guidance and wise counsel, I got away with murder.' One whole year later I was lying in a hot bath ruminating when the incident came back to me. Suddenly I was struck with horror. I jumped out of the bath and flew to the telephone.

'Tony?'

'Yes.'

'Ian. I say, you remember that cigarette-box I gave you on the first night of *The Gazebo*?'

'Yes.'

'I've just been thinking. About the engraving....'

He broke in with a guffaw of laughter.

* *The Very Merry Moira* (Hodder and Stoughton, 1969)

With Moira Lister in The Gazebo

'I didn't?' I burbled.

'You did, you know,' he said and he was roaring his head off.

I had spelt 'counsel' C-O-U-N-C-I-L.

The third leading part in *The Gazebo* was played by Michael Goodliffe, a lovely actor of whom both Moira and I were very fond. Dear Michael gave a delightfully relaxed performance, but he hated playing comedy. He just didn't know what to do when the laughs came. He was so completely honest about his shortcoming, it disarmed. Had he been anybody else but Michael, it would have driven us both mad, but as it was his hang-up became totally endearing. We were doing exceptionally good business with the play and every night he'd come down on to the stage before curtain-up, peep through the spy-hole and, seeing a packed auditorium, would turn away despondently and groan, 'Oh my God, they're all there again.' Michael adored mid-week matinées which were more sparsely patronised, hence the laughs would be fewer and lighter. In these performances he felt he could get on with the play. Laughs, to his ears, only held it up.

Moira had a circle of friends which embraced a wide social spectrum. A story that she has already recalled in her own book is one of which I am particularly fond.

One evening a friend who had been in to see the show took her over to the Savoy Grill for supper afterwards. He was, I understand, one of the chinless set. After telling her how much he'd enjoyed it, he referred to me.

'Tell me,' he said. 'This chap Carmichael; does he enjoy actin'?'

'I presume so,' replied Moira, 'otherwise I doubt if he'd do it.'

'Well, I do hope so,' said her friend, 'cos it must take up an awful lot of his time.'

But in the middle of this joyous run of *The Gazebo* personal disaster was looming up ahead of me and I was to rush into it unsuspecting at breakneck speed.

On 19 September I started another film, a comedy called *Double Bunk* in which Janette Scott was again my leading lady. The picture had an eight-week shooting schedule at Twickenham Studios and a certain amount of location work on the Thames. I was to be on call every single working day of the entire eight weeks but I had weighed it all up carefully and decided that I would be able to manage both the film and my evening performance of *The Gazebo* with no trouble at all.

Throughout the making of *Double Bunk* I took a room in a hotel in Richmond. Every night after my show at the Savoy I had a hire-car waiting for me which would whisk me down to it and there I would then study the following day's text and get to sleep as soon as I could. At some time between 7 and 7.30 the following morning a taxi would take me to the studio. After a hard day's shooting the hire-car would again pick me up at 5.30 and take me back to the Savoy where my very dear old Yorkshire dresser, John Mackie (of whom more anon), would bring me in a meal from a nearby restaurant. I would then, with luck, be able to put my feet up and grab half an hour's sleep before getting ready for the evening performance.

The Gazebo was a killer for me. It was a very physical show and I never left the stage throughout the entire evening. Eight weeks of this round-the-clock routine finally took its toll. It was not only that eight weeks actually, they merely put the kibosh on an ever-increasing work-load that had been building up since the day I came out of the army in

1946. I didn't know it but I had become both mentally and physically exhausted and, as a result, I had also, I believe, become even more impossible to live with than usual.

The moment *Double Bunk* finished I had a number of post-production chores to attend to and a long-playing record to make, all of which dragged my debility down further. No sooner had I completed this schedule than Pym announced that she had promised to go away and stay with my mother, who was also feeling a bit down, for a few days. In my extremely low state of health, I didn't want to be left alone. I became difficult and on the day of her departure, having most reluctantly taken her to King's Cross Station, I returned home angry and sorry for myself. At lunchtime I went into my local to have a couple of pints to drown my sorrows. I had nothing that in normal circumstances I could not have coped with at mid-day and still given a performance in the evening. The circumstances, however, were not normal and I arrived at the theatre that night frightened, shaken, demoralised and feeling as weak as a kitten. I went straight into Moira's room, poured out my woes, and told her that I was terrified that I wasn't going to be able to get through the performance. The curtain went up. I got through the first ten minutes, then, realising I was going to black out, I left the sofa where I was sitting with my dear leading lady, walked into the wings and collapsed.

The curtain was rung down, I was taken into my dressing-room and a doctor tried to administer brandy which I resolutely refused to accept. After about fifteen minutes I insisted on having another try. Inwardly by now I was feeling so terrified I knew the chances of rising above the terror were minimal. However, I tried. After a couple of pages I left the stage again and capitulated.

I spent the remainder of the performance on my back in my dressing-room sweating like a pig and shaking like a banshee. Moira refused to let me go home until the curtain was down, when she insisted on accompanying me back to Mill Hill. I shall never forget her kindness. It took her a good twenty-five miles out of her way, but she was gentle, solicitous and understanding.

The following morning Harold was on the blower to me practically before I had stirred. After enquiring after my immediate health, he ordered that I should not go back to the theatre that night, that I should go off with Pym anywhere we liked on an immediate fortnight's holiday and that furthermore he intended to foot the entire bill for both of us.

'Where do you want to go?' he enquired, but before waiting for a reply he continued, 'Think it over, ring me back and let me know and we'll arrange it all for you.'

It was just as well he didn't wait for a reply because I was speechless.

Pym and I had never been out of the country together in our lives. Where were we to go? It was 7 December, and after a quick conference on the telephone, the snow and fresh and bracing air of Switzerland seemed, as a snap decision, to beckon our tired and jangled nerves which, in both of us, had by now become a bit frayed.

Three days later we left Victoria on the Golden Arrow and that evening wandering round the cafés in the French capital was, to me, like novocaine. I was having the first free weekday evening that I could remember for months and the relief and total relaxation of being away from, not only the Strand, not only London, but right out of England altogether was magical. Somewhere about midnight we boarded a train for Zürich and ultimately, St Moritz.

The following day the last slow climb from the greenery of the comparative lowlands to the snow-capped heights around St Moritz produced a scenic change of the most breathtaking beauty. The gorges, the little isolated farms and chapels, the conifer-laden slopes, the rushing torrents of the rivers and streams and the whole landscape gradually becoming whiter and whiter as we ascended, left us speechless in wonderment. Finally, we stepped out at our destination to sunshine, the clearest of delphinium-blue skies and the deepest crisp, crunchy and detergent-white snow we had ever seen – it was Winter Wonderland.

The therapy was to prove all that I could ever have wished it to be. In the early morning, when usually it snowed, and before the sun rose over the mountain in front of the hotel, which was not until about 10.30, we just lay in bed reading and breakfasting off coffee, croissants and cherry jam. Later, with sun up and snowfall stemmed, we would rise, wrap up and walk for miles.

At about four o'clock every afternoon we arrived back in the centre of town for hot chocolate and the most delicious, figure-damaging Swiss pastries that were sold in a packed café right opposite the hotel. Then back home again we flaked out on the bed. At 6.30 we would rise once more, bath, take an apéritif in one of several adjacent bars and then, after an early dinner, we would be abed by ten.

We found St Moritz, captivating. For the general douching out of the cares, worries and aggravations of everyday life there is, to my mind, no physic like snow and mountains. The very texture of snow is a medicament in itself; it cannot fail to relax. It falls silently. When lain it deadens noise. It reflects light which is pure and unsullied and in the mountains,

Members of the 1960 South African touring cricket team at a party to celebrate the 100th performance of The Gazebo. *L. to r. Trevor Goddard, Jackie McGlew, Peter Carlstein, Roy Maclean*

of course, it is deep and crisp and even and totally devoid of its less acceptable by-product – slush.

I returned to the Savoy on 23 December armed with presents for the tolerant cast that had been so inconvenienced by my sudden departure two weeks previously. Under normal circumstances I would have considered exercising my right to leave *The Gazebo* early in the New Year, but after Harold Fielding's kindness and quite exceptional generosity I now had every intention of waiving that right and staying with the play at least until some further offer of substance came along.

Sadly, rejuvenated though I undoubtedly felt after my fortnight in Switzerland, I had been back with the play for only three days when, during the first house on the day after Boxing Day, my voice gave out completely and I was able to play Act I only.

One of the first things to affect the voice is tiredness, and though my throat specialist patched me up fairly quickly he told me that I should really get out of the play for a prolonged rest as soon as I could. I returned to the cast almost immediately but sadly, on doctor's advice, I had to hand my notice to Harold. I finally left *The Gazebo* for good on 28 January.

On my departure the company presented me with a beautiful silver magnifying-glass with which I could study my photographic negatives – the products of a long-standing hobby. It was much appreciated and is still treasured, despite the fact that a four-year-old grand-daughter has left indelible teeth marks on its handle. All things being taken into consideration, however, I don't really think I deserved it.

CHAPTER TWENTY-FIVE

ALL OVER THE PLACE

Enter THE VOICE OF REASON *accompanied by*
SOUND COMMONSENSE

I was now forty years of age, and considerably shaken by what had just happened to me. Hitherto I had always thrived on work. It had, I think, helped me to retain a youthful appearance that in fact belied my age. I now decided that I must pause for a deep breath and reassessment of my life-style, and in doing so I didn't very much like what I saw. I had a beautiful home, a loving and dutiful wife and two gorgeous daughters whom I worshipped and who were, by now, fast approaching the ages of fifteen and twelve, and yet we had never all been away together alone on a proper family holiday. In a few years' time the girls would be young ladies and, in the natural way of things, leaving the nest for good. I was horrified – it was rapidly becoming later than I thought.

It isn't all that easy for an actor who is also a family man to plan holidays. His breaks between periods of employment may not – in fact rarely seem to – coincide with school holidays. When he is free his children probably aren't and vice versa. Eric Barker once told me that after years of wrestling with this problem he had finally come to the conclusion that, if he ever wanted to get away with his family, something would have to give, and that he had eventually decided that in future, for better of worse, it was his work that would have to give.

I had no immediate offer of employment after my departure from *The Gazebo* so I decided to take Eric Barker's eminently sound advice.

Neither Pym nor I had ever been to the Côte d'Azur so we decided that that would be our goal. Tony Hayes – an old chum who had been playing the lead in *The Boy Friend* ever since its first performance at the Players Theatre in 1953 – recommended that we should sample Ville-franche, where there was, he said, a charming little hotel on the edge of the fishermen's harbour and overlooking the bay to Cap Ferrat. We booked, made all the travel arrangements and were due to leave England, taking the car with us, on 30 March.

February passed without incident. March arrived and all systems were still 'go' – it was a nail-biting few weeks. Never before had I said my prayers nightly with a plea that the good Lord should continue to ensure my unemployment until we returned on 13 April. The first week in March passed serenely by and we were well into the second when I was beginning to feel, with justification, that at last we were home and dry. How wrong I was.

On the Friday of that week the much-prized offer from Hollywood arrived: the leading part in a comedy opposite Tuesday Weld. Only half the script had been completed but if I accepted the job they wanted me to leave for Hollywood on 1 April. I was distraught. My assessment of the script was almost certainly jaundiced before I had even read page one. However, jaundiced or not, I told Richard that under no circumstances would I agree to fly out having seen only half a script; I would have to see the complete work before making a decision. In other words, I stalled.

We left England on time. The hotel was comfortable and friendly, the weather was all we could have wished for and for fourteen days we toured the countryside, lay in the sun, swam (all but me) and progressed lazily around the private beaches of Cap Ferrat on pedalloes. Each day that passed I breathed deeper. Not a word from Richard, not a word from Hollywood.

On the final day of our first week the remainder of the script arrived direct from the States. Also included was the instruction that if I wanted the part I would have to fly out in forty-eight hours. Crash – my world had collapsed about my ears. If my reading of the first half of that script had been jaundiced, my assessment of the remainder had to have been positively bigoted. I read it on a sun-drenched Mediterranean beach with my lovely family lying half-naked around me lapping up the first real holiday of our lives. How could I possibly remain unbiased?

I didn't go. Another actor, an old friend, went in my place and as a result established himself firmly in the Hollywood studios. I don't believe I ever saw the film when it eventually came out, but, as I remember, it didn't set the world on fire. What would have happened to me had I gone? A question impossible to answer. Do I regret not going? Never. I completed a holiday with the three girls who are dearest to me and we all enjoyed every minute of it; I wouldn't hesitate to make the same decision again, even with hindsight.

This was the beginning of my new approach to life. There are, I believe, two philosophies by which man can live after middle age. The first is that of he who wants to die with his boots on, and the second is that of the man who says 'Get out and enjoy yourself, it's later than you think'. Today I subscribe religiously to the second of the two.

I played a lot of cricket that summer – for the Lord's Taverners of whom I had become a member in 1957, for various charity games run by Harry Secombe, Brian Rix, John Boulting and Vic Lewis and for the odd county beneficiary such as Tom Clark of Surrey and Jack Mannings of Northamptonshire – all of which got me out in the fresh air, provided plenty of exercise (beneficial), several pints afterwards (not so beneficial) and generally got all the corpuscles on parade again and drilling with their old precision.

In June I had been invited by Peter Willes, then an executive producer at Associated Rediffusion Television, whom I had first met at Sandhurst in 1941, to do a play for them. I was asked to submit my choice. My first thought was to find something in which I could renew auld acquaintance with Moira, so I put my brain to steep and quickly recalled one that Binkie had offered me several years previously. It was a play by Lionel Hale called *Gilt and Gingerbread*. At the time it was offered to me I had been in my mid-thirties and I didn't think the time was yet ripe to appear in a piece in which I was saddled with a late-teenage daughter. Binkie seemed to accept this fact with equanimity and never pressed the matter. It was eventually presented several years later by John Clements who appeared in it himself with his wife Kay Hammond, and by that time the part of the teenage daughter had vanished.

I soon armed myself with a copy, re-read it and it made me laugh a great deal. Peter thought it 'rather old-fashioned' but nevertheless agreed to mount it for Moira and me.

Names have never been the lovely vicomtesse's strong point. We rehearsed the play for three weeks in a room at the back of a pub on the north bank of the Thames just above Hammersmith Bridge: a delightful spot when the sun shines and during those three weeks it did. The transmission was to be 'live' from Associated Rediffusion's studios in Wembley. On the morning we were to move into the studios and rehearse with cameras, the entire cast assembled at 10 a.m. with the exception of the leading lady. After fifteen minutes the director started to tap his foot; after half an hour he became decidedly tetchy and after three-quarters of an hour he was positively hysterical.

'Ring up her home,' he instructed his PA, 'and find out what has happened to her.'

The secretary returned with the news that the vicomtesse had left home over an hour ago as she had a television transmission that evening.

Ten minutes later she blew in. She had been at the studios well on time – unfortunately she had been at the wrong ones. She, also an old friend of Peter Willes, had rehearsed for three solid weeks under the impression that she had been working for the BBC.

A few weeks before my happy reunion with Moira, while searching for a new play for the West End, I had met an American agent called Milton Goldman at some social evening in London. Was there, I had asked him, anything new on Broadway that would be suitable for me.

'What about *Critic's Choice?*' he volunteered.

'What *about Critic's Choice?*' I questioned. I have always been a bad theatregoer, even in this country, and my theatrical intelligence is not, consequently, of CIA quality.

It was, apparently, a play by Ira Levin in which Henry Fonda had recently appeared in New York. Mr Goldman promised to send me a copy.

This had recently arrived and I was very taken with it indeed. It was another mammoth leading role, this time that of a New York theatre critic who is faced with the problem of reviewing his second wife's play which, if he does so truthfully, may cost him his marriage. It contained a great deal of comedy, some excellent dialogue – witty lines that I just had to speak instead of working myself to death with comedy business – but it was, in addition, a character with infinitely greater depth than anything I had played before. It was well within my range and I wanted to stretch myself further than I had been called upon to do to date. There was, however, no part in it for Moira. The role of the wife/playwright – the female lead – would not have been good casting for her. There was, however, a smaller part of the critic's first wife, a glamorous actress who had left him because he had told the truth about her acting, but the part was a subservient one with only two scenes which, though good, I wouldn't have dreamed of suggesting that she should play.

Feeling that, as a result of this, I would get a completely unbiased and detached assessment of the piece, I asked Moira if she would read it for me and let me know her views.

She returned it to me the following day and that evening, after the *Gilt and Gingerbread* rehearsal, we sat down to have a drink in the bar and I said, 'Well – what do you think?'

There was a pause and then she said, 'Why do you want to do it?'

Whatever else I had expected, it certainly hadn't been that.

'Because....' and I gave her my reasons.

She was, I could see, surprised. She was also, I think, mystified at, not so much my fondness for the play, but my attraction to the part.

It was a lovely summer's evening and we went for a long stroll up the river, Chiswick Mall way, discussing it at length. I don't think she ever fully fathomed my affection for and desire to impersonate Parker Ballantine, but after we had returned to our cars and before we said goodbye she completely took the wind out of my sails.

'If you really intend to go ahead with it,' she said, 'and if you want me and the management will provide me with two Balmain creations, I'll play the first wife.'

It was like the ads say: 'The Somebody's ring of confidence', 'The Somebody else's seal of approval'. I hugged her uninhibitedly and we parted.

The moment *Gilt and Gingerbread* was over I tore up to Fielding House clutching my one copy of the script, told Harold the news and asked him if he would present it for us. He agreed. Tony Sharp was again engaged to direct and soon we were into casting sessions.

It is seldom that everything runs smoothly and we had a disappointment to come. After a few days of deliberation and a friendly meeting in the office with Harold, Tony and me, during which my star seemed to be continuing ever more into the ascendant, Billie Whitelaw, I understood, agreed to play the female lead. Shortly afterwards, however, she went off on a holiday, I believe into the Lake District, from where she despatched a telegram saying, unhappily, that with regrets and apologies she had changed her mind. The part was eventually accepted by the diminutive, pert and enchanting Muriel Pavlow and it was a happy reunion.

We went into rehearsals on 9 October, after two weeks of which Moira was to give me her second body-blow in six weeks. The venue, I believe, was in one of the bars of the theatre in which we were rehearsing (the Vaudeville?) and she was, as I remember, dressed chicly in scarlet and black.

'I'm terribly sorry to have to tell you,' she said and then took a deep breath – 'I'm pregnant.'

I stood there aghast. Again! This, I reflected, was becoming a habit.

For Moira's sake I was delighted; she already had a daughter and, for a long time, had been dying to have another baby, but to me it was a bitter blow. Before I had time to say anything, however, she rushed on, 'Look, we have two more weeks' rehearsal which will be no problem and I can easily manage the four-week tour and also the first four weeks of the London run; that's ten weeks in all.' It was a *cri de cœur*. She desperately wanted to stay with us as long as she possibly could. Sad though I was to lose her, however, neither Harold, Tony nor I thought it would be wise for her to continue. To have to find a replacement of stature so early in a London run would, we reasoned, be neither prudent nor easy.

Critic's Choice opened in Oxford on 6 November with Moira's understudy, Anne Berry. Anne was an experienced actress and before joining our company she had been the leading lady at the Worthing Rep. She was a strikingly attractive, auburn-haired lass, and she gave the part considerable panache – all the extroversion, in fact, that must have been the last straw for her marriage to Parker. (When reviewing her performance as Helen of Troy, he had said that she would have been better cast as the Trojan Horse.) Everyone liked Anne's performance, so she was, quite properly, retained and the search for a replacement for Moira abandoned.

We opened at the Vaudeville Theatre on 6 December to, once again, a mixed Press, but I would assess a rather better one than had been accorded *The Gazebo*. Headlines such as 'This Critic's Choice' cancelled out with categoric clarity one that read 'But not this critic's choice'; and remarks in one paper describing it as 'witless' were somehow difficult to equate with those of one of our most revered and distinguished national Sundays' reviewers who said, 'The merit of the play is its wit.'

The underlying theme of *Critic's Choice* is, I suppose, a man's struggle to keep his integrity. During the course of the play, the author chose to take several cracks at theatrical critics, and on the evidence I am forced to the reluctant conclusion that, in the main, they humourlessly failed to see a joke when it was directed against themselves.

From a personal point of view I suffered the same anomalies that beset the critical reception of the play itself. Having received, over the previous few years, a surfeit of criticism for always playing the dithering buffoon I had deliberately selected Parker Ballantine for the opportunity it afforded me to get away from one. This, nevertheless, produced contradictory reviews such as '... Ian Carmichael ... has few opportunities to display the talents that won him a large personal following,' while another proffered the headline 'Ian Carmichael gives his best performance.'

The public, who are, after all the real touchstone, were, I think, rather like Moira, a little bemused as to why I had accepted the part. They, I feel, generally, never received quite what they wanted from me until I had a drunken monologue in Act III about my reasons for becoming

With Anne Berry in Critic's Choice

a critic. This was an exceptionally fine piece of comic writing and was riotously received every night. Many, quite erroneously, considered it was purely because of this solo that I had chosen to appear in the play.

Critic's Choice matched its New York run of six months where, I believe, it had received the same critical treatment. If I was to select one overriding factor for the public's lack of total enthusiasm for the piece, it would be because I doubt very much whether the general playgoer had any interest at all in the private problems of a theatrical critic. In other words, he was unable to identify with the inner turmoils of the principal characters. Personally, I have never had a single regret about choosing the part. I enjoyed every moment of every performance.

During the remainder of 1962 I was to be occupied making three films. Two weeks after *Critic's Choice* closed at the end of May, I returned to Hal Chester and Shepperton Studios to commence the first of them. It was called *Hide and Seek* and sadly it was to be a great disappointment.

For several years I had been trying to find a new sort of film role. All I was being offered (by the trunkload) were variations on the same old bumbling, accident-prone clot. The number in which I appeared were but a fraction of the ones I turned down. I was getting tired of them and so were the critics; it was only, I figured, a matter of time before the public would too. I was seeking romantic comedies, comedy thrillers along the lines of William Powell's *Thin Man* series but sadly the British studios were not making such movies, and even if the odd one did slip through the net, it was never offered to me. I was after the sort of roles that were being played so expertly by Cary Grant: the glossy, middle-of-the-road, domestic comedy at which the Americans excelled, or the superbly turned Hitchcock thriller like *North-West Passage*. *Hide and Seek* was one such. It was a splendid spy thriller with the most original twists and turns in the plot. It had been written by a young English novelist called David Stone and was one of the most exciting properties ever to come my way. Here at last was the gear change that I so badly needed to get me out of the Stanley Windrush mould.

Hal, as usual, put it all together with his customary flair. I was to play opposite the delightful little Janet Munro, who was tragically destined to die so young, and in two excellent supporting character parts he had cast Curt Jurgens and that larger-than-life Welshman Hugh Griffith. The director was Cy Enfield who had recently won acclaim for Stanley Baker's *Zulu*.

It was all there; it couldn't possibly miss. Unhappily it did. The customary pink and blue page amendments made their regular appearances and somewhere within the administrative machine disagreements developed and lethargy seemed to settle on the production. The shooting got farther and farther behind and towards the end of the ten- or eleven-week schedule, with a whole week's work still left to be shot, the money boys pulled the ladder up and instructions were issued that the picture had to be completed in the next forty-eight hours. Tiny sections of half a dozen or more sets were hastily erected all round one of the studio's stages and for a whole day linking shots to hold the remainder of the film together were grabbed at breakneck speed.

I don't think *Hide and Seek* ever had a West End showing; if it had it was in and out so quickly that very few people saw it. I believe it has appeared occasionally on television, but my big chance to show my paces in a different type of role and *œuvre* was torpedoed almost from the outset.

That summer the Boultings had launched themselves into John's *magnum opus* for Peter Sellers – *Heaven's Above*. As usual, the majority of the Boultings' Repertory Company were employed but on this occasion there was no part in it for me. The target for their barbs in *Heaven's Above* was, fairly obviously, the Church. The story was all based on a mistaken identity premise. Sellers, a plebeian Black Country parson, had, as a result of a clerical error, taken up a living in a sleepy little English hamlet in which the incumbent was always approved, if not actually selected, by the lady of the manor. The applicant to whom the appointment should have gone was a young public school churchman who had been cursed with the same name and who was the product of what might be referred to as 'a good family'.

As 'The other Reverend Smallwood' in Heaven's Above

INSET *Before orthodontic treatment aged twelve. I don't know why I bothered!*

Roy, who was producing and had done a certain amount of casting through Richard Stone, one day remarked to him on the telephone how sad they were that they had been unable to find a part for me in the picture. A few days later he called the Stone office again.

'Look, I've just been thinking,' he said. 'There is the tiny but important part of the young vicar to whom the living at Magna Parva [I think the village was called] should have gone. It's only about three days' work at the outside, but do you think Ian would like to play it?'

Was there ever any doubt? Two weeks later I joined John at the studios in Shepperton and, embellished with a top jaw full of protruding teeth and a pair of ears that stood directly out from the sides of my head like those of a dormouse, I committed to celluloid my performance of 'The other Rev. Smallwood'.

Later in the year at the same studios I appeared as the north-country Corporal Green, a regular army wide-boy, in the film version of the big stage success *The Amorous Prawn*. It was, for those statistically minded, the fifth film in which I had appeared with Dennis Price. Our big moment together was still to come.

The remainder of the year, what there was of it, was spent in negotiations with a rising young West End producer called John Gale for whom Moira and I were shortly destined to renew our partnership.

CHAPTER TWENTY-SIX

THE DOLDRUMS

Exit GOOD FORTUNE

John Gale, in 1962, was a tall, blond, good-looking, vital, up-and-coming young theatrical manager with offices on the top floor of the Strand Theatre in the Aldwych. Today he is one of our most senior impresarios and sartorially would appear to be the reincarnation of Hannen Swaffer. Of the many successes he holds to his credit I don't think he would be least proud of *Boeing-Boeing* and *No Sex Please, We're British*.

In the early sixties John was continually trying to persuade me to work for him. He had bombarded me with a succession of plays, many of them French, which seemed to be the 'in' drama of the day, but none of them had appealed to me. Now an actor's life, being what it is it always hurts to say 'No' to a prospective employer, but to say it continually seems to be nothing short of professional suicide. One day, having returned the previous night from viewing a play that he had sent me to see in Canterbury – another one that hadn't appealed – I thought I had really better put forward some counter-suggestions or it wouldn't be long before my page in *Spotlight* would be summarily ripped out of the volume in the Gale office and consigned to the WPB. With this in mind, I had lunch with him a few days later and took with me a copy of a play that Alan Melville had sent to me several months previously. I personally did not consider it to be one of Alan's best works, but it was, nevertheless, a splendid idea and many of its scenes contained good and amusing dialogue. I took *Devil May Care* to John, not to suggest that we should do it together but rather in an illogical attempt to make amends for having turned down so many of his own suggestions. Whatever its shortcomings, I considered it to be very much better than many of those I had been reading.

John took it away, read it then telephoned me the following day and said, 'When do we start?' Hoist with my own petard I think describes the situation to a T.

I then re-read the play myself and my decision to go ahead was, I'm afraid, based on two totally unsound pieces of reasoning and one enormous chunk of conceit. The unsound reasoning was occasioned first by the fact that I felt I just couldn't say 'No' to John any more – particularly with a play I had now taken to him myself – and second by the opportunity that it afforded me to work with Moira again. The conceit, I blush to say, was instanced by the thought that, if I was right about the play's shortcomings, Moira and I between us might, if she would agree to join me, be able to, in some way, make up its deficiencies. So, full of overweening self-delusion, having first ensured that Moira was game, I said 'Yes'.

The play began in hell where I, as a young devil, was being instructed by 'the guv'ner' himself to return to earth armed with a treasure trove of diamond bracelets and other materialistic temptations in order to win a few souls for him. 'Black Out'; then lights full up on a beautiful J. Hutchinson Scott set depicting the terrace of a luxurious hotel overlooking the bay at Monte Carlo. After several minutes I made my entrance in nothing but a bright scarlet towelling bathrobe. Shortly afterwards I was followed by the most ravishing blonde – my leading lady – in a virginal creation of the purest white. She, I then discovered, after attempting a pass in the name of my master, was an angel who had been sent down from above on exactly the same errand.

I had a song and dance with the female juvenile lead (Carole Mowlam) in Act II – a bit of a mistake, I think – and 'a double' (my conscience), identically dressed, in Act III, played by Simon Merrick. Again Tony Sharp was called in to direct.

Devil May Care toured for four weeks and played at the Strand Theatre for nine. The more dramatic effects during that period were, sadly, taking place off stage rather than on it.

During our penultimate week of rehearsals, I received news that my mother had had a stroke and was in hospital. Pym went up immediately and I followed by train after rehearsals on the Saturday evening, arriving in Hull shortly after midnight. I went straight round to the hospital. The weather was bitter; the countryside was enveloped in snow and ice and the streets of Hull were ankle-deep in slush. My mother was in a private room containing two beds – the second one was empty. When I arrived she had been unconscious for two days. I asked the sister if I could doss down on the other bed for the night in case she regained consciousness. I remained at the hospital the whole of Sunday and also throughout Sunday night and she never did. On Monday I had to return for our final week's rehearsal. She died on the Wednesday without ever regaining consciousness.

*Summer at 'Moat
Lodge'*

My mother was seventy. She had never really been fit or able to enjoy
life since my father died five years previously. She had missed him dread-
fully. She had always been a great believer and in accordance with her
faith she would, I know, be glad to be rejoining him.

The opening of *Devil May Care* in London was to instance one of those
extraordinary and totally inexplicable happenings that have peppered
Moira's life and my own since we got to know each other.

On the day we were to open in London I still hadn't found any suitable
gift with which to present her that evening. In a feverish last-minute
search during the morning I scoured Harrods. After at least three-quarters
of an hour in the store, still without luck, I was browsing round the Glass
and China Department when two milk-glass goblets that had been tucked
away at the back of a shelf caught my eye. I picked one up and the side
of it had been decorated with several bars of music from Gounod's *Faust*.
What could be more ideal? I bought it.

At the theatre that evening I went into her dressing-room at the half-
hour to wish her *bonne chance* and to hand her my gift. She reciprocated
and handed me hers. I returned to my own room and unwrapped it. It
contained the pair to the goblet I had bought for her.

As is the way of things in our business, I haven't seen Moira for several
years, but this sort of thing continues to happen. Last week Lee, now
married for ten years and living happily with her husband and three children, answered the telephone in their own home. A man's voice at the
other end of the line enquired, 'Helen?'

'No,' said Lee, 'this isn't Helen.'

'Er – oh! Is that—' and he supplied the number.

'Yes,' replied Lee. 'And I've lived here for eight years and there's never been a Helen in this house.'

The caller seemed momentarily nonplussed.

'Oh, dear,' he said; and then, rather oddly volunteering such information to a total stranger, he continued, 'Well, I'm trying to find Helen and Trevor Howard. I've got something for them that I've trudged half way round the world with; I'm only in England for a few days and I'm desperately trying to track them down.'

'Well,' said Lee, 'by an extraordinary coincidence, my dad happens to know them well; I could easily phone him and get their number for you if you like.'

'No, don't worry,' said the caller, 'I can probably trace them another way – I'm staying with Moira Lister.'

Lee and Sally at Eton Villas

Wondering what other novel twist the conversation could take, Lee then decided to declare her identity.

'This is ridiculous,' she said. 'I don't know if the name means anything to you, but my father is Ian Carmichael.'

'You're too right, it's ridiculous,' the stranger replied. 'Last time your father was in Johannesburg, he stayed with me in my house.'

And I had.

Generally speaking, the years 1963 and 1964 produced a recession in my professional life. The film scripts that had swamped me between 1955 and 1961 stopped almost as suddenly as they had started. This did not altogether surprise me. I had suffered enormous exposure in the cinema during those years and basically the sort of part I had been offered was always the same. Even if that in itself had not been damaging, to find scripts of the standard of some of my earlier successes became increasingly difficult.

On the theatre front I was receiving no shortage of offers but I could find no plays that appealed.

During those years I tried out another American success – *Sunday in New York* – at the Ashcroft Theatre in Croydon which 'Jolly' Jack Minster, who had staged it, wanted to transfer to the West End. My personal advisers, however, counselled against it, and rightly or wrongly I took their advice. I made a strange and abortive feature film that contained no dialogue in Copenhagen and I worked for some time, also abortively, with Cyril Ornadel and Philip Mackie on a musical version of *The Girl At The Next Table*. I toured for four weeks in a play of Ronald Harwood's called *March Hares*, a mad, surrealistic comedy with a large cast which included a clever young man called Michael Crawford; I played John Worthing in a very starry television production of *The Importance of Being Earnest* and I also joined Moira once again for our appearances as *Simon and Laura* in the same medium.

I was, during those whole two years, constantly searching for some new and impressive subject in which to display my talent, but it remained elusive. I had, I confess, become a little shy about taking risks, which possibly didn't help the situation.

In the event, the most significant idea that Richard and I discussed was the possibility of trying to sell someone the idea of mounting a TV series around the character of Bertie Wooster. The idea was, however, no sooner discussed than discarded. I considered that to have to return to the 1920s for subjects would lay me wide open to the criticism of being *passé*. It is only fair to add that, though I stuck to this view, I didn't carry Richard along with me.

During the summers I both watched and played a lot more cricket. The usual round of Sunday charity matches was ever prevalent and once again county beneficiaries such as Fred Titmus, Don Kenyon, Peter Loader and Ken Barrington asked me to lend them a helping hand, which I always enjoyed. By now I was on the cricket committee of the Lord's Taverners too, and such light-hearted but hard-working games (when off the field one was continually occupied on one of the many money-raising sideshows) occupied the majority of my Sundays during the season.

Towards the end of 1964, however, by pure chance, the occasion of Sir Winston Churchill's ninetieth birthday brought Michael Mills and me together again and, but for a brief and unhappy interruption which could have stymied the whole thing, my career was soon about to veer back on course.

CHAPTER TWENTY-SEVEN

NEW YORK

Re-enter MICHAEL MILLS − *an ever present help in trouble*

In late 1964, in conjunction with an American producer, John Gale was preparing a Broadway production of *Boeing-Boeing*, the French farce that ran in London for just over five years and which, when last heard of, was still going strong in Paris after eighteen. During the course of these preparations he asked me if I would go with it and play the lead.

Now this was not the first time that John had, over the years, asked me to appear in *Boeing* and, regardless of its enormous success, neither the play nor the part had ever appealed to me. It is a play which is all situation; there isn't a funny line in it from beginning to end and in addition I had never been able to find any character whatsoever in the leading role. I fully accept that this is a personal view and that many other performers have had a ball in it; nevertheless, it still remains one of my most unfavourite plays. When John approached me, therefore, I was in a welter of indecision. I had never played in New York, neither was there any other tempting offer lurking ahead. On the other hand, I was by no means convinced that it would be a guaranteed success on the other side of the Atlantic. The New Yorker is attuned to the slick and witty wisecrack as purveyed by the Neil Simons of their world and *Boeing-Boeing* was notable in its deficiency of such joys. Another disquieting factor was that, if I accepted the offer, I would have to remain with the production for a whole year. The thought of being separated from my family for so long a period filled me with gloom.

I chewed the problem over − with Richard, with John, with Pym and with Jack Minster who had directed the London production and was now about to reproduce it in New York. I tried to extract promises from him that, if I did go, I would be allowed to give my own performance and not a carbon copy of that being given by the actor then playing it on Shaftesbury Avenue. 'I may not get you every laugh that he is getting,' I explained, 'but I think I can compensate, if that is the case, by getting you several that are not there at the moment.' I wanted to be able to put more flesh on the character's bones. I wanted to dress him differently.

As I have already explained, because of that cigarette which was a permanent fixture in Jack's face it wasn't always easy to understand what he said, but I got the definite impression that, if I went, I would be given my head and allowed to create my own performance of 'Robert'. In view of this I finally agreed to go.

Before leaving England I tried hard not to be dragged into the Apollo Theatre one night to see the performance there (I'd already seen it twice over the years) but Jack insisted. What I did do, however, was to, quite openly, spend a couple of afternoons with Beverley Cross, the translator, who, most amicably, wrote in several new lines in order to give the character more substance, all of which he handed over to Jack who showed no sign of disapproval.

From England, I was joined by Gerald Harper in the second male lead and Maureen Pryor in the one female character part; the girls to play the three air hostesses were to be found in New York and Jack flew out ahead of us to do the casting.

On Friday, 18 December, Pym and the girls took me to London Airport. Never in my life have I had a more heartbreaking goodbye. I kissed and hugged them in the knowledge that I may not be seeing any of them again for a whole year. We were all in tears and were each fighting a losing battle not to show it. I doubt if any of us had ever been so miserable.

Now almost three weeks earlier, on 30 November of that year, Sir Winston Churchill celebrated his ninetieth birthday and the BBC decided to mark the occasion with a mammoth ninety-minute 'spectacular'. The show was to be called *Ninety Years On*. It was to be a birthday present for the great man from the world of entertainment, and it would link Sir Winston's life story with music and items from shows that he could have seen or heard during his lifetime.

Cicely Courtneidge played Vesta Tilley; Alma Cogan, Florrie Ford; Arthur Askey, Billy Merson; Margot Fonteyn, Anna Pavlova; Billy Cotton, Harry Champion; Ted Ray, Will Hay; Andy Stewart, Harry Lauder – Jimmy Edwards, Reg Varney, Anne Rogers, Edmund Hockridge, you name them they were in it. Twenty top 'names' in all, plus choruses of singers and dancers to boot. The narrator to link all the items together was to be Noël Coward who would speak a script written by Terence Rattigan ('This programme, ladies and gentlemen, is not for you. It is for you, Sir Winston') and the director and producer of the whole show was to be Michael Mills.

I was called upon to impersonate George Grossmith Junior and to perform, in the chic-est of grey morning suits with wing collar, cravate, *boutonnière*, top hat and silver-knobbed cane, 'Yip-Aye-Addy' from *Our Miss Gibbs*. I was given a chorus of beautiful girls to support me and, once again, another happy reunion after so many years, the routine was choreographed by Freddie Carpenter.

It was a great show to be connected with and it took four days to record. Such a galaxy of talent meant, of course, that only a select few could receive recognition in the following day's papers. I came out of it surprisingly well, but I hadn't, apparently, been mentioned in all the reviews; a fact, I discovered, that had been noted and recorded by others when, in the middle of the following afternoon, a telegram arrived for me at Moat Lodge from a man who, at that time, I had never even met.

SO UPSET THAT SILLY OLD AUNTIE TIMES NEVER MENTIONED YOU MUST TELL YOU THOUGHT YOU WERE PERFECT WARMEST CONGRATULATIONS AND KINDEST REGARDS – LARRY OLIVIER

It takes so little to make an actor feel 'the greatest'. That wire I treasure more than any review I have ever received.

However, it was during the making of *Ninety Years On* that, in the bar of the BBC Club on the evening after recording my number, Michael revealed to me his plans for the immediate future.

'I'm going to make a half-hour comedy series out of the P. G. Wodehouse Bertie Wooster and Jeeves short stories,' he said. 'And I'd very much like you to play Bertie. How would you feel about it?'

Astonishin', what? I told him that the idea had crossed my own mind a year previously and also why I had never pursued the matter.

'You're wrong, you know,' he said. 'Quite wrong.'

Michael, as I have mentioned before, is an articulate man and that fact, when harnessed to the expression of his firm convictions, can make him very persuasive. It wasn't long, therefore, before he began to fire me with considerable enthusiasm for the project.

'Well, we can go on nattering,' I said, 'but the matter is, unhappily, only academic as I have to leave for New York in two weeks' time,' and I told him why. 'And furthermore, if *Boeing* is successful,' I pointed out, 'I shall have to stay there for a whole year.'

'Well, we can't start till early next year,' said Michael. 'I'll leave the casting open till the last moment. If anything goes wrong over there, don't forget to let me know.'

I promised I would.

I arrived at JFK airport in New York somewhere about five in the evening. The first person I met in the concourse was Nigel Patrick who had also just flown in on another flight. He too was to appear in a play over there. Beyond that there was little else calculated to raise my spirits above the depths to which they had descended eight hours previously.

I had arrived with my old and very large school trunk which was brimming over with clothes both for the play and for my personal wear. (Have you ever tried to pack for a year?) The American customs man was rude and officious and he rifled it from top to bottom.

Reunion at JFK airport – with Nigel Patrick

I was then met by my American employer who escorted me into town in a chauffeur-driven limousine the size of a pantechnicon. Having settled in my seat, the first thing the latter did was to lock all the doors on the inside. When I asked why I was informed that it was always the safest way to travel in New York.

I checked in at the Algonquin, dined that night at Sardi's with Jack Minster and, feeling pretty whacked, returned to the hotel early and was in bed by eleven. The following morning the telephone beside my bed rang at nine o'clock.

'Hello.'

'Ian Carmichael?'

'Yes.'

A name was supplied which meant absolutely nothing to me.

'Who?'

The name was repeated and the caller continued, 'Can you have lunch with me today? Say 12.30?' And he named a restaurant.

I thought I'd better speak his language.

'Who is this?' I repeated.

He gave his name again. The voice had the urgency, push and no-non-sense of a high-powered salesman.

'I'm sorry,' I said, 'but I haven't the remotest idea who you are.'

'Aw, hell,' he exclaimed. 'We were together till two-thirty this morning.'

'I was in bed at two-thirty this morning,' I said.

'Aw, hell,' the voice growled on, now verging on the grotty. 'You know we were together – come on now.'

'Where were we together?' I enquired.

'Down town,' and as I didn't reply he narrowed it down a bit. 'At the Blackamore Club.'

I wasn't liking this call one little bit; it was sinister. If he had been with another man who by coincidence had had the same name as me, why should he ring the Algonquin?

'Look,' I said slowly and clearly, 'I arrived in New York at five o'clock yesterday afternoon for the first time in my life. I don't know your town, I don't know the Blackamore Club, I don't know you. Furthermore, I'm busy today and I can't possibly have lunch with you.'

'Aw, hell!' and the line went dead.

In 1964 I found New York a disturbing, violent city and I disliked it instantly.

We started rehearsals almost immediately in the Cort Theatre on 48th Street just off Times Square. It was 'dark' and gutted at the time and it was to remain so until we opened in it six weeks later. Because of my views on the play and the part I was apprehensive from the word 'go'. My morale was to sink lower, however, because having left London three and a half thousand miles away, Jack's attitude to my problem ('hang-up' if you prefer) became infinitely less flexible. The new lines that Bever-ley Cross had provided for me were swept aside as unnecessary and, as I was affeared would happen, I was called upon to give a carbon copy of the London performance. Hence, if Jack and I didn't actually cross swords, we had, to say the least, numerous heated and time-wasting argu-ments. I won a few points, like my 'wardrobe', for instance, but they were hollow victories, reluctant concessions given to someone who I am sure he considered to be an extremely difficult actor. As a result of all this my performance developed into an unhappy compromise that pleased neither myself nor my director.

By the end of our three-week rehearsal period I was, in consequence of my dislike of the city and my unhappiness in the play, at a very low ebb spiritually and my letters home became the most depressing documents.

Our opening week in New Haven and subsequent fortnight in Boston, however, cheered me considerably. Both towns I found more friendly, slower and in every way more attractive, but our stay in Boston was, sadly, to be marked by a most moving moment in English history – the death of Sir Winston Churchill. It was not the moment to have been on foreign soil. On the day of the state funeral I stayed in my hotel room the entire day watching the television presentation from London. I left it over lunch-time during a break in the transmission and went across to Jacob Worth's bar for corned beef hash and draught lager. I was very dewy-eyed and I got the impression that every Englishman in the United States – certainly those in Boston – were, on that day, looked upon by our American cousins with the kindness and sympathy that is normally reserved only for those who have just lost a close relative.

Boeing-Boeing eventually opened in New York on Tuesday, 2 February 1965, and during the morning of that day I had received a message from our stage director that Mr John Gale wished me to meet him in the foyer lounge of the Algonquin Hotel at 4.30 that afternoon. On time, I arrived to keep the appointment. There was no John Gale to be seen. Sitting there, however, as large as life and to my total astonishment and joy, was Pym. She had just flown in with a girl-friend – the result of a subterfuge between her and the Gale office. I was over the moon.

We opened and the first-night audience was appreciative. The management afterwards threw a large, expensive and star-spangled party at the El Morocco but the Press the following day turned out to confirm my worst fears.

Despite my unhappiness in the role I personally had been received well; considerably better, possibly, than I deserved to have been; nevertheless, this French farce, as I had suspected it might prove, was just not New York's *tasse de thé*.

Boeing-Boeing had a three-week run on Broadway and, to be truthful, nobody was more relieved than I to read those notices and realise that, consequently, the writing was on the wall for us. I was sorry for everyone

With Gerald Harper and Susan Carr in Boeing-Boeing

else and I had tried my best, but I think to have lived in New York for a whole year would have driven me out of my mind. At the end of the first week the statutory fortnight's notice was put up on the theatre notice-board and so I was able to say goodbye to Pym and her friend on the following day in the knowledge that, in only two weeks' time, I too would be returning to England, home and beauty.

The moment I had seen them off I cabled Michael Mills:

RETURNING ENGLAND 22ND FEBRUARY AM AT YOUR EXCLUSIVE DISPOSAL FROM THEN ON – IAN.

CHAPTER TWENTY-EIGHT

ENGLAND, HOME AND BEAUTY

Re-enter GOOD FORTUNE *accompanied by*
BERTRAM WOOSTER – *an amiable drone and*
PETER BRIDGE – *a compulsive theatre-goer*

Compared with what I had left behind, London, the centre of which can also at times be a bit of a flesh-pot, had never – except perhaps during wartime leaves – appeared to me so gracious, so clean, so friendly and so welcoming. The red double-decker buses, Eros and the dear old London taxis had never looked so beautiful before. For days when walking through the West End I felt I was living in the era of 'Sapper' or a Wilcox–Neagle–Wilding movie.

My cable to Michael had arrived at the *moment critique* if ever there was one; to be precise, at the very moment a conference was in progress at the BBC Television Centre during which it was to be decided who, in my absence, would be asked to play Bertie Wooster.

Over lunch a couple of days later, Michael told me we were to do six half-hours. The scripts were to be written, fifty-fifty, by Michael himself and Richard Waring – each of them being responsible for complete episodes. Filming for the series was to start in mid-April, by which time there would be a chance of some reasonable spring weather, the scripts would be finished, casting completed, music recorded and everything generally lined up for the off. Sandy Wilson had been engaged to write the incidental music, also a song which I was to sing out of vision behind the credit titles.

From the start Michael treated me as part of the whole creative team. He discussed the stories with me and together he, Richard Waring and I selected them. When the scripts had been written he always sent them to me first and invited my comments. My suggestions for amendments were always considered conscientiously and many of them incorporated in the final versions.

I think perhaps the most important nut that we cracked seems elementary in retrospect, but it wasn't at the outset. In his column in the *Evening Standard* in June of that year, Milton Schulman wrote:

No one ever thought it could be done. The property has been sitting there waiting to be exploited since long before television.... In my six years as an executive with commercial TV, I have sat in on innumerable programme conferences in which the possibility was discussed and invariably discarded. Jeeves and Bertie Wooster, it was always reluctantly agreed, were just not the stuff for a TV series.

One of the problems that had bugged so many potential producers of the Wooster/Jeeves books for so long, I venture to suggest, was that so much of Wodehouse's humour is in his narrative. The failure to evolve a satisfactory method of reproducing that narrative in a visual medium had, I believe, proved to be the reason why so many had eventually capitulated.

In time it suddenly struck us that vast tracts of this narrative could be transposed into dialogue without altering a line of it. For instance, when describing Honoria Glossop, one of Bertie's long line of designing flappers, Wodehouse's inimitable narrative stated that she was 'one of those robust girls with the muscles of a welterweight and a laugh like a squadron of cavalry charging over a tin bridge'. In due course it became abundantly clear how simple it would be to give the description to Bertie, unexpurgated, as a line of dialogue describing the lady to Jeeves. Once this simple fact had been realised the world was our oyster.

The next and most vital problem was to find a Jeeves. Michael had always considered the casting of he who, to many, is the true central character of the Wooster/Jeeves saga, of supreme importance, and as such he wished to 'read' several actors for the role regardless of the eminence of one or two of them. This proved to be a huge boon to me. I naturally read with them and the passage Michael had selected was quite a long duologue from the proposed first episode, the continual repetition of which, over two or three days, enabled me to get a pretty strong bead on how I would eventually play Bertie. It was at these readings that the speech hesitation with which I eventually invested the character developed, a mannerism which also owed a certain amount to an officer with whom I served during the last few years of the war.

The excellent Dennis Price was finally asked to assume the mantle of possibly the world's most celebrated gentleman's gentleman. It was a great day for us all when he agreed.

For me personally it was treasure of incalculable value. I have always taken rather longer than the average actor to perfect sections of a performance. Dennis had infinite patience. Never once did he complain at my request to practise things again and again and again. We were neither of us the speediest of studiers and, for some inexplicable reason, in those

'*Jeeves and the
Dog Mackintosh*'
– *with Dennis Price*

Wooster scripts we were both continually being provided with speeches
of inordinate length. Difficult to learn at any time, in five days every week
for six weeks a nightmare. Dennis's main 'pill' always used to come in
the last few minutes of an episode when Jeeves was asked to 'explain all'.
He always referred to these hurdles as his 'Gethsemanes'. In brief, we
both had an understanding of each other's problems and shortcomings
which made for harmony and compatibility.

The first episode of *The World of Wooster* – 'Jeeves and the Dog Mackintosh' – was transmitted at 9.50 on Sunday evening, 30 May 1965 and
was an instant and huge success.

Also immediately upon my return from New York a London theatrical
producer named Peter Bridge entered my life with all the force and impact
of a tornado. An actor invariably considers himself lucky when a prospective employer sends him a script. Within forty-eight hours of arriving
back Peter Bridge sent me six.

Peter was destined to become a close friend and to have a considerable influence on my life during the following five years. He was, in 1964, heavy. He was also dark, bespectacled and about five years my junior. Peter was totally and utterly in love with the theatre and all who performed in it. He lived it, breathed it and was like a lost lamb whenever he was away from it. He was of a restless disposition and rarely went home until the last theatre had emptied and quite frequently not until after Danny La Rue's Club had done the same. When not in London he would be travelling the country seeing plays and shows all over the provinces; frequently on business, but if that didn't call it would be for pleasure. He covered thousands of miles per annum on his progresses. Peter was also kind, generous, genuine and as straight as a die.

The plays he had just sent me were from an impressive bunch of authors, and I settled down to wade through them.

By the time I had finished reading number five there was one which stood out head and shoulders above the others. The last one, however, made me sit bolt upright from the very first page. It was a play for four characters – two males and two females – and was called *The Story So Far* and had been written by Keith Waterhouse and Willis Hall. Two hours later I picked up the telephone and rang Patrick Cargill to whom I knew Peter had also sent a copy.

'I've just finished reading *The Story So Far*,' I said. 'Have you read it yet?'

'I've just finished it myself,' said Patrick.

'What do you think of it?' I asked.

'I think it's hysterical,' said Patrick.

'Snap,' I said.

I then rang Peter and said, '*The Story So Far*, my dear old bean, is the first play I have ever read in my life on which I have never wanted a second opinion. I've got a TV series to do straight away which will occupy me till mid-June, after which I'm as free as a bird. Let's meet. Let's plan. I'm wildly enthusiastic.' Several days later we met for lunch to discuss it all; to consider the choice of director and the casting of the two ladies – Patrick was a foregone conclusion for the other man. It was at this meeting that, for the first time, I ran up against a strange idiosyncrasy of Peter's – one which was to recur with practically every play he presented except revivals of the classics.

'We'll have to change the title,' he said.

'What?' I exclaimed in horror.

'Oh yes,' he said. 'We'll have to change the title; we can't possibly use a title like that.'

I thought he must have had a bad night at Danny's the previous evening.

'You can't be serious,' I said.

'*The Story So Far*,' he repeated. 'What sort of a title is that? No, got to be changed. Got to be changed.'

The brilliance of Keith and Willis's title was that, on the final curtain, the audience, after having witnessed a splendid two-and-a-half hours' entertainment, suddenly realised that at the end of it all they had, in effect, only been watching an extended prologue. The play itself, had it been written, if you follow me, was just about to start.

In due course the authors and our director also joined me in battle with our intrepid employer but he remained adamant. As a result, immediately after I had finished what was to be, in fact, the first *World of Wooster* series, Patrick Cargill, Dilys Laye, Jan Holden and I went into rehearsals under the direction of a tall and strikingly attractive lady in her mid-thirties called Shirley Butler, and at the beginning of July we all opened at the Yvonne Arnaud Theatre, Guildford, in a play called *Say Who You Are*.

Say Who was a comedy about infidelity and it had a convoluted plot which was inextricably linked, with the most ingenious precision, to a complex composite set. The latter, handsomely designed by the admirable 'Jay' Hutchison Scott, included, all at the same time, the living-room of a flat on the top floor of a small block in Kensington, a section of the hall on the ground floor which embraced the bottom of the staircase and the entrance to the lift (practical), the façade of the pub just round the corner and a GPO telephone box which was situated outside it.

Say Who You Are was a zonking great success from the word go. It was that theatrical rarity – a sparkling, glittering gem of a comedy, complete from the moment it left the typewriter.

We did an unusually long pre-London tour as dear Peter, with commendable kindness and patience, was waiting for my revered Her Majesty's to become available. In due course his patience was rewarded and we opened, in the theatre that had been so lucky for me with *The Tunnel of Love*, on 14 October.

Say Who You Are repeated its provincial success and we dug in at the Haymarket for a long run during which Peter showered us with hospitality and presents. It was the theme of the play that had influenced his choice of first-night gifts. The cause and effect of practically every situation in *Say Who You Are* was the telephone link between the flat and the GPO box outside The Hussar – the pub on the adjacent corner. On

With (l. to r.) Jan Holden, Dilys Laye and Patrick Cargill in
Say Who You Are

this, because of the clandestine assignations which were permanently being made on it, everyone was more than guarded at volunteering his or her name; hence the new title which comes from the instructions in the telephone directory on how to answer the instrument correctly. Peter, therefore, having just returned from one of his progresses – this time to New York – staggered back through customs weighed down with five of those 'camp', kitsch, individually designed, call them what you like, telephones which were the trendy buy on Fifth Avenue at that time; one for each member of the cast and one for his office.

It was wonderful to get back into my old dressing-room once again, though the occasion was saddened because, for the first time in five plays, my dear old dresser, John Mackie, was unable to join me.

John and I had first joined forces in that very room for *The Tunnel of Love* and he had looked after me like a baby ever since. Sadly we were never to be reunited – but he will not be forgotten either by me or by any others in the companies in which we worked together.

John Mackie, though not cast in the Jeeves mould, was a treasure – the perfect theatrical retainer. He was small, had precious little flesh on his bones but a mop of wavy white hair which bushed out on all sides from under his brown trilby. He wore horn-rimmed spectacles and always arrived at the theatre in a heavy belted overcoat. Anybody seeing him pass through a stage-door could be excused for thinking that he was a member of the orchestra; the second bassoon, perhaps. He was a Yorkshireman and carried his brogue as to the manner born. He was also an old pro – a comedian who had married the soprano in one of the many troupes in which he had served. He was always at the theatre before me – as was, of course, fitting – and on my arrival my dressing-table would be immaculate and he would have changed into a lightweight biscuit-coloured jacket and sneakers.

John Mackie, was, I suppose, in his sixties but he had the brain of a teenager and the agility of a whippet. He was also an inveterate tea-maker. The kettle, his own, was always on the hob and a cup was placed in my hand the moment I arrived. A second cup was set beside me as I sat down to make up and a third was always waiting for me in the interval when a selection of biscuits in an old tin was also proffered. There would have been tea when the final curtain fell too had I not firmly put my foot down – 'A large whisky, please, old lad' – and that too was poured out for me and set down close to my right hand. How I ever got through those performances without having to leave the stage at regular intervals has remained a mystery.

John Mackie was ace at getting rid of visitors who overstayed their welcome ('Don't forget you are on call at Pinewood at 6.30 in the morning will you, Mr C.'); unwanted strangers never even got further than the stage-door. To get rid of *him* after the show, if I wanted to stay on and have a natter and a few jars with friends, was well-nigh impossible. However firmly I dismissed him – nay, ordered him to go home – he would, unless I actually ejected him personally through the stage-door, always stay lurking about somewhere in the building just in case he was wanted; he hated leaving until I did.

Between the shows on a Saturday during *The Tunnel* he would walk all the way from Her Majesty's to Wheeler's just off Jermyn Street and, on a tray covered in a cloth, he would bring me back a dozen oysters or a half lobster (that, of course, was in the days when such delicacies did not cost a king's ransom) plus fruit salad and cream. John Mackie, I repeat, was a treasure and was loved by all.

He died several years ago now in Kenya where he had gone on holiday to visit some baroness or other – an old friend – whom he repeatedly referred to as his partner; in what capacity I never discovered. His place was taken in *Say Who* by the admirable and resourceful Jack Parsons whom I shared with Patrick, and whose bone-dry cockney wit kept us entertained for hours.

Say Who You Are was as big a success as any with which I have ever been associated. It ran at Her Majesty's Theatre for a year and three months and only closed then because Peter had other plans for me; and, as I was leaving, the remainder of the cast decided that they too had had their fill and exercised their contractual right to leave.

We closed at Her Majesty's on Saturday, 8 January 1967. The following day Pym and I and Patrick Cargill flew out for ten days to enjoy the ever-relaxing and health-restoring powers of St Moritz.

Before leaving the story of *Say Who You Are* I must report that it was during this run – in March 1966 to be precise – that I received a letter from a theatrical agent, with whom I had recently formed an alliance, which read as follows:

My brother has come up with what might be a very interesting idea for a television series, namely the character of Lord Peter Wimsey in the Dorothy Sayers books. As you know, they were tremendously popular, and the character would, I think, fit you like a glove (or vice versa) and there is certainly quite a lot of material to draw on.

That was the beginning of an enterprise that was going to take me six years to get off the ground.

CHAPTER TWENTY-NINE

THE STATE OF MATRIMONY

Enter GOWER *– a Champion*

It was during the tour of *Say Who You Are* that I first realised the enormous impact that the Wooster series had made on the public. Wherever we went during those ten weeks I was always being asked, almost to the point of boredom, if I had brought Jeeves with me. If I was washing my car a stray passer-by would remark, 'Doesn't Jeeves do that for you, then?' If I appeared in a tie that was perhaps a trifle *outré* – a rarity, I might add – the comment would be, 'I don't think Jeeves would approve of that.'

There was also those who, strangely, would confuse the characters. When we were in a bar or a restaurant together, Patrick would frequently see someone indicate me and say to his companion, 'Look, there's Jeeves over there.'

The World of Wooster had undoubtedly scored a bull's-eye with old and young alike. Teenagers were trying to acquire 1920s-style clothes and many were the letters I received asking me where a monocle like mine could be obtained. It wasn't surprising, therefore, that the Beeb decided to do a second series and this we recorded almost as soon as we had opened at Her Majesty's.

The two years that my career had spent in becalmed waters were now well and truly behind me and to mark the occasion I decided to change my car once again. I now bought an elegant black-over-sand S3 Bentley just in time for it to be used to drive Lee and me to her wedding in St Paul's Church, Mill Hill, on 22 February.

A couple of weeks before the ceremony our future son-in-law came to have Sunday lunch with us at Moat Lodge. In the middle of the afternoon, while we were all having coffee, P. Bridge arrived. He was unexpected and, as was his wont, he swept in on his customary Force 9 gale of nervous energy. He had just returned from another progress to the United States and the main object of his visit that afternoon was to

Giving the bride away, 1 – Lee

present me with the long-playing record of a new Broadway musical which was, he said with burning enthusiasm, the very thing for me. It was called *I Do! I Do!*, was the musical version of *The Fourposter* and, like the play, contained a cast of only two people. Nothing would satisfy him but that we should play it there and then. So, innocuous though it may sound out of context, it was not, you may take my word for it, the time for poor John – Lee's fiancé – to have to sit there and listen to such lyrics as:

> My daughter is marrying an idiot.
> How could she stoop so low?
> My daughter is marrying a nincompoop,
> She loves him, but even so—

– with worse to follow in the same vein. We all had a good giggle, but it was a very self-conscious one. Dear Peter was oblivious.

The week before the wedding I had started rehearsals for Peter once again, this time for what was referred to as an 'all-star revival' (a horrid phrase) of George Bernard Shaw's *Getting Married*. Peter had engaged Frank Dunlop, a splendid non-eggheaded director, to referee and to generally marshal his considerable forces into some sort of cohesive whole. Mr Dunlop, in my eyes, immediately demonstrated his perspicacity and good taste by suggesting that I should play the dashing, cashiered officer, St John Hotchkiss.

The galaxy of a cast, first and foremost, heralded the happy return to the West End of the much-missed Googie Withers. Googie, I was to play opposite – if one can have an opposite in a conversation piece which is really what *Getting Married* amounts to – and to have so staunch, experienced and popular a leading lady to assist me through my first professional foray into the classics was fortune indeed. Also in the alphabetical list of players that surmounted the play's title on the bills were Alec Clunes, Raymond Huntley, David Hutcheson, Esmond Knight, Moira Lister (our fifth appearance together), Perlita Neilson, Margaret Rawlings and Hugh Williams. After several weeks in London, Hugh Williams, who had to leave us on health grounds, was replaced by Roland Culver. Below the title, poor lonely dears, who must not, however, be forgotten, were two excellent juveniles – Joanna Wake and Timothy Carlton.

Getting Married is two and a half hours' verbose dialogue on the subject of marriage, much of it poignant and witty. It does, however, change gear half way through and goes off, at what a friend of mine calls a tangerine, into realms of fantasy which appear to have little to do with the original theme.

After a five-week provincial tour we returned to town where, on 19 April, we opened at the Strand Theatre – about the only theatre with a large enough 'front of house' façade to accommodate ten names in lights. The Press reception was respectful.

To assemble a cast of such eminence, Peter accepted, in the planning stage, that it would be possible only if the project were to run for a limited period. He therefore informed us all at the outset that our services would be required for a maximum of six months.

We had a sensational tour, breaking the extant house record for a straight play at the Opera House, Manchester, on our first week, and we followed it by doing very nearly capacity business for our entire four months' season in London. Had not several of us had other commitments to fulfil later in the year, we would have undoubtedly run for a great deal longer.

I facetiously remarked that Frank Dunlop had been engaged to 'referee' *Getting Married*. Never has any company required one less. Never could there have been less friction between personalities who, on paper, might possibly have engendered potentially explosive situations. It was the most immaculately behaved, polite and theatrically generous company of which I could ever have wished to be a member. Characters, however, there were a-plenty.

Esmond Knight does a pretty nigh-perfect impersonation of Ralph Richardson. One matinée he gave his usual flamboyant, extrovert performance of the moustachioed, full-dressed, 1908 general in every detail as he had always done – with one exception. That afternoon, for the benefit of the cast and without warning a soul, he decided to play his entire role using Sir Ralph's voice. For those of us who have difficulty in controlling ourselves in the face of such behaviour – and Moira and I, certainly when we are together, are two such – it became a painful and exhausting performance.

Dear David Hutcheson, who died a few years ago, a great stalwart of Jack Buchanan's companies, was a splendid fellow, a man of infinite charm and jest, even in the face of the pain that invested his final years; he had crippling arthritis in both hips. David, during rehearsals, generally spent his lunch-breaks in an adjacent boozer where he would consume several large pink gins. One day I asked him if they were his usual tipple.

'No,' he replied. 'I drink gin at lunchtime and whisky in the evening.'

'Do you like gin?' I enquired.

'Hate it,' he said.

'Then why do you drink it at lunchtime?' I asked.

'Because it keeps me off the whisky,' he replied with a logic I found difficult to follow.

David was a quiet, dry-humoured man. He was a good listener and only really spoke when he had something worth saying. *Getting Married* was set in the stark, grey-stoned, Norman kitchen of the palace of the Bishop of Chelsea. The stage was occupied almost in its entirety by a long refectory table which ran parallel to the footlights and around which were ranged some ten dining chairs. When we came to the dress rehearsal the floor covering provided by our designer was a large carpet of coconut matting. Now this provided a hitherto unforeseen hazard; every time one of the players rose, unless it was done with infinite care, which was not always possible, the chair toppled over backwards. For fifteen minutes the rehearsal came to a halt while everyone offered suggestions as to how this disaster could be overcome. After innumerable impractical ideas, somebody said, 'Domes of Silence'; which, I suppose appropriately, brought the cacophony to a halt.

'What?' said somebody else.

'Domes of Silence; that's what we need,' repeated the instigator.

'What are *they*?' enquired a third party.

'They're small metal inverted domes that you screw to the bottom of each chair leg,' it was explained. 'Then, when you stand up, instead of the chair tipping over it slides back across the matting in the manner of a sledge.'

'Those aren't for chairs,' volunteered yet another member of the cast. 'They're for pianos.'

David Hutcheson, who had sat silently through the entire fifteen-minute exchange, thought it was time he offered some constructive suggestion.

'Well, why don't we dispose of the chairs,' he said, 'and get ten pianos instead?'

Getting Married closed on 26 August in accordance with our contracts, but when the final curtain fell its heart was still beating as strongly as an ox's. Nevertheless, when I left the stage-door that Saturday night my spirits were buoyant. I had what I considered to be a rosy, remunerative and well-balanced future ahead of me. I had followed *Say Who You Are*, a long-running modern comedy success, with a period classic of distinction. In two weeks' time I was to start a third series of *The World of Wooster* and, for production in early 1968, I had successfully wooed

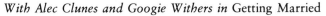

With Alec Clunes and Googie Withers in Getting Married

Binkie into offering me the hit Broadway musical *I Do! I Do!* which he was about to present in this country. A programme more beautifully balanced with contrasts it would be difficult to imagine.

The third series of *Wooster* was to embrace seven more episodes of the saga and, having already used up thirteen of the limited number of short stories that we considered suitable for adapting for television, this time we really did feel that we were scraping the bottom of the barrel. Find them, however, we eventually did and they were to be as instantly popular as their predecessors. When it was all over, nevertheless, we decided that that was to be the end. If our lords and masters required a fourth series we only had one option – to serialise a novel, and I, personally, was extremely dubious about the success of such a venture. Our audience had got attuned to a different story each week, each embracing the simple format of Bertie getting himself 'up to the neck in the old consommé' and Jeeves, after consuming a couple of kippers (fish, in the young master's eyes, you may recall, stimulated the brain), pulling him out of it. Would the 'cliff-hanger' ruse at the end of each episode work in comedy as it did in drama?

Michael, in due course, asked Richard Waring to write a trial episode of a novel called *The Code of the Woosters* so that we could examine it and try and estimate its chances of success. This he duly did and we all studied it.

I remained dubious. We had had a phenomenal success with the series as a whole, why risk running it downhill? Why not get out at the top while it was still popular?

We all decided that this was the course we would follow. So after twenty episodes *The World of Wooster* was finally laid to rest. It played for several more years all over the world, including many of the unlikeliest countries, all the way from Iceland to the darkest corners of Africa. How the inimitable Sir 'Plum', as he eventually became, suffered at the hands of his translators I dread to think. I would have thought he would have been largely untranslatable, but the fact that he was enjoyed so universally is a measure of his greatness.

I never met the man who supplied the material for one of my biggest successes, but I corresponded with him on several occasions. He wrote the most colloquial of letters which made me feel, practically from the first one, that I had known him all my life. Several years later, discussing this quality with Basil Boothroyd (who in due course also wrote a successful series for me), the latter said he agreed, and to illustrate the fact informed me that he had once received a ltter from the great man which began, 'I say, listen....'

'Plum' Wodehouse only ever saw two of our episodes. They were the first two we did and were consequently recorded before we had really got into the swing of things. Frank Muir, the BBC Head of Comedy at the time, took them over on 16 mm film to show him at his home on Long Island. I understand that after he had seen them he expressed his approval of our efforts. In any event, a long article about him in the *Sunday Times* Colour Supplement two years later, in which he was reported to have said that 'he found the BBC's Jeeves series rotten thanks to Ian Carmichael's middle-aged burlesquing of Bertie and Dennis Price's pasty face as Jeeves', drew an immediate letter from him.

Did you see that profile of me in the *Sunday Times* of 20 July? I have just got my copy, and was horrified to read that reference to you and the Bertie TV things. I can assure you that I never said anything remotely resembling what I am credited with there....

On a lighter and more characteristic note he continued: 'The last inter-view of me that appeared was in the *New York Times*, and my wife is frothing with fury because the man said she was 87 and she's only 84!'

Later that year he was to write and ask me to play Bertie in a new musical he had written with his old collaborator Guy Bolton; the music was by Wright and Forrest. In response to my reply saying that I had always been too old for Bertie and that I didn't want to press my luck any longer, he tried to persuade me to play Jeeves instead. I had no desire to follow so close upon Dennis's excellent and popular characterisation; neither did I feel that it would be a good idea to appear on stage with another Bertie when my own was, I hoped, still fresh in the memory. I politely declined and the production was never mounted.

I have one regret about *The World of Wooster*. It could have been yet another opportunity for Moira and me to work together.

Bertie had 'a surging sea of aunts', most of them Gorgons. There was one, however, who was different – Aunt Dahlia. Dahlia Travers was much younger and more beautiful than all the others, and to Bertie she was 'my good and deserving aunt', 'the old flesh and b', and 'the only decent aunt I've got'. All of which, in my eyes, added up to a tailor-made role for my favourite blonde. When approached by Michael, however, she was reported to me as having said, 'Look, I'll play Ian's wife, I'll play his girl-friend, I'll play his mistress, but I'm blowed if I'll play his aunt!'

Bertie Wooster and his creator Sir Pelham Grenville Wodehouse were very kind to me; I hope that, in some small way, I may have repaid the compliment.

I Do! I Do! was played on Broadway by two of its most popular artistes – Mary Martin and Robert Preston. It had been directed by Gower Champion who had, most recently, been responsible for *Hello, Dolly*, and it had been an enormous success.

Its story is a simple one. It is the story of a marriage – any and practically every marriage. It starts with the two characters going to the altar and finishes with them both in late middle-age when, their two children married, they finally leave their much-loved family home for somewhere smaller. It was a story with which practically every living soul, unless he or she was either too young or extraordinarily bent, could identify. The score, by Tom Jones and Harvey Schmidt, was a joy. The moment I heard the record I knew that I had to play it, and I went to work on Binkie like I'd never gone to work on anyone for years. Luckily he knew me well and my task wasn't a difficult one. Unless Gower Champion had some strong objection to me, I was home and dry. Fortunately, he didn't. For the first time in my life, I started taking singing lessons.

I had had several lunches with Binkie during the intervening weeks to discuss leading ladies. To find one who could sing, dance, act, look pretty and also have that indefinable charisma known as 'star quality' – an essential ingredient when there are only two of you to hold together an entire evening's entertainment – plus compatibility, a vital quality under such exceptional circumstances, meant that our short-list was a very short one indeed – Anne Rogers.

There was no shadow of doubt in my mind that *I Do! I Do!* was going to be the most enormous success. There was also no shadow of doubt that it was going to be a killer both mentally and physically: on stage all night, nineteen numbers, seven shows a week and no holiday at all until the end of the first year. At the conclusion of the *Wooster* series I had exactly three months before we were due to start rehearsals, so obviously the thing to do was to take a jolly good holiday. Europe, however, is apt to be unwelcoming in November and early December, so it looked like having to be a long and expensive trip to either South Africa or the Caribbean.

CHAPTER THIRTY

SOUTH AFRICA

Enter SEVERAL INFLUENTIAL MEMBERS OF THE PRESS

Moira Lister is South African, and for a long time she had been trying to get me to go out and see for myself the beauties of her homeland which she adored. To be fair, for a long time she had also been trying to get me as far as Calais – something she had at last succeeded in doing – but the more adventurous step I had not yet taken. I was now about to do so.

'I can fix you a couple of radio plays in Johannesburg,' she said, 'which will give you a bit of pocket money, and I've got plenty of friends who'll look after you while you're there.' In fact, she very nearly patted me on the head and said, 'So there's no need to be frightened.'

I had also, she advised me, while I was there, to go and stay at the Oyster Box, then a small hotel – now a much bigger one – right slap-bang on the beach at Umhlanga Rocks ten miles north of Durban, and if I was going to travel five and a half thousand miles, another eight hundred wouldn't make any difference, 'So pop down and see the Cape as well,' she instructed. 'It's gorgeous at this time of the year.'

'An excellent idea,' echoed Ken Barrington with whom I also discussed the project. 'Couldn't be better. How long would you be going for?'

'We haven't decided,' I said.

'Well, go – that's the first thing,' he advised, 'and if time is not of the essence, fly out and come back by sea. It's a wonderful voyage – fourteen days, twelve of them in glorious sunshine. You'll have the time of your lives.'

A few days later I toddled off to South Africa House and asked the tourist department to work out an itinerary for the three of us – Pym, Sally and myself. They did. It embraced a week in Johannesburg, during the first two days of which I would do the radio plays, and after that we would all pay a visit to the Kruger National Park. We would then spend two weeks sunning ourselves on the beach at Umhlanga Rocks and two more in Cape Town, at the end of which we would board the *Edinburgh Castle* and sail back to Southampton.

It was a long and expensive trip, but I had the time, I had also had a very good year and looked like having an even better one to come, and I did want to start *I Do! I Do!* feeling fit.

On the last evening in October, two days ahead of the girls, I flew out of a cold, wet and miserable London Airport *en route* for Johannesburg. Somewhere round about six the following morning, out of the port windows, I watched a spectacular dawn break over the mountains in Ethiopia, and several hours later I stepped out on to the tarmac at Nairobi. The heat hit me with all the power of a blow from a twelve-pound sledgehammer. From there we headed south again and landed at the Jan Smuts airport in Johannesburg at mid-day.

It was jacaranda time and the sun was shining brightly out of a cloudless sky on avenue after avenue of beautiful trees, all of which were crowned with a profusion of pale mauve blossom. The men were wearing lightweight suits and the womenfolk white or brightly coloured sleeveless summer frocks. It was a far cry from the miserable weather that I had left behind in London only eighteen hours previously.

I checked in at the Langham Hotel, unpacked and immediately made contact with Barry Whitehead, Moira's friend for whom I was going to record the plays. He greeted me and we made a date to meet socially that evening.

Shortly before leaving the hotel the telephone rang in my room. It was a most welcome and unexpected call. On the other end of the line was an old friend – the Worcestershire and England cricketer Basil d'Oliveira. He was in Johannesburg coaching and sounded as ebullient and irrepressible as ever.

'Can we meet for a drink?' I asked. There were obvious problems.

'Certainly we can,' he replied. He was, he explained, on friendly terms with the hotel manager who would let us meet in his private flat.

In actual fact we never managed it because he was busy that evening and on the following two I was tied up. It was, nevertheless, good to hear his cheery voice again.

Twenty-four hours later, before setting out for the recording studios, I left a note of welcome for Pym and Sally in the hotel bedroom and added that I would be back in the late afternoon as soon as I had finished work. Shortly after five I bounded into the room full of the joys of a South African spring. They were both sitting there in silence. I kissed them and received little if any response; not the flicker of a smile.

Something was wrong.

'What's the matter?' I said. 'Something wrong?'

Neither of them spoke.

'Well, come on,' I repeated. 'What's happened? What's the matter?'

There was still no response. Then I noticed a tear trickling down Sally's cheek. Despite my questioning and, by now, my concern, neither of them seemed able to speak. It took a good minute. I think it was Sally who burst first. They had had every stick of their luggage stolen at the Johannesburg air terminal.

It was November in London, you may recall, and they had each done special shopping for the trip. In addition, in Sally's case there had been a necklace of seed pearls that had been left to her by my mother. My heart bled for them.

'Come on, Sal,' I said. 'Let's go and have another search.'

She took me back to the terminal several blocks away. We scoured the place; I questioned everyone. There was no shadow of doubt about it, it had vanished. The poor kids had arrived on the first day of what was to be the holiday of a lifetime and, apart from their hand luggage, they had not a possession in the world except what they stood up in. Back to the hotel we traipsed mournfully.

I embraced them both again and did my best to console them.

'Cheer up,' I said. 'The first thing we do tomorrow morning is to go shopping. I'll buy brand-new outfits for both of you.' I then picked up the telephone, rang room service and ordered a bottle of champagne. That done, I picked it up again and rang the police.

The following day we went out shopping and I re-equipped them from top to toe including two new suitcases.

The day after that was Sunday and after a splendid generous and lingering lunch party thrown on our behalf by Barry Whitehead, at 8.45 that evening we boarded a train for Kruger Park. We immediately collapsed on our couchettes and were asleep practically before the train had pulled out of the station.

The following day we went out shopping and I re-equipped them from private limousine which we had hired for our exclusive use during our two-day visit.

Kruger Park is about the size of Wales. It is a game reserve of wild animals where the only thing that a beast has to fear is another four-legged predator. It is hot, it is parched, it is uncultivated and the landscape is at the same time both deadly boring and awe-inspiring.

It is so vast you can travel for miles without seeing a thing. By nightfall, however, we had seen impala and giraffe; impala and zebra; impala and elephant; impala and kudu; and impala.

That night we spent at the Pretorius Kop Rest Camp and when we enquired of our driver what time we should be ready for 'the off' the following morning, we visibly winced when he said he would call us with a cup of tea at four-thirty.

'Is that absolutely essential?' I enquired.

Apparently it was. It would be getting light an hour later and that, he pointed out, was the coolest part of the day and therefore the most likely time to see anything. At that time the animals were all out looking for their breakfast. By mid-morning, as has already been pointed out by Noël Coward, only mad dogs and Englishmen venture abroad.

The second day at Kruger was the same as the first – once you've seen one pyramid you've seen them all and the same applies with impala and giraffe, and impala and elephant, and impala and zebra.

That night, after a shower and a meal in a Nelspruit hotel, we boarded the sleeper and returned to Johannesburg.

At nine the following morning we were met on the platform by a jubilant Barry Whitehead and Sergeant Bronkhorst of the Johannesburg police; they had found all our lost luggage. It was now in our room at the Langham Hotel and would we go immediately to officially identify it and see if anything was missing? It had been found the previous day abandoned in some sleazy downtown bordello. Both cases, Sergeant Bronkhorst informed us, had been broken into but the contents looked reasonably intact. They were. Not a thing had been stolen. No jewellery, nothing. It was a miracle.

That afternoon we boarded a plane for Durban, Umhlanga Rocks and two weeks with nothing to do but laze by the sea.

Durban is humid which ensures an abundance of perpetual greenery; rubber plants grow in the gardens and the hibiscus, poinsettias and bougainvillaea seem to flower the whole year round. The taxi pulled up outside the main entrance to the Oyster Box and we piled out beneath a tree in which a colony of weaver-birds had set up shop and were procreating like Billy-oh. Their intricate and painstakingly built nests, each the size of a melon, were suspended from every bough and the air was full of bright fluttering yellow. We checked in.

Our rooms were delightful and a colourful arrangement of tropical flowers decorated the dressing-tables in both of them; these were kept fresh and were tended each day by a beautiful Indian lady in a white sari. In addition, Pym's and my room had a refrigerator fully stocked

Sally and Pym on the beach at Umhlanga Rocks – the Oyster Box in the background

with appropriate and welcoming bottles and lying there snugly in front of all the others was an ice-cold bottle of vintage Veuve Clicquot. We opened it instantly and sat down to drink it on our balcony gazing out over the white surf and the deep, almost electric, blue of the Indian Ocean. This, we decided, there and then, was paradise.

On 3 December we bid a fond farewell to Umhlanga Rocks and flew off for Cape Town.

The Vineyard Hotel nestles right under the lee of Table Mountain in Newlands. It was comfortable, cool, not too large, privately owned and, being inland and away from the coast, quiet and not crowded. It had its own large pool which we had to ourselves for the majority of the next two weeks and its grounds were massed with hundreds of prolific hydrangea bushes all in full flower.

I can't believe that we could have picked a better month to visit Cape Town. The central reservations between the dual carriageways leading from Newlands into the centre of town were packed with blue and white agapanthus, the botanical gardens at Kirstenbosch were just one vast pincushion of proteas, huge trees with bright scarlet blossoms looked as if they were on fire against the beautiful white, Cape Dutch architecture in the suburbs, and everywhere seemed to be draped with sprawling bougainvillaea and hibiscus. Table Mountain, whose top was a mass of tight little yellow alpine flowers, was majestic against a clear blue sky and Signal Hill and Lions Head seemed to be throwing out their chests, like the proudest of pouter pigeons.

A few morning after our arrival, breakfast was brought into our room on a tray with the morning paper. We opened it and read banner headlines right across the front page. The previous day Dr Christian Barnard had performed his first human heart transplant operation at the Groote Schuur Hospital but a mile from our hotel.

During the next two weeks we hired a car and drove all round the Cape to see everything there was to see. I adored South Africa, which is not to say that I condone its racial policies, but the country, the scenery and the climate I found sensational. The friends we had made there and the hospitality we had received – largely thanks to Moira and Ken Barrington – were of the most generous I have received anywhere. It was, therefore, with infinite sadness that during the afternoon of 6 December we went down to the docks to board the *Edinburgh Castle* in which we were to return to England.

We sailed somewhere about six o'clock, and to look back over the stern of the ship at the slowly receding image of Cape Town tucked so snugly into the side of that magnificent Table Mountain is a sight never to be forgotten.

Ken Barrington had been dead right about coming back by sea. There was absolutely nothing to do during the daytime but lie in the sun and play deck games. As we approached the tropics, lunch was served up on deck and in nothing but bathing costumes and shorts we ate crayfish and drank Nederburg Riesling while watching the flashing silver slivers of the flying fish as they accompanied us for miles.

I had had a marvellously lazy five weeks and, as work was now looming up on the horizon once again, I thought a bit of toning-up was necessary. I therefore spent a certain amount of time each day in the gym going long cycle rides and I also took a daily four-mile walk round the deck – sixteen laps, if I remember correctly. During the latter the majority of the prone, flaked-out passengers, I am quite convinced, thought that I was stark raving mad.

It was a wonderful voyage and it wasn't until we hit the Bay of Biscay – which obliged by resembling the proverbial millpond – that the crew abandoned their whites and shorts and reverted to full navy blue.

Sad, though infinitely refreshed, we docked at Southampton in a damp and thick morning mist during the early hours of 18 December. We then boarded a quayside train for Waterloo where we were met by John and Lee.

The production of *I Do! I Do!* was a quite brilliant conception on the part of Gower Champion. The setting was spartan in its simplicity and it remained so throughout the evening. Against a plain backcloth – in front of which were eventually dropped three isolated and purely decorative flats – there was one chair, one chaise longue and a specially made, large, oak double bed. The orchestra pit had been covered in to form an apron stage and the orchestra itself was situated behind the backcloth, the musical director having to keep in touch with his artistes solely by means of earphones and a closed-circuit television screen on which was relayed a picture shot by a camera fixed to the front of the dress circle. He could see us all right, but we could never see him.

As the curtain rose at the beginning of the evening, the stage was empty except for the bride and groom, each dressed for the wedding and each sitting terrified on either side of it in a single spotlight. The opening five minutes were all in song, dance and mime, and they took the action from those initial few moments of embarrassed fright to the altar for the wedding and finally into the bridal chamber.

Immediately after the ceremony in church the accompaniment, which had, until that point, been provided by a solo piano (two in New York), swelled to embrace the entire orchestra and, as the lights came full up to complement the crescendo, a shower of confetti fluttered down from the flies. Then, and with a better entrance than either of us had all night, on came – self-propelled – the bed. It entered from one of the wings and, describing an arc, it finally came to rest dead centre stage, where we both collapsed on to it still in our wedding gear.

Gower Champion's bed was almost human. Not only did it move about the stage on its own, it also possessed a central pivot on which it could be spun round like a cartwheel. In addition it had fixed to its foot an ottoman box which contained many of the props required throughout the performance. It was, in fact, quite impossible to rehearse without it. The furniture, however, was not the only rehearsal requisite demanded by Gower's intricate and unorthodox production.

I Do! I Do!, as already explained, contains only two characters, both of whom, during the course of the evening, pass from their early twenties

I Do! I Do!
(1) *Wedding day*
(2) *Wedding night*
(3) *The first child*
(4) *The 'Honeymoon is Over'*
(5) *Reconciliation. Finale
Act I*
(6) *New Year's Eve –
several years later. 'Where
Are the Snows of
Yesteryear?'*
(7) *The children both
married*
(8) *Darby and Joan*

to late sixties. All the changes of costume, therefore, had to take place either at breakneck speed in the wings while the other character was singing a song or, as frequently happened, on stage during the course of action. This then also necessitated all the costumes being available for rehearsals which in turn added yet another expense item to the budget; as every change was a quick one, it was impossible to make them without the assistance of a dresser. Both our dressers, therefore, had to be on parade every day throughout the entire period of rehearsals too.

We rehearsed *I Do! I Do!* for six weeks. The first two, which took place in some private hotel on the Bayswater Road, were occupied solely in learning the score. The remaining four were conducted in a large first-floor drill hall in the Wellington Barracks in Chelsea and by the end of them I had lost a whole stone in weight, one contributory factor being a built-in sweat-box that I had to wear during the whole of Act I.

At the end of the opening sequence, we both had to undress and prepare for bed – I on stage in full view of the audience.

The action opened at the turn of the century, so underneath my morning suit I was wearing a pair of heavy woollen combinations with long sleeves and long-legged pants. During Act One I performed ten numbers, many of which contained, if not an actual dance, a wealth of frenetic movement. I also had six changes of costume, but never did I have time to remove those debilitating combinations. They stayed on me for the entire act. During the interval an hour and a quarter later they were peeled off me sopping wet and steaming; I was like a race-horse immediately after it had passed the post at the head of the St Leger.

I Do! I Do! opened in Oxford on 13 March where it received rave notices. After two weeks in Oxford we played two more each in Newcastle, Edinburgh and Brighton – it was rapturously received in each town by both the paying public and the Press. On the Monday and Tuesday of our opening week at the Lyric Theatre in Shaftesbury Avenue we gave two charity performances, the first of which I had arranged for the Lord's Taverners. Again the receptions, notoriously bad at charity performances because everybody has paid so much for his seat, were exceptional.

We opened on Wednesday, 16 May, and the following day the national Press, to a man, slaughtered us. The opening salvoes were repeated at the weekend and in the weekly and monthly magazines. The target for their venom was the piece itself. They found it totally unacceptable American saccharine. 'Two stars gooed up in treacle.' (*Daily Express*); 'They Do, I Don't' (*Daily Sketch*); 'It's a Rotten Cliché for Two' (*Daily Mail*); 'Bedroom Scenes to Sleep Through' (*The Sun*); 'Fifty Years and it *Does* Seem

a Bit Too Much' (*Evening Standard*); and plenty more besides. Felix
Barker in the *Evening News* found it

... just about the most outrageous dollop of sentimentality ever aimed at the
tearducts of the West End.... Now I'm not denying that for many there is
a genuine pathos in the business of growing old. But I resent so frontal an
onslaught on our hearts – the seeking of private tears in a public place....
Probably it will run for years.

It didn't; after such a savage attack it had about as much chance of survival as the victims of the St Valentine's Day massacre.

I never saw Gower to say goodbye, so I wrote to him immediately.
He had left London the day following our opening night and my letter
was waiting for him when he arrived home in Beverly Hills. In his reply
he said, 'I must confess right off that I simply did not read the London
reviews. I somehow smelled it coming and wasn't going to put myself
through the agony.'

More than for anybody I was sorry for Gower. His conception and
production was a brilliant one. What's more, he was amenable and infinitely more flexible than many other less gifted directors when recreating
their work for different players. This time, where things that he had given
to Robert Preston were obviously not right for me, he changed them instantly.

The audiences adored *I Do! I Do!* We hung on to see the effects of
a television excerpt but the chop came exactly two weeks to the day after
its transmission. We closed on 24 August after a run of fourteen weeks.
Had Harold Fielding presented the show I believe there would have been
every chance of it running for two years.

It is only of academic interest that when a limited-run revival of *I Do!
I Do!* was presented at the Phoenix Theatre in 1976, with Rock Hudson
and Juliet Prowse, the gentlemen of the Press did not revise their
judgement.

It was a great disappointment but in the words of some Hollywood
script writing hack 'that's show business'. There were, nevertheless, great
compensations; had it not been for *I Do! I Do!* neither Pym, Sally nor
I might ever have seen South Africa.

CHAPTER THIRTY-ONE

TO CANADA AND BACK

Enter PETER LLOYD JEFFCOCK – *a latter day saint*

Major Donald Neville-Willing, who after the '39–45 war became general manager of the Café de Paris in Coventry Street until its sad departure in 1957 robbed London of its last really chic night spot, claims to have an infallible cure for the blues.

'Whenever I feel depressed,' he once told me, 'I go out and buy a Rolls Royce.'

The moment *I Do! I Do!* closed, I decided to emulate the Major.

One morning a few days later, I filed into showrooms in Berkeley Square and at peak central traffic time with a rather grand pin-stripe-suited salesman in the back and a liveried chauffeur sitting beside me, I drove off through Mayfair and into Hyde Park in a beautiful, refrigerated, astral blue Silver Shadow. Twice round the park we went and returned via Hyde Park Corner – or Duke of Wellington Place as some local government official has now seen fit to rechristen it – down Piccadilly, up one of those streets on the left and back to the showrooms. As we rounded the final curve of Berkeley Square I felt the chauffeur exhale and for perhaps the first time since we started out, relax back into his seat.

'You know you drove that rather well,' he said in utter astonishment as we pulled up at the kerb. I tried hard not to show offence at such lack of faith. Three days later I took delivery and Donald Neville-Willing had been quite right. It *was* an infallible cure for the blues.

The remainder of 1968 went by painlessly. 1969, however, started out for me with a totally exhausting yet hilarious two weeks in Canada. Towards the end of the previous December a charming young Canadian called Lewis Roberts had arrived in England. Lewis Roberts is the son of Billie Houston – for anyone old enough to remember the Houston Sisters – and he worked for the Canadian office of the British Travel Association. At that time BOAC and Air Canada were running a package deal, a fortnight's holiday from Canada to London called 'London Show Tours', its main object being to draw visitors to London's Theatreland at advantageous prices. The object of Lewis Roberts' visit was to recruit a small party, representative of the West End theatre scene, to go on a two-week coast-to-coast promotional tour of the country.

He had, apparently, already recruited J. Hutchinson Scott, the commercial theatre's leading designer, Milton Shulman, the drama critic of the *Evening Standard* and himself a Canadian, and I was now asked if I would join the party. I had never been to Canada; I had a few weeks free and as the offer was inclusive of first-class expenses throughout, it seemed to be a heaven-sent opportunity to see a bit of the country.

'I'd love to,' I said.

'Splendid,' he replied. 'Now I've only got to find one more member of the party. I must have a suitable girl.'

That was enough for me; in I waded, knee-deep, almost before the words were out of his mouth.

'Moira Lister's the lass,' I said. 'Beautiful, charming, amusing, superb hostess, a celebrated actress and excellent company. What more could you want?'

'Who's her agent?' he asked.

'Blow her agent,' I replied. 'Cut out the middle man. Here's her private number, give her a buzz.'

Moira too was available for the weeks in question, thank the Lord, and being an inveterate globe-trotter she required no persuading.

So, on Sunday 5 January, this most unlikely quartet flew out of Heathrow for Montreal. Moira and I both knew 'Jay' but Milton Shulman was new to us and actors and their critics are not always the most compatible company, particularly if the latter happen to be the ones who are, let us say, astringent – if you will forgive the euphemism – and Milton Shulman could be one such. However, the ice was soon broken, and by the end of the trip he had become known to the pair of us as 'Giggles' Shulman; our last evening together was celebrated with a particularly alcoholic dinner at the Panorama Roof Restaurant in Vancouver by which time we had all become firm friends.

During those two weeks we travelled the entire breadth of Canada in thick snow – all the way from Montreal to Vancouver with stops in Ottawa, Toronto, Hamilton, Winnipeg, Edmonton and Calgary.

In each town we appeared at a press conference, various receptions and also on a succession of radio and TV chat shows starting as early as 9 a.m. Many of the latter were daily programmes and were, strangely, conducted in the reception foyers of hotels. The natives were so used to this form of presentation, apparently, that they took not a blind bit of notice of live television transmissions taking place right under their noses while they went about their daily business. These programmes Milton Shulman was soon to refer to as 'Lobby Spectaculars'.

In Toronto we were given a day off, and Moira and I went to Niagara. It was a magnificent sight. The countryside was shrouded in snow and the American Falls in particular were framed in gigantic stalactites of ice. We stood but a few yards from the edge of the Horseshoe Falls and watched huge chunks of ice, six inches thick and the size of table tops, thunder over the edge on thousands of gallons of water the colour of thick glass. Moira was wrapped up in lynx and I was swathed in lambswool, but the air was still bitter and tingling.

After lunching in the revolving restaurant on top of the Skylon 775 feet above the falls, we returned to Toronto and that night went to see a play in the vast O'Keefe Theatre, in which I was destined to appear myself in only six months' time.

A month after I returned to England I went to work for Peter Bridge once again. Peter had acquired a play called *Birds on the Wing* in which I was to assay the part of a very sharp, smooth-talking, sartorially correct, utterly charming confidence trickster. It was a play and a part that I fancied very much. It was unfortunate therefore that, having committed myself to Peter, Binkie came along only two days later and offered me an equally good part in a new Joe Orton play which he was about to present with a most distinguished cast. Well, at least my commitment to Peter saved me from having to make a murderously difficult decision.

Birds on the Wing was a marvellous idea and it possessed all the ingredients with which to concoct a first-class theatrical soufflé, but somehow or other it just never rose. We worked like beavers throughout the entire tour (which in addition to many English provincial cities also took me back to the O'Keefe Theatre in Toronto), yet we never really succeeded in getting it right. By then, having lost confidence in the piece, I asked Peter if he would release me from my contract and he very kindly agreed. It was no particular consolation to me either that in due course when the Orton play reached the West End, it received a surprisingly bloody mauling by the critics, and as a result its run was short-lived.

In June of 1969 Michael Mills, who had by then become Head of Comedy at the BBC Television Centre, produced another fascinating idea for me.

The subject was the life of an extraordinary gentleman called Peter Lloyd Jeffcock.

Peter Lloyd Jeffcock is my own age. He is a bachelor, stands 6 feet 3 inches, is lantern-jawed and has become a Roman Catholic convert. On leaving the air force after the war, he went into estate management in the Driffield area of what used to be known as the East Riding of York-shire; the part of the country in which I had been born and bred.

When he was young Peter had had a comfortable and happy home life, and after settling down in Civvy Street once again, he developed a burning desire to give to children who had been less fortunate than him-self the same happy and contented upbringing. In pursuit of this aim he eventually sank his entire gratuity, personal savings and inheritance.

To start with it was a long struggle. The welfare authorities were most reluctant to allow a bachelor to foster young children. Eventually, how-ever, he wore them down and he was asked to accept John, an eleven-year-old who was at that time unsettled, having been shifted from one institution to another.

It wasn't long before Peter convinced the authorities of his sincerity and he was asked to accept four more – two brothers and two sisters, aged six to eleven – from a convent in Mill Hill that I had passed every day of my life during the previous twelve years.

Soon Peter's 'family' grew until he had six boys and six girls. This brood he reared entirely on his own in a house he bought in Horley in Sussex. Unaided, he shopped for them, cooked, sewed, darned, dress-made, washed, ironed, nursed, ensured that they all had a sound educa-tion and provided them with succour and affection.

All Peter's charges were products of broken homes and he never split up a family of children – if there were more than one, he took them all. Another inviolate rule he imposed upon himself was that if the authori-ties telephoned to ask him to accept a child or children, he would make up his mind on hearing the case history alone; his decision was always made before he saw any of them.

In 1969 his 'family' was in the late teens and early twenties, and on the verge of going out into the world leaving him lost, lonely and wonder-ing what to do next.

Now an attractive young actress who was a friend of Michael's and who had inherited a considerable amount of her successful father's busi-ness acumen, having learned of Peter's story, thought to acquire it legally and to market it for the mutual benefit of both Peter and herself. A film of his life was mooted and a stage musical was also to be written, but neither project came to fruition. Olga Franklin, on the other hand, wrote a book which was published in due course, and Michael Mills, on behalf of the BBC, acquired the rights of Peter's story for a television series. I was now asked to impersonate Peter Lamb, alias Peter Lloyd Jeffcock.

There was only one thing about the project that worried me. Peter's story was a marvellous one; it was touching and it was poignant but it had been bought for the purpose of making a *comedy* series. An integral part of his astonishing story was what had motivated the man and this aspect would, I felt, be left unprobed in a series in which the only real *raison d'être* was to raise laughs. My worries, though not assuaged, diminished as the series progressed but there were, nevertheless, several occasions when I felt that we were guilty of treating a very sincere man's life work, his philanthropy and humanity, with levity. I must report immediately, however, that I don't think this ever crossed Peter's mind for a second.

Richard Waring, possibly the most experienced and consistently successful situation-comedy writer for television in this country, was engaged to write the scripts, and as salve to my fears, he kept assuring me that they would contain 'plenty of moving moments' – and, true to his word, they did. There were, nevertheless, several problems he had to overcome. First of all the series would essentially have to be a slow starter if Peter's initial winning over of the authorities was to be established, and this, in turn, would necessitate his 'family' being built up gradually. Secondly, Richard felt that, from a purely dramatic point of view, Peter had to have some other adult character with whom to discuss his problems. I was, therefore, provided with a daily woman – a Mrs Pugsley – who was played by that delightful comedy actress, Joan Hickson. We had worked together several times before and it was a joy to have her around again.

Richard's final problem (no, his final problem was probably me – but apart from that one) was the stories themselves. All but one – the one in which, when pressured by his children, Peter entered a local cake-baking competition, which, as the only male entrant surrounded by housewives, he won – had to be the products of his own fertile imagination. The series was, in fact, only biographical as far as the concept as a whole was concerned. All the characters (with the exception of Peter himself) were fictitious. No attempt was ever made to make accurate impersonations of any of the others.

Bachelor Father took to the air early in 1970. The first series embraced thirteen episodes and in it we employed three boys and two girls of whom

With my enchanting family in the first series of Bachelor Father. *My arms are round Ian Johnson and Briony McRoberts.*

the most important was the first arrival – Ben. He it was who had to set the scene for all that followed.

We auditioned dozens of children. The very first to read was a young lad called Ian Johnson. I can't remember his age but I think he was about twelve. He was a canny, well-mannered lad and read with sincerity and charm. As he left the room I said to Richard and Graeme Muir, our director, 'We'll never do better than him.' We saw children every day for a week and we never did. Ian Johnson was a charmer and was in every way suited for the role he played. He became the leader of the family both fictionally and in fact. Because of his total naturalness and sincerity he was an absolute joy to work with. He, more than anyone, understood my problem of the pages of Richard Waring I used to have to learn every week (Richard always over-wrote and vast tracts had to be exorcised at the final rehearsal) and was always patient, helpful and considerate when he saw me struggling for lines while having to cook and serve breakfast for five all at the same time. I remember Ian Johnson with affection. I don't know if he decided to become an actor on leaving school – I doubt it. I think he really wanted to play for Arsenal; or was it West Ham?

I am, of course, frequently asked all the old cliché questions about acting with children. I can only say that anyone who doesn't realise the reflected glory in which one can bask when they are good – and all mine were – must be extraordinarily unperceptive. I just encouraged them, 'fed' them, tried to help them and let them get on with it. They really did all the work for me.

By the press, the series was at first received guardedly. Ultimately I think they accepted us, but those who had a built-in resistance to child actors we never really won round. With the public generally, the series was popular. It was clean, wholesome, family viewing; frequently funny, occasionally moving, and at its worst, inoffensive. The powers-that-be obviously felt the same way because in the following year Richard was asked to write thirteen more. He was, however, anxious. He didn't find the subject an easy one and ultimately said that he could only manage seven. In the event he wrote nine.

For the second series a few of the children had to be replaced – some were growing up too fast, others were unavailable. Ian Johnson remained, however, as did Briony McRoberts, our elder girl, and on this occasion we were joined by two pretty little identical twins which gave Richard a few more ideas for comedy fodder.

When we finished we had done a total of twenty-one episodes (excluding a special Christmas Day edition) – four less than the BBC had asked for – and yet the series was never repeated.

In addition to *Bachelor Father*, the next two years were exceptionally busy ones for me professionally. The main thing that occupied my time during that period, however, had nothing to do with my professional life at all. In 1957, after several years of being let down by well-meaning friends whose promises to put me up for membership of the Lord's Taverners never materialised, I was finally elected to its ranks. In 1970 I was invited to become its Chairman. I accepted with a mixture of excitement and trepidation and held the post for the next two years, the second of which coincided with the association's twenty-first anniversary.

CHAPTER THIRTY-TWO

ST JOHN'S WOOD AND ST JAMES'S

Enter MARTIN BODDEY – *a visionary*

The Lord's Taverners was founded in 1950 by an actor and singer named Martin Boddey. Its membership was restricted to members of the arts who revered the game of cricket and to cricketers who held a similar affection for the arts. Its early recruits came, almost entirely, from a group of actors and broadcasters who used to watch cricket from in front of the original Tavern at Lord's – hence its name. The objects of the association were to raise money to plough back into the game that had given its members so much pleasure.

The Lord's Taverners' first President was John Mills, its first Chairman was the founder member, Martin Boddey, and its first council meeting was held on 3 July 1950 in the Royal Circle bar of the Comedy Theatre in London – a fact which is commemorated by a bronze plaque fixed to one of its walls.

A few weeks previously, Captain Jack Broome, an early member, who had served in the Royal Navy with Prince Philip, suggested that His Royal Highness might be interested in the formation of the Lord's Taverners. As a result, after some enthusiastic co-operation from Lieutenant-Commander Michael Parker, then Prince Philip's Equerry-in-Waiting, Martin Boddey and Jack Broome were invited to meet His Royal Highness at Clarence House. Prince Philip listened attentively and suggested that he might do something to help. When it was cautiously put forward that he might consent to become the association's first President, he replied, it is reported, 'I couldn't do that. If I became your President I should expect to chair your meetings – indeed, I should insist on doing so – and I really haven't the time. But I will be your Patron if you like.' The overjoyed visitors prepared to take their leave but before doing so they casually mentioned that the honorary and honourable position of Twelfth Man had been hopefully left vacant. His Royal Highness, perhaps with his tongue in his cheek, enquired the significance of the position. He was told that the traditional duties of that indispensable member of a cricket side are (a) to carry the bag from the station, (b) look after the score-book, (c) bring out the drinks, (d) 'sub' in the field, and (e) run for anybody who didn't feel like it after lunch.

'Exactly what I thought you meant,' said His Royal Highness, and thereupon claimed the right to fill the role.

The original Lord's Taverners had nothing if not panache. One of the first fund-raising functions the council decided to mount was a ball to be held at Grosvenor House. Furthermore it was to be a ball with a difference – a game of cricket would be played on the ballroom floor. Despite expressed doubts from some quarters, the idea took shape. A team of Test Match players were persuaded to play against a Lord's Taverners Eleven. The field of play, it was agreed, would be surrounded by great nets to protect the spectators at the tables. The hotel was *not* in favour of such a thing. It had never been done before: but when the Taverners were able to say that not only would their Twelfth Man be present but also HRH Princess Elizabeth, as the Queen then was, all objections melted away. Even so it was a near thing. When the President asked at a meeting how much it was all going to cost, he was told that for the hire of the ballroom, the dinner and the bands, the Lord's Taverners would have to cough up £2,000. He then enquired the state of the association's current assets.

'Our present cash in hand,' reported the Hon. Treasurer, 'is £14 4s 8d.'

The President promptly offered his resignation. It was not accepted.

The ball was held on 30 April 1951 and was a glittering success. Not only was it graced by the presence of Princess Elizabeth and His Royal Twelfthmanship, but also by HRH Princess Margaret, and the Earl and Countess Mountbatten who took their own table. The evening made a net profit of £1,000. The Lord's Taverners Ball was to become, and remain, an annual event of great distinction in the London social calendar.

The original conception of the Lord's Taverners was very much a child of its day. I doubt if it could have been conceived in the 1970s. Apart from the fact that the original Lord's Tavern was demolished in 1966, the present working climate for actors is so totally different from that prevailing in 1950; and it was this that helped so much to band together the early members of the association.

Before 1955 the country had only one television station – dear old Auntie BBC. Viewing time was also extremely limited and the output of programmes consequently much smaller. This meant that there was a great deal less work around than there is today. What then did the London thespian do with the daytime hours during those summers? Well, those of us who were cricket lovers spent them almost entirely at Lord's. For the modest sum of two shillings (for a county match) one could sit in the sun for seven hours and watch star players from all over the world playing our national game – and with Compton and Edrich at the wicket for the majority of the season, what happier way was there of whiling away an otherwise unproductive day?

The Tavern was, of course, the great vantage point. There one could quaff one's ale and in addition to enjoying the game rub shoulders with other actors and swap grape-vine chat about what new plays were being cast, who was casting them and all the information requisite to finding future employment. It was a grand coterie. If you were miserable, lonely, depressed, or if you had just landed a plum role and wanted to shout about it, you always knew – in those days – that you would find a mate to talk to outside the Tavern at Lord's.

I remember watching a game round about lunchtime one Saturday and in our group on that occasion was a leading member of the Old Vic company. He was appearing in *Othello*, alternating the title role with that of Iago (generally considered to be the longest role in Shakespeare) with another actor, turn and turn about. We had all downed a considerable number of pints and my turn had come round once more.

'Same again?' I enquired of all concerned. I then said to this actor, 'Shall I skip you this time?'

'Certainly not,' he replied. 'Why?'

'You've got a matinée, haven't you?' I asked.

'Yes,' said Richard Burton, 'but it's only Iago this afternoon.'

The Welsh have great constitutions.

Such then is the background to Martin Boddey's brain-child which, since its birth in 1950, has ploughed hundreds of thousands of pounds back into the game of cricket – until 1971, almost entirely through the agency of the National Playing Fields Association; each year a cheque was ceremoniously handed over at an annual Spring Luncheon held at the Café Royal at which the new season's visiting Tourists were always the Guests of Honour.

The money was raised by a variety of functions from dances to race meetings and charity shows and premières, but principally by such annual events as the Grosvenor House Ball, a Harry Secombe Pro/Am Golf Tournament, a boxing evening also held at the Café Royal and ten to a dozen Sunday cricket matches played all over the country each summer.

The members who turned out to play in the latter – who willingly got up early on a Sunday morning, perhaps their only day off, and travelled long distances in support of the Lord's Taverners – were such stalwarts as Tony Britton (who invariably shared the wicket-keeping honours with Clement Freud), Roy Castle and Brian Rix (two useful all-rounders), Michael Craig, Leslie Crowther, David Frost (when not globe-trotting), Bill Franklyn (a hasty opening bowler), Julian Holloway (another), Harry Secombe (occasionally employed between innings as a heavy roller), Bill Maynard, Nicholas Parsons, Bill Simpson, Henry Cooper, Mick McManus and many others.

The professionals from the game itself – except for the one who was annually elected our Cricketer of the Year and was, as a result, offered Honorary Membership – were not eligible to join our ranks until they had retired from the first-class game. This temporary exclusion was instigated to give membership of the Lord's Taverners a certain cachet within the county dressing-rooms. Any professional wearing the association's tie, in those days, had won it by merit. It was an accolade. Despite this legislation, however, the county cricketers rallied generously to our cause. Many of them on what was also their only day off (this was prior to the advent of professional Sunday cricket), not only turned out for us but also treated us kindly into the bargain. We – that is to say the likes of myself – they always appreciated not only had to appear on stage or in a studio the following day, but also that our reactions were probably not quite as keen as those of six-day-a-week, trained athletes. I once fielded at first slip to Alec Bedser bowling off a shortened run and I only thank my lucky stars the batsman never got a tickle. On another occasion one of our thespian cricketers – I forget whom, which is a pity because his name should be recorded – showed commendable valour (and faith) after arriving at the wicket and taking guard opposite Frederick Sewards Trueman who was augmenting the opposition's attack.

'Stand still,' said Mr Trueman. 'Stand perfectly still. Don't move a bloody muscle.'

He then walked back and took his full county match run up. The next delivery whistled its way through the air; the batsman courageously did as he was bid and the ball took the bat clean out of his hand. Roars of laughter from a delighted crowd.

But the discretion of our professional colleagues was always impeccable and to be appearing on the field with them – our idols – in addition to raising money for charity, was always an exhilarating and treasured experience.

A Lord's Taverners Sunday cricket side: Sir Leonard Hutton, Umpire (?), MacDonald Hobley, Richie Benaud talking to Colin Cowdrey (hidden), Alf Gover behind Tony Britton, Bill Maynard, self, Alec Bedser, Raman Subba Row, Eric Bedser, Tom Graveney. Lying down Richard Hearne (Mr Pastry)

Sadly, in more recent years, irreconcilable differences of opinion concerning the policies of the Lord's Taverners developed between Martin and I and one or two others (including its Trustees) on the one hand, and a majority of the council on the other. As a result of those differences the Panel of Trustees later ceased to exist and towards the end of his life the situation became so intolerable to the man who had founded the movement, that he saw no alternative but to resign – a decision which practically broke his heart. Fortunately for the Lord's Taverners he was not to be allowed time to do so. I, on the other hand, tendered my resignation in October 1976. Pym and I had many friends in the Lord's Taverners and we had worked hard and willingly for them for almost twenty years. It was a sad day for us both when we had to say goodbye.

In 1970 and 1971, however, I was proudly shouldering the administrative responsibilities of an association which one of our prime ministers once described as being 'an estate of the realm'. The President during my first year of office was Brian Rix and during my second – our twenty-first anniversary year – appropriately, Martin Boddey.

During the anniversary year, three events stand out in my memory. The first was a cricket match against the RAF at Cranwell in July where the Prince of Wales was attending a course. Much to our joy he had agreed to turn out for the opposition. On the appointed day, when it was his turn to bat, he joined in the spirit of the occasion by, unbeknown to all but his closest confidants, approaching the wicket completely padded up, mounted on a magnificent chestnut horse. It was the most regal of entrances.

During the afternoon Martin and I debated whether we could, without embarrassing him, approach His Royal Highness and ask him to do us the honour of joining our ranks. The last thing we wanted to do was to take advantage of his generosity in agreeing to play in our match – a gesture which was undoubtedly responsible for producing a crowd of twelve thousand. We sought the advice of his aide, who thought it would be quite all right.

I think it was during the tea interval that Martin approached His Royal Highness and asked him if he would be prepared to consider becoming our Honorary Member Extraordinary. The invitation was graciously accepted. In 1975 and 1976 The Prince of Wales was also to accept the Presidency of the association.

Prince Philip's fiftieth birthday also fell in 1971, an occasion which made the council put on its thinking-cap in search of a suitable gift. Over the years, many of the Lord's Taverners' bright ideas were initiated by its founder – he was now to produce another one out of the hat. The association's half ton birthday present to its Twelfth Man, he suggested, should be a book – rather a special book which Martin himself undertook to edit. It was his intention, he said, to approach a number of distinguished authors, artists, cartoonists and celebrities over a wide field and ask each one of them to contribute a new work. These would then be bound into an anthology; the original copy, in which each item would be signed by the contributor, would be presented to His Royal Highness and in due course a published edition would be put on sale to the public. It was also Martin's intention, after consulting with the royal recipient, that all the royalties from the latter would be returned to swell the Lord's Taverners' coffers.

The finished article with a foreword by the Prince of Wales contained items by fifty-six contributors. They included HRH Prince Bernhard of the Netherlands, John Betjeman, Daphne du Maurier, Paul Gallico, Nicholas Monsarrat, Mary Renault, Gerald Durrell, Basil Boothroyd, Annigoni, Giles, Graham Hill, Ronald Searle, Laurence Olivier, Edward

Seago, John Snagge, Peter Sellers, Jim Laker, Roger Bannister, Sheila Scott, Robin Knox-Johnston and many more. It was called *The Twelfth Man* and was published by Cassell.

On 9 June 1971, Martin, Kenneth Parker – a director of Cassell – and I went to Buckingham Palace to present the Twelfth Man with his birthday present. We were received in an annexe to his study where Martin made the presentation which also included a cheque for advance royalties; this was immediately handed back to us and the following day the published edition went on sale to the public.

But perhaps the crowning event of that year took place in July. Being our twenty-first birthday year it was decided that we should have an anniversary dinner and we began searching for a suitable venue. As I have already explained, the Lord's Taverners – in those years anyway – had nothing if not élan. In council such locations as Hampton Court Palace, St James's Palace and the Mansion House were bandied about as if they were the Connaught Rooms and all we had to do was to ring up and place a booking. Their unavailability, or the nerve of even considering them, never crossed our minds for a second. Unofficial enquiries were made about all three venues and each was received with gracious consideration. In due course, however, it became clear that the most suitable was going to be the Mansion House, so our unofficial enquiries became official ones and luckily for us the Lord Mayor of London in 1971 was Sir Peter Studd. Sir Peter, who had scored a not out century for Harrow against Eton at Lord's in 1935 and had captained Cambridge University in the last season before the war, was, as might be imagined, sympathetic to our aims. Permission was generously granted. Perhaps it is not without interest either that one of the Sheriffs of that year was Sir Hugh Wontner, Chairman of the Savoy Hotel Group, whose father had been a distinguished actor.

It was a star-spangled occasion. VIPs from the world of the arts and sport were thick on the ground and the pomp and circumstance dictated by City of London protocol added hugely to the theatricality of the evening. The demand for tickets was so great that guests had to be restricted to one per member, and all 317 available seats were soon subscribed for. Excellent wines were specially imported and I made myself personally responsible for recruiting the very best after dinner speakers I could lay my hands on – a task which was helped considerably by Prince Philip kindly agreeing not only to attend the dinner but also to respond to the toast to the Lord's Taverners. I made a special point of asking all speakers (with the exception of His Royal Highness) to restrict themselves to ten

The Mansion
House dinner:
Martin Boddey,
The Twelfth Man,
self, Lord Mancroft

minutes only. The point was taken. In the *Daily Telegraph* a week or so later E. W. Swanton wrote as follows:

From time to time over the years I have had a dig at speakers who spoil club dinners by long speeches – when practically everyone present awaits impatiently the renewal both of his glass and of old acquaintance, probably in that order.

In this respect the Lord's Taverners dinner at the Mansion House earlier in the month set a precedent that is worth recording. We had six speeches, all first-class and all beautifully brief, from the President (Martin Boddey), the Lord Mayor (Sir Peter Studd), Harry Secombe, Frank Crozier, Lord Mancroft and, finally, the Duke of Edinburgh.

All was over and done with in fifty-seven minutes. If speakers of the top class can modestly restrict themselves to about eight minutes why should others, much less digestible, presume to prattle on for twenty minutes or half an hour? How have we all suffered!

In due course Decca marketed a long-playing record of the occasion which also benefited the association's funds.

My last duty for the Lord's Taverners was a sad one. Dear Martin Boddey died of a heart attack on 24 October 1975 and I made a special request to the council that I should be allowed to arrange his memorial service. They agreed.

It was held on 7 April 1976 at St John's Wood Church which stands on St John's Wood circus adjacent to the nursery end at Lord's – the nearest I could get it to the cradle of his beloved organisation. Amongst those present on the occasion was John Snagge, member No. 9. John – a past President, Chairman, Secretary and Trustee – had been deputed from Buckingham Palace to represent the Twelfth Man.

And so ended an era.

CHAPTER THIRTY-THREE

DUKE'S DENVER

Enter LORD PETER WIMSEY – *an aristocrat extraordinary*

To pick up the threads of my professional life, we must return to 11 March 1966 when, during the run of *Say Who You Are*, I received that letter suggesting the Wimsey novels as a possible subject for a television series. The moment I read it bells rang and lights flashed; I knew immediately the idea was a good one.

I had read a few of the Wimsey books when I was in my teens and shortly before the war I had also seen the Hull repertory company give a performance of *Busman's Honeymoon*. I knew, in fact, sufficient about His Lordship to realise that this was the best idea to have come my way for a very long time. Unfortunately, a very long time was exactly what it was going to take to bring that germ of an idea to full flower.

On receipt of the letter, I immediately rang up Harrods and asked them to send me copies of the complete Wimsey canon.

'How many books are there?' I asked.

'Fourteen,' came the reply after a few moments' research.

'In *paper*back,' I added hurriedly.

Someone once described a Yorkshireman as being a Scotsman without the generosity. Unfortunately my ancestry is allied to both clans.

Now I enjoy reading for pleasure very much indeed, but reading for professional reasons is an entirely different matter – that I invariably find a complete chore; largely because seventy-five per cent of it is wasted effort. So it was with mixed feelings that I sat down to read fourteen novels on the trot. In the event, rarely, before or since, has such a daunting job of work given me so much pleasure. With no effort at all I read them, one after the other, in chronological order, without even stopping to pick up so much as a copy of *Playboy* magazine to act as a mental douche between stories. I had been right – and so had Herbert Van Thal, the originator of the idea – Lord Peter Wimsey was undoubtedly the ideal subject for me.

The next six years were to be possibly the most frustrating of my professional life.

I first approached the BBC Light Entertainment Department, for whom I had just finished playing Bertie Wooster and immediately hit the first of a long line of obstructions which were to be strewn across my path like tank-traps for the next five years. It came in the form of a letter from the head of the department.

The very first snag, I was informed, was an insuperable one – money. The BBC, apparently, had no risk capital whatever at that time to invest in projects, however optimistic they may be about potential profits. In addition the overseas sales advisers had expressed the view that the subject would by no means be an easy sale across the Atlantic. The character of Lord Peter Wimsey, they professed, was not very well known in the States, nor, in their opinion, did Dorothy L. Sayers's literary and literate style fit in very well with the current trends of filmed series.

Mumbling into my metaphorical beard several phrases like 'lack of foresight', 'no imagination' and 'false assumptions' I refused to be put off. So – girding up my loins – I then approached the Drama Department of the same station, the head of which was an old friend and neighbour.

One evening during the act interval of *Say Who You Are*, I telephoned him to ask if I could call in and have a chat on my way home after the show. He agreed and an hour-and-a-half later armed with a large whisky, I started my sales spiel.

'Do you know the Wimsey books?' I asked.

'Look behind you,' he said; and there on a bookshelf behind my head was every one of them. Obviously I had found a fan. My spirits rose.

He then went on to tell me that they were, indeed, at that very moment being considered as a possible follow-up to a very successful and long-running series that had just come to an end. My spirits rose even higher. They needn't have done. It was to prove yet another disappointment. The powers-that-be opted for one of the alternatives that were being considered at the same time. From a morale point of view it was as well that I didn't know then (I was to find out about a year later) that the producer who had been championing the Wimsey saga had not wanted me in the part. Whether this had influenced the overall decision to drop the idea, I know not; I very much doubt it.

The wisdom of casting Ian Carmichael as Lord Peter Wimsey was, perhaps, not, if the truth be known, questioned by only one man. The success of the recent Wooster series was now, paradoxically, about to work against me rather than in my favour. Throughout nearly all my initial efforts to sell myself there was, I always felt, by some, an air of doubt about accepting me in the role. The fear that I would play Peter Wimsey with the same idiocy with which I had endowed Bertie Wooster was never really far from the surface. Even when the series was finally mounted and underway there was still, I sensed, a feeling of distrust in my perform- ance which was to persist until the first novel was behind us and I had, so to speak, proved myself. All of which was not destined to help my chances of a breakthrough in the early stages of trying to get the project off the ground.

However, having drawn a blank at the BBC, I then decided that a more professional approach should be made to the commercial stations. As a result I sat down and drew up a twelve-page sales brochure on the sub- ject with which, in due course, like the best door-to-door salesman, I set out to tout around the lot of them. Each in turn showed a similar lack of enthusiasm. I received such dismissive answers as:

'After careful reflection we do not think there is an international market for the Peter Wimsey idea.' And:

'It's not our scene.' And:

'The Americans will never go for an *effete* [a strange adjective for Peter Wimsey] Englishman.' Or:

'The Americans will never buy a serial, only a series.'

Simultaneously my advisers and I had been having talks with the Sayers estate to discover the availability of the TV rights, and here we encountered further problems. The executors were, at that time, only pre- pared to sell the rights of the complete works in one package. They were not interested in discussing the purchase of individual books one or two at a time, and this, I knew, would not endear the idea to the British TV moguls, regardless of their other prejudices.

Disheartened, I let the matter drop for a year and got on with something else. In 1968 I became more depressed as I heard that a film company was showing interest in the properties and consequently the Sayers people were no longer prepared to entertain the possibility of a television series.

Impasse.

In 1969 I received information that the film project was off, so I started knocking at the BBC's door once again – this time with considerably more success. A producer was assigned to the job – albeit the one who had not wanted me in the first place – scriptwriters were put to work and all the novels were to be presented in chronological order in three series of thirteen episodes each. Excelsior! That was the way I had always wanted them to be presented. But 'when troubles come' etc. – nine months

With Donald Eccles in The Nine Tailors

later the producer left the BBC to produce a feature film, and all was off once again.

One year after that (and if you are finding this monotonous, think how I was feeling) I again tried to persuade them to resurrect the project. Apart from anything else, I was getting concerned that when and if we ever did get it off the ground, I would be too old for the part. By this time the Sayers estate had withdrawn its original condition of selling the complete works as a package, and plans were made to do one novel in five episodes to see how it was received.

You would have thought that by then I was home and dry, but oh dear no – which novel to start with was the next hiatus.

'Number One, *Whose Body?*' I opined.

'Not a bit of it,' said the authorities. 'We must start with a well-known one. Let's start with *Murder Must Advertise.*'

'But that's halfway through the canon,' I protested. 'We shall get into a frightful mess from a chronological point of view if it is a success and you want to do more.'

Impasse again.

Finally a compromise was reached and we agreed to start with book number two, *Clouds of Witness*.

It was, then, early on a cold January morning in 1972 – almost six years to the day after I had received Herbert Van Thal's letter – in the heart of Howarth Moor in Yorkshire, that Wimsey and Bunter got into a green 3½ litre Bentley and drove off past camera. At last we were on our way.

During the next three years we also recorded *The Unpleasantness at the Bellona Club, Murder Must Advertise* and *The Nine Tailors.*

In late 1974 *Strong Poison*, the first of the Harriet Vane novels, was scripted and was all ready for the off when the whole of the BBC's schedules became retarded as the result of a strike. When the industrial action was lifted there was such a backlog of productions looking for studio space, *Strong Poison* was postponed and *Five Red Herrings* hurriedly mounted in lieu. The latter could be shot almost in its entirety on location in Scotland and the little studio work that was required it was possible to accommodate in the BBC studios in Glasgow.

In January 1975 in Glasgow, after the final shots of *Five Red Herrings* were committed to video tape, the fifth book was completed. Since then the series appears to have been abandoned and Harriet Vane has never appeared on a television screen. The number of letters I have received from avid fans awaiting her entrance are considerable – but it was not to be. Why? I have no idea. Finance, I suspect, but I have never been told.

For those who don't know, Peter eventually married Harriet Vane (*Busman's Honeymoon*), the girl he got acquitted of murdering her lover (*Strong Poison*) and by whom he eventually had three sons (*Striding Folly*). So criminology, bibliography, music and cricket were obviously not the sum of his talents.

I loved Wimsey. He was me – or what of him was not me was what I would have liked to be me. I think I was rather like a child playing dressing-up games. I dressed up as Wimsey and played 'let's pretend' because I admired him; I envied him his life-style, his apparent insouciance, prowess and his intellect. He was never, as some people will have it, a snob and an anti-semite – one of his closest friends married a Jewess, the daughter of a long-standing friend of his family. Peter Wimsey was everybody's friend.

I am often asked why, with my firm belief in the project, during all those years of frustration, I never bought the rights myself. How could I have done so? I am, if nothing else, an honest man. To raise sufficient money I would have had to form a consortium, and how could I have approached my fellow men and asked them to invest in something that I knew from my initial researches nobody wanted to buy?

As a tailpiece to the story, however, it is perhaps interesting to note how wrong thoughts had been on the viability of the sale of Lord Peter Wimsey on the other side of the Atlantic. The Americans have lapped him up and, certainly the aficianados, are continually crying out for more.

CHAPTER THIRTY-FOUR

HOME AGAIN

In my late forties grass roots started to stir in my soul. My 'it's later than you think' philosophy began to assert itself more and more aggressively and the laziness that had marked my first twenty years began slowly to return. At the same time I found I was becoming increasingly disenchanted with the 'big city', and a yearning to return to Whitby and the North Yorkshire moors became compelling. My in-laws were getting no younger and unless we acquired a place of our own in the area, a time would come, I reasoned, when we might never return to it again. That didn't bear thinking about, so we started to search for a holiday home.

Over the next few years we looked at property after property. We knew the area well, which helped considerably when scanning the local paper at a distance of two hundred and fifty miles. If we saw anything that looked a likely prospect, one of our many friends up there would give it the preliminary once-over for us and if their report was favourable, one or both of us would make the journey to see for ourselves. I had always fancied being on the sea whereas Pym preferred one of the little moorland villages a few miles inland, but we considered everything.

One day in 1973, having found nothing that appealed, a local estate agent asked us if we would be prepared to consider a freehold flat – there was one, apparently, available. It was on the second floor of what had once been a large hotel, built just before the turn of the century, on Whitby's north promenade; it was the hotel in which the entire Westminster Dragoons had been housed during my stay in the town in 1941. We knew the present occupants slightly – an elderly, retired Teeside store-owner and his wife – and we made a date to view it at 11.30 the following morning.

We arrived. Coffee and biscuits were on offer, or would we prefer something stronger? As the question was posed a drinks cupboard was thrown open with an expansive gesture. Pym accepted the coffee – one of us had to keep a clear head – I opted for a gin and tonic. An unopened bottle of Gordons was then set down in front of me accompanied by a glass, a small tonic and a genial invitation to help myself.

In estate agents' parlance and within the context of Whitby, the property could, I think, fairly be classed as a luxury flat. It had a huge, L-shaped, split-level living-room, two double bedrooms, a sizeable hall, a spacious kitchen with dining area and a well-appointed bathroom. The whole was double-glazed, embraced a long balcony and looked straight out to sea with nothing between the building and the edge of the cliff. It had a one hundred and eighty degree panoramic view of the coastline and the side windows completed an extra ninety degrees across the rolling countryside towards Scarborough and the moors. It was not what we had been looking for, but the price was fair, the position excellent, and it would provide us with a bridgehead in the area from which to pursue further operations in the future. We bought it.

During the next three years we enjoyed many breaks from work in our new home, and in it, and in the company of our many local friends, I found total peace and relaxation. Whenever I was there, I never wanted to return to London.

In October 1974, Sally, who was by then a make-up artist with BBC Television, married a young man called Christopher Hennen – a member of

*Giving the bride
away, II – Sally*

'The Young Generation' group of singers and dancers – and Pym and I were left to rattle round Moat Lodge all on our own. I had always sworn that I would never leave our beloved family home until I was carried out of it in a box, but now I was becoming older (if not wiser) and the situation, and my approach to life generally, were changing perceptively.

One night, while we were all asleep in bed, three weeks after moving into Moat Lodge in 1958, a most expert thief broke into three of our downstairs rooms and cleaned us out of every piece of silver we possessed – which was a lot. I was the son of a silversmith and most of our wedding presents from relatives had been silver. He had also helped himself to my two treasured presents from Robert Morley and Robin Fox which marked our partnership in *The Tunnel of Love*. The following day I went out and bought an Alsatian. We never had any more trouble with intruders until the day we left. However, as a result of the attention that such marauding gentlemen continued to accord to properties in the Mill Hill area, we were never able just to lock the door of our castle and drive up to Whitby without forward planning. With security in mind, we always had to find (and pay) caretakers – rarely easy at the drop of a hat – so opportunities to get up and go on impulse were sadly restricted.

As the months rolled by facing this problem, it became more and more clear to me that the sensible thing to do would be to reverse our whole lifestyle; to sell both our London and our holiday homes and in their place to buy a new permanent residence in the Whitby area and a small pied-à-terre in Town from which to work.

The decision to act on this logical premise was both a murderous and a lonely one. Firstly, for an actor to move two hundred and fifty miles away from London, the hub of his professional wheel, seemed on the surface to be crazy. I had, however, for some time wanted to take life more easily; wanted to have more leisure time. The theatre, per se, no longer provided me with the stimulation that it had done in days of yore, and films and television, which could take me anywhere, would, under the proposed new order, provide no problem. Secondly, and this was perhaps more important, all my womenfolk were, to say the least, pretty half-hearted about the idea. They were understandably concerned about breaking up the family. I was convinced that it could be made to work and also that, if it did, their fears would be unfounded. Furthermore, and possibly selfishly from Pym's and my points of view, it would, I tried to persuade her, provide us with the best of all possible worlds.

We started searching once again and one weekend, Pym being otherwise engaged, I drove north on my own. On the Sunday I was taking a lunchtime glass in a charming little country pub in the area, when an old acquaintance who lived in Whitby but worked throughout the week as an estate agent in Wetherby some sixty odd miles away, asked me what exactly I was looking for. I told him.

'I think we've got the very place for you,' he said, and he mentioned the name of the village – it was four-and-a-half miles inland from Whitby in the Esk valley.

'Tell me about it,' I asked.

'It has an acre of land,' he continued, 'about a quarter of which is a paddock and is at the moment let off to a neighbour who keeps a few hens and geese on it. It is secluded, and has, at the foot of the garden, a magnificent salmon pool with three hundred yards of fishing rights.'

'Lead me to it,' I said.

An appointment was made that evening and I went to view it the following morning.

It was a beautiful August morning and the owner, a widow, greeted me warmly and said, 'Let's have some coffee in the summer house, shall we?' (That's how they are in the Whitby area.) She led the way into the garden. We rounded the end of a tall, thick, masking yew hedge and there was a large, revolving, Canadian cedar summer-house. The moment we sat down I knew my search was over. The view was captivating. The garden, which faced due south, stood high above the salmon pool and the summer-house looked straight down over the wooded banks and bubbling waters of the River Esk. It was a dream position.

The house had once been a farmhouse. It is about two hundred years old and is situated on the site of a priory built there in the second year of King John – much of the old stone being utilised in the present building. That night I telephoned Pym.

'I've found it,' I announced triumphantly, and the following day she came north to confirm my judgement.

As with our previous homes there was a great deal of modernisation and renovating to be done, but this had never frightened us before so there was no reason why it should do so now. Madame drove up full of apprehension, but unlike her nocturnal arrival at our first house in Gloucester Avenue twenty-five years previously, the conditions for her first view of this one were ideal – it was another glorious summer's day. The following week we bought it.

After gaining possession at Easter 1976, the workmen moved in and we immediately put Moat Lodge and the Whitby flat on the market. All we could do then was to be patient and just hope and pray that the sale

Home

of each would dovetail neatly with our eventual move to our new home. We had many anxious moments, but were saved, ironically, by the workmen in Yorkshire who kept abandoning us in favour of other jobs. Work which was originally estimated as requiring two months to complete, in the event took nine. Eventually, however, on the morning of 26 January 1977, amid copious and understandable tears, we moved the last remaining effects out of the house that had been our home for nineteen years, locked the door, handed the key over to the estate agent and set off for the north.

The weeks that followed were highly emotional ones for our whole family and I carried away with me to Yorkshire a guilt complex the size of the Houses of Parliament.

Now, two years later, things have settled down as I had hoped, and we have indeed attained the best of all possible worlds.

The Whitby area generally, breathtakingly beautiful in summer, has, despite bitter and hostile weather in the winter, a hypnotic attraction to many who have strayed so far off the beaten track to find it. As an example

I need look no further than the purchaser of our flat on the North Promenade. It was bought by a retired Lieutenant-Colonel in the USAAF who had served a term of duty at the nearby Fylingdales Early Warning Station – a location in the heart of the North Yorkshire moors that is frequently completely cut off by snow in the winter. On retirement, this American officer, whose home was in sunny California, had fallen so much under the spell of the countryside that he chose to return and settle here. He was neither the first nor the last retiring officer from Fylingdales to do so.

And so, having reached the age of fifty-eight, I am still married to the same girl and with a tally of, to date, four enchanting grandchildren, I can truly claim that my life has come full circle.

I have been incredibly lucky. I have had the most tolerant, steadfast and loving of wives, two most beautiful daughters, and professionally I have achieved much of what I set out to achieve. I have also been to places and met people that, had I adopted any other calling, I would never have been fortunate enough to either visit or become acquainted with.

Today, once again I find myself asking the same question that I asked myself all those years ago in Germany – 'Whither Carmichael?' Now, however, I am less worried. Something will crop up – it always has – and even if it doesn't, I am more than contented in my Yorkshire Shangri-la.

INDEX